To Bishop Patrick Walsh
With deep gratitude
and kindest regards

Sr Marie Duddy, RSM

The Call of the North

A History of the Sisters of Mercy, Down and Connor Diocese, Ireland

The Works of Mercy

From the original painting by Sister M. Clare Augustine Moore (1808–1880)

The Call of the North

A History of the Sisters of Mercy, Down and Connor Diocese, Ireland

from the founding to the Mercy Irish National Union, 1854–1994

SISTER MARIE DUDDY, R.S.M.

ULSTER HISTORICAL FOUNDATION

First Published 2010
by the Ulster Historical Foundation
Charity Ref. No. XN48460
E-mail: enquiry@uhf.org.uk
Web: www.ancestryireland.com
www.booksireland.org.uk

Printed by MPG Biddles
Design by Cheah Design

To the Sisters of Mercy
Down and Connor
past, present and future

CONTENTS

PREFACE

This is a work long in maturation. Several decades ago, as a young religious, and a historian, I was given charge of the archives of my community. That was not an onerous responsibility at the time as my brief extended only to the documents and other archival material of the community of the Sisters of Mercy of Belfast which had been handed down over the previous hundred years. In the 1970s, Sister M. Brendan Blanche, who had retired from teaching, took over the task and organised, and added a considerable amount of historical and archival documentation to, the original small stock.

When Sister M. Brendan could not longer continue with this task, I again inherited the job of archivist. We, the Sisters of Mercy of the original St Paul's Convent, Crumlin Road, owe a great debt of gratitude to Sister Brendan for the foundational work that she did.

When Crumlin Road Convent closed (for reasons outlined in the following history) the archives were brought to Ballysillan House, and, in due course, moved on to the provincial archives in the Mercy Convent, Bessbrook, and eventually to the Mercy Central Archives in Dublin, where the archives of the Irish Mercy convents are stored.

In the early 1990s, the superior of my community, Sister M. Emilian Maloney, asked me to write up the history of our then Down and Connor Mercy Congregation. Changes had already taken place, and were to continue to do so, in the structures of the Sisters of Mercy in Ireland and worldwide. It was important to conserve the valuable history of the foundations and early days of the local communities. I willingly undertook the task – a 'spare-time' work of research in an otherwise very busy and full-time teaching schedule. So the project was an ongoing one of well over a decade. When I was asked by my congregation to have it published, that brought up another agenda for me. Hopefully the whole undertaking will have been worthwhile and prove of value and interest to all who read the story.

I gratefully acknowledge my indebtedness to all who helped me to bring this book to fruition. In the first place, I wish to thank Andrew Boyd who, as far back as the 1960s, encouraged me to research and write up the story of the Mercy Sisters in Belfast and passed on to me some valuable historical information relating to the topic. Thanks to Sister M. Genevieve Martin, RSM, and Sister M. Carmel Laverty, RSM, for reading chapters of the draft in its early stages and making helpful comments; to Monsignor Ambrose Macaulay, Historian of Down and Connor Diocese, for permission to use some references from his book, *Patrick Dorrian*, and for advice on some other topics; to Mr Frank D'Arcy, head of the Department of Humanities of the University of Ulster, Magee College, Derry, for providing me with very valuable sources of information on female adult education in Ireland in the mid-1850s. I also wish to thank the archivists of the Mercy International Archives and the Mercy Central Archives, Dublin, for research information; the archivists of Mercy Convents Bermondsey (London) and Handsworth (Birmingham) for welcoming me to do research there, and Sister Agnes Gleeson, RSM, Melbourne, Australia, for providing me with information about the Warrnambool, Geelong and Colac foundations. I thank my Mercy Congregation for encouraging me to present this work for publication and friends who have supported me in seeing this task to completion.

Finally I thank Monica McErlane, Deputy Librarian, Linen Hall Library, Belfast, for her advice regarding publication and for directing me wisely to the Ulster Historical Foundation; Fintan Mullan, Ulster Historical Foundation, for accepting the manuscript for publication; Deirdre Brown (UHF) for reading the original version and making helpful suggestions; and a very special thanks to my meticulous editor, Alicia McAuley who straightened out inconsistencies and put the final text into order, and to Jill Morrison, graphic designer, for the final layout.

INTRODUCTION

This is the story of the Sisters of Mercy of Down and Connor Diocese, Ireland, from their arrival in Belfast in January 1854 to the creation of the Union of the Sisters of Mercy of Ireland and South Africa in 1994.

The Sisters came to Belfast at the invitation of the bishop and the Catholic people of the town to undertake the education of children and women and to care for the poor, the sick and dying, the homeless and people in any other sort of need. In 1855 a foundation was also made in Downpatrick. These foundations became involved, within a brief space of time, in the setting up of schools, evening classes and the care of young women in distress. The Sisters were also invited to teach in, and undertake the administration of, some parish schools.

The year 1883 saw the beginnings of the Mater Infirmorum Hospital on the Crumlin Road, Belfast, and for over a hundred years the Sisters administered, nursed and undertook nurse training in the Mater and, in time, in associated establishments.

Over the years the apostolate of education expanded into all levels and the Sisters also became involved in missions abroad.

An important and, indeed, fundamental part of this story is the history of the Mercy Sisters in their day-to-day lives in community, community events, and important public events and historical occasions (for example the two world wars and the outbreaks of sectarian strife).

There is also built into the narrative local background where appropriate for the realistic setting of the life and work of the community over 140 years. January 2004 marked the 150th anniversary of the coming of the Sisters of Mercy to Belfast. Over those years about 300 Sisters who belonged to the Mercy Congregation of Down and Connor Diocese have contributed much to their local areas and further afield. This story is an attempt to give an account of what they have achieved and what they hope to carry forward into the future through their good work and tradition of prayer and service.

ABBREVIATIONS

ADA   Armagh Diocesan Archives

APF   Archives of the Sacred Congregation
           of Propaganda Fide, Rome

DCDA   Down and Connor Diocesan Archives,
           Down and Connor Curia, Somerton Road, Belfast

MCA   Mercy Central Archives, Herbert Street, Dublin

MIA   Mercy International Archives, Baggot Street, Dublin

MIHA   Mater Infirmorum Hospital Archives, Belfast

PRONI   Public Record Office of Northern Ireland, Belfast

SMD   Sisters of Mercy, Downpatrick

SPCMB   St Paul's Convent of Mercy, Belfast

DIOCESES OF IRELAND

BOUNDARIES

Provincial ——————
Diocesan – – – – –
United Diocese ●●●●●●

ENCLAVES

A Ardagh
C Clonfert
L Lismore
O Ossory
T Tuam

RAPHOE

DERRY

CONNOR

DOWN

ARMAGH

DROMORE

CLOGHER

KILLALA

ACHONRY

ELPHIN

ARDAGH

TUAM

MEATH

GALWAY

CLONFERT

KILDARE

DUBLIN

KILLALOE

KILLALOE

OSSORY

LEIGHLIN

CASHEL

FERNS

LIMERICK

EMLY

LISMORE

KERRY

CLOYNE

CORK

ROSS

Map of Irish Dioceses – Patrick O'Neill, MA

1

BEGINNINGS

I hear that there is a nunnery in this district. The nuns are ladies as can be known by their neat turn of ankle and footwear.

Mary Ann McCracken[1]

On Monday, 16 January 1854 Sisters M. Philomene Maguire, M. Ignatius Crolly and Mary Lister, accompanied by a young monitress named Kate Molloy, started out from the Convent of Mercy, Baggot Street, Dublin, to found a convent in Belfast in the north of Ireland. These Sisters of Mercy would be the first nuns to come to the diocese of Down and Connor since the reign of Queen Mary (almost 400 years earlier).

During the course of the previous year preparations for this foundation had been under way in the motherhouse of the Sisters of Mercy. As early as 17 March 1853 a leader for the little band of pioneers had been appointed, Sister M. Philomene Maguire, one of a family of four Sisters who had committed themselves to the new Institute of the Sisters of Mercy, founded by Catherine McAuley in Dublin in 1831.

Negotiations between Belfast and Dublin had been in train for some time and eventually more concrete plans began to materialise, as we learn from a letter of 22 November 1853 from Mother M. Vincent Whitty, superior in Baggot Street Convent, to the bishop of Down and Connor, Dr Cornelius Denvir, regarding the actual building of a Mercy convent in Belfast.[2] However, before this ambitious project could be undertaken, temporary accommodation was offered and in January 1854 final arrangements were completed and the first group of Sisters prepared for their journey north:

Convent of Our Lady of Mercy,
Baggot Street,
15th January, 1854

Right Rev & Dear Dr. Denvir,
Having heard from Mr. Loughran last week that the convent is nearly ready I have decided upon sending three Sisters by the 10 o'clock train in the morning to Belfast. Knowing your Lordship would wish us to get in quietly I thought it better to divide our party and not let anyone know of our arrival until the morning of the day we would come to

Belfast. I will bring two Sisters with me on Tuesday and as Dr. Crolly of Maynooth is coming at the same time it is just as well not to let anyone know when he will come.

I am sending Mr. Loughran word to have a car at the station tomorrow to meet the Sisters.

Begging your prayers for the success of our Mission in Belfast I am, my Lord, your faithful servant,

Sr. M. Vincent Whitty.[3]

The cautious note of the letter, implying the need for quiet and even secrecy, may sound rather shocking in a letter dated 140 years ago, but already the north-eastern corner of the island was known as the 'black north', a place where Roman Catholic nuns and papist prelates would not be particularly welcome. Secrecy was maintained so as not to provoke unnecessary antagonism. However, the Sisters discovered during their earliest days in Belfast that their fears were unfounded. They were well received. Nonetheless, they never attempted to conceal the purpose for which they had come – to care for the poor, the sick and the ignorant, without distinction of class or creed, wherever the need became apparent.

What challenges were the Sisters to expect as they journeyed north into the unknown, and what was the significance of the mission they were invited to undertake? By 1800 Belfast was a thriving town, the fifth largest in Ireland, with a population of around 20,000. In the 1850s this had increased to around 119,000. The growth of Belfast was the most obvious example of urban development in nineteenth-century Ireland. Most of the people had migrated to the town in the 1830s and 1840s, looking for work in the textile mills, the backbone of Belfast's prosperity.

The cotton mills, which had begun Belfast's industrial revolution, were replaced after 1828 by flax-spinning mills. With the market for linen growing in England and in the Americas, the number of people employed in the trade increased by over 60 per cent between 1850 and 1860 and the majority of them were women (over 70 per cent). This period also saw a great advance in shipbuilding, which provided work for men. Belfast gave, to the mid-nineteenth-century passing observer, every appearance of industrial prosperity, its 'numerous tall and thin chimneys … [and] the volumes of smoke that issued from them giving unquestionable tokens of full employment; while its vicinity to the ocean removed at once all idea that the labour was unwholesome, or the labourers unhealthy'.[4]

However, if the visitor had pursued his or her investigations further he or she would soon have met sights less favourable. The flax-spinning mills were built on greenfield sites away from the central area of Smithfield, where the cotton mills were located – that is, along the lower Falls and Shankill

Roads. The influx of new workers met a marked shortage of housing. The town centre, which was both residential and commercial and by now overcrowded, could not provide the low-cost housing the mill workers badly needed. Gradually, as commerce was concentrated in Donegall Place and the White Linen Hall, originally the prime residential areas, the middle and upper classes began to move away from the dirt and congestion of the town centre southwards to the more attractive outlying areas such as Malone and Stranmillis. New residential streets, such as Joy Street and Eliza Street, were laid out at this time in a less populated area behind the White Linen Hall and the merchants from High Street moved there. The growing industrial character of Belfast was widening the gap between the well-to-do and the poor.

The older parts of the town – Smithfield, Hercules Street (now Royal Avenue), Millfield, Sandy Row, Carrick Hill and the Pound – were occupied by the many thousands who had been forced off the land by the famine of the 1840s and who had flocked in for employment in the factories and shipyards and all the labouring jobs and services associated with the main industries. This influx into the town created many problems. The newly arrived, driven by poverty and need, were compelled to accept whatever accommodation was available and often found themselves living in cramped and unhealthy houses in narrow streets, entries and courts where resistance to disease and epidemics was weak. The basic requirements for health and hygiene were lacking. The water supply was inadequate and most workers' families had to live in houses with no sanitation. It was typical for families of ten or more to share two tiny rooms, earth floored and dank. These conditions of deprivation and hardship inevitably nurtured a complex of social evils that added to the hardships of the poor. By the mid-nineteenth century it was very obvious that while the lot of tradesmen and the middle-class was improving, thanks to the economic boom, that of the immigrant mill workers and of the unemployed was radically deteriorating:

> An industrialised society forced communities to face, on a large scale, what had hitherto often been the isolated problem for the individual and his family. And poverty, disease and crime were the most prominent of these social problems.[5]

In confronting the massive problem of the poor and marginalised the onus fell on private charity which, it was assumed, would carry the burden of the needs of an impoverished labouring class. The Poor Law Amendment Act of 1834 was totally inadequate in the circumstances and even the Irish Poor Law of 1838 made little difference. In time the mill owners stepped in to try to better the living conditions of their employees. The result was that the archetypal red-bricked, two-up, two-down kitchen houses, which later became standard in the working-class streets of Belfast, were built.

Before these improvements were made, the conditions of the poor were dire indeed. In 1850 the poverty stricken were so numerous among his congregation in Belfast that the Catholic bishop of Down and Connor enlisted the help of the Society of St Vincent de Paul, which up until then had not been represented in that diocese. A year later the society in Belfast reported to their General Council in Ireland:

> The work of looking after half the city is too laborious. We have 30 mills here employing 33,000. There is a vast amount of accidents, of sickness and other misfortunes that a vast congregation of trades people must produce. If you consider the large draughts of people seeking employment here and pouring in from the surrounding counties, often looking to us for employment or for sustenance until they could become skilled operatives, if you could count the number of unfortunates landed on our quays penniless and friendless, your Council would not hesitate in granting permission to make our organisation more complete.[6]

Given these circumstances, early in 1853, 22 years after the foundation of the Institute of the Sisters of Mercy in Dublin, a deputation of Belfast Catholic gentlemen sought an audience with the bishop, Dr Cornelius Denvir. Their mission was simple and commendable: to obtain his lordship's consent to their appeal that he should invite the Sisters of Mercy to come to the town and set up a convent there.

It was not the first time that the subject had been broached. In the latter part of 1852 Reverend Bernard McAuley, parish priest of Downpatrick, with the consent of Bishop Denvir, had gone to Baggot Street and asked for a few Sisters of Mercy to found a convent in Downpatrick, promising a free house and an annual collection in the parish of Down towards their support. He also proposed that they would take charge of the girls' schools and that any funds accruing should be allocated to the Sisters. Reverend Bernard McAuley, although no relative, was a great admirer of Catherine McAuley and her work for the poor in Dublin. He liked to visit Baggot Street Convent and was always pleased to remind people that he had been the first to say Mass in the new chapel of the House of Mercy in 1828. When he became parish priest of Downpatrick in 1836 he asked the Sisters of Mercy to come to his parish. As the story shows, he had to wait for almost 20 more years for this to happen. By a strange coincidence Father Bernard died on 11 November 1863, the same date of the month on which Mother McAuley had died.

In 1853, the gentlemen who requested that Bishop Denvir send the Sisters to Belfast instead represented to the bishop that they considered the need for nuns in Belfast far greater than in Downpatrick – in fact, that they were a necessity for the Catholic population of the town. They proposed that when the Sisters were established in Belfast they could send four or five of their members to Downpatrick as a branch house. (This, in fact, happened in June 1855.)

Welcome to the diocese of Down and Connor

No doubt, then, as the Sisters set out for Belfast, they anticipated a warm welcome there. One of the community annalists gives an imaginary account of what their departure from Baggot Street must have been like that January morning:

> One can well imagine the excitement that day as the little band of pioneering Sisters prepared for their journey to Belfast. They would have arisen at the usual time, 5.30 am, lighted their candles and recited the Morning Offering which that day would have had a greater significance for them than possibly any other day in their lives, as they were about to embark on a journey to an unknown town a long distance away. Many were the distractions and heartaches as they thought of their new home a hundred miles to the north, which would take them away from their companions with whom they had shared a warm affection and understanding over the years. Besides, their roots were in the southern counties, and they would be leaving the proximity of parents and family.
>
> Immediately after community prayer and Mass at 7.00 am, the Sisters who were travelling would have breakfasted probably on porridge and milk as tea was scarce and expensive in those days. One of the benefactors of the community would have sent her carriage to bring them to Amiens Street Station so that they would arrive in time to board the morning train.[7]

The Sisters and their young companion set out on a journey which was, by today's standards, long and wearying. Arduous journeys were no new challenge to the missionary-minded early Sisters of Mercy. Pioneers had already travelled, since the founding of the institute in 1831, to England and much further afield: to Newfoundland (1842), Pittsburg, Pennsylvania (1843), Australia (1845), New York (1846), New Zealand (1849) and even through Central America to the Pacific Ocean to found the first Mercy convent in California in 1854. Each journey had its dramatic moments, not least the first journey to Belfast.

In the earlier part of the nineteenth century it had taken eight hours to travel from Dublin to Belfast, a journey which entailed the alternating use of train and horse-drawn omnibus and a walk over the wooden footbridge across the River Boyne at Drogheda. In 1853, however, in preparation for the Great Dublin Exhibition (masterminded by the railway contractor William Dargan), the Dublin–Belfast Junction Railway had the scaffolding over the Boyne strengthened to allow trains to pass at a reduced speed and a rail journey between Dublin and Belfast became possible. The new Boyne Bridge, the completion of which had been held up by a shortage of iron in the 1840s, was eventually opened on 5 April 1855. However, this was more than 12 months after those first Mercy Sisters had travelled to the north. In January 1854 the journey was still slow and precarious. No wonder, then, that the new founders encountered some hitches along the way.

On the appointed morning the three Sisters left Dublin on the early mail train. As we know, Bishop Denvir had been advised of their arrival in a letter from Mother M. Vincent Whitty, sent only the day before. This arrangement was uncertain and, to complicate matters, the journey did not go exactly according to schedule. Sister M. Philomene got so ill that she and her two companions were obliged to get out at Lurgan. She was not well enough to continue the journey when the train left. They would proceed later on in the afternoon train. Kate Molloy, however, who was travelling third class in a slower train, knew nothing of Sister M. Philomene's illness. When the train arrived in Belfast she was surprised not to find the Sisters on the platform. The carriage of the Protestant bishop happened to have come to meet the train. Kate, innocently thinking that the Catholic bishop had sent it for the Sisters, got into it. When the mistake was discovered she was kindly left down at the residence of the Catholic bishop in Donegall Street. One can imagine the dismay in the bishop's house when he and the priests learned that the expected Sisters were missing.

However, all ended well. Two of the gentlemen instrumental in inviting the Sisters to Belfast, Alexander O'Rorke and Henry Loughran, met the next train and conducted the Sisters who came in it to the home of Mrs Dowling, who lived nearby. Mrs Loughran, Mrs Pelan and other ladies were there to welcome them. After some refreshment these ladies conducted the Sisters to their new abode.

This was a fine residence, 2A Donegall Square North, which had been rented for the Sisters and refurbished from funding provided by Henry Loughran and other local Catholic businessmen. In the 1880s this and neighbouring private dwellings were demolished and replaced by a handsome red-brick structure that became the headquarters of the Belfast Water Commission (the Water Office). The original Mansard roof of this building was destroyed in the Belfast Blitz of World War II. This building is now part of Marks and Spencer's retail premises. At this time Donegall Square was still the hub of the residential area for the prosperous businessmen of the town. It was built around the old White Linen Hall, which itself was built in 1784 (on a site where the City Hall now stands). A picturesque description of Donegall Square is given by Cathal O'Byrne:

> The gardens of the Square were used as a People's Park, and the main walk around the old building was a fashionable promenade for the wealthy townsfolk. A military band performed for two hours in the central garden at the entrance gates, a Sunday evening being a favourite time.[8]

At the same time, this fashionable quarter was no great distance from the factories and mills that lined the banks of the Blackstaff River, the second of Belfast's main arteries, at that time flowing down what is now Ormeau Avenue, its insalubrious mudbanks now the site of the British Broadcasting Corporation.

It was to this house in Donegall Square North that the weary Sisters were conveyed. Gradually the new arrivals settled in and some memories and homely anecdotes about their first days have been handed down to posterity. The Sisters, it is recorded, were amused that their house had been furnished with mirrors and some other 'luxury' articles. These were graciously returned, since the Sisters considered them unseemly furnishings for a convent. Other items were more acceptable. Among the first gifts were a large roll of Indian matting from Mrs Bernard Hughes and a mahogany cross, without a figure, about 18 inches long and made to hang up, which was handed in at the door without the donor's name being given.

Another simple anecdote which has been passed down gives an insight into the novelty of having nuns as neighbours. The room to be used by the Sisters as a refectory happened to be the upper storey of a return (the kitchen being on the second storey since the room below was to be used as a school). The windows of this refectory were of clear glass, so that the Sisters were clearly visible from the next house (Mrs Dufferin's), where a number of children lived. They, of course, peeped and saw the Sisters at tea. They ran to their mother, saying, 'Mamma, Mamma, the nuns eat just like anyone else!' Mrs Dufferin took great enjoyment in relating this story to her friends.

The Mercy charism[9]

Who were these Sisters of Mercy who were awaited in Belfast with such high expectations? The Congregation of the Sisters of Mercy was founded by Catherine McAuley, a Dublin woman, in the mid-nineteenth century. In 1827, two years before Catholic emancipation was granted in Great Britain and Ireland, on 25 September, the feast of Our Lady of Mercy, Catherine, a woman of prayer and compassion, opened a house in Baggot Street, near the centre of fashionable Dublin, for the relief, protection and education of the poor. Her charitable work included the visitation of the sick and people in prison, the care and education of poor and neglected children and the shelter and training of unemployed girls and young women. She did not have in mind the founding of a religious congregation. Her ambition was to serve God's poor as a lay woman. However, Providence decided otherwise. On the urgent recommendation of her ecclesiastical superiors, and in keeping with the Catholic Church's understanding at the time regarding women who wished to live a regular life of spiritual exercises and apostolic service in the community such as Catherine and her companions envisaged and, indeed, were already putting into practice, she and two of her companions made a novitiate under the direction of the Irish Presentation Sisters in their convent in George's Hill, Dublin. They took their religious vows on 12 December 1831. This date marks the foundation of the Institute of the Religious Sisters of Mercy, under the patronage of Our Lady of Mercy.

In 1835 Pope Gregory XVI gave his approval and blessing to the institute for its dedication to the work of 'helping the poor, relieving the sick in every possible way and safeguarding, by the exercise of charity, women who find themselves in circumstances dangerous to virtue'.[10]

In time, Catherine's community of religious Sisters became the largest congregation of women established by an English-speaking Catholic. At the time of her death, 11 November 1841, the number of her associates had grown from two to 140, and her institute had established 13 branches in Ireland and England.[11] In the same year, 1841, Pope Gregory XVI formally approved the rule and constitutions of the institute. Less than a hundred years later, in 1926, its status as an institute of pontifical rite was confirmed by the Holy See. Catherine was proclaimed Venerable in May 1986. The naming of a candidate as venerable is the first stage of the process towards the canonisation (proclamation of sainthood) of a person noted for his or her sanctity and outstanding Christian commitment.

The story of Catherine McAuley is the story of a heroine who marked out a path for women who would vow to serve Jesus Christ and people who were enduring poverty, deprivation and suffering in any form they had the power to alleviate. She was an idealist in her conception of the power of women for the betterment of society. She was also a realist with a prophetic vision and a great heart, evinced in a personal concern for humankind. She was a woman of prayer, penance and humility, with an unbounded confidence in God.

Catherine's image of a member of the Sisters of Mercy was expressed in her own words:

> Besides an ardent desire to be united to God and to serve the poor, she must feel a particular interest for the sick and dying, otherwise the duty of visiting them would soon become exceedingly toilsome. She should be healthy, have a feeling, distinct, impressive manner of speaking and reading, a mild countenance expressive of sympathy and patience. And there is so much to be required as to reserve and recollection[,] … caution and prudence in the visits that it is desirable aspirants should be rather young, before habits and manners are so long formed as not too likely to alter.[12]

However, ever a realist, Catherine continued:

> I beg again to remark that this is what *seems* generally necessary. I am aware exceptions may be met, and where there is a decided preference for the Order and other essential dispositions, conformity in practice might be accomplished at any period of life.[13]

It would appear that Catherine's vision did coincide with God's plan. Today more than 15,000 Sisters carry on an extensive educational, medical and social apostolate in keeping with Catherine's creed of service, that 'the poor need help today, not next week'.

Imbued with these ideals, and with Catherine's dedication to 'the poor, the sick and the ignorant' (the traditional vow formula for the Sisters of Mercy), the Sisters from Dublin responded to the call to contribute, as best they could, to the welfare of their sisters and brothers who were flocking into the new industrial town of Belfast in the 1850s in search of employment and what they hoped would be the promise of a better life. The need for the works of mercy, both spiritual and temporal, that marked their apostolic dedication was glaringly obvious in a rapidly expanding urban industrial community. They immediately set themselves to the task of carrying them out.

1   Mary Ann McCracken, writing as a member of the Board of the Charitable Institute, Clifton Street, Belfast (*c.* 1859), quoted in M. McNeill, *The life and times of Mary Ann McCracken, 1770–1866: a Belfast panorama* (Belfast: Blackstaff Press, 1988).

2   See Chapter 2.

3   DCDA (D.54/1).

4   Account of a visit by Mr and Mrs S.C. Hall in the 1840s in A. Jordan, *Who cared? Charity in Victorian and Edwardian Belfast* (Belfast: Institute of Irish Studies, Queen's University, 1993), p. 15.

5   Ibid., p. 12.

6   Society of Saint Vincent de Paul, *Centenary volume* (Belfast, 1951). See also P. Rogers, *St Peter's Pro-Cathedral, Belfast, 1866–1966* (Belfast: Howard Publications, 1967), p. 11.

7   M.M. Cummins, 'The coming of the Sisters of Mercy to Belfast', *St Malachy's Convent Primary School Centenary Brochure, 1878–1978* (1978), p. 49 (edited).

8   C. O'Byrne, *As I roved out: a book of the north* (Belfast: Blackstaff Press, 1982), p. 54.

9   The 'charism' of a religious order or congregation is the special quality or gift that indicates the spirit of the congregation and the purpose for which it was founded. This is usually inherited from the vision of the founder.

10 Catherine McAuley to Very Reverend John Rice, 8 December 1833. Very Reverend John Rice, brother of St Ignatius Rice, was then in Rome. (See Appendix to Chapter 1.)

11 Sisters of Mercy, 'Directory of foundations, 1863–1913' (MIA).

12 Letter, Catherine McAuley, 5 September 1836, in Bolster, A., *Correspondence of Catherine McAuley, 1827–1841* (Cork, 1989).

13 Ibid.

2

THE EARLY DAYS

The day after the arrival of Sister M. Philomene and her companions, Reverend Mother Vincent Whitty, superior of the Convent of Mercy, Baggot Street, Sister M. Gabriel Sherlock and Sister M. Aloysius Brady (a novice), accompanied by Reverend Doctors Crolly and Murray of Maynooth College, arrived in Belfast around midday.[1] Dr Crolly celebrated Mass the following day in the front parlour, and on the feast of the conversion of St Paul Sister M. Philomene and Sister M. Ignatius made the first visitation of the sick to one or two homes, Kate Molloy leading the way for them. The schools would not be ready for about a fortnight, but the Sisters were not idle. The entire evenings were employed in receiving visits from the mill girls and factory girls. They came in batches and fortunately the hall held a good number. The Sister 'on show' usually asked what they thought of the nuns, and each girl was sure to say, 'I think well of you, ma'am.' When the novice, Sister M. Aloysius, was sent to them it was a common thing for her, as soon as she turned the stairs, to see all the persons in the hall fall on their knees. They imagined that as she was unlike the rest, with her white veil, she must be the reverend mother.

As soon as the schoolrooms were ready the day schools opened with very large numbers under the charge of Sister M. Gabriel. Then a report spread through the town that the nuns would have a night school. This was to have its first opening at seven o'clock on a particular evening. The Sisters had tea at 6.30 p.m. in the refectory, the end window of which looked out over the back lane which led into Callender Street and into which the school door opened. While at tea, the Sisters were attracted by a strange sound from the lane and heard a hum of voices 'so deep and so mighty' that Reverend Mother Vincent became alarmed, not knowing what to think, yet knowing that the school girls were assembled at the door for admittance. Fortunately a carpenter was at work in the house and on investigation discovered that the hum came from the dense crowd below in the lane. He was asked to take charge of the school door, but the press of the young women seeking admittance was so great there appeared to be a danger that lives might be lost. The man had to exert all his strength to pull each girl into the hallway

I leave and bequeath to the said Rt. Rev. Cornelius Denvir and such other person or persons as from time to time for the time being forever hereafter shall successively officiate as Roman Catholic Bishop within the said Diocese of Down and Connor according to the rights and discipline of the Roman Catholic Church the sum of Four hundred pounds sterling so lent and advanced by and to the Corporation for improving the port and harbour of Belfast as aforesaid Upon Trust to expend, lay out and disburse the said two principal sums of Six hundred pounds and Four hundred pounds (making together the sum of One thousand pounds) in building, erecting, establishing, purchasing or maintaining a suitable house and premises as an Institution to be conducted by a Body of females of a religious Order professing the Roman Catholic Faith for the moral and religious education of poor female Children as the said Rt. Rev. Cornelius Denvir and such other person or persons as from time to time for the time being forever hereafter shall successively officiate as Roman Catholic Bishop within the said Diocese of Down and Connor according to the rites and disciplines of the Roman Catholic Church shall think necessary and useful and it is my will that no part of the said sum of One thousand pounds shall be laid out or expended in the Purchasing of Building Ground as a site for the said intended Institution but that the entire sum shall be so expended in its erection, completion and fitting up or in the purchase and maintenance of a house suitable for such an Institution as aforesaid as the Rt. Rev. Cornelius Denvir and such other person or persons as from time to time for the time being forever hereafter shall successively officiate as Roman Catholic Bishop within the said Diocese of Down and Connor according to the rites and discipline of the Roman Catholic Church and by whom as such Roman Catholic Bishop the said two sums of Six hundred pounds and Four hundred pounds or either of them shall be received in pursuance of the bequests aforesaid may think most expedient for securing the moral and religious education of such poor Children as aforesaid, and I hereby direct and my Will is that my said Executors and trustees shall as soon as convenient after my said Wife's decease or Marriage make sale and absolutely dispose of all my estate and interest in the said hereditments and premises situate in Annette Street, Abbey Street and North King Street as aforesaid and in such manner as they shall consider most beneficial, and pay the monies that may be realised by such a sale to the Rt. Rev. Cornelius Denvir or such other person or persons as from time to time and for the time being forever hereafter shall successively officiate as Roman Catholic Bishop within the Diocese of Down and Connor to be by him or them applied towards the maintenance and for the benefit and advantage of the said Institution upon such trusts and for such purposes as are hereinbefore declared and stated with regard to the said sum of One thousand pounds provided always that the person who for the time being shall officiate as the Roman Catholic Bishop within the said Diocese of Down and Connor according to the rites and discipline of the Roman Catholic Church shall offer up or cause to be offered Masses for the eternal happiness of my soul …

Will of James Duffy leaving one thousand pounds on trust for the establishment of a charitable institution to be run by females religious from out of the crowd. This process occupied him for full two hours before the crowd was cleared.[2]

The feast of St Patrick, 17 March, was the day fixed for the installation of Sister M. Philomene Maguire as superior of the new community, and the previous day Mother M. Xavier Maguire (her sister), Sisters M. Angela Boland, M. Borgia Fortune and M. Aloysius Gonzaga Morrin arrived from Dublin for the occasion. This was an event of great formality, the canonical installation of the new community in Belfast. The appointment was made by the bishop:

Act of appointment
On the Feast of St. Patrick, 1854, the Community of the Sisters of Mercy assembled in Choir when Sr. M. Philomene Maguire was appointed Mother Superior for six years by his Lordship the Right Revd. Dr. Denvir in his Diocese and in the town of Belfast.

(Signed) Sr. M. Vincent Whitty

The above named Sr. M. Philomene Maguire was on this day appointed by us Mother Superior of the Convent of the Sisters of Mercy in the Town of Belfast for six years in the presence of the Community assembled in Choir and in the presence of the Revd. Joseph Fagan, Chaplain of the said Convent, and the Revd. Edward Kelly, Professor, Diocesan Seminary.

+ Cornelius Denvir
Dated on the Feast of St. Patrick,
17 March, 1854
Patrick J. Fagan
Edward Kelly.[3]

The earliest entry in the Acts of Chapter of the Belfast community contains a brief record which indicates that Sister M. Philomene Maguire had already been appointed superior of the new foundation in Belfast when it had been projected in the motherhouse in Baggot Street ten months previously, probably following the visit of the Reverend Bernard McAuley at the end of 1852:

On 17th of March 1853 the Community of the Sisters of Mercy were assembled in Choir when the appointment of Sr. M. Philomene Maguire …[4]

Such an appointment would have been made by the mother superior of the community in Baggot Street Convent, from which the new foundation was being made. When a community was established elections for a new superior were held every three years. The record is incomplete but can only relate to this appointment having taken place in her original community in Baggot Street. This conjecture seems further confirmed by the 'Act of Election' of 9 June 1859:

> Sister Mary Philomene Maguire, having completed her six years term of office, the Chapter assembled for the election of a Mother Superior …[5]

A few days after this historic occasion Mother M. Xavier Maguire returned to Dublin with Mother M. Vincent Whitty, while the others remained in Belfast, Sister M. Aloysius permanently. In August 1854 Sisters M. Angela Boland and M. Gabriel Sherlock also returned to Baggot Street. Sister Mary Lister, one of the original pioneers, returned in August 1855.

The first bazaar for furnishing the new convent was held in the community room and parlour. It lasted for two or three days and was a great success. The Sisters had arrived.

While living in Donegall Square North the Sisters attended Mass each morning in St Malachy's Church. This church, near Cromac Square, was the third Catholic church in Belfast and had been opened in 1844 by Bishop Denvir. It had been built to accommodate the needs of the estimated 30,000 Catholic inhabitants of the town who could not all be provided for by the two existing churches, St Patrick's and St Mary's.[6] Immediately after the arrival of the Sisters of Mercy in Belfast a chaplain was appointed to them, Reverend Joseph McGrane, a native of Balbriggan, County Dublin, and he continued with the community until the beginning of 1856, when he was obliged, through sickness, to return to his native place. He died there a few months afterwards at only 30 years of age. A stained-glass window of St Joseph was erected in one of the oratories in St Paul's Convent and was inscribed, 'This window was erected to the memory of the late George Joseph McGrane, chaplain to the convent, who died on the eve of the Ascension, May 16th, in the year of Our Lord 1856; on whose soul, sweet Jesus, have mercy.' After the Sisters moved out of St Paul's in 1992 the window was transferred to the oratory in Ballysillan House (614 Crumlin Road, Belfast – a community house). The first chaplain to St Paul's Convent, Crumlin Road was Reverend Jeremiah Ryan McAuley, C.P. He had a very interesting career.[7]

The national schools in Hamilton Street were handed over to the Sisters and two of them went there daily to teach. They had already commenced visitation and visited many poor families who were crowded in the narrow entries between Donegall Square North and High Street, where sickness and infant mortality were common and the ministrations of the kindly Sisters were gladly welcomed. Their evenings were occupied with classes, when crowds of mill and factory girls assembled to receive instruction in both secular and religious subjects. Soon all the works of the Mercy apostolate were in successful operation in the town. Several munificent benefactors appeared to aid the Sisters in the promotion and extension of their work and the witness of their zeal soon attracted new members to join the community.

The evening schools

It would seem appropriate at this point to give some details about the innovative work undertaken by the Sisters from the outset of their residence in Belfast – that is, the evening school for working girls and young women. The *Irish Quarterly Review* in 1856 published an article by Patrick (later Sir Patrick) Keenan, a school inspector in the Belfast area for the Commissioners of National Education in Ireland, on the subject of female adult education, which was for the most part an extended report on his visit to the evening school run by the Sisters. Keenan later went on to be the chief official of the national-school system.[8] This work was indeed innovative because, although there were in existence various philanthropic societies for the promotion of learning in addition to the provision of day schools, these were mainly for young men of a higher class. Where evening schools for females did exist they were, to all intents and purposes, schools for working female children who could not attend school during the day. They did not attract the older mill girls or women. The existence and success of an evening school for women in connection with the convent could, according to Keenan, 'only be traced to the zeal and enterprise of its own conductors'.[9] The Sisters saw the plight of the mill girls and decided to make the problems of these poor girls their responsibility, insofar as they could. Keenan further commented:

> The Sisters of Mercy in Belfast are the first who, on a scale of greatness and national efficiency, conceived the idea of education of adult females.[10]

Keenan reported that the school 'offers those who are ignorant of book learning and industriously employed during the day an opportunity of obtaining a literary education. In this respect it may be regarded as the complement and converse of ordinary industrial schools.' He pointed out that, though statutory provision had been made by the National Education Board for evening classes, these classes were very poorly attended in most areas. Thus, he was deeply impressed by this educational venture undertaken by the Sisters so recently established in the town:

> Few institutions which we have inspected afforded us anything like the pleasure and satisfaction we derived from a visit we made to the Evening School for Female Adults conducted by the Sisters of Mercy in Callender Street National School. This school was established for the purpose of extending the blessings of education to grown females, especially to those who are employed in the mills of the town.[11]

At this time there were 33 mills in Belfast and its neighbourhood, giving employment to more than 32,000 persons. According to Keenan, thousands of young women, 'who have never played at the apron strings of a mother, or heard their names called over by a father's voice, worked in the mills from half-past five in the morning until six o'clock in the evening'. Having started work at a very early age, they had had no opportunity for schooling and were, for the most part, illiterate. Their working conditions were in most cases very inhumane; their health was being eroded and their dreary existence gave little promise of betterment in the future: 'Physical hardship and moral peril are the conditions of the poor mill girls' life,' Keenan reported.

The education of these girls was considered impracticable by the Education Board. In simple terms, no one wanted to bother with them. One excuse was that to encourage them to leave their homes at night in order to attend classes was to expose them to the dangers and temptations of the streets. Better ignorance and innocence, it was said, than knowledge and vice. There was one group of people who did not accept these excuses and did not agree with the adage. The Sisters of Mercy conceived the idea of educating these young girls and women in order to help them confront the challenges of their condition in life, to achieve literacy and combat ignorance, and so to raise their sense of self-esteem and even better their prospects for whatever employment they might aspire to.

And so the evening classes officially commenced at the beginning of March 1854, a mere two months after the arrival of the Sisters in Belfast. Premises had become available in Callender Street which could serve as schoolrooms. A brief word has already been said about the first opening of the school. Keenan gave a vivid account worth quoting:

> The crowd of grown females that sought admission on the first night amounted to about twice the number the school could accommodate. The Sisters made every exertion to reduce the number by excluding those who could read or write, no matter how imperfectly; but the attempt was ineffectual on account of the persevering eagerness of *all* to remain. They rushed and pushed and cried and begged to be permitted to stay in the school. Organization, classification, arrangement of any kind were accordingly out of the question, and at the end of the first

week the Sisters thought it the safest and most prudent course to close their doors altogether for a time. They hoped that the temporary closing of the school would allay the ardour of some of those who fought so hard to be admitted, and that the novelty of the thing would soon, in a measure, pass away.[12]

The school was reopened about a month later, but the number of applicants had not diminished. Rather, they had brought with them new recruits, eager as the first to obtain admission. This time the Sisters had recourse to a strategy for handling the unmanageable numbers. They divided them into two classes, one class consisting of those who could read tolerably (about 250 in number) and were anxious to learn writing, arithmetic, etc., and another (about 300), most of whom did not even 'know their letters'. Equally, the evenings were divided up – Tuesdays and Thursdays for the first group and Mondays, Wednesdays and Fridays for the second. The pupils of both classes were adults, and many of them were married women.

It was obvious that these evening classes had a great attraction for the working girls and women. Keenan reported that his first visit took place 'on a cold, rainy, cheerless evening … an evening when it would be more than difficult to drag oneself away from home and fireside after twelve hours' work in a mill'. However, to the observer's surprise (for he expected to find no one), when he entered the schoolroom at seven o'clock:

> there were 205 young persons there assembled; their work in the mills had ceased, and in the meantime they had gone home, washed themselves, arranged their hair and dress and then made their way, dark and stormy as it was, from various remote parts of the town, in all comeliness and cleanliness, to school.[13]

Not only literacy was taught in these evening classes but also writing, arithmetic, history and political geography, according to the aptitude of the pupils. Because of the accommodation problem (the school could only adequately cope with 300 students), the most advanced (those who had attained fourth-class standard) were periodically asked to leave the school in order to make room for the newcomers who had to start at the beginning. On average, the students achieved this top standard within five months. The girls attending the evening school paid one penny per week and received instruction, books, pens, slates and other requirements free. The school was well equipped with maps, charts and all kinds of helpful visual aids. Education was not only academic but social. Personal cleanliness, discipline, good moral behaviour and general propriety and responsibility were

SISTERS OF MERCY, CALLENDER STREET SCHOOL. July 1855

Notes and General Remarks upon School inspected by Mr Keenan

Date of Visit: 9th, 10th, 13 July
Name of School: Callender Street, Belfast.
Roll No.: 7.059
County: Antrim
Average Number on Books for 12 Months: 403
Average Attendance for 12 Months: 260.6
On Rolls at time of Visit: 441
Average Age: Males - ; Females: 9
Income from: Board: £53-7-6   School Fees: £49-4-8   Other sources: -   Total:£102-7-6

 Callender Street

1. Two commodious rooms; light and ventilation good.
2. Furniture excellent and well arranged; large supply of prints, charts, maps and tables; cabinet of objects, large globes, etc.
3. Time-table good; accounts neat and accurate; children remarkably clean and orderly; simultaneous instruction employed in teaching geography; large supply of books and requisites.
4. Teachers: the Sisters of the Convent of Mercy; highly qualified for their duties; system of teaching intellectual and effective.
5. Reading excellent; fait proficiency in all other branches; industrial work very superior and very practical.
6. This is one of the best organised and most useful schools I have ever visited; the infant department is particularly interesting; manners and demeanour of the children most becoming; every thing so well arranged that the business goes on like clockwork.

ADULT FEMALE EDUCATION

There was an average on the school rolls of 425, and an average attendance of 275, for the last year. On the evening that we visited the school there were, as we have stated, 205 females present. Of these -

13 were 12 years of age	29 were 18 years of age
12 were 13 years of age	19 were 19 years of age
19 were 14 years of age	14 were 20 years of age
26 were 15 years of age	9 were 21 years of age
24 were 16 yeasr of age	4 were 22 years of age
28 were 17 years of age	8 were 23 and above

The average age is then about 18 1/2 years - the very period of female life when moral danger is most imminent, when the affections and the passions are most active and least fixed, and the enemy to virtue sees in woman his richest prize. At such a stage in her life, Knowledge is offered as a shield of sweet protection, and the school in which the offering is made is as thronged as theatres in gayer places on gala nights. Of the moral phases of the school and the inducements to attend it, however, more presently. The employments during the day of those present were varied as follows: -

Working at mills	180	Muslin Workers	2
Servants	5	Fruiterer	1
Waistcoat maker	1	Book-binder	1
Dress makers	5	Not employed	10

The classification, according to the proficiency of the pupils, was as follows: -

25 in first Book (still unable to read)
63 in second do.
42 in sequel to second Book
46 in third Book, and
29 in fourth Book.

One hundred and seventeen were engaged at writing on paper, and, for apparently sound reasons, the nuns had relinquished in the evening school the practice of writing on slates - 176 were learning the arithmetical tables - 151 were learning the easy rule of mental arithmetic - 29 were working at commercial arithmetic upon slates, and the latter girls were also employed in the study of the rudiments of grammar and political geography. The classes were examined, and we found 4 who could read with care and expression, and about 90 who could read with as much clearness and intelligibility as the general mass of educated people; 59 of those who were able to read with sufficient fluency and expression as to be characterised 'fair readers' had entered the school ignorant of the very letters of the alphabet; 22 girls had learned a fair share of the rudiments of grammar, and 29 were intimately acquainted with the outlines of the maps of the world, Europe, America, Ireland, etc.; 30 girls were able to write a free and agreeable hand and there were a few who had attained to a bold, clear and gentlewomanly style.

The order, attention and neatness of the pupils were amongst the many remarkable and satisfactory features of the school; and the whole tone and 'ensemble' appeared to be an expressive picture of industry, skill, efficiency and happiness.

The were seven Sisters present on the occasion of the Commissioner's visit. Mother M. Philomene was Superioress, Sr. M. Borgia Fortune was 'superintendant of the school'. Report, p. 179

Notes and general remarks upon schools inspected by Patrick Keenan, Commissioner for Education, during the year 1855 expected, and the industrial employers invariably commented on how these young women who attended the nuns' school appeared to raise the tone of their place of employment. Also, evidence showed that the manufacturing proprietors preferred employing those who had some basic education.

The Sisters had certain principles governing admission to the school. Their objective was to reduce ignorance and illiteracy and so preference was given to those who needed to start at the lowest grade, simply to learn the rudiments of reading and writing. It was 'to make the ignorant wise and not the wise wiser that the school was opened', and it was open 'to persons of all persuasions'. They had a fundamental rule of non-compulsion and non-interference in matters of religion. Though each evening session ended with a brief period of prayer, the Sisters held that in the schoolroom their task was 'to teach, not preach; to reform, not to proselytise'.[14]

Even with the evidence of such a highly successful and unquestionably valuable educational enterprise, the Board of Education was slow to recognise the school's claim. Although in April 1855, when the school was in perfect working order (according to the opinion of the authorised inspector), the Sisters applied to have recognition and funding for their evening department from the board, this recognition was not given until 14 months later. The funding which accompanied the recognition was minimal: £7 per annum for every hundred adults actually attending nightly (the average nightly attendance was, for a variety of material reasons, usually little over 50 per cent of the numbers on roll, as was also the case in most day schools of the time). Consequently the grant came to something less than a penny farthing per head per annum, or about £3 10s for every hundred on roll. At this period, throughout the country, the question of maintaining convent national schools out of public funds was a major and controversial one. It was generally assumed that the nuns had ample means for the maintenance of their educational institutions. In actual fact, the reality of the situation was very different, particularly for those who worked for the poor and conducted non-fee-paying schools and yet were expected to meet the standards of staffing, facilities, services and equipment of the maintained national schools. In spite of this, reports show that in all requirements the convent schools, in most cases, far surpassed those provided by the other schools.[15]

Growth and expansion

The first accommodation of the Sisters in Donegall Square North was understood to be only temporary. From the time the decision had been taken in Baggot Street to send Sisters to Belfast, negotiations had been going on between Reverend Mother M. Vincent Whitty and Bishop Denvir with regard to the building of a convent in the town. It is interesting to note that some years later, on 16 April 1858, the *Building News* reported that in 1852 it had been announced that active arrangements were being made for the erection of 'a suitable building for conventual purposes' on a portion of ground adjoining the residential quarters of the Catholic seminary (St Malachy's College, founded on 3 November 1833), which was situated on the leased site of Vicinage. Vicinage was quite an extensive estate on the outskirts of Belfast, within about half a mile of the town, above the poor house on Clifton Street. It had been owned by the McCabe family and in the 1820s was in the possession of Thomas McCabe, grandson of the original owner and relative of William O. Putnam McCabe, who had been a noted figure in the United Irishmen. It was leased in 1832 (and purchased later, in 1837) by the bishop of Down and Connor, Dr William Crolly, and the diocesan seminary was opened there in November 1833.[16] The purchase of Vicinage was the beginning of what was to become an extensive site, between the Antrim Road and the Crumlin Road, of the Catholic Church's most important and impressive educational and medical institutions in the diocese: St Malachy's College and Seminary, the convent of the Sisters of Mercy and their schools and orphanage adjoining, and the Mater Infirmorum Hospital, whose frontage, aligning the Crumlin Road, is a landmark up to the present time.

However, everything was not plain sailing, as we can gather from a letter of 22 November 1853 from Mother M. Vincent to the bishop:

> Convent of Our Lady of Mercy,
> Baggot Street.
> November 22nd, 1853
>
> Right Revnd. and Dear Dr. Denvir,
> As you cannot give us the ground at the Vicinage for building would you have any objection to our getting it in any other locality and building the convent by subscriptions? Although this house[17] is such a good one it would not, of course, answer the purposes of a *settled* Convent and before we go it would be well to see the best means of doing the good work permanently.
>
> I am sorry to give you, my Lord, all this trouble, but I think you will be better pleased with me when we say beforehand all that is necessary.
>
> On reflection we have been thinking that two acres of ground might be *quite* enough for our wants – of course we would not purchase this ground until we would be settled in Belfast.
> Hoping for an early answer, I am, my Lord,
> Your faithful servant in J.C.,
>
> Sr. M. Vincent Whitty[18]

The Sisters did settle in Belfast and their work flourished, and the question of a permanent convent again arose. Providence had unfailingly stepped in to lend a hand in the form of a very generous bequest in the will of James Duffy, by which he left in trust to Bishop Denvir £1,000:

> to lay out and disburse … in building, erecting, establishing, purchasing or maintaining a suitable house and premises as an Institution to be conducted by a body of females of a Religious Order professing the Roman Catholic Faith for the moral and religious education of poor female children as the said Rt. Rev. Cornelius Denvir … shall think necessary and useful.[19]

This bequest was made on 23 September 1854 – the eve of the patronal feast of the Mercy Institute, the feast of Our Lady of Mercy.

This will, along with the promise of donations from some of the wealthier Catholics of Belfast – whose numbers were expanding steadily in keeping with the new commercial prosperity of the town and who were willing contributors towards the needs of their church – and funds from the dowers of the Sisters themselves – that is, the money brought by the young women who joined the community – made it possible to plan for the building of a 'settled convent'.

As we can see from the letter above, at first Bishop Denvir was unwilling to give any Vicinage land for the building of a convent. In the light of the Duffy will, however, he eventually gave two acres. Later an adjoining site was purchased, subject to head rent, by Belfast gentlemen from a Mrs Law (a Protestant) for the building of schools. This was on the Crumlin Road, on the immediate outskirts of the town, to the north. At that time the Crumlin Road was the only road out of the town to the north, the old coach road passing through the villages of Ardoyne and Ligoniel and crossing over Squire's Hill to Crumlin, Glenavy and eventually Lough Neagh. In May 1855 Bishop Denvir laid the foundation stone of the new convent of Our Lady of Mercy, later to be known as St Paul's, Crumlin Road and work began the following year. The architect chosen was J.J. McCarthy of Dublin and the builder was Thomas Byrne. According to the plans, the convent was eventually to be a fine quadrangular structure, but only the front portion was erected at first. The wings and cloisters were added in 1859. While the convent was being built a good-sized house was acquired in Hamilton Street, not far from the Sisters' original accommodation in the town centre and off May Street. The Sisters remained there for a few years until their new home was ready.

Mother M. Philomene Maguire's next initiative was the opening of a convent in Downpatrick. The original invitation to the Sisters of Mercy in Baggot Street had been to make a foundation in Downpatrick, but this had been deflected on the plea of the greater need for Sisters in Belfast.[20] Downpatrick – the parish of Down – had for 13 centuries been the mensal see of the bishop.[21] Its strong associations with St Patrick and the origins of Christianity in Ireland had made it a noted ecclesiastical centre. However, when the parish priest of Belfast, Reverend William Crolly, was appointed bishop of Down and Connor on 31 January 1825, he persuaded the pope, with the support of his fellow clergy and laity, to transfer the episcopal parish to Belfast, where he still held the position of parish priest, as his successors do to this day. Bishop Crolly was the first Catholic bishop to be ordained to the episcopate in Belfast – in St Patrick's New Chapel, Donegall Street. He later became archbishop of Armagh. But sadly, Belfast's gain was Downpatrick's loss.[22] Sisters M. Aloysius Brady, M. Borgia Fortune and three other Sisters formed the group that made the new foundation in Downpatrick and took up residence in Irish Street. They were warmly welcomed by the Catholic people of the town and, from the beginning, very richly blessed in their energetic exercise of the works of mercy. In February 1860 this community was constituted an independent convent. Its history will be followed up in later chapters of this story.

Meantime the small founding community in Belfast was growing. Already, by the end of 1854, the first two postulants[23] had arrived, Louise Reynolds and Charlotte Geraghty. Louise Reynolds received her votes for reception on 23 October of that year but she did not remain in the community. Charlotte Geraghty also was accepted, on 26 December, to receive the Mercy habit. She persevered and went on to have an interesting career in the congregation.

In the summer of 1854 Sister M. Aloysius Brady, who had come from Baggot Street as a novice with the superior, Reverend Mother M. Vincent Whitty, the day after the arrival of the first Sisters in Belfast, made her profession as a member of the new community. The actual date of the profession ceremony is not recorded, but 23 June is given as the date when she received the votes of the community to be admitted to profession. This must have been quite a momentous event for the pioneer Sisters and their friends and benefactors. Unfortunately the details of this first profession ceremony are not recorded in the annals, so we can only conjecture that it must have been quite a private affair, with only community and friends present. This is understandable, since the Sisters would not yet have been sure of how they had been accepted by the mainly Protestant population of the town.

In December 1854 the novitiate group was joined by a 'white novice'[24] from Baggot Street, Sister M. Mercy McCann. Their numbers were further expanded by the entrance, in the course of 1855, of Mary O'Hara (Sister M. Vincent, who went to Downpatrick), Eliza Walsh (Sister M. de Sales) and Anna Houlahan (Sister M. Joseph). These Sisters were to figure prominently in the later history of the community. In 1856 came Maria Sharman (who did not stay) and Mary Anne Byrne (Sister M. Vincent). Nannie O'Brien (Sister M. Philomene) and Caroline Hayes followed in 1857, though Caroline did not persevere.

It would be interesting to know if any of these young women were northerners, or even natives of Belfast. The records of the earliest days are, in many cases, incomplete as to family details. We know for sure only one who was local – or nearly so – Mary Anne Byrne, daughter of Michael and Catherine Byrne of Muckamore, County Antrim. Eliza Walsh was from Cappoquin, County Waterford and, in Belfast, found herself a long way from home. We know nothing of where the other Sisters came from.

After the Sisters had moved into the new convent on the Crumlin Road (1857) they were further blessed by the arrival of more new members: Louise Grace, Ann McQuillan, Margaret Sherman and Mary Maher. By the end of 1858 13 young women had entered the Belfast community. Of these, nine were professed on the completion of their novitiate and joined, with youthful spirits and generous hearts, in the service of the poor, the sick and the uneducated, and of all those in any sort of need.

The powerhouse behind the success and growth of the Mercy missions in Belfast and Downpatrick was the leader of the first band of pioneers, and the first superior, Mother M. Philomene Maguire. We have a contemporary pen portrait of this remarkable woman in the description given by Patrick Keenan on his visit to the schools in Callender Street:

> The Superior was affable, learned and accomplished; she had a countenance expressive of an enduring enthusiasm; no project that was destined to make her fellow-creatures wiser and better was too formidable for her; no check, no baulk, nor cross, nor frustration could apparently sink her heart or diminish her hopefulness. Her voice was of that right womanly kind, it was sweet, firm and impressive; and she moved from class to class amongst her devoted pupils with the dignity and gentleness of a hostess passing from guest to guest, and had a smile and a word for each, that all might feel the assurance of her welcome and her desire to make them happy.[25]

Future history was to bear witness to these qualities so acutely observed by the visitor. Mother M. Philomene's influence was to extend far beyond Belfast, but at this date she found more than enough to absorb her talents and enthusiasm in her formidable task of enabling the Mercy Congregation to take root in the industrial capital of Ireland.

[1]   A note on the Sisters' names: at her formal reception into the community (usually after about six months' probation or postulancy) a Sister was given the name of a saint as her patron. This was usually prefixed by the name Mary (often abbreviated to M.) in honour of the Blessed Virgin Mary, who is considered a special patron of all religious. A religious is the official name by which a vowed member of a religious institute or congregation in the Catholic Church is known.

[2]   Sisters of Mercy, 'St Paul's Convent of Mercy, Belfast: annals' (MCA) (hereafter Annals, SPCMB).

[3]   Sisters of Mercy, 'St Paul's Convent of Mercy, Belfast: acts of chapter, 1854–1911, 1923–1994' (MCA) (hereafter Acts of chapter, SPCMB), vol. i.

[4]   Ibid.

[5]   Ibid.

[6]   J. O'Laverty, *An historical account of the diocese of Down and Connor, ancient and modern*, (5 vols, Dublin: Duffy, 1878–95 and Belfast: P. Quinn and Co., 1945), vol. ii, p. 424.

[7]   Ibid., p. 407.

[8]   P. Keenan, 'Female adult education' *Irish Quarterly Review*, no. 21 (1856).
      I am indebted to Mr Frank D'Arcy, head of the Department of Humanities in the University of Ulster, Magee College, Derry, for a copy of this very valuable article, and the information about its author.

[9]   Ibid.

[10] Ibid., p. 168.

[11] Ibid., p. 165.

[12] Ibid., p. 168.

[13] Ibid., p. 169.

[14] Ibid.

[15] See *Special reports of the Commissioners of National Education in Ireland on the convent schools*, HC 1864 (46) xlvi.

[16] O'Laverty, *op. cit.*, vol. ii, p. 435.

[17] 2A Donegall Square North.

[18] DCDA (D.53/39). It could be assumed from this letter that already in 1853 Mother M. Vincent Whitty had visited Belfast and seen the accommodation offered to the Sisters.

[19] Last will and testament of James Duffy (DCDA, 20 September 1855).

[20] See an early register of foundations: 'Convent of Our Lady of Mercy, Mount St. Patrick, founded in 1855 from St. Catherine's, Baggot Street, Dublin, through Belfast, by Mother M. Philomene Maguire,' in M.J. Gately, *The Sisters of Mercy: historical sketches, 1831–1931* (New York: Macmillan, 1931).

[21] The term 'mensal' in the Roman Catholic Church is applied to the benefice – church, land, etc. – set aside for the maintenance of the bishop of a diocese.

[22] *The Irishman*, 6 May 1825.

[23] A postulant is a young woman who presents herself as a candidate for a religious congregation or institute. After about six months' candidacy or apprenticeship, she and the congregation decide whether she will continue as a member and undertake the further training required (up to six or nine years) before she takes perpetual religious vows.

[24] The novitiate (or noviceship as it was sometimes called) was a period of two years' spiritual formation in religious life which followed postulancy. A 'white novice' was so called because she wore a white veil during her novitiate, receiving the black veil on making her religious profession.

[25] Keenan, *op. cit.*, p. 178.

3

Saint Paul's Convent Of Mercy, Crumlin Road

In the autumn of 1857 the new convent on the Crumlin Road was ready for occupation and opened under the patronage of St Paul, on whose feast, 25 January, the Sisters had formally taken up residence in Belfast. That feast was traditionally held thereafter as foundation day. It was indeed a fine building, the only work in Belfast of the 'Irish Pugin', as the great Gothic revivalist, James J. McCarthy, was known. It was more colourful than usual for McCarthy's work, being built in red brick with blue-brick relieving arches and Scotch sandstone details, and a distinctive feature was some fine tracery windows. It was planned around four sides of a central garden. A notice in *The Builder*, 27 March 1859, gives a further account of the progress of the work. By that date the south wing of the convent was finished and occupied by the nuns, and the schools, to accommodate 600 children, were also complete and in operation. The orphanage, for 50 children, was to be finished the following month. The cloisters and north, east and west wings of the convent were being built and would be finished before the end of the year. The style throughout was 'decorated Gothic of a monastic and collegiate character'. The contractor was Thomas Byrne of Belfast, and the cost of the contract was £10,000.[1]

The joy of the Sisters in taking occupation of their new and beautiful convent and commodious schools was to be short lived. They were not unaware, we can assume, of the extent of the financial undertaking, but they had confidence in the plans the bishop had had in mind when he invited them to Belfast. In order to supplement the legacy left by James Duffy, from the year 1855 public collections were being made in Belfast for the new convent, school and orphanage. The original outlay, £6,000, was formidable, and as the initial appeal had brought in less than £1,000 there was still a considerable sum to be accounted for. At this time the diocese was also trying to collect funds for the construction of a new church to serve the large Catholic population of the Pound area of the lower Falls Road. St Peter's Church was opened in October 1866 and later became the cathedral of the diocese of Down and Connor under the Most Reverend Dr C.B. Daly in 1986.

Convent crisis

Though the people contributed as generously as they could to the erection of the convent and schools, the financial undertaking had been so large that by the middle of 1861 the Sisters had got into serious difficulties about meeting the cost. This signalled the beginnings of a major crisis which was to have a very traumatic effect on the community, with reverberations echoing down through many years. Even towards the end of the 1850s, as the buildings were being brought to completion, there were intimations of the problems ahead. The community was being pressed by the builder for payment. The Sisters did not have the funds. Mother M. Philomene, the superior of the community, saw a lawsuit looming and sought to avoid it at all cost. She appealed to the bishop with a suggestion. There were wealthy Catholic businessmen and tradesmen in the town who would have been willing to take on the burden of the debt and organise the necessary fund-raising. Bishop Denvir, however, was unwilling to trust this project to such a body because, as one of his closest associates remarked, his 'natural turn of mind would not relish what he considered dictation from the laity'.[2]

As a result, after the first response to the appeal, no further donations were forthcoming.

Mother M. Philomene wrote, in January 1861, to Charles Cavanagh, a solicitor of Harcourt Street, Dublin, for advice. Cavanagh, noting the absence of a contract with the builder allowing for a delay in payment, could only inform her that she was 'all at sea and at his [the builder's] mercy'.[3]

Despite this daunting reply, she was determined to leave no stone unturned in her attempts to 'keep out of the law'. She was anxious not to be compelled to borrow money at a rate of interest which the convent could not pay back, as indicated in a letter to Archbishop Dixon, the primate of Armagh, in which she stated her fear that 'Dr Denvir would just raise money in the bank and the whole expense would be more than paid in interest and the principal still lying there'. She made a suggestion to the archbishop:

> if the bishop would take the portion of the debt due upon the schools as a Parish or Town debt and the Priests to collect for it, I think they would get a good part of it at once and perhaps with this, and the prospect of soon getting the rest of the money due for the schools, Mr Byrne would be satisfied and, please God, in time we would be able to pay the portion due on the Convent.[4]

When Dixon duly communicated Mother M. Philomene's suggestion to Denvir, his reply was that the nuns were being too troublesome, and he was determined not to concede to them: 'Wiser people than I have told me not to mind them. The way is to keep away from them …'[5]

By the end of 1861 a crisis had been reached. The building contractor, who had invested a lot of money in the project, found that there were no funds from which he could receive payment. He was owed the very substantial sum of £2,500 and he felt unable to continue the work without reimbursement. In his predicament he too consulted Archbishop Dixon, for whom he was then building the cathedral in Armagh. Dixon referred the matter to Cardinal Cullen who, as apostolic delegate, held a special responsibility for the religious orders in the country, asking him to use any influence at his disposal to obtain payment for the harassed contractor and thereby relieve him of the necessity of instituting legal proceedings. Naturally the cardinal was of the opinion that the responsibility lay in the hands of the bishop of the diocese. But Bishop Denvir was intransigent and would not come to the help of the Sisters in any way.

This state of affairs greatly distressed Dr Patrick Dorrian who, in 1860, had been appointed coadjutor bishop in Down and Connor. He was forced to watch helplessly from the sidelines as the processes of law were set in motion and the sheriff was about to take possession of the convent. Deeply hurt by the public humiliation which the church in Belfast was being made to suffer, and chafing at his own impotence to prevent or undo the scandal, in his helplessness he wrote frankly to the archbishop of Armagh:

> 2 Adelaide Place, Belfast
> February 21st, 1862
>
> My Dear Lord Primate,
> As your Grace is already aware of the state of Mr Byrne's claim against the Convent here and of his application to his Grace of Dublin, which your letter to Dr Denvir made me aware of, you will not think it strange, I trust, that I should drop a line or two to your Grace on the pass to which things are now come. Not that I can see what your Grace can do, but for fear that I would be guilty of any omission in not doing so.
>
> The suit has been put into the hands of the Sheriff and execution will be made [at] we know not what hour. The Schools of the Convent are dismissed and steps have been taken to make provision for the nuns in town for the time being; for the nuns must leave the moment the Sheriff's men enter.
>
> The spirit of the Catholics has been dampened enough already, but the state of things arising from this scandal is appalling, and the effects on religion incredible now and hereafter.

Dr. Denvir is exerting himself driving about but from what I see and hear he will *not* do the only thing that can meet the crisis. Last night I went so far as to tell him that he himself was morally responsible, that he let the works go on when it was his business to have stopped them, and that any effort now was only putting off the evil without meeting it, unless some Catholics would join him and secure the money in one of the Banks till time would have it paid – and that if *he* would do this, Catholics would join him. But he answered, 'I will not. I nearly lost my life before by that.'

Now, of course, he alone can do anything. Nor ought anyone else to interfere, for he might, and would, be left in for it without any help.

The Bishop has no committee and will have none. People hold aloof and will now say, as they do say, 'This is what comes of leaving our money affairs in the hands of the clergy who know nothing about business matters'. Whatever may turn up the effects must be disastrous to religion. The Bishop blames Mr. Byrne. I do not.
Believe me, your Grace,
Most faithfully,

+ P. Dorrian.[6]

Without any cooperation from the bishop the financial problem appeared insoluble and on 18 February 1862 the bailiffs proceeded to take possession of the new buildings and the Sisters had to leave. When Mother M. Philomene informed Archbishop Dixon officially that the convent had been taken over and the community dispersed, he regretted that he himself was unable to give any financial help and advised her to consult Archbishop Cullen about the Sisters leaving Belfast temporarily. He declared that he considered this to be 'the saddest affair for the Catholics of Ulster' that had happened in his lifetime, and could only foresee that 'the Catholics of Belfast especially will not be able to hold up their heads for many a long day to come'.[7]

Meanwhile, provision had to be made for the community, who found themselves without a home, the bailiffs having taken possession not only of the convent but also of the branch house, 15 Hamilton Street. The period of occupation of the convent by the bailiffs was from 18 February to 21 May 1862:

On 18th February 1862 legal proceedings were entered into by the Builder of Saint Paul's Convent, Belfast, against the Superioress and Community to recover his claim of upwards of three thousand pounds on the Building. The Bailiffs, having taken possession of the Convent, and the Branch House, No. 15 Hamilton Street, the Community were unhappily obliged to accept Mr James Connor's charitable invitation to his house in Great George's Street; and on 1 March twelve of the

Community removed to Saint Patrick's Convent, Downpatrick, the Superioress and professed Sisters to 17 Hamilton Street, until the 21st May when they all were recalled and re-established at Saint Paul's Convent, Crumlin Road, by His Lordship, Right Reverend Cornelius Denvir, Bishop.[8]

Several of the Sisters were welcomed by Mrs James Connor into her home in Great George's Street, and others were taken into the homes of other friends. An amusing anecdote from this time is recorded in the annals:

Sr. M. Gabriel McKenna (a member of St. Paul's community), granddaughter of this worthy woman (Mrs Connor), often spoke of her grandmother's joy at having the Sisters, and socks darned by the Sisters (during their stay) were never worn again and needlework or small gifts were locked away in a bottom drawer.[9]

Such was the veneration in which the Sisters were held!

On 1 March 12 members of the community moved to St Patrick's Convent, Downpatrick. These included the novices, Sisters M. Genevieve McQuillan, M. Magdalene Malone, M. Augustine Sherman and M. Catherine Dowling. Subsequently these novices were required to wait for an additional three calendar months before being admitted to profession because of their interrupted novitiate. The superior and two other Sisters went to 17 Hamilton Street.

The public embarrassment provoked by the eviction of the Sisters from the convent spurred the wealthier Catholics of the town to come to their rescue and to ensure that sufficient money was forthcoming to redeem the present debt. Eventually the community were enabled to return to St Paul's on 21 May 1862. But the financial difficulties were not all solved, and Mother M. Philomene still faced an uphill struggle to see the buildings completed. After the community was reinstated she made a suggestion to Dr Dorrian that a profession ceremony, which was due at this time, be held in public in the hope of raising funds. This profession ceremony was most likely held in St Patrick's Church. Though the immediate financial crisis had passed, the community were still left with a considerable debt for some years to follow. On 19 February 1865 Bishop Butler of Limerick preached a charity sermon in St Malachy's Church to raise money to pay off the £500 the convent still owed to the bank. More than £400 was collected.[10]

Dr Dorrian advised Mother M. Philomene to write to Bishop Denvir. This evoked an immediate reaction from the bishop, who came post haste to Dorrian to demand (in Dorrian's words), 'What did these nuns want now? Did I think but he would not object to them?', and added, 'This convent must go down.' Dorrian tried to reason with him, explaining that the community had £150 a year to pay in taxes, their dowries had nearly all been paid away to defray the debt and that now they had only the proceeds of the school to support them; and they must go to the wall if he (Denvir) did not look into the matter and suggest some remedy. Eventually the bishop conceded: 'It ended by his giving consent for this one thing' (the public ceremony). Dorrian concluded:

> In reality I don't know whether this is the best thing, and I gave no opinion to the Reverend Mother on the subject. But it can do no harm, and it is better to be doing something than nothing.[11]

It did not alleviate the problems of the Sisters of Mercy to know that, not only in his dealings with them but also in his handling of other responsibilities of his diocese, Dr Denvir was, at that time, either unwilling or unable to take on his obligations. As coadjutor, Dorrian did his best to make the bishop take action, not only on behalf of the convent and the adjoining schools but also for the sake of the other Catholic schools that were threatened with closure through lack of funds. However, the bishop seemed unwilling to take any advice whatsoever. Dorrian commented:

> There is no satisfaction nor use in speaking to him about schools, convents or chapels. He seems to think that we have some designs on him and that nobody understands anything but himself.[12]

No wonder this was a difficult time for Mother M. Philomene and her community.

The strain of the situation was telling severely on Mother M. Philomene. Though the crisis had passed and the Sisters were resettled in the convent and the schools again, the legal proceedings dragged on and she felt she was coming to the end of her resources. She wrote to Archbishop Dixon again:

> Mr Macken wrote to me again for money to go on with these law proceedings, and I wrote to Dr Dorrian to know what I should do. I enclose you his answer. It will give you an idea of how truly friendless I am. I really know not what to do. Would it be wrong for me to ask Dr Cullen to take me back to Baggot Street?

She then, surprisingly, admitted to some personal responsibility for the misunderstanding with the bishop:

I think if I were away the Bishop would perhaps do more for he has a great feeling against me, as having built the convent. I came here knowing we would get nothing from Baggot Street, and would not tell him. Do, my dear Lord, tell me what I am to do and most willingly I will do it.[13]

This crisis, and her very strained relations with Bishop Denvir, were to bring another turning point in Mother M. Philomene's career, as her subsequent story will show. But with this hurdle crossed the community set down firm roots which ensured the growth of future years. When the Sisters returned to the convent it can be assumed that they appreciated their new home more than ever. They had learned from sad experience and with careful management their work flourished in many new institutions, spreading through the city and beyond.

The motherhouse

St Paul's Convent became the cherished motherhouse and was to remain so for the next 130 years. In view of the fact that the Sisters are no longer in residence there, some further details as to the appearance of the convent will be of interest.

A contemporary report described the building as follows:

(It was) basically a functional structure, built to hold large numbers of people. The problem was to avoid a barrack-like appearance, which McCarthy did by having projecting bays break up the wall surfaces, and gables interrupt the roof-line, and by making a feature of a large traceried east window … The ecclesiastical flavour was further developed by having pointed windows, some traceried, some in pairs. What gives the building an unusual exotic appearance is the use of strong polychrome … McCarthy rarely uses such highly coloured materials.[14]

Over the years extensions were added. In 1867 Calvary Garden was designed, a spacious central cloister garth enfolded on three sides by the wings of the convent building. Here a beautiful stone Calvary group was erected on a small mound, surrounded by flowers and shrubs and creating a focal point for the daily life of the community.

As the community grew in number, the original chapel was no longer adequate. In the early 1900s a beautiful new one was built, adjoining the convent and alongside the avenue. The space between the outside sanctuary wall of the chapel and the road accommodated a pretty little garden of lawn, trees and flowering shrubs named Hamill Park after the benefactors, the

Hamill sisters, whose generous donations made possible the building of the new convent chapel, a spacious place of worship for the expanding community. St Anthony's Oratory was opened in 1910. See Chapter 13.

Extra storeys on the north wing in 1925 and on the south wing in 1937 were added by Frank McArdle, architect, completing the three-storey cloistered building surrounding the inner quadrangle. A handsome gate lodge was built at the entrance to Convent Avenue, principally from the proceeds of a bequest left by a benefactor named Warren Curran of Bridge Street, who died in 1875. Further extensions would be made before the convent reached its completion and these will be described in later chapters.

1   *The Builder*, 27 March 1859.
2   Archbishop Dixon to Reverend T. Kirby (then rector of the Irish College in Rome and agent of the Irish bishops) regarding the possibility of an arrangement between the nuns and the builder, Mr Byrne, which might prevent the matter going to court (DCDA, D.61/3, 10 June 1857).
3   C. Cavanagh to Mother M.P. Maguire (DCDA, D.61/11). The seriousness of the matter can be seen from the fact that also, in February 1861, Archbishop Dixon attempted to intervene with Bishop Denvir, requesting him seriously to consider 'if an arrangement could be made (with the builder) which would prevent the matter from coming to the courts' (DCDA, D.61/3).
4   Mother M.P. Maguire, St Paul's, to Most Reverend Dr Dixon (Primate Dixon Archive, Armagh, n.d.).
5   Archbishop Dixon to Bishop Denvir (Primate Dixon Archive, Armagh).
6   Primate Dixon Archive, Armagh.
7   Dixon to Mother M.P. Maguire (Primate Dixon Archive, Armagh, 27 February 1862).
8   Acts of chapter, SPCMB, vol. i.
9   Ibid.
10   *Belfast Morning News*, 20 February 1865.
11   Dorrian to Dixon (Primate Dixon Archive, Armagh, n.d.).
12   Ibid.
13   Mother M.P. Maguire, St Paul's, to Most Reverend Dr Dixon (Primate Dixon Archive, Armagh, n.d.).
14   *Building News*, 16 April 1858.

4

THE WORKS OF MERCY –
PENITENTIARY AND ORPHANAGE

With the traumatic experience of the eviction behind them the Sisters settled in the convent on the Crumlin Road and resumed their work of teaching and visitation. A few years previously (September 1858) a branch house had been opened at 15 Hamilton Street, attached to a larger building which was used for the next 20 years as a school. A house adjoining the schools was rented and made ready for the reception of young women who were homeless or, for one reason or another, had been rejected by their families. These penitentiaries were sometimes called Magdalene asylums. In the context of the repentance of prostitutes this dated back to the tradition (not solidly founded) that Mary Magdalene, 'a sinful woman', repented and followed Jesus. They were for the welfare of 'erring and repentant females reclaimed from the course of prostitution ... and willing to work for their support'. The problem of prostitution was an almost inevitable consequence of the rapid growth of a new industrial town. It is recorded that in the 1850s there were already two penitentiaries in Belfast, a Presbyterian one and an Episcopalian one, 'for the churches played an important role in the work of reform'.[1] A Magdalene asylum, sponsored by the Church of Ireland, had been opened in Donegall Pass in 1849 and a large number of Catholic women had found refuge in this establishment. It was considered that the Catholic Church itself needed to make some provision in this regard.

On the feast of St Patrick 1860 the house adjoining 15 Hamilton Street was taken with a view to opening a Belfast Catholic penitentiary under the patronage of the bishop, Cornelius Denvir. The bishop appointed a committee of local priests to watch over its spiritual and temporal needs while the Sisters of Mercy took responsibility for the day-to-day running of the house. The provision of refuge for distressed women had been a priority for Catherine McAuley, and so the Sisters willingly undertook this great work of charity.

The penitentiary provided residential care mostly for teenage girls described as 'wayward ... and in moral danger, or disowned by their families'.[2] These girls were generally referred to the Sisters by the parish priest or by their own families who were not willing to keep them in their homes if they got into trouble. Unlike the Ulster Female Penitentiary or the Magdalene asylum in Belfast, the Sisters took in young girls who were not necessarily prostitutes but who had committed an offence that was not serious enough to warrant a sentence at a reform school. Refuge in the penitentiary gave them an escape from their deprived surroundings and the moral dangers to which they were tempted to succumb through the pressures of poverty, unemployment and often homelessness.

The young women in the penitentiary were instructed in needlework, laundry work and other household skills, and the produce of this contributed to their upkeep. The sense of achievement in doing worthwhile work and earning their keep was very important for the young residents, most of whom had had little success and little sense of self-worth in life.

The apostolate progressed favourably. However, it was found after a short time that the house in Hamilton Street was unsuitable, being too small to accommodate both the residents and the laundry, which was their main source of income. On 1 January 1863 they moved to a larger dwelling, Bankmore House, Dublin Bridge, which was a little more distant from the centre of the town and had a few acres of land attached.[3] The outhouses were converted into washhouses, a laundry and other offices. It gave fair accommodation for a small number.

Three Sisters generally remained in charge of the penitents and two went daily to teach in one of the schools in town. The penitents, if left too much to their own devices, were inclined to become unruly and troublesome and after some years the Sisters realised that they could not manage them together with attending to their other duties of teaching and visitation. They prayed that God would send them some religious order dedicated to this type of work. Their prayer was answered, as the annals of the Good Shepherd Sisters testify:

> On 24 May 1867 a letter from the Most Rev. Dr Dorrian arrived in the Good Shepherd Convent, Limerick, expressing his Lordship's wish to have the Good Shepherd Sisters come to his diocese. On receiving the letter in New Ross the Superior set off for Belfast with Sr. M. Magdalene Coleman. On reaching Belfast they were cordially received by the good Sisters of Mercy who would have them remain in their convent – the upper part of the town – until arrangements with his Lordship for this foundation were finally made. The Sisters of Mercy of Bankmore House returned to St. Paul's. Two more Sisters came from Limerick and made a community of three.

They took up residence in September 1867. But scarcely five weeks had elapsed when Sister M. Magdalene Coleman died. This was a great blow for the new community. A solemn requiem Mass was celebrated for her in St Malachy's Church.

While the Good Shepherd Sisters remained at Bankmore House their health suffered from the dampness of the place (it was situated near the insalubrious Blackwater River) and the bishop gave them permission to spend time occasionally with the Sisters of Mercy in St Paul's Convent, Crumlin Road. Unfortunately this did not solve the problem. Flooding from the nearby river frequently invaded the cellars of the house and infection from the polluted flood water meant that the Sisters and most of the girls were stricken with the dreaded typhoid fever. One of the affected Sisters died, the second to die within a few months. The Sisters of Mercy gave what help they could at this sad time. There was no Catholic cemetery yet in the town, Catholics of the town being buried in Friar's Bush cemetery on the southern outskirts of the town – what is now Stranmillis Road. The old cemetery is adjacent to the Ulster Museum. The two Good Shepherd Sisters were interred in the small plot in the garden of the Crumlin Road convent. The second Sister to die was Sister M. Dominic (Catherine O'Brien). Born in Tipperary, she entered the Good Shepherd novitiate in England and was professed there on 12 June 1853. She died of typhoid fever in Bankmore House on 8 February 1869 at 50 years of age. In 1992, before the Sisters of Mercy moved out of St Paul's Convent, Crumlin Road, the remains of the Good Shepherd Sisters were exhumed and reburied in their own cemetery.

Eventually new accommodation was found for the penitents and the Sisters caring for them on the southern outskirts of the town, in Ballynafeigh, where the great pastoral work of the Good Shepherd Sisters flourished for many years to come.

The orphanage

The care of the homeless and the orphaned was a work particularly dear to Catherine McAuley's heart. While still living at Coolock House in Dublin she had adopted her godchild Teresa Byrne, the youngest child of her cousin Ann Conway, and two orphans, Mary Ann Kirwin and Ellen Corrigan. Teresa Byrne joined Catherine's community in Baggot Street and, as Sister M. Camillus, went on the mission to Baltimore, USA, where her devotion to the sick and poor for over 25 years was legendary. Mary Kirwin made an unhappy marriage, despite Catherine's good advice, but could still always turn to Catherine in times of distress. Ellen Corrigan also joined Catherine in Baggot Street, being professed as Sister M. Veronica. She was destined for the Carlow foundation but, to Catherine's great grief, died within a month of her profession.

Catherine also undertook the care of her two nieces and three nephews when they were orphaned by the death of their parents, her brother James and his wife Mary, who died within six months of each other in 1828 and 1829. All these young people remained very dear to Catherine McAuley as long as they and she lived, and their happiness and welfare were always of concern to her.

Later, as Catherine undertook her charitable work in Dublin, her scope of care for the homeless knew almost no bounds. A primary reason for building the House of Mercy in Baggot Street was:

> to lodge poor servant girls who, owing to the prejudices of heretical employers, or other misfortunes, found themselves deprived of employment, as well as others who, though they have some trade or profession, are unfortunately not able to find work and therefore stand in need of food and help.[4]

The care of poor orphaned children, then, which was entrusted to the Sisters of Mercy four years after their arrival in Belfast, was an apostolate truly in keeping with Catherine McAuley's spirit. In Belfast, as in the Dublin of Catherine's day, needy and homeless children and young women were among those who certainly deserved any care and attention the Sisters could give.

In Belfast, because of the high mortality rate among the poor of the city, the welfare of orphaned children was a matter of concern to all. The need for some provision for them was urgent, as the only alternative was the workhouse, and conditions there were so basic and severe that the poor were deeply reluctant to go there except as a last resort. In a report from the 1850s, Reverend A. McIntyre described an experience he had on the Belfast streets on one specific occasion:

> 1 September 1853: Spent the forenoon of today in getting two poor children into the Union Workhouse. I met these two little boys on the Queen's Bridge. The first thing that arrested my attention was the circumstance of the elder abusing the younger. He was dashing his head on the crib stones. I interfered. A woman who was passing at the time stated that the elder was drowning, and would have drowned, the younger two days before but that some boys had prevented him. I learned that the name of these children was Nixon, that their father was killed by some accident a few years ago in this town, that the mother

and children had been in the workhouse some year or so ago but that she had come out and brought the children with her and that lately she has had to go to the hospital being taken ill of dropsy and that now the children have no-one to look after or take care of them. They are both all but naked, and when I saw that the elder had to carry the younger one on his back and beg whatever they got, I could not think it strange that he should sometimes be driven by hunger and fatigue to acts of cruelty and desperation.[5]

The better-off people of Belfast could not but be aware of the destitution of the poorer classes and, in fact, did not shirk responsibility for them. There were many charitable societies conducted both independently and by church-sponsored bodies. In the 1840s the three main churches in Belfast had orphan societies for their own denominations. St Patrick's Orphan Society was founded by the Catholic Bishop Denvir and was managed by a committee of ladies, who for some time most conscientiously carried out the work of the institution and supplied a much-felt need. The objectives of the society were 'to afford the means of support to destitute orphans, to bestow on them a religious education, and to implant the seeds of virtue in their tender minds'. In many cases the orphaned children had been boarded out with foster parents until they were up to five years of age, but it was reported that in general the Catholic hierarchy (particularly after Archbishop Cullen came to Dublin) preferred that they go to religious institutions and believed that the Sisters of Charity, the Sisters of Mercy and the Presentation Sisters were most successful in raising good Catholic children.[6] So a year after the Sisters of Mercy had settled in Crumlin Road (that is, in 1858) an orphanage was built on a plot of ground adjoining the Crumlin Road Convent National Schools and placed under their care, subject to the control of the bishop and a committee appointed annually. A site was acquired to build an orphanage and later schools between the convent and the Crumlin Road. The land was bought by Henry Loughran, a generous benefactor of the community.[7]

To this new building, called St Patrick's Orphanage, the female orphans, who for many years had been located in a small house in May Street, were transferred on 1 January 1859. There were 80 children on the roll. A matron was appointed with a salary of £60 yearly. The orphanage was to be supported by voluntary donations but, as time went by, when it became difficult to manage in this manner and after the passing of the Industrial Schools Act (Ireland), the Sisters applied to the government for recognition. The orphanage was certified as an industrial school in December 1869 and began to receive funding.

Meanwhile, the care of the sick and dying, a work assumed immediately by the Sisters upon their arrival in Belfast, was continued on a regular basis and, as the occasion arose, they provided whatever material help they could to those in need. It is recorded that when the young working girls came to the evening schools in Callender Street, they appealed not only for basic education for themselves but also for the needs of their families and relations at home to be met. The same Patrick Keenan who described so vividly how the schools were run witnessed a further service the Sisters provided nightly when the classes concluded:

> [W]e observed a large number of school girls standing waiting in the hall; they were waiting for ointments, plasters etc. which the nuns were distributing amongst them for their maimed or sick relatives at home, or for ailments of their own … Thus (he concluded) do these Christian teachers complete the beautiful mission of their lives by adding the last link to the long chain of the attributes of mercy.[8]

The Sisters continued this tradition of serving the poor who came to the convent doors in each convent throughout the years with dedication and diligence.

---

[1] C. Clear, *Nuns in nineteenth-century Ireland* (Dublin: Gill and Macmillan, 1987), p. 153 *et seq.*

[2] Ibid.

[3] Bankmore Penitentiary, 'at the left hand side of the Dublin Road at what is called the Old Dublin Bridge' (according to Bishop Dorrian in a deposition to the police following the riots of November 1864) is mentioned in the *Belfast Directory* of 1864. The name Dublin 'Road' does not appear in the directory until that year. Bankmore House was situated in Basin Loney. The Basin provided Belfast's water supply at that time. It was obviously, for this reason, a suitable place to have a laundry, but as a dwelling place it was very unsuitable, as the future history of Bankmore House was to show.

[4] Petition to the Apostolic See for approval of the institute, quoted in A. Bolster, *Positio: documentary study for the canonisation process of the servant of God, Catherine McAuley, 1778–1841* (Rome, 1985), p. 86.

[5] Reverend A. McIntyre, *Diary of visits to the poor in Belfast, 1853–6,* quoted in Jordan, *op. cit.,* p. 17. Reverend McIntyre was a missionary with the Domestic Mission, a non-subscribing Presbyterian organisation.

[6] J. Robbins, *Lost children,* p. 293, quoted in ibid., p. 158.

[7] See Sister Marie Duddy to John Gordon, solicitor, Sisters of Mercy, 'St Paul's Convent of Mercy, Belfast: archives' (MCA (hereafter Archives, SPCMB), 2003).

[8] Keenan, *op. cit.,* p. 179.

5

EARLY MISSIONARY EXPANSION

In June 1859 Mother M. Philomene Maguire had completed her six years of office as superior and was elected for a further three years, there being a sufficient number of professed Sisters now in the community to constitute a quorum (six) for a valid election. At this same date Sister M. Aloysius Crolly was elected to the double office of mother assistant and mistress of novices, and a little later Sister M. Raphael Flanagan was elected as bursar.

When Downpatrick Convent became independent (in 1860) Mother M. Borgia Fortune, who had been mother assistant under Mother M. Philomene, went as first superior to the newly autonomous community, replacing Sister M. Aloysius Brady, who had been appointed first local superior when Downpatrick Convent was set up as a branch house of St Paul's (in 1855).

By mid-1862, when the Sisters were reinstated in their convent, the community had been expanded with the addition of several more young women who had been attracted to the Mercy way of life. By this time there were six young professed Sisters and six novices. It is interesting to note that among them was Ellen Savage (Sister M. Philomene), who had been accepted for the mission in Geelong, Australia, where Mother M. Philomene's sister, Mother M. Cecilia Xavier Maguire, had made a foundation in 1858. In the event, Ellen was invited in 1860 to remain in the St Paul's community and accepted.

One can well believe that the experience of being evicted must have had a traumatic effect on the young community. Mother M. Philomene had been superior during the time of the crisis and had struggled hard to hold the community together, to maintain morale and to try to find a solution to the financial problem. One can imagine the stress and strain, during that trying time, in the relations between the superior and the bishop, with whom there could be no dialogue and from whom there seemed no hope of sympathy or understanding. It is no wonder that, as her third term of office drew to a close at the end of May 1862, Mother M. Philomene may have felt that her patience and endurance were at an end. She welcomed the invitation to take her talents and dedication to a new field of endeavour when the bishop of Birmingham requested her to send Sisters to make a foundation in Worcester, England. For Mother M. Philomene it was time to move on.

Worcester and Ballyjamesduff

As has been demonstrated in the story so far, Mother M. Philomene was a remarkable woman. She was the second eldest of four sisters who had entered the Convent of Mercy, Baggot Street, shortly after the death of the foundress. They were the daughters of Richard Maguire, a wealthy grazier from Newgrange, County Meath, and his wife Margaret. Annie, born in 1827, followed her older sister Elizabeth's footsteps and entered Baggot Street Convent, where she was received and professed on the same dates as Elizabeth, and given the name Sister Mary Philomene. Her name was to be inextricably bound up with the Mercy foundations in the north of Ireland, in England and in Australia.[1]

As has been recorded, on 17 March 1853 Sister M. Philomene Maguire was appointed to lead the new mission to Belfast, which she did early in January 1854.[2] The following year, on 21 June, she founded a branch house in Downpatrick, County Down, which became an independent convent in 1860. The new community in Belfast and its works flourished under her guidance for nine years. On 24 May 1862 Bishop Denvir received her resignation from the office of mother superior and by 5 June she had left to make a foundation in Worcester, England, accompanied by Sisters M. Ignatius Crolly, M. de Sales Walsh and two novices. The St Paul's acts of chapter include the entry:

> On 24 May 1862 Sister M. Philomene Maguire resigned the Office of Mother Superior of this Convent into the hands of his Lordship, the Right Reverend C. Denvir. Having received his Lordship's permission she left this community to found a Convent in Worcester, England. Accompanied by Sister Mary Ignatius Crolly and Sister Mary de Sales Walsh. (Signed) + C. Denvir, Bp.[3]

There was a great need for the works of mercy in England, to where thousands of Irish people had emigrated in the post-famine years and were there absorbed into the expanding industrial urban milieux. Poverty, destitution and sickness were the lot of these dislocated people when they were worn out with labour or left unemployed. There were several reasons for these painfully adverse conditions. The influx of Irish Catholic labourers in the early and mid-1800s was strongly resented, even by 'old' English Catholic families who were staunchly faithful to the Roman Catholic tradition and had continued to practise their faith in private (though not with impunity) since Reformation times. They particularly feared a Protestant reaction such as had led to the terrible Gordon riots in London in 1791. This kind of resentment was expressed, for example, by Thomas Arnold, headmaster of Rugby School, as early as 1834, when he wrote to a friend that '[t]he tremendous influx of Irish labourers into Lancashire … is tainting the whole population with a more than barbarous element'.[4] The immigrants were also accused of carrying fever and various diseases consequent on the conditions of the Irish famine.

Such was the prejudice against the impoverished immigrants who, it can be imagined, had enough to suffer as they undertook the back-breaking labour of building the railways, docks and factories so essential to England's industrial prosperity, while enduring the abominable hardships of insanitary work camps and persecution from the indigenous labour force, who felt themselves deprived by competition from the Irish, who were prepared to accept lower wages and conditions of employment in order to earn a subsistence livelihood.[5]

The 1860s in England were years of great social and religious unrest, fuelled by the slow pace of economic and political reform and residual, but nonetheless highly flammable, anti-Catholic feelings following Catholic emancipation in 1829, the Oxford Movement of the 1830s and 1840s and the restoration of the Catholic hierarchy in Great Britain in 1850. The anti-Catholic agitation reached its climax with the 'no popery' riots that flared up in the docklands of the East End of London, culminating on Easter Sunday 1860 with many outrages.

It was into this unwelcoming situation that Mother M. Philomene and her companions had been called, for the sake of their fellow countrymen and women, in the summer of 1862. Harassment increased over the ensuing years, with some of the most violent anti-popery riots in Birmingham and other midland towns. However, the Sisters persevered in Worcester for about seven years, in the face of a considerable amount of hostility, intolerance and even physical violence. These conditions were possibly aggravated by the notorious Great Convent case (Saurin v. Starr), involving the Hull Mercy community, which was held at Westminster Hall, London in February 1869 and which received wide adverse publicity throughout the whole of England.[6] Eventually sectarian feelings rose so high that the local priest advised the Worcester community to leave.

In 1864 there had been a second exodus from St Paul's Convent, Belfast, to a new mission in Ashton-under-Lyne in the diocese of Salford in England. This was led by Sister M. Bernard Geraghty, and she was accompanied by Sisters M. Joseph Houlahan, M. Philomene O'Brien and M. Joseph Aloysius

Maguire. Sisters M. Bernard, Joseph and Philomene had been among the first postulants to enter the Belfast Mercy community, and Sister M. Joseph Aloysius Maguire (youngest sister of Mother M. Philomene) had come as a novice from Baggot Street and been professed in the community of her adoption.

Charlotte Geraghty had been born in Kingstown (now Dún Laoghaire), County Dublin, in 1830, the only child of wealthy parents. Her choice of vocation was no doubt influenced by the example of the Sisters of Mercy in her home town and she came to join the new community in Belfast during the course of 1854. She received the religious habit and the name Sister M. Bernard in 1855 and, while still a novice, went to the new foundation in Downpatrick at the end of July of the same year. She returned to Belfast to make her profession at the end of December 1856 or in early January 1857.

On 18 August 1860 she was elected to the office of mother assistant in St Paul's community. On 5 June 1862 she was reappointed to this post (the appointment was made by Bishop Denvir, 'there being, at this stage, only six vocals in the community').[7]

As regards the Sisters who accompanied Sister M. Bernard, Anna Houlahan (Sister M. Joseph) received votes for reception on 8 December 1855 and received votes for profession on 27 November 1856; Nannie O'Brien (Sister M. Philomene) received votes for reception on 8 December 1857 and received votes for profession on 6 February 1860; Sister M. Joseph Aloysius Maguire entered the Mercy Institute in Baggot Street and in October 1861 joined the Belfast community as a novice. She completed her novitiate there and received votes for profession on 19 October 1861.

Sister M. Bernard resigned from office on 3 August 1863 and, along with Sister M. Joseph Houlahan and another Sister, went to make a foundation in the west of Ireland.[8] This foundation does not appear to have flourished, for all three Sisters were back in the Crumlin Road convent before the end of 1863.

In February 1864 Sister M. Bernard and three companions applied to the bishop for permission to leave the Belfast community in order to respond to the request from Father Crumbholme, parish priest of Ashton-under-Lyne, who, early in 1864, had appealed to St Paul's for Sisters to teach in the schools of his parish. The bishop's permission was granted and the little band of Sisters, in a rather final way, cut their links with their home community and stepped out, with true missionary spirit, into the virtually unknown. We have a record of the Sisters' arrangements for their departure and new venture:

We, the undersigned Sisters of St. Paul's Convent of Mercy, Belfast, have, of our own free will, and full consent and desire, arranged to go out on a new foundation under the jurisdiction of the Bishop of Salford at Ashton-under-Lyne and hereby, on receiving our Dowries or other annuities from this convent in Belfast, give up and resign any further claim in that Institution and on the Diocesan Bishop of Down and Connor beyond his future wish and agreement.
Belfast, February 19th 1864

> Signed: Sister Mary Bernard Geraghty
> Sister Mary Joseph Houlahan
> Sister Mary Philomene O'Brien
> Sister Mary Joseph Aloysius Maguire.[9]

The bishop of Salford, for his part, confirmed his commitment to his side of the transaction. He welcomed the new community, undertook to provide them 'with a house suitable for a convent', financial support as necessary, and to oversee their freedom to live their religious life according to the Mercy rules and constitutions:

We, William, Bishop of Salford,
Hereby declare that we accept the Mother Superior and Sisters appointed by the Ecclesiastical and Local Superiors of the Convent of Our Lady of Mercy, Belfast, to found a New Convent under our jurisdiction in Ashton-under-Lyne. We undertake to become the guardian of their Rule and Constitutions, Approved and Confirmed by the Holy See, the observance of which we will see enforced in all practical respects according to the Customs of the Congregation.

We promise to provide the community with a house suitable for a Convent, wherein regular discipline can be maintained, and also a reasonable competency for their simple and religious manner of living independently of anything that may accrue from their own exertions. We will not permit them to be interfered with, either in the admission or discipline of subjects, but with our consent and approval, or in their internal or external mode of government, nor will we withdraw any Sister from the community either to make a new foundation or for any other similar purpose without the free consent of the Mother Superior and the Diocesan Bishop.

We further guarantee to pay to the four Sisters thirty pounds per annum to be paid quarterly, and to defray the travelling expenses to Ashton-under-Lyne, and also to pay the taxes of the house.
Dated the 18 February 1864[10]

It appeared that they soon settled into their new home in Ashton-under-Lyne. Shortly after their arrival the little community agreed to the appointment, by the bishop of Salford, Most Reverend Dr Turner, of Sister M. Bernard as their superior and Sister M. Joseph Aloysius Maguire as her assistant. In September 1864 their number was increased by the arrival of a postulant from Belfast, Eliza Jane Molloy. However, as time went by the situation in Ashton-under-Lyne must not have looked too promising. Within three years they had moved to Bolton, where their new address was given as St Joseph's Convent, Crook Street. They had been joined by new members during these years. Sister M. Joseph Aloysius Maguire was appointed mistress of novices (September 1867) and when the Sisters left Bolton a short time later they were a community of seven. They had, meanwhile, happily kept in contact with the Sisters in Worcester.

Sad to say, England was not always a hospitable place for Roman Catholic nuns at that time, and the fate of the Bolton community matched that of their Sisters in Worcester. Many obstacles were put in the way of their carrying out works of mercy and the struggling parish was too poor to support them. But providence, it seemed, was guiding them to their true destination. While they were tussling with the difficulties of life in south Lancashire the parish priest of Annagh, in the diocese of Kilmore, Ireland, Reverend James Dunne, was appealing to the Mercy motherhouse in Baggot Street for Sisters to start a foundation in the town of Belturbet, County Cavan. This was early in 1868. The Baggot Street community had no Sisters to spare but, knowing the conditions of the young foundations in the north-east of England, they directed Father Dunne to apply to the community in Bolton. His application was considered favourably and, on 23 August 1868 the Bolton community, seven Sisters in all, moved back to Ireland.

The Sisters who made the Belturbet foundation comprised the original four who had left St Paul's, Belfast, and those who had joined them in England – Sisters M. Stanislaus Molloy, M. Magdalene Clancy and M. Martha Finnegan, the latter two still novices (they were professed in Belturbet at the end of 1869). They were made very welcome by the bishop of Kilmore, Dr Nicholas Conaty, and the local people. They flourished in Belturbet, running schools and caring for the sick, the poor and orphans, and a short time later opened a branch house in Ballyjamesduff (also in County Cavan). Once again Mother M. Bernard Geraghty was superior of her community, but not for long. She died at the very young age of 39, on 27 May 1869, in only the sixteenth year of her religious life. It was a short life, but one full of enthusiasm, zeal, action and firm confidence in her calling.

Meanwhile, when it became obvious that Mother M. Philomene and her community had to leave Worcester, an appeal came to them from the Belturbet community to return to Ireland to take over the convent in

Ballyjamesduff. Mother Bernard's death had depleted the community and the Belturbet Sisters felt that they could not sustain the Ballyjamesduff foundation. Canonically, the minimum number of Sisters required to form a community at that time was three, so the two Sisters left in Ballyjamesduff had to withdraw from there after the death of Mother M. Bernard in May 1869. In June 1869 Mother M. Philomene and her companions arrived to take their place. (Apart from Mother M. Agnes Graham, Mother M. Philomene's assistant, we do not know how many Sisters accompanied her to Ballyjamesduff. We do know that of the group of Sisters who went to Worcester only one, Sister M. de Sales Walsh, returned to St Paul's Convent, Belfast.) The newly arrived community, besides caring for the sick and the poor, extended the convent facilities with the full and wholehearted encouragement of the bishop, Dr Conaty, in order to make accommodation for schools and 'take in poor and neglected female children and give them a course of education',[11] which would help them, especially if they were to emigrate (emigration seemed to hold the only future for poor children in a rural area at the time). The efforts of the Sisters were generously supported by the parishioners and the clergy.

Warrnambool
However, Mother M. Philomene's residence in Ballyjamesduff was not to be of long duration. Her eyes were set on more distant pastures. About eight months after their arrival, Mother M. Philomene and all her community left Ballyjamesduff to set off for the Australian mission. (The Poor Clare Sisters from Newry took over the convent and school vacated by the Sisters of Mercy, and 6 February 1872 is held as their foundation day there.) Their destination was Victoria, where Bishop Goold was in great need of Sisters to work with the Irish immigrants who had settled in the western district of his jurisdiction and who had established a flourishing farming community there. Mother M. Philomene's response to this need was most probably largely influenced by the fact that her sister, Mother M. Cecilia Xavier Maguire, had made a foundation in Geelong in 1859, also at the request of Bishop Goold, after she had finished her term of office in Baggot Street. She had no doubt invited her sister on many occasions to join her there. The call for Mother M. Philomene to the Australian mission was more direct, however. It is recorded in the annals that Bishop Goold happened to visit Baggot Street Convent (as was his wont when in Ireland) some time in 1870, after attending the Vatican Council, and there he was introduced to Mother M. Philomene. His representation of the needs of his diocese did not fall on deaf ears. Mother M. Philomene was already planning her next 'missionary

The ship, Windsor Castle, of Messrs. Green's Blackwall line, which passed Cape Otway on Sunday night, entered Port Phillip Heads yesterday morning, and reached Hobson's Bay about noon. The Windsor Castle is on her first visit to this port, but her antecedent career in the India trade is well known, and as a fast sailer and a comfortable passenger ship she was considered a great favourite. Her accommodation for passengers of all classes is ample, the 'tween decks especially being very roomy and well ventilated, and the salon is after the same style as the other well-known ships of her fleet. With the exception of heavy weather encountered for several days after leaving the land, and occasional gales in running down the longitude, the voyage has been marked by fine pleasant weather, but by no continuance of favourable winds. The ship has brought a large cargo and a number of saloon and 'tween-deck passengers who expressed themselves well pleased with the ship, commander, and officers. Captain Dinsdale, well-known here when in the Roxborough Castle, of the same line, has command of the Windsor Castle, and of the passage out. He reports leaving London on February 7, and landing the pilot off Start Point on February 11. The ship has then to contend for about a week against violent S.W. gales and stormy weather, followed by variable winds to the equator, which was crossed on March 10 in lon. 24deg.W. The S.E. trades were not fallen in with until March 16, in lat.4deg.S., and from thence moderate breezes prevailed until passing the meridian of the Cape of Good Hope on April 8 in lat.42deg., moderate variable winds (with the exception of one of two stiff gales) prevailing until crossing the meridian of Cape Leuwin. Since then the ship has been delayed by light S.E. and S.S.E. winds. On arrival in the bay, the Windsor Castle was berthed alongside the railway pier, Sandridge to discharge cargo with all despatch, and load again for London. On the voyage the ship Jerusalem was signalled on March 6, and again on March 14, being in lat. 2deg.S. on the latter date.

(The clipper ship Jerusalem, of the Aberdeen line, entered Port Phillip Heads yesterday and anchored.)

THE ARGUS, TUESDAY, MAY 7, 1872

WINDSOR CASTLE, ship (Messrs Green's Blackwall line) 1,074 tons, Chas. Dinsdale, from London February 7, Start Point February 11.

Passengers – cabin: Misses Graham, J. Graham, O'Mara, Wingfield, Howard, Flood, and Cousins (Sisters of Mercy), Mrs Elizabeth Stodart, Mrs Louisa Stodart, Mrs. Maguire, Mr. And Mrs. Pritchard and family (8), Miss Stodart, Miss Reidy, Miss Steggles, Dr. Thomas Somerville, Messrs Robt Stodart, Burton; and 27 in the second and third cabins. J. H. White and Co., agents.

PROJECTED DEPARTURES
WINDSOR CASTLE, Lincolnshire, early; Moravian, June 5.

PORT PHILLIP HEADS
(By Electric Telegraph)
Arrived – May 6
Windsor Castle, ship from London.

It is stated by The Argus that seven Sisters of Mercy, who arrived on Monday in the Blackwall liner Windsor Castle, from London were landed at Queenscliffe, and then proceeded overland to Geelong to the convent there.,
THE GEELONG ADVERTISER, Wednesday, May8, 1872

Seven Sisters of Mercy who arrived yesterday in the Blackwall liner Windsor Castle, from London, were landed at Queenscliffe, and then proceeded overland to Geelong to the Convent there.
THE ARGUS, Tuesday, May 7, 1872

Reports of the voyage from Ireland to Australia, 1872

journey'. The Sisters were allocated to the town of Warrnambool in the recently created diocese of Ballarat.

So it was for Victoria that the Sisters set sail, probably in January 1872. Passenger lists tell us that eight Sisters arrived in Queenscliff, Victoria, on the ship *Windsor Castle*, after a three-month voyage from London. They were Mother M. Philomene Maguire, Sisters M. Catherine McQuillan, M. Agnes and M. Philomene Graham, M. Stanislaus Aldridge, M. Joseph Howard, M. Xavier Flood, a novice, and Brigid Cousens, a postulant. From Queenscliff they were conveyed on the *Silver Eagle* to Geelong, their first destination.

It is interesting to note that, of the new arrivals in Australia, Mother M. Philomene seems to have been the only one that was a member of the original group that had left the Belfast community ten years earlier. In the annals of the Sisters of Mercy of Victoria she is described as being 'tall and well-built, her bearing graceful and dignified, her manner gracious and affable'. She was now 45 years of age and an experienced leader.[12] The numbers of that original group had been swollen by the Sisters who had entered Baggot Street for the English mission and had gone to Worcester – for example, Sister M. Agnes Graham of Belfast and Sister M. Stanislaus Aldridge of London. It is possible that others had joined the community in Worcester and during the Sisters' brief stay in Ballyjamesduff (for example Sister M. Philomene Graham). Still others may have joined specifically for the mission to Australia – for example, Sister M. Xavier Flood and Sister Brigid Cousens.

After a stopover at Geelong, where Mother M. Philomene had the joy of being reunited with her sister, and then at the Mercy convent in Fitzroy (founded by Mother M. Ursula Frayne), the pioneering party travelled on, still by coastal steamer, the *Edina*, to Port Fairy, in the shire of Belfast (what a coincidence!) and thence to Warrnambool. The new arrivals were allocated a 'comfortable, eight-roomed stone dwelling on ten acres of land, situated conveniently within one mile of Warrnambool'.[13] Soon a notice appeared in the *Warrnambool Examiner*:

> The Sisters of Mercy beg to announce that they will open a day and boarding school for young ladies at the Convent of Mercy, 'Wyton', Warrnambool, on 1st July 1872. For further particulars apply personally or by letter to the Superioress, Convent of Mercy, 'Wyton', Warrnambool.[14]

Eventually a convent, St Anne's, was built, which was said to be modelled on St Paul's Convent, Belfast. Most of the money for this came from the fortune of Sister M. Stanislaus Aldridge and from money that had been given by the other Sisters' families when they had left Ireland. The Sisters did not confine their apostolic activity to the schools, though that would appear to have been the priority in a town which was described as educationally the weakest link in the new diocese. They were also straight away involved in other works of mercy, in particular the care of sick and of orphans and destitute children whose fathers, Irish miners, had died from the inevitable 'black-lung' disease, a consequence of deep lead mining on the Ballarat fields, and whose mothers, now left without support, had drifted into the seemingly greater security of their national community groups and settled in and around Warrnambool.

Nine years after the Sisters arrived in Warrnambool a branch house was established in Ballarat by Sisters M. Agnes and M. Philomene Graham, M. Xavier Flood, M. Joseph Howard and Brigid Cousens (1881). It became independent in 1885 and eventually became the motherhouse of the Ballarat East Congregation. In 1888 Sisters from there established a separate foundation in Colac, where Sister M. Agnes Graham became the first superior. She died there in 1894 at the age of 55. The second Warrnambool branch house was established in Terang in 1907. All the foundations flourished, in their membership and in their apostolic undertakings, 'setting a shining example for future generations to follow'.[15]

Eventually hard work and illness began to take their toll on the health of Mother M. Philomene. She was a strongly built woman but, like her sister, Mother M. Cecilia Xavier, for the last several years of her life she was confined to a wheelchair with an arthritic condition. From there, a 'formidable invalid', she continued to exercise her literary talents, composing poetry and plays for the school concerts and tutoring the schoolgirls who came to rehearse their parts. She knew each one by name. She retired to spend her closing days with her friend, Mother M. Agnes Graham, in Ballarat East. Eventually the sad news was reported in the *Warrnambool Standard* on Monday, 18 June 1888:

> General regret was felt in Warrnambool on Saturday when it became known that Mrs [sic] Maguire, the Mother Superioress at Wyton convent, had died during the afternoon. The deceased lady had been ailing for some time past, and death took place between eleven and twelve o'clock on Saturday morning. All those who were acquainted with the Mother Superioress spoke highly of her kind disposition and she was beloved by the inmates of the Convent, as well as by the children who attended Wyton school. The Office and Mass will take place at ten o'clock this morning and at twelve o'clock the remains of the deceased will be interred in the convent grounds.[16]

After many wanderings, and 16 years after arriving in Australia, Mother M. Philomene died on 16 June 1888, aged 61. Quite remarkably, according to the lack of records on the subject in the archives of the Sisters of Mercy of the diocese of Ballarat, Mother M. Philomene seems never to have talked about her years in Belfast and Worcester. Some cloud of secrecy seems to have shrouded her memories of these very important years of her life so that, unfortunately, she left no account of them in Australia, either in oral or written form. Furthermore, there is no record in the Belfast archives of her having kept any contact with the Belfast community after her departure, either from Worcester, Ballyjamesduff or Warrnambool.

Mother M. Philomene was survived by her great friend, Mother M. Agnes Graham, by only by six years. Mother Agnes was remembered in her community as a painstaking, gentle, patient nun, a model Sister of Mercy, and was greatly missed by her community, past pupils and many friends after she passed away on 7 December 1894.

Overview
The early years of the 1860s seem to have been a restless time in the Belfast community. This is very understandable in the circumstances. The community was recovering from the very distressing experience of the eviction and a certain amount of breakdown in communication between the bishop, who had invited them to this difficult mission in Down and Connor, and themselves. In 1862, when their strong superior, Mother M. Philomene, had completed her third term of office she went, accompanied by four others, to England. Then, a short time later, Sister M. Joseph Houlahan and two other Sisters left Belfast for the west of Ireland (of this venture we have no details). They returned from there after a short sojourn, only to leave again, with Sister M. Bernard Geraghty, for England. By the autumn of 1864 the number of professed Sisters in St Paul's community was considerably reduced.

Because of these vicissitudes the history of the Belfast community so far could appear rather negative and its future survival questionable. However, there were more positive influences at work in the courage, generosity, optimism and perseverance of the Sisters, qualities characteristic of the members of the young institute wherever they went. The 1840s, 1850s and 1860s were years of extraordinary expansion for the infant Mercy Congregation and reports flooded in of ventures across the Atlantic and Pacific Oceans to Canada, the United States and Australia, often carrying off the youngest of the Sisters, even novices, who were being entrusted with great responsibilities in these unknown territories and far-distant lands.[17]

Indeed, the foundress never had any hesitation about giving responsibility at an early age.

1   See Appendix 1 to Chapter 5.
2   Acts of chapter, SPCMB, Book 2, end pages.
3   Ibid.
4   Quoted in S. Usherwood '"No-popery" under Queen Victoria', *History Today*, vol. xxii, no. 4 (April 1973).
5   Ibid.
6   M. McClelland, 'The first Hull Mercy nuns: a nineteenth-century case study', *Recusant History*, vol. xxii, no. 2 (1994). A full report of this case was given daily in the *London Times*, 3–24 February 1869.
7   Acts of chapter, SPCMB, Book 1. A 'vocal' was a professed member of the community who had a 'voice' in chapter and the right to vote.
8   By some oversight the actual location was not recorded in the annals.
9   Acts of chapter, SPCMB, Book 2. See there also another document drawn up by the Sisters, most probably earlier, in February 1864, but from which, strangely, the name of Sister M. Joseph Houlahan is missing. She must have joined the little party in the interim.
10 Ibid.
11 Report of a charity sermon preached by Reverend J. Boylan on 28 September 1870, *Anglo Celt*, 1 October 1870. See A.H. Leaden, 'The Sisters of Mercy in Kilmore (1868–1968)', *Breifne: Journal of Cumann Seanchais Bhréifne*, vol. iii (1969).
12 See M.G. Allen, *The labourers' friends: Sisters of Mercy in Victoria and Tasmania* (Melbourne, Australia: Hargreen, 1989), M.F. Larkins, *A Mercy way of life: Colac 1888–1988* (Colac, Australia: Colac Herald Press, 1988) and M. Quill (ed.) *The end of an era, 1872–1990: St Ann's College, Warrnambool* (Warrnambool, Australia: St Ann's College, 1990) for brief biographies of other pioneering Sisters.
13 *Warrnambool Examiner*, 1 March 1872. Also Allen, *op. cit.*, p. 101.
14 Quill, *op. cit.*, p. 6.
15 Quill, *op. cit.*, p. 9.
16 Ibid., p. 7.
17 See supplementary manual to Gately, *op. cit.* See also the bibliography for the many fuller accounts of these foundations.

6

THE BELFAST MERCY
COMMUNITY AND EDUCATION

As the 1860s progressed the Belfast community, now depleted in numbers, struggled on. Shortly after the departure of Mother M. Philomene Maguire and her companions Bishop Denvir appointed Sister M. Gonzaga Morrin superior of St Paul's community, 'the appointment of the said Superior having devolved upon us (Dr Denvir), there being, at this date, only six vocals in the community'.[1] This took place on 5 June 1862. On this date also Sister M. Bernard Geraghty was appointed assistant and Sister M. Raphael Flanagan bursar.

Since Bishop Denvir was, at this time, still loath to face up to the many issues needing attention in the diocese, including those concerning the Sisters of Mercy, Dr Patrick Dorrian, his coadjutor, who had proved a firm friend and supporter of the Sisters, took upon himself responsibility for the future well-being of the community and in particular the spiritual welfare of the novices who had been evacuated to Downpatrick with the consequent disruption of their canonical or spiritual year. With this in mind we find him writing to Dr Paul Cullen, archbishop of Dublin, expressing his concern and putting forward a specific recommendation:

> 2 Adelaide Place, Belfast
> July 27th, 1862
> My dear Lord,
> Your Grace is aware, I know, of the unsatisfactory state of our Convent,[2] and that some time as well as some change in its mode of management will be necessary to bring things to a healthy condition. The Sisters are now on Retreat after which, I hope, a better spirit will be evinced, for there has not been up to this the right sort among them.
> The present Rev. Superior is afraid that the spirit of those, who in a few days will have finished their Novitiate after Profession and whose privilege it will be to join the community then, is not such, from past training, as would be promising to the future usefulness of the Order here, and it would seem desirable, if practicable, to have them some time longer in the Novitiate under a proper Mother of Novices. But in this community there is, at present, no properly qualified member to appoint to that office, and it is necessary to look elsewhere.

Our Rev. Mother is assured that a very competent and proper person could be spared and would be granted for a time out of the community in Baggot Street under your Grace, if your Grace would grant permission to the Rev. Mother of Baggot Street to lend her for a time to this community.

After talking the matter over with Dr. Denvir and Fr. Vincent who is giving the Retreat I am desired by his Lordship to state the case to your Grace and in his name to ask your Grace to have the kindness to let Rev. Mother send us a Sister for this purpose. We only ask her for a time, as I have said, and because our community has been thrown into a state most unsatisfactory which every effort will be necessary to restore.

If your Grace will kindly assent to this, the sooner Sister M. Walburga would come to us the better, as the term of Novitiate will soon expire; and it is thought that the sisters here might volunteer to stay under her if she had reached us before their leaving the Novitiate.

I know I have hurriedly and unsatisfactorily explained the state of things here, but from what your Grace already knows you will be able to supply my omissions.

I beg to remain,
My dear Lord Archbishop,
Your Grace's Humble Servt.,
P. Dorrian.[3]

This letter would certainly seem to express doubts as to the leadership in the community as it had been exercised in the previous months. It is hardly fair to make a judgement on this, considering what the Sisters, and the superiors, had come through. But it was obvious that there had been serious disruption and that help was needed to bring reassurance and harmony back to the community as a whole.

And so Sister M. Walburga Grace joined the Crumlin Road community and was, on 3 August, appointed mistress of novices for three years. This day was also the date of the resignation of Sister M. Bernard Geraghty from her office as assistant superior (see Chapter 5). Sister M. Vincent Byrne was appointed to succeed her for a term of one year. When Sister M. Walburga had been secured to assure the proper training of the novices, Bishop Denvir stipulated that they should continue in the novitiate for three additional calendar months before being admitted to profession.[4]

In order to further strengthen the community, in October 1862 Mother M. Gonzaga Morrin, with the approval of her council and the consent of the bishop, applied to Baggot Street to get Sister M. Juliana Delaney, who was then local superior in Hull, England (a branch of Baggot Street), to come to St Paul's Convent, Belfast. Sister M. Juliana was a younger sister of Mother M. de Pazzi Delaney, who had been a close friend of Mother

Catherine McAuley and had succeeded her as superior in Baggot Street after the foundress died. The Delaney sisters were born of wealthy parents, William and Eliza Delaney of Castle Durrow, County Offaly, and both had entered Baggot Street. Ellen (Sister M. Juliana) entered on 15 August 1841, just three months before Catherine's death. On the occasion of her profession (19 March 1844) her sister, Mother M. de Pazzi, gave her Mother Catherine McAuley's ring, which she wore until her death and which was ever after treasured by the Belfast community. (The Belfast Mercy community presented the ring to the Mercy International Archives, Baggot Street, Dublin, in July 1997.) While still in Baggot Street, Sister M. Juliana served for different terms as bursar and as assistant superior until she went, in 1860, to join the Clifford foundation in Herefordshire, England. She subsequently became superior in Hull, from where she seems to have come willingly to Belfast in October 1862, and was soon to exercise a strong leadership role in the community. It may be of interest to add that Sister M. Juliana brought with her not only Mother Catherine's precious ring but also, with the permission of the archbishop of Dublin, the income on her dowry of £500 (no mean sum in those days), which was a welcome asset to the Belfast community's meagre funds. Sister M. Juliana was elected to office of mother assistant on 23 September 1863; she was appointed mistress of novices on 2 February 1866; she was elected as superior, Octave of the Ascension, in 1868 and re-elected in 1871, 1877 and 1880.[5]

Internal affairs being settled, the Sisters concentrated their energies with renewed vigour on the works of the apostolate, which was primarily focused on the needs of 'the poor, the sick and the ignorant'. Taking the order in reverse, we will first look at their educational undertakings.

Education in the mid-nineteenth century

'We have a model school and nunnery in Belfast,' wrote Mary Ann McCracken in 1859. She continued, 'They are both well worth seeing. I have visited both, and was quite delighted with them, they were such spacious buildings, and the nuns are so pleasing in their manners.'[6]

She was referring to the new national schools, which had been built beside the convent on the Crumlin Road and were under the management of the Sisters of Mercy. These were the first convent schools in the diocese of Down and Connor. They were part of the building project that suffered financial difficulties in 1862, but Reverend John McAuley, a lifelong friend of the Sisters of Mercy, then working as an energetic young priest in the Belfast parishes, had helped raise the money to clear off the debt on the orphanage and schools so that the Sisters would no longer be burdened with them. By the early 1860s the schools were functioning fully and provided for the education of over 600 pupils.

The education of the Catholic children was one of the greatest concerns of the bishop, of many of the clergy and of the wealthier Catholics in the diocese. Though education was needed at all levels, the most urgent need was to provide some form of schooling for the poor. There was already in existence in Ireland, since 1831, a national system of education, intended to make resources available for the education of children irrespective of denomination. The aims of the National Education Board were:

> to provide a system of combined literacy and separate religious education. No pupil would be required to attend any religious exercise, or to receive any religious instruction to which his parents objected, and the clergy of each denomination were to be given the opportunity of imparting religious instruction to the children of their respective creeds. The system was to be one 'from which should be banished even the suspicion of proselytism'.[7]

One of the main objects of the system was to unite children of different denominations in school, and the board would be required to look with favour on applications to aid schools made jointly by Roman Catholics and Protestants. Local managers were to have the right to appoint and dismiss teachers, but the right of dismissing any teacher was to rest with the board if it felt such action necessary.

This legislation appeared to respond to the need for a suitable education system but, in fact, in many ways it was impracticable. In the first place, it benefited mostly the more well-to-do classes and urban families; the level of poverty of the Catholics, and their dispersion throughout the most remote parts of the country, made school attendance virtually impossible. Secondly, there were problems concerning the allocation of finances for the provision of books and other resources, the appointment of teachers and the vesting of school property. Thirdly there was the very controversial matter of religious education in the schools. The Church of Ireland claimed, in fact, that since it was the official church of the country it should have the entire care of the education of all youth, and even saw as its duty the conversion of Catholics to the established church. The Presbyterians had their own insurmountable objections to the system and reacted accordingly in order to obtain certain concessions.

The Catholic Church was very aware of and alert to the dangers of proselytism. (Frederick Street Lancastrian Schools in St Patrick's Parish were well known for their proselytising practices. Bishop Denvir became a member of the National Education Board in March 1853. Active in the Whately controversy,[8] he wrote a letter of complaint against the evil of proselytism in schools.) They saw some benefit in applying for the financial aid offered by the National Education Board and in the diocese of Down and Connor there were many examples of cases where this was availed of. A specific example is the first school officially sponsored by the Catholic community in Belfast, which had been opened in 1829 beside St Patrick's Church in Donegall Street and for which, as for the other Catholic schools, the income normally came only from voluntary contributions.

However, distrust of the National Education Board increased in the mind of the Catholic Church over the decades following the 1831 legislation, in particular with the introduction of the model schools in the late 1840s. These schools were intended to attract the most able students who eventually would become teachers. They were trained through a monitorial system, introduced by Joseph Lancaster (1778–1838) by which senior pupils assisted in the discipline and education of younger pupils. The National Education Board had exclusive control of the model schools, of the appointment of teachers there and of the allocation of schoolbooks and any other financial resources.[9]

While the education controversies dragged on, conditions were becoming more and more acute in the centres of urban population and particularly in the rapidly expanding industrial melting-pot which was Belfast. Here, as the mid-century years crept by, the matter called for urgent attention. Several schools for Catholic children had been set up in the city and had attracted thousands of children. However, attendance necessarily fluctuated. Many children were employed in the textile mills and, the majority of Belfast Catholics being in the lowest income group, education was of very minor interest to them when compared with the problem of securing a livelihood. Bishop Denvir had, in 1850, called on the St Vincent de Paul Society. They set up and took responsibility for schools which were under parish management, though they received virtually no aid and next to no encouragement from the clergy (who, to give them credit, surely had many other problems to deal with) and there was an immediate danger of the schools being closed.

So, in spite of all the society's zealous efforts, the provision was inadequate, as they themselves realised only too well. With the continuous influx of impoverished Catholic families looking for work in the town after the ravages of the famine years, numbers steadily mounted. By the 1860s it was calculated that there were approximately 12,000 Catholic children in Belfast who needed schooling. But the parish schools were overcrowded and teachers were working in very deprived conditions. The schoolrooms were often private homes converted for the purpose, having minimal furnishings and equipment. The children suffered from undernourishment. Even then only about ten per cent of the Catholic children were attending these schools on any kind of a regular basis. One explanation was that the parents, poor, and coming from rural areas where they had never attended school themselves, were mostly illiterate and as yet did not recognise the value of educating their children when more urgent human needs such as making a living had to be attended to. On the other hand it was believed that, with only about 2,400 children attending schools managed by Catholics, a very large number of Catholic children were attending national schools under Protestant management. In these conditions the bishop tried to provide some religious education for his flock by organising Sunday-school classes, where religious instruction was given by members of the Confraternities of Christian Doctrine and of the Blessed Virgin Mary.[10]

The Mercy convent schools

When Bishop Denvir and the Catholic gentlemen of Belfast had originally called upon the Sisters of Mercy they had had in mind primarily the provision of a better system of education for the Catholic community. Already the Sisters of Mercy were renowned for their dedication in this field, especially with regard to the education of the poor. Mother Catherine McAuley had been particularly keen on founding Catholic schools, which she regarded as the antidote to proselytism, a serious threat to the faith of Catholic children and young people in mid-nineteenth-century Ireland. She had been much impressed by the example of her father, who had gathered local children around him at Stormanstown House to instruct them in their faith. It was probably this example that had helped her to persevere in her own faith when, as a young woman, she was thrown into the heart of Protestant society life in Dublin. Her Catholic faith was scorned and she was urged to abandon it, as were some of her closest relatives.

Apart from her own personal experience, Catherine's work among the poor in Dublin gave her evidence, at first hand, of the great inroads proselytising societies were making among the Catholic poor there. For a time she worked in the Parochial Poor School in Middle Abbey Street. In 1824 she decided that something more was needed and leased the land at the corner of lower Baggot Street and Herbert Street. There she invested her inheritance in building a house intended as a school and a refuge for women in need. While religious instruction took first place in Catherine McAuley's schools, she insisted that general education should be solid. As early as 1825 she devoted much attention to studying the education system used by the schools of the Kildare Place Society. Not satisfied with the monitorial systems commonly used, she visited France to study methods for the instruction of large classes in the poor schools of Paris. When the National Education Board was set up in Ireland in 1831, she, like Archbishop Murray, favoured cooperating with it, hoping that this would raise the standard of pupils' work. On the whole, Catherine McAuley was a visionary with regard to the value she saw in education for the raising of the dignity of the poor – in particular, of women. Wherever they went, her Sisters were examples themselves, and leaders for others, in this field.

In Belfast the Sisters rose quickly to the challenge before them. As we have seen, as soon as they arrived in the city they opened a school at their first residence, 2A Donegall Square North, where they converted the ground floor of their dwelling into schoolrooms. These expanded into Callender Street and evening classes were instituted for the mill girls who worked during the day and any other women who cared to attend, an attempt to overcome the prevailing illiteracy among the poor and to open for them the possibility of a better life. These classes continued to function until the community moved to their new convent on the Crumlin Road. But they did not abandon the town centre. By the end of 1858 a day school was well established at 15 Hamilton Street, which continued even after the opening of the Convent National Schools on the Crumlin Road. The new convent schools were built to accommodate 600 pupils, and by 1865 the Sisters were running the largest schools in Belfast – those beside the main convent and the other adjoining the branch convent at 15–17 Hamilton Street. In all, their pupil enrolment numbered over a thousand.

The Young Ladies' School

It seems also that while the priority for the Sisters was the needs of the poor, they were also urged to offer some provision for the daughters of the wealthier Catholic families – to whom they were indeed indebted. A notice appeared in the *Belfast Morning News* of Friday, 10 April 1857:

THE SISTERS OF MERCY
propose opening their
DAY SCHOOL FOR YOUNG LADIES
on Monday, 20 of April.
The course of education will comprise the various branches of English and French Literature, Music, Dancing, Plain and Ornamental Needlework, and every other accomplishment and branch of knowledge essential to the complete education of a young lady.

Terms: 4 guineas per annum, to be paid quarterly in advance.
Extra charges: Music, Dancing and Stationery.
For any further information regarding the school, apply to –
THE SUPERIORESS, CONVENT OF MERCY, BELFAST.[11]

The Young Ladies' School was a fee-paying day school, or 'pension' school, such as were to be found associated with many Mercy national schools in the country and had been introduced by the foundress herself.[12] In establishing pension schools for the daughters of the well-to-do middle class Catherine McAuley was responding to a genuine need in nineteenth-century Irish society, as well as to an almost prophetic insight into the value of a well-educated woman:

> The Sisters shall be convinced that no work of charity can be more productive of good to society, or more conducive to the happiness of the poor, than the careful instruction of women; because, whatever be the station they are destined to fulfil, their example will always have great influence; and wherever a religious woman presides peace and good order are generally to be found.[13]

Such schools were not the primary work of the institute, but Catherine stipulated that:

> In localities where there is no good Catholic school for children whose parents could not afford to send them to a convent boarding school, there such may be undertaken … Such schools ought to be regarded as concessions to meet the exigencies of a locality rather than as belonging to the spirit of the Institute.[14]

The pension schools also took in boarders when this was a necessity. In Catherine's time, and for many decades afterwards, secondary education on a residential basis in Ireland was almost exclusively confined to Protestant endowed grammar schools (and those were only for boys) and to a few girls' schools of private enterprise. Sister M. Angela Bolster, in her study of the pioneer education work undertaken by Catherine McAuley, tells us that the foundress's breakthrough in this field was first tried in Carlow in 1837–8. She set up a day school to provide secondary education for the daughters of townsfolk for whom the fees charged in existing boarding schools were prohibitive, yet who were ambitious for their daughters to have something above what was offered in the national schools.[15] In the brief ten years of her life as a Sister of Mercy, Catherine McAuley founded more pension schools than houses of mercy for working girls.[16] One possible explanation for this is, of course, that houses of mercy were generally confined to cities like Dublin, Cork and Limerick and the larger towns, where the need was greatest. Pension schools were found in most of the towns where the Sisters of Mercy were established. Within a few years of the opening of the Young Ladies' School at St Paul's Convent, Belfast, 'about twenty better-class girls from Belfast and the surrounding counties' were in attendance. Some of these girls boarded because of the distance from their homes.

Younger children, too, were sometimes taken in as fee-paying boarders. They were taken only when there was an occasion of special need and they shared the same accommodation as the orphans (the intention being that the orphans should not feel inferior to those pupils who had families). However, this concession failed to retain the approval of Bishop Denvir, who wished to emphasise the exclusively charitable status of the convent junior schools. This is evidenced in a correspondence, in 1859, between a Mrs Johns of Carrickfergus (County Antrim) and the bishop:

> Mrs. Johns presents her compliments to the Rt. Rev. Dr. Denvir and begs to trouble him in regard to the case of Mary Anne Darcy, the child of Mrs. Johns' cook, who has been for some months past a Boarder in the school attached to St Paul's Convent of Mercy, Belfast.
>
> Mrs. Johns has been made aware that his Lordship has directed that the school shall, for the future, be confined to destitute orphans and that therefore the children for whom the relatives or friends have hitherto made some payment will be sent away, and she does not at all desire to trouble his Lordship with any request that Mary Darcy should be made an exception to the rule.
>
> But since there are still at the school several boarders whose terms have not expired Mrs. Johns begs that his Lordship will allow Mary Anne to remain at the orphanage as long as any of the others; and whenever they are sent away Mrs. Johns undertakes that Mary Anne shall be brought home and paid for up to the time of her removal.
>
> The reason for the present request is that there is no similar establishment in this neighbourhood conducted by members of the Roman Catholic religion – and, indeed, Mary Anne Darcy might almost claim to be received as a 'poor orphan', her mother's wages being a scanty provision for both and the child's father being dead. No such application, however, is intended to be made.
> Carrickfergus, Wednesday …[17]

An important fact can be deduced from this example: that parents or guardians of children who lived at a distance from Catholic schools were anxious to have them educated in a Catholic environment. Many of these would be the children of parents in service in a Protestant household whose employers would be good enough to be concerned about the children's education in their own faith. Such, we assume, was Mrs Johns. Also, of course, a boarding school provided for the day-to-day care of the child, leaving the mother free for full time employment.

The pension schools, then, provided for young girls who had completed their elementary education. They were later called colleges, high schools or academies, and were established wherever the Sisters of Mercy went throughout the world. (In Ireland they were often called 'secondary tops'.) In fact, they were the forerunners of the post-primary education that later became available to all. Many pupils of these schools later joined the Mercy Congregation. Normally a fee, or pension, was paid for tuition, but Catherine McAuley provided that 'The proceeds should be applied to charitable purposes.' However, it was invariably the rule that the fee could be waived in the case of especially promising young pupils when their parents could not afford it (usually in the form of scholarships).

The Young Ladies' School continued and in later years took on the important task of training young women as teachers. There was no provision for Catholic teacher training in Belfast at this time and trained teachers were an urgent requirement for the Catholic schools in the latter half of the nineteenth century.

For the Sisters of Mercy in Belfast, therefore, there was no discrimination with regard to means, class or creed. In fact it is worth noting that, when the Convent National Schools opened, for the first several years many of the children attending were not Catholics.[18] The Sisters were responding, then, as best they could to the needs of the time as they presented themselves. This adaptability gave vision and energy to their apostolate and they were ever open to new challenges, as the further account of their story will show.

---

[1] Acts of chapter, SPCMB, Book 3.
[2] This was a consequence of the disruption caused by the eviction.
[3] Bishop P. Dorrian to Archbishop P. Cullen, Belfast (MIA, 27 July 1862).
[4] Acts of chapter, SPCMB, Book 1, 3 August 1862.
[5] Letter in 'Early letters, St Paul's Convent of Mercy' (MCA, 21 February 1863).
[6] McNeill, *op. cit.*
[7] *The Vindicator*, 20 January 1841.
[8] At the height of the controversy about the national education system in Ireland in the mid-1800s and its implications for denominational education, Richard Whately, the Anglican archbishop of Dublin, published four volumes of extracts from scripture and a book entitled *Introductory lessons on Christian evidences*, which were promoted by the National Education Board for use in all schools at the time. Some saw the latter publication as an instrument of proselytism. For more on this subject see

A. Macaulay, *Patrick Dorrian, bishop of Down and Connor 1865–85* (Dublin: Academic Press, 1987), Chapter 9.

[9] *St Vincent de Paul Society Centenary Magazine*, pp. 14, 15, quoted in Rogers, *op. cit.*, p. 10, col. 2 and O'Laverty, *op. cit.*, vol. ii, p. 433.

[10] Rogers, *op. cit.*, p. 11, col. 2 and n. 12.

[11] *Belfast Morning News*, 10 April 1857.

[12] The term 'pension' is from the French *pension*, which describes this type of school.

[13] Sisters of Mercy, *The rule and constitutions of the religious called Sisters of Mercy* (Dublin: Browne and Nolan, 1866 (repr. 1926)), Chapter 2, Section 7.

[14] Sisters of Mercy, *Guide for the religious called the Sisters of Mercy* (Dublin: Browne and Nolan, 1888), Part 1, p. 22.

[15] Bolster, *Positio, op. cit.*, p. 724.

[16] Ibid.

[17] DCDA (D.59/1).

[18] Annals, SPCMB.

7

VISITATION: THE CARE
OF THE SICK AND DESTITUTE

During the latter years of his episcopate Bishop Denvir had felt much overwhelmed by the sectarian conflicts that blighted the lives of the people of Belfast and in particular caused much suffering to the Catholic population. He retired in the summer of 1865 and, on Tuesday 11 July 1866, just a year afterwards, died in the parochial residence in Donegall Street. Reverend Mother M. Gonzaga Morrin and Mother M. Juliana Delaney had remained in attendance upon him during his last night. Bishop Denvir was succeeded by his coadjutor, Patrick Dorrian, who had, in fact, been carrying the burden of the diocese for some years.

Great encouragement was brought to the struggling church of Down and Connor when, in October 1866, Belfast had a visit from the newly elevated cardinal-archbishop of Dublin, Dr Paul Cullen. The Sisters of Mercy had the privilege of hosting the cardinal, who had come for the dedication of the new St Peter's Church on the Falls Road (Sunday, 14 October). It was a most memorable occasion, attended also by 11 other bishops including Dr Ullathorne, bishop of Birmingham, who preached the sermon at the Pontifical High Mass at which the cardinal presided.

The cardinal visited the convent the next day, where a reception was held. For this the convent refectory, the largest room in the house, was used, and it was tastefully arranged and decorated for the occasion. Here the cardinal, attended by Bishop Dorrian, Bishop Ullathorne, Bishop Butler of Limerick and other important personages, received many congratulatory addresses, since it was just four months since he had been made a cardinal – the first in the history of the church in Ireland. After the crowd had departed the cardinal and friends partook of a lunch served in the community room. The schools were then visited and memoirs have recorded that 'when a little child from the infant school presented his Eminence with a bouquet of flowers he seemed much pleased and gave her a medal'.[1]

Meantime, visits of another kind, which had become the hallmark of the Sisters of Mercy from the earliest days of the institute, were being made. The apostolate of the visitation of the sick, the dying, poor families and those in prison was of primary importance wherever the Sisters were to be found. The Sisters, once settled on the Crumlin Road, continued the charitable work that had been started shortly after their arrival in Belfast. From St Paul's Convent they visited the poor and the sick in their homes in the crowded streets of St Patrick's Parish. This area was home to many of the mill and factory workers, mostly women and girls, and men employed in regular or casual labour. The families were usually large, with very little by way of material resources. The territory of visitation was widespread, comprising on the one side Great and Little Patrick Streets, Great George's Street and the many small streets that had found space between the busy parallel thoroughfares of North Queen Street and York Street as the labouring population expanded north from the town centre, and on the other side the older district of Carrick Hill and the new terraces of workers' houses, which were being built by the more benign mill owners between the Old Lodge and Crumlin Roads and directly facing the convent. From both these districts came most of the children who attended the convent schools.

Rapid industrial development, especially in the middle decades of the century, had brought many social problems, in particular with regard to the housing of the thousands of migrant workers. These were compelled to accept any accommodation they could find and many records from this period give vivid descriptions of the appalling living conditions many had to endure. Reverend William Murphy O'Hanlon, minister to the Congregational Church in Donegall Street and a man of keen social conscience, in his book *Walks among the poor of Belfast*, described what he witnessed in the area around St Patrick's Parish – the districts 'bounded by Donegall, Academy, Great Patrick, Corporation and Waring Streets'. It was by no means, he estimated, the worst quarter of the town, but one of the most densely populated:

> Street after street, alley after alley, courts and by-ways, very numerous, meet us in this direction … mostly overcrowded with human beings in the lowest stage of social wretchedness and vice … Brady's Row lies off Gratton Street, and I can assure you that the aspect and odour of this place will quickly put to flight all sentimental benevolence. Here my companion and myself fixed upon two houses as specimens of the whole. In one of these we found that seven persons live and sleep in the same room – their beds, if such they may be called, lying upon the floor. The desolation and wretchedness of this apartment – without windows and open in all directions – it is utterly impossible to describe.[2]

This description could be repeated in many variations, according to O'Hanlon's evidence. Such conditions not only made the maintenance of the most basic social standards virtually impossible but when to these were added long hours of unhealthy work in the factories, the prevalence of child labour, the lowest wages, the very poor health standards and the practically non-existent sanitary arrangements, it is not hard to believe the susceptibility of the densely packed population to epidemic diseases and a very high mortality rate. J.L. McCracken has recorded, in his account of conditions in early Victorian Belfast, that in the 1850s this was one in 35, the average age at death being nine years and half the living population being under 20 in certain areas.[3] The 1830s and 1840s had seen outbreaks of typhus and cholera with which the municipal authorities could hardly cope. The consequent fatalities numbered hundreds.

Many generous efforts were made, of course, to respond to the extreme needs of the poor. These were mainly initiated by church bodies, in which the well-to-do ladies of the town played a leading role. These charitable ladies visited the sick in their homes to assess for themselves their circumstances:

> They collected the (voluntary) subscriptions and went into the back streets to investigate applications for help … Like the Clothing Society, they divided the town into districts and visitors were appointed to each so that they got to know every case.[4]

Though the conditions of the poor in Belfast, a rapidly developing industrial town, may have had aspects with which they were not quite familiar, the 'ladies from Dublin', as the Sisters were called by the local Belfast people, found themselves in not unfamiliar surroundings. Those who had commenced their religious lives in Baggot Street Convent had tested their vocations in the lanes and alleyways of the poor in Dublin, giving material help where they could or at least, by their presence, bringing comfort and consolation to all. Catherine McAuley had said, 'There are things which the poor prize more highly than gold, though they cost the donor nothing. Among these are the kind word, the gentle, compassionate look and the patient hearing of sorrows.'[5] At an early date Archbishop Murray had inserted into the Mercy constitutions the commitment to undertake the visitation of the 'sick poor', thus distinguishing the new congregation from the more enclosed communities who were equally involved in the corporal and spiritual works of mercy but within the confines of their own convents. This insertion, though outside the norm, had gained the approval of the Holy See. The opening chapter of the rule and constitutions of the Sisters of Mercy named the visitation of the sick among the primary works of mercy in which the Sisters pledged to engage themselves:

Mercy – the principal path marked out by Jesus Christ for those who desire to follow him – has, in all ages of the Church, excited the faithful in a particular manner to instruct and comfort the sick and dying poor, as in them they regard the person of our divine Master who has said: 'Amen I say to you, as long as you did it to one of these, the least brethren, you did it to me.'[6]

The following sections of the chapter – with which many generations of the Sisters of Mercy were very familiar up until recent times – give quite a vivid picture of the image the Sisters must have presented as they set out on visitation along the streets of Belfast:

> Before the Sisters leave the convent, they shall endeavour to understand perfectly the way they are to go – and if some places cannot be found without making enquiries it will be most prudent to go to a huckster's or baker's shop where the poor are generally known; always speaking with that gravity which insures respect … No Sister shall go out unless accompanied by another Sister. The greatest caution and gravity shall be observed in the streets; walking neither too slow nor in a hurried pace; not stopping to converse with or salute those whom they meet; keeping close together without leaning on each other; preserving recollection of mind as if they expected to meet their Divine Redeemer in every habitation of the poor …[7]

During the lifetime of the foundress, no less a personage than Daniel O'Connell paid tribute to this work in a public speech at the time. No doubt what he gave was a rather romanticised picture of the Sisters of Mercy as they were familiarly seen in the streets of Dublin. But his words registered with Catherine McAuley, who recorded them (rather amusedly, we can imagine) in a letter written on 17 November 1840 to Sister M. Catherine Leaghy in Galway:

> Look at the Sisters of Mercy, wrapped in their long black cloaks. They are seen gliding along the streets in their humble attire, while a slight glance at the foot shows the accomplished lady … They are hastening to the lone couch of some sick fellow-creature, fast sinking into the grave with no-one to console, none to soothe. They come with consolation and hope and bring down, by their prayers, the blessings of God on the dying sinner, on themselves and on their community.[8]

The Sisters soon became known as the 'walking nuns', and in the 1860s the Sister of Mercy was a familiar sight on the streets of Belfast as she passed from house to house in the slums in visitation.

The Sisters robed themselves suitably for the occasion in black bonnets and long, black visitation cloaks covering their religious habits. The veils were worn only indoors as it was considered prudent not to appear too conspicuous in the streets of the town, where their presence might be met with some antagonism. Gradually circumstances changed. A letter of June 1900 to the superior of the St Paul's community from the motherhouse in Dublin, gives us what now seems an amusing glimpse into the conditions of the times:

> Convent of the Mother of Mercy,
> Carysfort Park, Blackrock,
> Co. Dublin.
> 27th June, 1900
>
> My dearest Rev. Mother,
> I see no objection to the Sisters wearing the indoor dress when travelling by mail. The Limerick Sisters have abolished the out-door dress altogether and wear the Visitation veil over their *faces*.
> Soon, please God we shall do the same, for it is a *remnant* of the *Penal times*.
>
>
> With best love and blessings to you all,
> Believe me always,
> Your loving and devoted Sr. in Ct.,
> Sr. M. Ligouri Keenan.[9]
>

And so the Sisters would set out, with decorous demeanour, the junior carrying the basket and walking at the left side of the senior, 'unless they carry an umbrella, in which case she may walk at the most convenient side'. The main intention seems to have been the spiritual welfare of the sick and dying – 'The good of souls is what the Sisters shall have principally in view' – though the *Rule* clearly stated that 'they should act with great tenderness, and when there is no immediate danger of death it will be well, first, to relieve distress and to endeavour, in every practical way, to promote the cleanliness, ease and comfort of the sick person' and 'when ... the subject turns on procuring relief for the indigence of the sick person's family, let them promise, as far as depends on them, to attend to it in the manner their state permits'.[10]

The prison
The visitation was not confined to the poor. The Sisters also endeavoured, whenever possible, to visit the prison. They had every opportunity for this. The building closest to the convent, sharing a boundary wall, was the Crumlin Road Jail.[11] This was the main prison for the north of Ireland and,

with the courthouse facing it, presented in the mid-1800s an ominous presence on the still relatively suburban Crumlin Road. Of particular concern to the Sisters were the prisoners facing the death penalty. This, sad to say, was not a rare circumstance at the time, as is clear from contemporary social history and also from an instruction given in the guide to the rule and constitutions:

> Prisoners under Sentence:
> When prisoners are under sentence of death they should be visited as frequently as possible, and every effort made to aid them to sanctify their awful doom, and to turn this most precious time to the fullest profit.[12]

We have a tragic record of just such a case in the community annals of around this time – a newspaper report (dated 1894) possibly written by one of the Sisters on 'The death (execution) of an unnamed prisoner in Crumlin Road Jail':

> For more than a week previously he was visited regularly each day by two Sisters of Mercy from the Crumlin Road Convent, and he was always glad to listen to their pious exhortations and to join with them in fervent prayer, so that his conduct and devotional disposition have given those appointed to promote his spiritual welfare much consolation. His habits for the past month were extremely regular. Each morning he took for breakfast some tea and a little toast, and in the evening he took the same for supper. His dinner consisted of potatoes and a little meat, of which he ate very sparingly. Very often his dinner was brought from him much in the same condition in which it was left with him. He slept well each night, but his night's rest never exceeded four hours. On Tuesday he was visited twice by Fr. Hamill, and also by the nuns, and after he was left alone in the evening he continued his devotions during the night until three o'clock the next morning, when he retired to rest, after requesting the warder to wake him at half-past five. He slept soundly during those two and a half hours and after being roused by the warder at the appointed time, he immediately got up, and as soon as he had dressed he resumed his devotions in his cell, and continued thus until six o'clock, when he assisted at Mass, which was celebrated by the Rev. Fr. Hamill, and received the Holy Communion. Two of the Sisters of Mercy, along with Fr. Hamill, remained with him in prayer to the last moment. Breakfast was brought to him at the usual hour, but he partook of none, and it was only by the persuasion of the chaplain that he was induced to take any supper on Tuesday evening. He prayed in the most fervent manner all yesterday morning, and it will be a source of some happiness for his spiritual director to feel that as his end approached he seemed to make a good preparation for the life

hereafter. The prisoner expressed his most sincere thanks for the earnest and constant attention which his spiritual advisers paid to him, and also desired Fr. Hamill to convey his thanks to the Governor of the jail and the officials for their kindness to him. The only matter which troubled his mind was that he could not be buried in consecrated ground.[13]

Serving the poor

The fact that the Sisters were familiar with the families in their local districts became a great advantage as generations of poor families turned to them for help, support and consolation in times of need. For their part, the Sisters were delighted to see many of those families succeed in improving their circumstances, especially when steady employment came the way of the breadwinner. While visiting the homes, the Sisters urged the parents to send the children to school, believing that even a basic education was the first step out of the degradation of poverty. In many cases sending the children, especially the older ones, to school was a sacrifice. Some families depended on even the meagre earnings of the young to keep hunger at bay.

Visitation was a two-way traffic. Parents were invited to the convent to collect clothing and food as the need arose. Christmas was a time of bounty, when special food parcels were prepared and delivered, and some cash was handed out for an extra treat. Parties in the school were very popular events, as can be imagined.

In all Mercy convents a reception area for 'men and women of the road' was a regular feature. In St Paul's, after the building of the new chapel, 'the porch' became an institution. This was an enclosed hallway where all day, every day, a few or several wayfarers could be found (sometimes in various stages of inebriation) awaiting tea and bread or, on a cold winter's day, nourishing soup. Many went away with packages of food or parcels of clothing. Money was always in demand, but this had to be administered prudently as, in many cases, it was wont to disappear in the nearest pub. The Sisters took turns serving in the porch. It was always a salutary new experience for a young novice, whose energy and ingenuity would be comprehensively exercised in running back and forth from porch to kitchen, keeping the food and drink supplied on demand. But the visitors' favourite request was for the reverend mother. They knew where the funds were most likely to come from.

Whatever the cost, fidelity to the needs of the poor who lived in their midst or arrived on their doorstep was a priority that every young woman joining the community was brought up to respect. She was reminded, from her earliest days in the convent, of the primary charism of the congregation, defined by Catherine McAuley as follows:

The spirit of our institute is MERCY. Mercy can operate only in proportion as destitution, suffering, ignorance and other miseries call it forth. Charity embraces those who abound as well as those who are in need; but Mercy finds exercise only in proportion to the necessity of its objects.[14]

As society has changed over the decades, the form of this response of Mercy has had to adapt. But the primary focus for the institute, the service of the poor, has never been abandoned.

[1] Annals, SPCMB, 1866.
[2] W.M. O'Hanlon, *Walks among the poor in Belfast, and suggestions for their improvement* (Wakefield: S.R. Publishers, 1971).
[3] J.C. Beckett and R.E. Glasscock (eds), *Belfast: the origin and growth of an industrial city* (London: BBC, 1967), p. 93.
[4] Description of the work of the Society for the Relief of the Destitute Sick, founded in 1826 by Reverend Dr Edgar, in Jordan, *op. cit.*, p. 183.
[5] C. McAuley, *Familiar instructions of Rev. Mother McAuley: foundress of the Institute of the Religious Sisters of Mercy, Dublin, Ireland* (St Louis, USA: Carreras, 1888), p. 137.
[6] Sisters of Mercy, *op. cit.* (*Rule*), Section 8.
[7] Ibid., Section 12.
[8] I. Neuman (ed.), *Letters of Catherine McAuley* (Baltimore, USA: Helicon, 1969), p. 255.
[9] Sister M. Ligouri Keenan to Reverend Mother, St Paul's Convent, Belfast (Annals, SPCMB, 27 June 1900).
[10] Sisters of Mercy, *op. cit.* (*Rule*), Chapter 3 and idem., *op. cit.* (*Guide*), Part 1. Here many detailed instructions are given for the carrying out of this apostolate.
[11] Marked on a map of the time (1861) as the 'County Jail'; built by Charles Lanyon in 1843–5, with additions in 1849–50.
[12] Sisters of Mercy, *op. cit.* (*Guide*), Part 1.
[13] *Irish News*, February 1894; Archives, SPCMB.
[14] Sisters of Mercy, *op. cit.* (*Guide*), Part 1.

8

TAKING ROOT

A description of life in Belfast would be incomplete without mention of a recurring hazard: sectarian riots. This was one major problem with which the growing town had to contend from the mid-1800s onwards. Up until the early 1800s the different denominational communities in Belfast – Roman Catholic, Presbyterian and Church of Ireland – had lived in considerable harmony and in fact had much in common on many political and social issues. However, as the years unfolded, various factors emerged to replace harmony with distrust and intolerance. It would appear that the incipient fears of Ulster Protestants rose to a crescendo with the passing of the Act of Catholic Emancipation in 1829 and they took a defensive stance in the reinforcement of the strength of the Orange Order.

Towards the middle of the nineteenth century, apprehension was fuelled as the established Belfast Protestant (mostly Presbyterian) community witnessed the growing prosperity of the Catholic business and professional class on the one hand and the increase in the Catholic population of the town resulting both from their migration from rural areas and the growing numbers employed in the mills, the factories and in the shipyard ancillary services on the other. As Bernard Hughes, a leading Catholic businessman, saw it, these Catholics had become the 'bone and sinew artisans of the town'.[1] With this growing Catholic population came the expanding presence of the Catholic Church, which displayed itself in the building of churches, schools and institutions and the arrival of members of religious congregations of Sisters and Brothers to administer the same. As Alison Jordan expressed it:

> Any doubt as to the growing wealth of Catholics would be dispelled by
> the sight of their large Gothic style churches which rose in all parts of
> the town in the last quarter of the nineteenth century.[2]

Though the two main religious groupings in Belfast differed fundamentally in their beliefs and understandings, the destructive antagonism that now emerged was a new development. For example, the building of the first Catholic church in Belfast since the Reformation, St Mary's, in the town centre, had been well supported by the leading Protestant businessmen of the town, and at its opening in May 1784 'the Belfast Volunteer companies

… lined the chapel yard in full dress uniform and presented arms to the parish priest, Fr. Hugh O'Donnell, whom they followed into the Chapel to hear Mass.' In return they received the 'grateful thanks of the Roman Catholic congregation' who knew not 'in what adequate terms to express their feelings, excited by the attendance of so respectable a Protestant audience … the impression of which mark of regard is never to be effaced.'[3]

It was similar with the opening of the first St Patrick's Church in 1815, after which the following was printed in the *Belfast News Letter*:

> the Catholics of Belfast, impressed with the warmest feelings of gratitude for the unexampled liberality which they experienced from their Brethren of the different religious persuasions … feel a duty … to express publicly our grateful acknowledgements for the disinterested generosity which they manifested at the consecration of the new Chapel.[4]

In Belfast sectarian fears and suspicions were added to the usual disruptive forces that come in the train of population shifts that occur too rapidly and haphazard industrial growth with its attendant evils of unemployment, homelessness and destitution. So it was that, as the 1800s progressed, the balance of population and power between Protestants and Catholics changed steadily. At the beginning of the century the proportion of Catholics was small, about one in ten. By 1835 they were one in three. With this demographic development the tolerance that had characterised Protestant attitudes in the early decades turned to mistrust; by the 1850s the peace of the town and the well-being of the inhabitants were endangered by periodic outbursts of violence which reached peak points around the Twelfth celebrations. Nor did the more rebellious elements of the town's Protestant population want for encouragement and provocation. J.J. Campbell, in describing the recurrent disturbances which became, sadly, so characteristic of the town, noted that since the time of Reverend Dr Cooke, the great orator, who died in 1868, Belfast had been the scene of periodic sectarian rioting. He quoted the words of the noted social geographer, Emrys Jones:

> The support which was given to the extreme anti-papist attitude of Henry Cooke was probably an expression of Protestant dismay at the great increase in numbers of the sect [Catholics]. Tension certainly rose as their numbers increased.[5]

Most of the rioting took place around Sandy Row and the lower Falls areas, but periodically church and convent property elsewhere came under attack. In August 1857 the newly built convent on the Crumlin Road was under threat as gangs of shipwrights (Orangemen and Orange supporters), armed, made their way up Clifton Street in that direction. It was feared that they were bound for an attack on the convent. They diverged, however, and turned their attention to the partly built St Peter's Church not far away. In the summer of 1864, however, the Sisters did not get off so lightly. That August saw one of the worst outbreaks of rioting, leaving many partisans dead and injured. It seemed that this was triggered by the celebration of the unveiling of a monument to Daniel O'Connell, the 'Liberator', in Dublin. O'Connell had engineered Catholic emancipation and called for a 'Catholic parliament for a Catholic people'. This appeal appeared to signal the rebirth of a Catholic nationalism, alien to the ideals of 1798 and recalling, for Ulster Protestants, memories of earlier nationalist resurgences that had spelt persecution for their coreligionists. Many violent incidents took place in Belfast that summer month and a contemporary report gives a vivid account of 'the wrecking of Bankmore House' on Thursday, 11 and Friday, 12 August:

> Many of the rioters and wreckers who had been roaming through Belfast all night were unemployed; many more had jobs but did not turn up for work on Friday morning. Indeed, by this time the disturbances had seriously disrupted the commercial and industrial life of the town. Some of the mills had closed, mainly because the workers were afraid to venture near them. The shops, even in the centre of the town, kept their shutters up all day. And although Friday was market day, few farmers brought their produce. Many of those who did regretted it for mobs of people met them on the road in, overturned their carts, and stole what they had. That weekend the price of food in Belfast rocketed. The markets committee lost the substantial sum of £50.
>
> The mobs roamed through town all day Friday. At ten o'clock in the morning they chased two Catholic curates into Dr Dorrian's house in Howard Street and then smashed all the windows and plate glass in the front door. The bishop was in his study at the time wondering how he could get protection for Patrick McCabe, caretaker of Friar's Bush, and for the nuns in Bankmore House. Little did he realise that Bankmore House was at that very moment under attack.[6]

The only people in Bankmore House were a few of the Sisters from St Paul's Convent, 25 young women residents who earned a living by washing and sewing under the supervision of the nuns, and an old man who did odd jobs about the place and kept the grounds and garden tidy. The mob from Sandy Row broke down the entrance gate, broke all the windows, smashed the shutters into splinters and caused extensive damage. Something must then have alarmed them because they suddenly retreated and ran back to their own district. That, however, was only the first attack. The second, a few days later, was to be much worse. This took place on Monday, 15 August:

> About five o'clock the area all round St. Malachy's [Church] was thick with people. They thronged in thousands on the Dublin Road. They invaded Bankmore house, set fire to the haystacks, and again threatened the nuns and the women in their care.[7]

Luckily no one suffered any bodily harm but the cost of the damage amounted to a considerable sum. And it was a terrifying experience for the Sisters and their charges.

Outbreaks of rioting continued into the 1870s and 1880s, inflamed on the one hand by partisan parades and marches and on the other by desperation as employment, wage cuts, lockouts, totally inadequate living conditions and near starvation drove the poorest sections of the population to extreme measures of protest against injustices in which both sides of the religious divide found common cause.

Despite the periodic disruptions that became so characteristic of life in Belfast, daily life in the town continued with, on the whole, a remarkable degree of normality. The last three decades of the century were years of rapid development in the life and work of the Sisters of Mercy in the town and in the diocese. This can be seen from the expansion of their undertakings in the field of education.

Industrial schools

The Convent National Schools had been functioning for some years and St Patrick's Orphanage, adjoining the schools, had opened on 1 January 1859. Within the next ten years the government had accepted the concept of the industrial school, an institution which had, since the late 1840s, been promoted by a group of women, the Ladies' Relief Association of Belfast, who believed that the best way to help the orphaned and the poor was to prepare them (particularly, in this case, young females) to earn a living by their own handiwork, mainly needlework.

The Sisters of Mercy in Belfast supported this idea with enthusiasm because it was so similar to the ideas that Catherine McAuley had put into practice in the House of Mercy in Baggot Street, Dublin. Following the enactment of industrial-schools legislation (1868) the government was prepared to recognise the existing orphanages as industrial schools. Thus the orphanages could become eligible for grants from the scheme, 'for services provided'. Consequently the Sisters of Mercy in Belfast made application and St Patrick's Orphanage was certified an industrial school for

80 pupils in December 1869. Industrial schools, to which neglected or delinquent children were sent by the education authorities, were set up in the later 1800s. They were residential and their main purpose was to give the pupils some technical training so that they could take up some useful occupation on leaving school. The industrial school at the convent could accommodate 90 girls aged between 7 and 14 years. By the turn of the century, with 88 children enrolled, the school was receiving a government grant of £1,450 per year. In 1896 a second industrial school was opened beside the convent at Abbeyville, which could accommodate 120 girls.[8] With 95 residents it received a government grant of £1,558.

The school was run very successfully and soon a grant for 20 more pupils was given as the building and the school's administration more than met the inspectors' requirements. Eventually it was placed as a first-class school. It had a fine, large workroom in which the main occupation was the making and embroidering of church vestments and the repair of the same. The school employed several skilled workmistresses and almost every church in Down and Connor and in the neighbouring dioceses gave it their custom. The pupils of the school were given excellent training and the income from their work gave sufficient means to pay the employees and to cover expenses.

But it was not all work. The Sisters rented Parkmount, a house at Greencastle (706 Park Row) on the north-eastern outskirts of the town and close to Belfast Lough, to which the girls could go for a short holiday, accompanied by some Sisters and a teacher. The holiday house was much appreciated by pupils and teachers alike. It gave welcome opportunity for country walks and the benefits of fresh sea air.

Teacher training

Meanwhile, other educational developments were taking place. At the end of the 1860s Mother M. Gonzaga Morrin, having been left a legacy of almost £3,000 by her brother, asked the bishop if she could use the money to build a preparatory school on Convent Avenue (beside the Convent National Schools) for girls who wished to become monitresses but who did not have an adequate foundation. She suggested that they could pay a small sum for their support and be trained in the Convent National Schools. The bishop agreed and a two-storey building was erected adjoining Our Lady's Pension School (opened 1857), consisting of a dormitory and dining room and having direct access to the classrooms of the Convent National Schools. When completed, this new building gave accommodation to 16 aspiring young monitresses, most of whom completed their training and entered upon a successful teaching career.

This work developed into teacher training when, in 1877, Bishop Dorrian asked the Sisters to undertake the training of young women to become teachers in Catholic schools under the National Education Board. This provision was in response to the circumstances surrounding teacher training at that time. Up until the 1860s the majority of teachers being trained in Ireland under the National Education Board were Catholic. The Catholic bishops did not approve of the training provided by the national system and showed their disapproval by passing a decisive resolution, in 1862, directing priests to stop, from the beginning of the following year, sending any person to be trained as a teacher either to the model schools or to the training college in Marlborough Street, Dublin – despite the fact that teachers who had not been through the approved training were not eligible for payment from the government. The clergy were also instructed to cease employing, in the schools under their management, teachers who had received training in either of these two institutions. This resolution was followed by a demand for denominational training colleges to be financed by the government (a demand with which the leaders of the other churches in the country would have agreed). Eventually a response came from the government and the Powis report, published in 1870, recommended that one-system training should be phased out and that the establishment of denominational training colleges be encouraged and supported in recognition of the fact that a distinctly dual-denominational school system existed.

However, although the government originally accepted the recommendation, a subsequent government reneged on the commitment and no funds were forthcoming. So the problem of providing teachers, trained or untrained, for the national schools remained. Since about five-sixths of the teachers in those schools were Catholic, the issue was a major one for the Catholic hierarchy. If they did not wish to have their future teachers trained in the establishment college (and, as we have seen, the bishops had banned Catholics from attending the training college in Dublin), they would have to set up their own, with or without government aid. The bishops pursued their policy, continuing to struggle with the government on the matter of funding for the Catholic teacher training colleges they had already established.[9]

Already the Sisters of Mercy in Dublin had a female teacher-training institution attached to the convent in Baggot Street, and for this the Catholic bishops sought approval and funding in 1880. The Sisters in Limerick had also undertaken teacher training. And so the Sisters in Belfast willingly applied themselves to this important task, and many future female teachers for Catholic schools in the north were trained in the Belfast Mercy convent schools. They continued this work for about 20 years until, because of the pressure of many other apostolic commitments (in particular more involvement in the education of children and hospital work), they handed it over to the Dominican Sisters, who had come to the Falls Road in 1870. St Mary's Teacher-Training College for women students was established in 1900 and was, at that date, the only teacher-training college in the north of Ireland. St Mary's, Belfast, was for women; St Patrick's, Drumcondra, Dublin, was for men. After 1922 the young men from Northern Ireland went to St Mary's Teacher-Training College, Strawberry Hill, London, in order to have recognition for teaching in Northern Irish schools.

The intermediate examination

In the 1870s the issue of secondary schooling for Catholic youth came to the fore. No government support was given to secondary schools under Catholic management until the Board of Intermediate Education (which administered secondary-level education) made payment to the schools according to the results of the intermediate examination. This was under the Intermediate Examination Act (1878), which promised to reward teachers in proportion to the academic success of their pupils in the public examinations. Though the act was designed to benefit secondary schools, the distinction between primary and secondary was not drawn so finely as to exclude primary schools from preparing their senior classes for the examination. This move was welcomed by the Catholic bishops as they saw the benefit for diocesan colleges for young men – secondary-level colleges that Catholic bishops were required by Rome to set up in each diocese for the education of boys. They were intended to give a basic classical education to boys who might later desire to train for the Catholic priesthood. These colleges, for the most part, had been in operation for several decades. However, the bishops did not envisage the same legislation being extended to the education of girls. Bishop Dorrian, for example, thought that the education of young women should be quite different. He could not approve of 'an attempt to subvert society to establish a blue stocking in every family by the introduction of a system of education which would not be in keeping with the positions of females'.[10]

Undaunted, however, the Sisters of Mercy decided to enter the intermediate examinations. In the first year of the examinations (1879) a class began in a room of the convent for senior girls who wished to sit them. Reverend Michael H. Cahill, a very energetic young curate in St Patrick's Parish and editor of a Catholic newspaper, *The Examiner* (founded by Bishop Dorrian), undertook to teach the girls, assisted by Sister M.

Columba Larkin. Father Cahill was born in Kilkenny in 1844. He was curate in St Patrick's Parish from 1868 until his death in December 1881. Every morning he began work at nine o'clock and left at half past three in the afternoon. So successful were the results that one young lady, Annie Blaney, gained the gold medal for first place in Ireland with the highest mark for girls. The following year her sister, Mary Blaney, gained the same distinction. In the ensuing years many other girls won exhibitions and prizes, amongst them Annie Johnston, later of literary fame (as Ethna Carbery).

Nurturing faith

As soon as the Sisters had settled in Belfast (1854) an evening school had been opened in Callender Street, where mill girls and other young workers were instructed in literacy, religion and other subjects (see Chapter 2). After the community moved to the Crumlin Road, and when the Convent National Schools were in operation, the Sisters continued this work. As well as attending the evening classes, the Sisters encouraged both young and older working women to come to the convent three times a week, at seven in the evening, for general instruction on the sacraments and other religious subjects. The community annals record that Reverend Mother M. Gonzaga Morrin was especially adept at this and held the attention of the young women with her simple talks and instructions in Catholic doctrine. The young girls and women came regularly from every part of the town to attend these classes. Many adults who had missed the sacraments earlier through ignorance were confirmed, sodalities of Our Lady were organised and the Sisters got in touch with many people who had been negligent of their Catholic duties. The instruction of converts was always the duty of at least one member of the community in each house. (Most of those who came took instruction in view of marriage to a Catholic partner.) This work, along with instruction of adults desirous of adopting the Catholic faith, continued until recent times. Retreats for women were also conducted annually at the convent and were open to all who wished to attend, according to a contemporary local newspaper:

CONVENT OF OUR LADY OF MERCY
CRUMLIN ROAD, BELFAST
THE ANNUAL SPIRITUAL RETREAT
for ladies living in the world
will commence on October 6th
and terminate on Saturday the 10th.
Ladies who propose attending will please send in their names to the
Superioress before 1st of October.[11]

The House of Mercy

Meanwhile, the apostolate of the Sisters was ever widening. In the early spring of 1889 a house had been purchased on Royal Terrace, close to the convent, and in April it was opened as a house of mercy,[12] providing temporary accommodation for girls in service and in retail employment who had come up from the country until they were able to find themselves suitable permanent accommodation. Though Royal Terrace was, in November 1898, absorbed into the site for the new Mater Hospital, this work continued, in various forms and at various sites, for the next hundred years.

By the end of the 1880s – just over 30 years after their arrival in Down and Connor – the Sisters of Mercy in Belfast were working to their full capacity, with most of the works of mercy – education, care of orphans and of the homeless, visitation of the poor the sick, the elderly and people in prison, teacher training, instruction in the faith – in hand. The early 1880s saw an exciting new venture into the field of nursing and medicine, when the first Mater Infirmorum Hospital was founded on the Crumlin Road.[13]

This expansion was possible because of the many generous-minded young ladies who had joined the community in the first 30 years, and its inspired leadership. Between 1854 and 1889 70 young women had tried their vocations in the community. Some did not persevere but the majority (42) did. Some went, in the 1850s and 1860s, to fresh fields and pastures new – Downpatrick, Worcester, Ashton-under-Lyne and even Australia. In leadership, after the founding Sisters, were such great women as Mother M. Juliana Delaney, Mother M. Genevieve McQuillan, Mother M. Magdalene Malone and Mother M. Aloysius Phelan. The Downpatrick community was flourishing under the very able leadership of Mother M. Borgia Fortune, and to its story we now turn.

1. *Belfast News Letter*, 27 October 1857.
2. Jordan, *op. cit.*, p. 193.
3. O'Laverty, *op. cit.*, p. 410.
4. *Belfast News Letter*, 10 March 1815.
5. Beckett and Glasscock, *op. cit.*, p. 144.
6. *Belfast News Letter*, 12 and 15 August 1864. For a very full account of the sectarian riots in Belfast see A. Boyd, *Holy war in Belfast* (Belfast: Pretani Press, 1987).
7. Ibid.
8. See Chapter 18.
9. See also M. O'Connell, 'Convents in the north of Ireland from mid-nineteenth century to mid-twentieth century' (MA dissertation, Queen's University Belfast, 1992).
10. *Belfast Morning News*, 20 July 1878.
11. *Ulster Examiner*, 24 September 1874.
12. Sisters of Mercy, *op. cit.* (*Guide*), p. 56.
13. See Chapter 15.

9

DOWNPATRICK FOUNDATION, 1855–70

On the Feast of St Aloysius, June 21, 1855, Saint Patrick's Convent of Mercy, Downpatrick, was founded as a branch house from St Paul's, Belfast, an affiliation from the parent house, 1854. Three Sisters took possession of the neat house which their father and friend, Dr McAuley, had prepared for their reception. By an unforeseen circumstance, it happened that the Very Rev. Dr McAuley was the first priest who ever offered the Holy Sacrifice in the original choir of Baggot Street Convent, Dublin, in 1828 – a circumstance which he often mentioned with considerable gratification.[1]

The arrival of the Sisters in Downpatrick was to be another significant event in the history of the diocese of Down and Connor. Downpatrick is one of the oldest Irish towns, originating from a Bronze-Age fortress on what is now Cathedral Hill (the site of the Church of Ireland cathedral of the diocese of Down), whose noble tower dominates the surrounding countryside of rolling drumlins and fertile fields, a welcome landmark to the visitor approaching along the broad, straight road from the north. The early fortress commanded the marshes of the River Quoile to the west and defended the prosperous lands of Magh Inis or Lecale against invaders from the east. Celtic tradition associates the early settlement on the hill with Celtchar, hero of the Red Branch Knights and contemporary of Conor Mac Nessa, king of Uladh, who reigned at Emain Macha near Armagh. From Celtchar's stronghold on the height above the placid Quoile comes the first half of the name of the present town, *'an dún'* – the fort.

Christian history relates that, in the fifth century, St Patrick landed at Saul and commenced his missionary work in Lecale – the valley of the Quoile. An unshakeable tradition holds that the great patron saint of Ireland was laid to rest on the hill of the fort on which, it has always been assumed, he built one of his first churches. There a monastery and schools flourished until they were plundered by the Vikings. On recovering from the Viking invasion the town continued to prosper and, by the time of the synod of Rathbreasil in the year 1111, when a diocesan episcopate was established for the whole of Ireland, it was considered sufficiently important to be the see of the diocese for the territory of Ulidia. Some years later the second bishop, St Malachy, known as bishop of Down, repaired the church on the hill and introduced a community of Augustinian canons in 1138.

Down continued to be the mensal parish of the bishops of Down and Connor for over 700 years, until Dr William Crolly, in 1825, petitioned the pope to change the episcopal parish from Downpatrick to Belfast. The intervening centuries were rich in history for the territory of Down. John de Courcy, a leader of the Anglo-Norman invasion of Ireland's north-eastern shores in the late twelfth century, settled on the banks of the Quoile and, it is said, in order to ingratiate himself with the native Irish, renamed the ancient fort of Celtchar (Dún Celtchar) and the surrounding town Dún Pádraig. De Courcy also promoted the tradition that not only the bones of St Patrick but also those of St Brigid and St Colmcille had found their last resting place on Cathedral Hill.

Downpatrick grew in importance as a place of Christian pilgrimage and monastic learning as well as economic prosperity, because of its rich agricultural hinterland. With other Irish settlements it suffered from the purges of the Protestant Reformation and the Penal Laws. Catholic emancipation brought relief and the fervent Catholic character of the historic town was gradually restored. Gardiner's Relief Act of 1782 allowed Catholics to acquire leasehold property. Five years late three prominent Downpatrick Catholics – Edward O'Donnell, William Sawby and John Dougherty – approached the Southwell estate for the lease of a hay yard in Stream Street. The first small post-Reformation Catholic church was built on this site late in 1787. Since post-Reformation times the venerable Church of Ireland Cathedral of St Patrick dominates the town from its eminence on the hill, a symbol of the veneration which that church holds for the patron saint of Ireland.[2]

It was to this historic town that the Sisters of Mercy had been originally invited by Reverend Bernard McAuley, parish priest of Down between 1836 and 1863. His dream for the restoration of a community of nuns to Downpatrick was not fulfilled until a year after the founding of the Mercy convent in Belfast.

Despite Downpatrick's glorious history, it was to an impoverished town that the Sisters were called. The area was struggling to survive the ravages of the great famine, which had afflicted the rural areas of Ireland so severely. The Downpatrick workhouse, refuge for the destitute, was home to almost 900 men, women and children during the late 1840s, while the fever hospital desperately strove to cope with the victims of typhus, dysentery and other fatal illnesses that were rapidly spread by hunger, malnutrition and poverty of all descriptions.

White Linen Hall, Donegall Square. Entrance and part of north façade *c.* 1890
(W10/21/58) © National Museums Northern Ireland 2010. Welch Collection, Ulster Museum
Photograph reproduced courtesy the Trustees of National Museums Northern Ireland

Donegall Place and the Royal Hotel, mid-1800s
Lawrence Collection. Courtesy of the National Library of Ireland

St Paul's Convent of Mercy, Belfast

Crumlin Road Mercy Convent Schools

Sussex Place Mercy Convent Schools

Calvary garden, St Paul's Convent

The garden and cemetery, St Paul's Convent

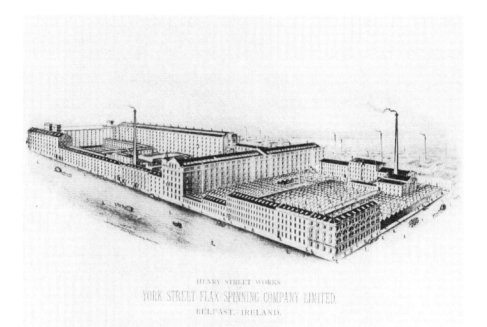

York Street Flax Spinning Mill, *c*. 1905
Reproduced with the permission of the Controller of Her Majesty's Stationery Office
and the Trustees of National Museums Northern Ireland

Mill girls – doffers and half-timers. © Belfast Exposed

Pottinger's Court, off Pottinger's Entry
Reproduced with the permission of the Controller of Her Majesty's
Stationery Office and the Trustees of National Museums Northern Ireland

Dunlop's Place, off Cromac Street, 1968. Courtesy of A.C. Merrick

St Patrick's Convent of Mercy, Downpatrick

Downpatrick Convent chapel

Downpatrick Convent community room

Sectarian strife in Downpatrick added to the sufferings of the poverty-stricken Catholic population. If the Catholic people of the town gave the Sisters a rapturous welcome, however, their reception by the opposite section of the population was compromised even before their arrival. An ardent spokesman declared that 'They are greatly misrepresented if proselytism be not the chief task to be undertaken' and called on the Protestant ladies of the town to ensure that 'if Romanism is to be taught in all its strength … let scriptural religion be enforced more and meet the agents of Rome. Moreover, he went on, the aforesaid ladies should match the 'zeal, vigilance and activity' of the nuns by visiting, comforting and relieving the poor with greater dedication.[3]

Such negative publicity did not quench the Sisters' enthusiasm as they prepared for their new venture into County Down. On Thursday, 21 June they set off by coach from Belfast (the rail connection between Belfast and Downpatrick was not completed until 1859) to take the road south. It was a journey of possibly two hours, but the discomforts of travel may have been tempered by the beauty of the pleasant rolling countryside and an occasional distant view of the majestic mountains of Mourne on the southern horizon. At a certain vantage point the sight of the cathedral on the hill would have signalled their approach to the town and almost simultaneously they would have found themselves passing over the calm and peaceful waters of the Quoile, stretched over flood meadows, home to graceful swans, gliding water hens and the many varieties of estuary wildlife that abounded on the marshes.

When the Sisters arrived in Downpatrick they received a joyous welcome from the people of the parish. Reverend Mother M. Philomene Maguire accompanied the little band of Sisters who had been chosen for the new foundation. These were Sister M. Aloysius Brady, Sister M. Gonzaga Morrin and Sister M. Borgia Fortune. The Sisters' first residence was in Irish Street (a house later numbered 112), on the rise of the hill overlooking the main crossroads of the town. During their first week they settled in and gradually got to know the people of the parish. On Sunday 1 July, Reverend Dr McAuley celebrated Mass in the little oratory of the new 'convent' for the first time.

We could not do better at this point than to insert a first-hand account of the new foundation given by one of the foundresses herself.

Mother M. Aloysius Brady's account[4]

I begin in May 1882 to recall that day ever memorable to me, Thursday, 21 June, 1855, when, about 3 pm, we drove up the hill of Irish Street and caught the first glimpse of the stone-built house set apart for us as 'the convent'. The sun shone brightly, doing its best to make the house look cheerful. This was not an easy matter though the green Venetian blinds gave it a respectable appearance. The same blinds were a very historic article as they had figured in a lawsuit between some occupiers of the house many years previous to our entrance there. And I believe they still do their duty as veterans, notwithstanding the several changes of occupants since we left it for our own convent on Mount St. Patrick.

Here Mother M. Aloysius recalled the inception of the Downpatrick foundation:

We (the Sisters of Mercy) were not a fortnight in Belfast when the Very Rev. Bernard McAuley, P.P., Vicar General of Down, came expressly from Downpatrick to pay us a visit and to renew his application for a foundation in Downpatrick. It is well to note here that Dr. McAuley happened to be in Dublin collecting for a church in his parish at Ballymena at the very time that Mother McAuley had added her Choir to the new convent in Baggot Street.[5]

Dr. McAuley, though no relative, made his acquaintance with her and was the first priest to say Mass in the Choir of our Mother House. From that time he wished to have a convent of our Sisters in Down, and had, from time to time, though unsuccessfully, applied for a foundation from Baggot Street. Belfast held out a wider field for supporting a community, and for these continued reasons it was supplied first with Sisters.

To return to Dr. McAuley's visit, I remember well that I was called to the parlour to see him, and heard him pressing Mother Vincent Whitty to send him Sisters at once. She urged that she could spare no-one at that time from Baggot Street, and that it would be impossible to give them out of our few in Belfast, and I well remember how he said in reply, 'We have not here a lasting city'. However, it ended by arrangements being made that Mother M. Vincent and Mother M. Philomene would go to Downpatrick at once to see the house which he had purchased for the convent, and that a foundation should go to him from Belfast in less than a year and a half. Little did I then imagine that my destiny was as closely woven with that visit. The promised visit was accordingly made to Downpatrick. The house was found satisfactory, and on the following June twelve-months I found myself the Local Superior of the convent in Downpatrick on 21 June, 1855. It was a grand day for Down when, after nearly three hundred years, religious had once more a roof over their heads on the once-favoured spot of St. Patrick.

We did not select 21 June for our journey. We expected that event to take place a week earlier but, owing to delays with painters, the house was not ready for us, and I need scarcely say that I was overjoyed that my dear saint's Feast (Aloysius) should be now made with us one of such importance. Owing to the anticipated break-up of our small community in St. Paul's, Donegall Square, Belfast, Reverend Mother allowed us to anticipate the 21st on the 20th, and gave us a free day which we really did enjoy.

But to return to 21 June. The covered car in which we arrived was occupied by Rev. Mother M. Philomene Maguire, Sr. M. Gonzaga Morrin and myself.[6] When we arrived at the house no greetings awaited us. The door was open as the painters were at work within and we entered as quietly as if we had been only out for a drive. We then sent one of the men to acquaint the priests of our arrival. They came over immediately to welcome us.

Although we seemed to be unnoticed when passing up through the town, the news spread quickly and we were scarcely an hour in the convent when Margaret Keown of Scotch Street sent us up our first present, a goodly parcel of tea and sugar, two bottles of wine and some nice biscuits. There being no obstacle, the servant made her way up through the house and found us all in the room afterwards known as the community room. This servant was, of course, quite proud to be known as the first person who spoke to 'the nuns'.

The painters having still to finish the staircase and choir papering, we located ourselves as best we could upstairs and went over to the church each morning for Mass until Sunday, 1 July, when we had the happiness of having the first Mass in our own little choir celebrated by the Very Rev. Dr. McAuley, P.P., V.G. who, on that occasion, before concluding the Mass, addressed the Sisters and told them that, although in his life he had erected many churches and rebuilt many altars, he never before experienced such happiness as on that morning, nor did any of these altars afford him such consolation in their erection as this present one in the Convent of Mercy in Downpatrick.

From that day we had Mass regularly every morning except on Sundays when we were obliged to attend the parish church, each of the curates having to duplicate his Mass as the P.P. became too infirm to do duty beyond the first Mass in the church. Dr. McAuley arranged, too, that in consideration of our convent not being endowed in any way, we should have the advantage of the services of a chaplain without having to pay a salary for it. Consequently, up to the present, the priests have been most considerate and attentive to these points. Rev. Fr. O'Kane, when appointed parish priest, carried out the same interest and care of the community as his predecessor, only in a more intensified degree.

Now to return to our foundation day. It will be interesting to know how we found the house and its contents:

All clean – walls white, gas arms ready for use, four handsome iron bedsteads with mattresses, no curtains, three presses with a drawer in each. The furnishings:

Community Room: 12 cane-bottomed chairs, 1 small sofa, 1 low table. Parlour: 1 card table, 6 hard-bottomed chairs, 1 easy chair, fender, hearthrug.

Kitchen: 1 chair, 1 frying pan, 1 iron spoon, 1 three-legged pot.
Stairs: an eight-day clock.
Choir: an altar.
First and second storey windows: Venetian blinds.

Such was the interior state of things, and as all our luggage came in the car along with ourselves, the reader may infer we were not overburdened with the things of this world.[7]

Mother M. Aloysius later wryly remarked:

It was all very well, at the beginning of our foundation, to imagine, or see in perspective, what we should require for the house, to select gasaliers and room paper and have them well hung, to order [choir] stalls [and] consider how long it would take to make them, to require a kitchen table and order one. Yes. Draw on the bank. But our banker was Fr. McConvey, C.C., the holder of one cheque left to him by a Margaret McClure, R.I.P., for the nuns, and the amount of that cheque was £50.[8]

After describing the residential accommodation, Mother M. Aloysius continued with an amusing glimpse into some domestic experiences of the first days:

I shall describe something of our first Sunday's dinner, as my duty lay in cooking it. Our good parish priest, having failed in his most pressing invitation that we should dine with him, as next best thing he sent us a fore-quarter of a lamb. On some two previous days your humble servant, the cook, managed some dinner at a small grate upstairs, but today the kitchen grate, for the first time, beheld a nun before it, one who was far from being adept at her work. Well, how to do it, that was the question. She stuck a nail into the wall, suspended the fore-quarter from it by a piece of cord tied to the meat, set the pan on top of the pot and basted with a shallow spoon. This latter operation was a tedious and hot affair for a June day, but 'cook' was drawn now and then from her post by increasing exclamations from rosy faces at the window, for all the children of the town must have arranged to take turns at the small window and so get a peep at the nun. Whenever cook turned her head towards the window or moved near it, the little folk would fly off as if shot, but return to the show in a few minutes. Thus was celebrated Sunday number one in Down, June 1855.
    During the following week dinner had to be cooked, visitors received, cell curtains made, various things, in fact, accomplished, and at the end of the week our numbers were increased by the arrival of Sr.

M. Bernard Geraghty (novice) and Sr. Eliza [Walsh] (postulant). The latter is now Sr. M. de Sales. Sr. M. Bernard died a few years later as Reverend Mother of Ballyjamesduff, R.I.P. They assisted on 2 July at the opening of the schools. Rev. Mother and Sr. M. Bernard then returned on Tuesday, 3rd, to Belfast, leaving the writer as Local Superior, assisted by Sr. M. Gonzaga who had charge of the National School, and Sr. Eliza, the useful one between both.[9]

The schools

On Monday, 2 July the Sisters began teaching in the schoolhouse. This little building, sited in John Street, had been built by Dr McAuley pending the Sisters' arrival. It was structured according to a plan given him by Reverend Mother M. Philomene Maguire, consequently earning the name St Philomene's. Later it was to be known as John Street National School and served for the education of the children of the parish until the new convent schools were opened in 1876. A contemporary record gives us a description of the schoolhouse and the first pupils:

> [It] consisted of two rooms – one 37' by 24' containing ten desks and a blackboard; the other 22' by 20', to be divided into classrooms, hall and cloakroom.[10]

The schoolhouse was not quite completed when the Sisters arrived in Downpatrick, but a week later they determined to begin classes. The main classroom – known as the national-school room – was adequately furnished. The other schoolroom had no door and no desks, only a few borrowed forms. Sister M. Gonzaga, the Sister in charge of the school, was rather small and was obliged to use a candle box as a rostrum in order to have a view of all her pupils, an expedient which caused great amusement to her charges and any visitor who happened to drop by.

During the first week the attendance was 20 boys and 109 girls; during the second week there were 26 boys and 122 girls. Some of the children were barefoot. The pupils paid one penny a week if they could afford it. The sum total of the income from the school for the month of July was £2 13s 10d.

As the accounts show, the children were poor. Though the hinterland of Downpatrick was agriculturally prosperous, little of it was in the hands of the Catholic population until the passing of Gardiner's Relief Act of 1778 permitted Catholics to take leases of land. At the time of the Sisters' arrival Downpatrick was, according to historic accounts, a 'ghost town'. It was essentially a market town but trade, reduced by the local conditions of destitution and disease occasioned by the famine, was slow to revive. Among the poor, unemployment was high:

> [I]f a man lost his job he must stand in Market Street on Fair Day, with a straw or other mark in his hand so that a farmer, or other employer, might hire him for six months … To the Registry Office went the girls who wished to be accepted as maids to the gentry of the district.[11]

This kind of 'hiring fair' was common in all market towns in Ireland at the time. A few years later, in 1859, conditions began to improve commercially for the people of Downpatrick with the completion of the rail link to Belfast. Farm produce could then be transported more quickly and more regularly on the three daily trains to Belfast, where there was a ready market. The parish of Downpatrick became less isolated and, in general, its economic conditions improved.

Attendance at the schools was very encouraging indeed for a beginning. Something that had to be dealt with as soon as possible was correspondence with the Commissioners of National Education so that the schools would be accepted into the system. This presented no difficulty and 'Mrs Louisa Brady' (Mother M. Aloysius) was recognised as the schools' manager. Also, efforts were made to secure exemption from taxes for the convent but these failed. All was to be taxed except the schools.

Religious instruction played an important part in the education programme. The Sisters started giving classes on Sunday evenings in the school and at other times instructed young people and adults in the convent. Mother M. Aloysius recounted:

> On the evening of the first Sunday after the schools were opened a course of Religious Instruction was commenced in the National Schools. The female portion of the congregation almost entirely wended their way from the parish church immediately after the Rosary direct to the schools where an appointed Sister met them. She read and explained a chapter of Butler's Catechism, spoke in detail of the coming Feast or Feast Days, etc. For many years these instructions were so well attended as to have the room filled and it was both consoling and edifying to see assembled there members of all the principal families not only of Downpatrick but also of the neighbouring parishes, the better-off not disdaining to mix with the poorest people. All were eagerly seeking the bread of Religious Instruction at the hands of the Sisters.[12]

At the end of nine or ten years the attendance on Sunday evenings dropped and, as these instructions had attained their end – that of educating adults in the faith – it was considered advisable that they should be discontinued and the labours of the Sisters given to the increasing needs of the schools. However, it is worth noting that during the years 1855, 1856, 1857 and 1858 there was also a course of instruction for men after the last Mass on each Sunday for the purpose of giving practical help to those who had not had the opportunity of receiving instruction in their youth. These classes were always attended by about 60 men, who valued the additional information they received and derived great benefit from it.

The Sisters were soon immersed in their familiar apostolates. Reverend Mother M. Philomene had returned to Belfast on 3 July, assured that the community was well established and that the works of mercy were well under way. Sister M. Aloysius Brady had taken up her charge as local superior and Sister M. Gonzaga Morrin as assistant and Sister in charge of the schools. In the last week of July, Sister Eliza Walsh returned to Belfast and was replaced by Sister M. Bernard Geraghty, then a novice. Besides teaching in school, the Sisters undertook the visitation of the sick and the poor in the town. The patients of the hospital were not neglected, but in a short time it was made clear to the Sisters that they were not welcome in this institution. Within a few months the *Downpatrick Recorder* reported that the governors of Down Infirmary and Fever Hospital explicitly forbade nuns to visit patients under their care and, a year later, by a unanimous verdict, the Board of Governors who had charge of the workhouse extended this prohibition with regard to the residents there.

In time the Sisters started a fee-paying (pension) school for the daughters of the more well-to-do families. For this the stables at the rear of the convent were converted and, as Mother M. Aloysius recounted, 'with good-sized windows and nicely papered walls, it presented a rather cheerful appearance'.[13]

In the course of time it had the addition of a good ceiling and the same room served as a temporary chapel for great occasions owing to the smallness of the convent choir. It was the scene of the Holy Thursday and Good Friday liturgies, the annual retreat was held there and it served for the reception and profession of more than one Sister of Mercy. Here Sister M. Vincent O'Hara professed her vows.

An autonomous community

By 1859 Sister M. Borgia Fortune had returned to St Paul's, Belfast, where she was elected assistant superior. On 14 February, 1860, the Downpatrick community, being now considered well established and self-sufficient, became independent of the motherhouse in Belfast. On 21 February Sister M. Aloysius Brady was appointed superior of the newly autonomous community by Reverend George Conway, C.C., on behalf of Bishop Denvir. The appointment was witnessed by Mother M. Philomene Maguire. On 23 February 1861 Mother M. Aloysius retired from her position as superior, which she had held for almost five years (from the time of her appointment as local superior in 1856) and Sister M. Borgia Fortune was transferred from St Paul's by Bishop Denvir and appointed superior of the Downpatrick community in her stead. Meanwhile, Sister M. Bernard Geraghty rejoined her former community in Belfast where, on 18 August of the same year, she was elected to the office of assistant superior, which had been vacated by Sister M. Borgia. She held that office for the next two years. Sister M. Gonzaga Morrin also returned to Belfast and in June 1862, after Reverend Mother M. Philomene Maguire's resignation, became superior there. She was appointed superior by the bishop – an unusual procedure, but one that was necessary on this occasion. At that time there were only six professed members with the right to vote in the election of a superior remaining in the St Paul's community.

Mary Kathleen O'Hara had entered St Michael's Mercy Convent in Athy, County Kildare, on 8 September 1858. From there she had transferred as a novice to Downpatrick to support the new community. On 24 September 1861, as Sister M. Vincent O'Hara, she made profession of her religious vows and became the first religious to do so in Downpatrick since the Reformation. There she spent 40 very fruitful years until her death in 1899. While teaching, she published *The Catholic child's and youth's Bible history* for use in schools. This was widely used throughout the whole of Ireland, and further afield, until at least the 1950s.

Five other dedicated young women joined the community in the course of the next ten years. These were: Sabina Margaret Kirwan (Sister M. Joseph Aloysius); Catherine Maguire (Sister M. de Sales); Catherine M. O'Kane (Sister M. Alphonsus); Margaret Catherine Mullan (Sister M. Ignatius); and Elizabeth M. Russell (Sister M. Xavier). Two were natives of Downpatrick and the others were from Dublin, Belfast and County Antrim.

The year 1863 brought the first sad loss for the Sisters of Mercy in Downpatrick, with the death of their revered and beloved founder, friend and pastor, Bernard McAuley. The Very Reverend Dr McAuley, a native of the Glens of Antrim, had been parish priest of Downpatrick for 27 years. He had served as curate in Belfast, later becoming parish priest first of Drummaul and then of Ballymena, where he erected the parish church in 1827 and the parochial house the following year. On transferring to Downpatrick he rebuilt the chapel at Ballykilbeg and also built Downpatrick parochial house. Perhaps what he would have considered his greatest claim to fame was establishing the Sisters of Mercy in that parish. He had been their inspiration and their strength over the first eight crucial years and had seen his protégées mature into an autonomous community, firmly rooted in the hallowed soil of County Down. When he died on 11 November, 1863, though he had lived to the venerable age of 92 years, he was sadly mourned. He died on the same date as his namesake, the Mercy foundress, whom he greatly admired.

[1] Sisters of Mercy, *Leaves from the annals of the Sisters of Mercy* (New York: Catholic Publication Society, 1881). It is important to note that, though the annals of 1881 record Downpatrick Convent as a branch house of Belfast, the Downpatrick community traditionally consider themselves as founded from Baggot Street Convent, since the first request for Downpatrick and the foundation there were made by Mother M. Philomene Maguire.

[2] J. Magee, *St Patrick's Church, Downpatrick, 1872–1993: a souvenir of the dedication of the extension and new shrine of St Patrick, 23 May 1993* (Downpatrick: St Patrick's Church, 1993).

[3] *Downpatrick Recorder*, 5 May 1855.

[4] Sisters of Mercy, 'St Patrick's Convent of Mercy, Downpatrick: annals' (MCA) (hereafter Annals, SMD).

[5] The private chapel of a community was often called the 'choir' as the seating was in the form of monastic choir stalls in rows facing each other.

[6] Sister M. Borgia Fortune must also have accompanied them as she is recorded in the Downpatrick annals as one of the foundresses.

[7] Annals, SMD.

[8] Ibid.

[9] Ibid.

[10] Ibid.

[11] *Downpatrick Recorder*, 12 April 1856 and 12 December 1857.

[12] Annals, SMD.

[13] Ibid.

10

DOWNPATRICK, 1870–1911

On 17 March 1872, the feast day of St Patrick, Bishop Dorrian laid the foundation stone of the new St Patrick's Convent of Mercy. Building work began in July. The construction of the convent was made possible by a legacy of £4,000 left by a most generous benefactor, John McIlheron of Downpatrick. McIlheron had died on 9 February 1871. A plaque to his memory was erected in the entrance hall of Downpatrick Convent.

The recently completed parish church, built between 1868 and 1872, shared its site with that of the new convent, a picturesque hill overlooking the town, to be known from that time on as Mount St Patrick. A rather romantic, if somewhat inaccurate description of the new ecclesiastical structures is given in the early annals of the Sisters of Mercy:

> The Downpatrick Convent was erected on holy ground – the site of the old grey cloisters of the past ... A loving Providence watched over the sacred spot, and it was soon once more covered with monastic buildings ... To its sunny cloisters the Sisters migrated from their temporary home on 1 November 1873. The Convent of Our Lady of Mercy and St Patrick's Memorial Church stand on a gentle eminence in the midst of picturesque scenery, bounded by the Mourne range and the lofty summit of Slieve Donard, and opposite the sacred hill on which St Patrick erected his first church. The [Church of Ireland] Cathedral rises on the site of the ancient cathedral, close to the spot which tradition reveres as the triple shrine of Ireland's greatest saints:
>
> > 'In Down three saints one grave do fill,
> > Patrick, Brigid and Columb-kille.'[1]

The convent, designed by Mortimer H. Thompson, is a handsome, three-storey, decorated Gothic structure in red brick with stone facings. (There is an early engraving of the convent building in Downpatrick Convent.) The elegant front entrance is surmounted by a well-proportioned and crenellated bay window on the second storey, which gives a magnificent view of the Mourne Mountains on the southern horizon. To the right of the entrance is an imposing tower tapering to a graceful spire, which tops a belfry, the tower itself rising to one storey above the roof-line of the main building. A large niche at second-storey level houses a statue of the patron, St Patrick.

The building connects at its eastern wing, which mainly comprises the convent chapel, with the apse of the parish church – whose walls, together with those of the south-facing main wing of the convent opposite, surround a delightful enclosed garden (originally monastically named the cloister garth) onto which look the wide, mullioned-windowed cloisters of the ground floor on two sides. The building is spacious, but not so large as to look institutional. The warmth of the red brick creates a homely and welcoming atmosphere, which is not belied by the experience of those who visit. A century later, fine extensions were added to the rear, but these did not detract from the elegant proportions of the original.

The Sisters took occupation of the new convent on the feast of all saints 1873 and the first Mass was celebrated in the main cloister (St Malachy's corridor) by Reverend Patrick O'Kane, who had succeeded Dr Bernard McAuley as parish priest. The dedication of the convent chapel took place on 8 December and at six o'clock on Christmas morning, two years later, the Angelus bell in the handsome bell tower echoed over the sleeping town for the first time. It had been presented as a gift by Bishop Dorrian. (In the 1980s this bell was given to St Colmcille's Church, the Flying Horse estate, Downpatrick.)

The first decade of the life of the Downpatrick community was not without sadness. A short few months after their revered parish priest had passed from their midst they suffered a further great loss on the death of Mother M. Borgia Fortune, a founding member and unfailing source of inspiration and encouragement to her companions. Sister M. Borgia had entered the Mercy community in Baggot Street on 8 May 1848. Margaret Fortune, daughter of John and Margaret, had been born in the parish of Saints Michael and John, Dublin (the date is not recorded). She received the religious habit in Baggot Street Convent on 13 December 1848 and was professed there on 14 January 1851. She had come with the first group of Sisters to Belfast and was given charge of the evening school they had started in Callender Street soon after their arrival in the town. An inspector from the National Education Board, who visited the school in January 1856, was very impressed by this charming and competent woman:

> The Sister who had charge of the school was one of the cleverest and most practical teachers we ever met. Her brow was radiant with intelligence; she was thoughtful, inventive, and eminently perceptive; her features were naturally vivacious, but subdued and softened by discipline and religion. She knew the name, and could tell something interesting, of every pupil in the school; her heart and soul were lost and absorbed in the glorious mission of her life; and her mind was of that delicately cultivated order that she was esthetical [sic] whilst saying or doing the most commonplace things.[2]

Sister M. Borgia gave herself wholeheartedly to the foundation in Downpatrick, being recalled there as superior in 1861 on the resignation of Mother M. Aloysius Brady. Dedicated to the visitation of the poor and the sick, she succumbed to the dreaded typhus fever then prevalent and died after a short illness on 10 May 1864. She was only in her thirteenth year of religious life. She was buried in the grounds of the convent in Irish Street. Later her remains were transferred to the community burial ground on Mount St Patrick after the new convent was built.

On the death of Mother M. Borgia, Bishop Dorrian again appointed Mother M. Aloysius superior, with Sister M. Vincent O'Hara as assistant (14 July 1864). On completion of a three-year term of office Mother M. Aloysius was reappointed with Sister M. de Sales Maguire as assistant. On 29 May 1873 she was elected by the community and continued as superior for a further term of six years. By May 1879 Mother M. Aloysius had completed the full term of her office allowed by canon law. By a special rescript from Rome, requested by Bishop Dorrian and bearing the date 'May 16, 1879', she again became eligible and was duly elected. By renewed rescripts from Rome, and repeated re-elections, she continued in office until May 1891, a total of 25 years.

On the Octave of the Ascension, 14 May 1891, Sister M. de Sales Maguire was elected superior and Mother M. Aloysius Brady became assistant.

The apostolate of education

The 1870s and 1880s were years of growth for the Downpatrick community. On 3 June 1876 the newly built schools adjoining the convent opened. The building of the schools was made possible through the further generosity of John McIlheron and his wife, who had bequeathed £300 for that purpose, and above all to the indefatigable zeal of Reverend P. O'Kane, then parish priest. Father O'Kane collected the additional £2,350 necessary by questing throughout the United Kingdom, by preaching charity sermons and by various other means until the full debt was finally paid off by the proceeds of a grand bazaar in 1877.[3]

The new schools, which were constructed behind the convent with the entrance on Stream Street, were known as the Mount St Patrick Convent Schools. Sister M. Vincent continued as principal. What became the middle portion of the school was built first, but before long much more accommodation was needed and for this two cottages which were beside the school were acquired and demolished to provide the additional buildings. The community annals provide some local colour:

> [One of the cottages] was occupied by the caretaker of the church and
> school and the other by two sisters, the Misses McCormack, known as

Anne and Rose Bud, the latter because she wore a white bonnet with rose buds. From the well in their yard she carried buckets of water to the neighbours by means of a hoop. This water she sold for a penny a bucket.[4]

(The pump was retained when the garden was eventually incorporated into St Michael's Home.)

The extension was added to the school in 1904. These schools were to serve many generations of children for the next hundred years, after which time they were replaced by the present modern premises on Edward Street.

In the 1880s private boarders were accepted in the convent for St Columba's Private School, which young daughters of prosperous parents could attend before going on to convent boarding schools elsewhere. Even though Mercy schools primarily served the poor, and paying (or pension) schools were 'foreign to the spirit of the Mercy Institute', they did come into existence as 'concessions to meet the exigencies of a locality'.[5] Consequently, at the end of the nineteenth century a large proportion of Mercy convents were running parallel schools for non-paying and paying pupils, the income from one helping to finance the needs of the other. However, the double-tiered system was never happily accepted by all the Sisters because of what appeared to be its discriminatory character.

Some former pupils of this school later joined the community: Margaret (Sister Margaret Mary) Nelson (1870–1960) and Anna Maria (Sister M. Brendan) O'Neill (1875–1972). In 1894 an orphanage was opened and more spacious accommodation was acquired for it when, on 26 April 1899, the Sisters of Mercy bought a large house on Irish Street for the sum of £775. The house had been built by Thomas Henry in the early years of the nineteenth century and had gardens stretching down the hill to what is now St Patrick's Avenue. Along with two adjoining houses, it had been constructed on the site of a seventeenth-century castle built by Thomas Cromwell, Viscount Lecale, when he was granted 'the town of Downe, alias Down Patrick' and about 14,000 acres of land in the surrounding area, by a royal patent on 13 July 1638. The castle surmounted rising ground and its orchards and gardens swept downhill to Loch Cuan, which then flooded the flat meadows now occupied by St Patrick's Avenue, Russell Park and the playing fields of the town along Ballydugan Road. Cromwell's castle was burned down at the time of the 1641 rising and lay in ruins for the rest of the seventeenth century. Its remains passed down to a Lady Elizabeth, the last of the Cromwells, who married Edward Southwell, chief secretary for Ireland, in 1703. His agent, living in Downpatrick, built himself a residence there in the early 1700s which became known as the Manor House. As the years went by other houses were built alongside it and passed into the hands of various owners from among the town's most prominent families.

Eventually one of the houses came into the ownership of the Gardner family, from whom the Sisters of Mercy bought it.[6]

This new property was named St Michael's Home and it provided accommodation for paying boarders, 'children of respectable parents'. These were mostly children who came from country areas and for whom regular attendance at school was difficult. Residence near the convent gave them the opportunity to avail of a full-time education at the national school and to continue, if they wished, at the private school, where they received further instruction fitting them for positions suitable to their capacities – as monitresses, etc. The private school taught additional subjects – music, elocution, drawing, painting and languages (French and Irish). It was attended also by many non-Catholics of the town, who took advantage of the refined education it provided.

St Michael's became well known as an important part of the Mercy presence in Downpatrick for the next 80 years. Over the years it served as a boarding school and, for a time in the 1920s, as a home for elderly ladies. In the 1940s a commercial school for girls (opened on 25 September 1939) was conducted there, which provided education in business studies for young ladies who had completed Standard 7 in the national school. This school could be seen, in many ways, as the forerunner of St Mary's High School, which opened in 1957 under the administration of the Sisters of Mercy.

The monitorial system

An important part of the work of the Sisters of Mercy in Downpatrick, as in St Paul's and Sussex Place Schools in Belfast, was the training of monitresses, or pupil-teachers. The monitorial system was very beneficial to teachers of large classes such as were prevalent at that time. This apostolate they inherited from Catherine McAuley, who saw the importance of proper training for those who would undertake the education of the young. As early as 1836, Catherine McAuley was supplying monitresses to schools around Dublin and further afield, on application. In Baggot Street she had introduced courses in training for education in order to qualify promising pupils who wished not only to take up positions as governesses in middle-class homes but also to become teachers in schools. To a certain extent this initiative arose out of necessity in relation to the rapid increase in Mercy foundations in Ireland. The primary undertaking in any new foundation was the setting up of a school, and the number of Sisters available for teaching in any one school was not always adequate to meet the demand. Higher education was not open to women until after the Intermediate Education Act (1879), which allowed girls, for the first time, to sit a public examination and consequently to go on to study for higher qualifications. The young Irish women who did have higher education had received it abroad, particularly in France. These would have included several of Catherine McAuley's first companions, and the National Education Board inspectors' reports bear witness to the erudition and competency of these Sisters in the many convent schools around the country.[7]

In 1825, before embarking upon her own education system, Catherine McAuley and her friend and companion, Fanny Tigue, had gone to France to study education techniques there – for example at St Cyr, where many Irish girls had received their education, and at the schools of the Ursuline Sisters and other teaching orders in Paris. In addition, for the training of pupil-teachers, Catherine had borrowed ideas from the methods of the Kildare Place Society in Dublin. That society used a modified form of the Lancastrian system, which had proved successful with the very large classes of the schools of that time. In the 1830s and 1840s in Ireland there was a great scarcity of teachers, especially with the expansion of schooling under the new Education Acts. The only form of teacher training then available in the country was that given in the model schools, which only opened in 1833. The Central Training School in Marlborough Street, Dublin, did not open until 1838, and even then it catered exclusively for male students. (In 1844 a college for women was added.)

In adopting the pupil-teacher system Catherine McAuley was well ahead of her time. It proved very successful and pupil-teachers formed an essential component of the teaching staffs of convent and other schools. Their competence and skills were also highly commended by visiting schools inspectors.[8] In addition, Catherine stipulated that monitresses' salaries be paid from the grants allocated to the national schools by the National Education Board in the Mercy schools throughout the country, and this was carried out for several years before the board ratified such salaries in 1845.

Catherine McAuley was far sighted in that hers were the first religious schools to join the National Education Board system (they did so in 1839). Her intention was to motivate the children: 'We will place our schools under the Board because our children will improve much more when expecting examination.'[9]

After Catherine's death her school in Baggot Street was officially recognised as a teacher-training centre, the first for Catholic teachers and specifically for females. This expanded over the next 150 years into the famous Mercy Teacher-Training College (Sedes Sapientiae) at Carysfort, Blackrock, County Dublin, which trained many women teachers for schools in Ireland and abroad and which was a model for the other Mercy teacher-training colleges in Ireland and throughout the world.

And so the Sisters of Mercy in Down and Connor carried on the tradition in Belfast and Downpatrick. When St Mary's Teacher-Training College, conducted by the Dominican Sisters, opened in Belfast in 1900, formal teacher training commenced there. One of its first students was Sarah Dumigan, a monitress from Mount St Patrick's Convent School. She was the first student president of the college, something of which her former teachers were justly proud. The training of monitresses continued in the convent schools for several decades, until a formal teacher's certificate was required of every practising teacher within the education system. However, the schools continued to hold in great esteem the wonderful members of staff who had come up under the monitorial system and who had shown such devotion and dedication to the generations of children who had come into their care.

As the century drew to a close, the community in Downpatrick was firmly established and the works of mercy were flourishing. In the last two decades the community increased considerably in number. In that period 22 young women joined. These years also saw the death of eight Sisters, some of these, sadly, at a very early age. In 1882, for example, Sister M. Philomene Grene, older sister of Mother M. Ethna Grene, died at the age of 28; in 1886 Sister M. Teresa Aloysius Russell, the second of the three Russell sisters to join the community, died at the even earlier age of 26; in 1890 Sister M. Patrick Polley died at the age of 35.

The 1890s saw the deaths of two more members of the original founding community – Sister M. Aloysius Brady, who died in 1893 at the age of 64, and Sister M. Vincent O'Hara (who had come to Downpatrick as a novice), who died in 1899 at the age of 66. Mother M. Borgia Fortune had died in 1864. Of the five founding Sisters, Mother M. Philomene Maguire (superior, Belfast) and Sister M. Gonzaga Morrin had returned to Belfast when the new community had got established. In 1897 Sister M. Ignatius Mullan died in her forty-sixth year and Sister M. Joseph Kirwin died in 1899 at the age of 62. These Sisters left behind them a great tradition in Downpatrick of the service of 'the poor, the sick and the ignorant', which was carried on by their youthful followers into the twentieth century. The Sisters became well known, not only in the schools but also on visitation throughout the parish wherever the poor, the sick or the lonely could benefit from their presence. Visitation became a particularly important apostolate for the Downpatrick Sisters of Mercy, who, in visitation cloaks and bonnets, baskets on their arms, became familiar sights on the streets and alleyways of the busy market town.

1   Sisters of Mercy, *op. cit.* (*Leaves from the annals*), p. 494.
2   Keenan, *op. cit.*, p. 178.
3   Memoirs of Mother M. Aloysius (Sisters of Mercy, 'St Patrick's Convent of Mercy, Downpatrick: archives' (MCA) (hereafter Archives, SMD).
4   Annals, SMD.
5   Annals, SMD.
6   I am indebted to the late John Magee's historical research on Downpatrick for much of this information.
7   *Special reports of the Commissioners of National Education in Ireland on the convent schools*, HC 1864 (48) xlvi, p. 67.
8   See registers of convent national schools (Crumlin Road Convent Schools; St Malachy's, Sussex Place; Star of the Sea, Halliday's Road; Downpatrick Convent Schools) (PRONI, Education section, 6/1/3/3, 1,840 *et seq.*). The employment of monitors to supplement the fully trained teaching staff ceased in Northern Ireland in 1929.
9   R. Burke-Savage, *Catherine McAuley: the first Sister of Mercy* (Dublin: Gill and Sons, 1949), p. 270.

11

FURTHER GROWTH

By the 1880s the convent national schools in Belfast and Downpatrick were flourishing and requests were made to the Sisters to undertake the administration of schools in other places. As the Sisters understood that their priority in education was that of the poor and the least privileged, they stretched their personnel resources to meet the demand. Many requests were made to the community around this time to establish convents in other parts of the diocese and even beyond – Ballymena, Kilkeel, Larne, Ballycastle, Ballymacarret, Donaghadee and Magherafelt. These requests were most likely in the hope that the Sisters would set up convent schools within the national education system since, as yet, many towns lacked Catholic parochial schools. Catholic children there largely attended mixed national schools – a situation the bishop, the clergy and those parishioners who wanted a church-sponsored education for their children considered very unsatisfactory. However, the Sisters decided to confine themselves, for the immediate future, to Belfast and Downpatrick so as to give their full commitment to their undertakings there.

The name Sussex Place will not easily be forgotten by any of the Sisters who have lived in the Belfast community. Next to the Crumlin Road Convent Schools, the school in the Markets area (the streets adjacent to St George's Market on May Street: Cromac Street, Cromac Square, Hamilton Street and Sussex Place) was one of the community's most successful educational establishments, and the convent was second only to the motherhouse.

The school the Sisters had started in a house in their first parish, St Malachy's, in the centre of Belfast, was greatly in need of better premises and of the facilities necessary for the proper functioning of a school that was in operation both during the day and in the evening. Matthew Bowen, a prosperous Catholic businessman (owner of the Royal Hotel and several other properties in the city), bequeathed a large sum of money for religious and educational purposes in the parish through his executor, Reverend Geoffrey Brennan, the administrator of St Malachy's Church. His wish was that a new school should be built, which would be put in the charge of the Sisters of Mercy, and that the Sisters should be in residence and have a convent suitable for the accommodation of a community of eight.

Accordingly, a site was purchased in the locality, at Joy Street, not far from May Street, one of the main thoroughfares in the centre of the city. There the Bowen Schools were erected.

It was to this spacious new building that, on 24 September 1878, the Sisters transferred from the old school in Hamilton Street. This school was to cater for the female children of the Markets, where there was a strong and active Catholic population, and many children also came from families in the lower Ormeau Road, another Catholic enclave and part of St Malachy's Parish.

When the new schools in Joy Street were opened the Sisters who went to teach there lived in a rented house in Alfred Street until the new convent was ready. The convent was to be built at Sussex Place, a site conveniently adjoining that of the schools in Joy Street, and in July 1879 Bishop Dorrian laid its foundation stone. The architect was Alexander McAlister (two of whose daughters, Sister M. Austin and Sister M. Baptist, later joined the Mercy community). The convent, dedicated to St Joseph, was opened on the feast of the patronage, 19 March 1880. The bishop performed the dedication, celebrated Mass in the pleasing little chapel and blessed the house. It was a quiet and unpretentious ceremony according to the Sisters present who, besides those engaged in the school, included the superior from Crumlin Road and a novice who had come to accompany her, Sister M. Gertrude McAuley, a future annalist of the community, who left us a first-hand report. Sister M. Teresa Dorrian was appointed the first local superior.

The establishments erected through Matthew Bowen's bequest became known as the Sussex Place Convent Schools. Besides the national schools, a room in the building was set apart as a private school, known as the Young Ladies' School, where parents paid a small fee for their daughters to be tutored in French, music and drawing as well as the basic elementary curriculum. This private school continued until the turn of the century, when it was closed because the rooms were needed for the growing national schools, children then remaining at school until the age of 14. Pupils who wished to stay on to become monitors were welcomed and many took advantage of this offer, laying a foundation for future careers as teachers.

The new schools and community were richly blessed in the many years of their fruitful apostolate in the Markets, as the story of Sussex Place will record. Matthew Bowen's generosity was far reaching. He left two residential houses in Royal Terrace towards the upkeep of Sussex Place Convent. To supplement the income a bazaar was held in Easter Week 1881 at St Mary's Hall, Berry Street, to obtain funds to pay off the debt on the building of the convent. This produced the welcome sum of £1,530.

A further educational undertaking was assumed within the decade. In October 1889 the administrator of St Patrick's Parish, Reverend Robert Crickard, asked the Sisters of Mercy in Crumlin Road to take charge of the Star of the Sea Girls' School. This was part of a new school building in the New Lodge area, on Halliday's Road off the Antrim Road, for which Father Crickard had purchased a site from Andrew McErlean in 1887, for £397. It was named the Star of the Sea Boys' and Girls' Schools and was administered under the National Education Board. Beside the schools he had built a teachers' residence as he had applied to the board for funds for the employment of two lady teachers who, he hoped, would be able to conduct evening classes for the young women of the parish – 'mill workers, factory girls, confectioners, house-keepers and some with no occupation at all'.[1] The evening classes took place and had considerable success, the numbers attending proving very satisfactory. Those who could do so contributed two pence per week. For those who could not, tuition was free. The young women were instructed in reading, writing and spelling, as illiteracy was seen as the greatest drawback to the betterment of the poor in Belfast.

The girls' school was actually the upper floor of the two-storey building, approached by a stairway from a separate entrance on the street, next to that of the boys' school. Separate playgrounds helped to maintain harmony between the two school communities. Sister M. Bernard Connolly was appointed headmistress of the school and Sister M. Gabriel McKenna her assistant. This latter Sister was a granddaughter of a great old lady, Mrs Connor, who had given hospitality to some of the Sisters when they were evicted from St Paul's in 1862. Indeed, the Connors and McKennas, related by marriage, were genuine friends and most generous benefactors to the community from the earliest days.

The Sisters walked to the school each day from the convent in Crumlin Road and became well-known figures in the New Lodge area. Because the girls' school was in the Sisters' charge it was often (though incorrectly) called the convent school.[2] The boys who had been attending the Crumlin Road Convent School were removed to the Star of the Sea Boys' School in the 1890s. The Sisters would continue to teach on Halliday's Road for the next 97 years.

A question of funding

The national schools were poorly paid by small grants according to the number of children attending the school (capitation), and the children who could afford it brought a small fee every Monday, ranging from one to four pence according to the classes they were in. The fee-paying pension school at the convent, for the daughters of more well-to-do families, brought some income, and an annual collection in the churches and all over the city was organised for the same purpose.

In response to the problem of funding, Reverend Tom Quin, while a curate in St Patrick's, Belfast, wrote to the National Education Board in Dublin demanding better payment for all the nuns engaged in the national schools. The Sisters were seriously underpaid in comparison with other teachers who had been trained and were employed within the government system and who did not have to rely on capitation for what they might earn. Because of the dispute over denominational teacher training in Ireland at this time, most of the Sisters in the Crumlin Road Convent Schools would have had no formal training. However, it would appear that owing to their usually quite wealthy backgrounds they would have received a good, even an advanced, education before they entered, and would have been well qualified to teach in the schools. In the 1860s state-school teachers received an average salary of £20 a year. The Sisters in St Paul's, Crumlin Road, received no more then £11 and depended for their funding mainly on voluntary donations.[3]

Father Quin also wrote strongly worded letters to the press, pointing out the handicaps the Sisters had to contend with and stating that, according to inspectors' reports, the schools in which the Sisters of Mercy taught were equal to any of their own 'pet' model schools. This argument was corroborated by the inspectorate of the time. One report stated, in relation to the Crumlin Road Convent Schools, that despite the Sisters' lack of formal qualifications, 'Their appreciation of the Inspector's questions to the advanced classes and monitresses, as well as their aptness in detecting any error in the answer, fully testifies to their literary competence'. It went on, 'for an unembarrassed and composed method of communication instruction, and a methodical organising power, I have always thought them rather remarkable'. In the same report the pupils were described as 'docile', 'orderly' and 'perfectly happy', and the school, in fact, was said to be superior to any lay Roman Catholic school in the district.[4]

The case put by Father Quin did not fall entirely on deaf ears and he finally succeeded in getting the capitation raised for all convent schools in Ireland. Some years later the same case was given consideration in the Powis Commission, set up in 1868 to look into education in Ireland and obliged to give attention to the strongly expressed dissatisfaction of the Catholic bishops. One of commission's recommendations, made in 1870, was that the distinction between convent schools and the other national schools should be ended and that the teachers in convent schools and in Christian

Brothers schools should be classified in the same way as any other teachers and enjoy equal benefits under the national system.[5]

Another bone of contention between the Catholic authorities and the National Education Board was the failure to grant aid towards the payment of assistant teachers in the convent evening schools. Bishop Dorrian put this to the Powis Commission, stating that the evening classes afforded opportunities for girls who were forced by necessity to earn their living in factories and mills to acquire some education after finishing their daily work. He spoke feelingly of the grim working conditions and appallingly long hours to which the 500 girls who attended the evening schools at the Convent of Mercy were subject. On leaving the factories and mills, those workers, aged between 11 and 20, went to class for two hours each evening during the winter and were taught reading, writing, religion and deportment. Were it not for the beneficial influence of the nuns, he said, the girls would have been exposed to the gravest dangers, yet the board refused to pay salaries to assistant teachers or monitresses for them.[6]

Leaving aside the financial problems, the Sisters' concern for their pupils, and also for their pupils' families, was obvious to all who passed through their hands. An inspectorate report stated of the Crumlin Road schools that 'The attention of the nuns in visiting the Roman Catholic families has greatly increased their attendance at this school.'[7] An account given by an inspector who had visited the Mercy school in Enniskillen could well have been applied to any other:

> The nuns belong to the order of the Sisters of Mercy in which capacity they frequently visit the sick and dying belonging to the most destitute classes. During these visits they turn to good advantage the opportunities which occur for inducing parents, hitherto careless about the education of their children, to send the latter to school. But these poor children must generally be supplied with some articles of clothing before they can attend school. This the nuns accomplish by means of their Industrial School.[8]

Time and experience had shown that education and visitation went hand in hand for the Mercy apostolate, especially to the poor. Not only were the Sisters to be found in the classrooms, they were also involved in much wider pastoral care of the poor and the needy in the parish.

Community life as a century closes
In 1880 St Paul's Mercy community experienced their first sad bereavement. Sister M. Bernard O'Hanlon, who had joined the community in 1878, died

of consumption (tuberculosis). As she had not yet been admitted to religious profession, she had the privilege of pronouncing her vows on her deathbed. After an extended illness Sister M. Bernard died on 16 February 1880. No record has been left of the young woman's last days, nor of the moving event for her community and family that her deathbed profession must have been, but we have a record of the funeral obsequies as they were reported in the local newspaper:

Death of a Sister of Mercy
16th February, 1880

On yesterday morning, in the chapel of the convent of the Sisters of Mercy, Belfast, a Solemn Requiem Mass was celebrated for the repose of the soul of Sister M. Bernard O'Hanlon. His Lordship the Most Rev. Dr Dorrian presided at the Office which was chanted by the Rev. Fr Cahill and Rev. Fr McArdle.[9]

The account named 34 priests from St Malachy's College and many of the surrounding parishes who had come to attend the requiem Mass, as was the custom. The report continued:

At the Mass the Very Rev. Canon Keogh was celebrant, the Very Rev. Fathers Henry and McGreevy deacon and sub-deacon, and the Rev. George Conway Master of Ceremonies. His Lordship the Bishop pronounced the absolution, and the remains of the good Sister were borne to the grave, where the last rites of the Church were performed. Thus at the early age of twenty-three years, with her hands full of works of Mercy, Sister Mary Bernard Josephine passed from a world she had early learned to look upon as a place of banishment, and not her true home. No more will her gentle voice be heard in the schools in which she laboured so long as health permitted, teaching the little children both by example and by word how sweet it is to walk in the way of virtue from earliest childhood. R.I.P.[10]

Sister M. Bernard was interred in the new little cemetery that had been carefully laid out in the centre of the garden at the back of the convent and recently consecrated by Bishop Dorrian, assisted by eight priests. This little graveyard was to be the last resting place for many of the community in the years following, until it had reached its full capacity and a new burial site was purchased in Our Lady's Acre at Greencastle.

By 1880 the community in St Paul's, Crumlin Road had increased to 22 Sisters. Between 1854 and 1855 three young women had joined the original four of the founding community and been professed, bringing their number up to seven. In June 1855, when four Sisters had left Belfast to make the foundation in Downpatrick, the numbers were again reduced. However, between 1855 and 1862 ten other young women had made their novitiate and been admitted to profession, increasing the numbers in the new St Paul's to 13. No further members joined between 1862 and 1864 but in the course of those years seven Sisters left for the English mission (see Chapter 5). The number of professed Sisters in the Belfast community was again reduced to six, although there were several novices and also some postulants who had come to test their vocations, all of whom would have been involved in the works of the community according to their capacities. Thus the early 1860s were years of struggle for the young communities, yet they attended energetically and zealously to their undertakings in schools, penitentiary and orphanage, to the visitation of the sick and those in prison. Between the mid-1860s and the end of the century the Belfast community grew steadily. In all, 48 new members had joined and made profession, but the vicissitudes of sickness and age took their course and so by the turn of the century 16 Sisters had died. Some of these had died young. Besides Sister M. Bernard, Sister M. Regis O'Rorke died at 30 years of age and Sister M. Cecilia Murray at 32. But most of those who died did so in the fullness of their years, a rather unusual achievement in the later nineteenth century.

It was not the luxury or ease of life which made survival possible. The Sisters followed a strict and demanding daily horarium considered to be the foundation of a well-regulated religious life, assuring time for prayer, work, meals, rest and recreation in such a way as to be best conducive to the 'Common Life' and apostolate. Prescription for this was laid down in the rule and constitutions:

> In every house there shall be a fixed horarium, suited to the circumstances of the place and the duties of the Congregation, and approved by the Ordinary.[11]
>
> The hours to be marked on the horarium are those for the spiritual exercises to be daily performed in community ... those for breakfast, dinner and supper, for recreation, for rising and for returning to rest. The ordinary time allowed for sleep is seven hours and a half.[12]

Normally arising with the 'call' bell at 5.30 a.m., the Sisters' day started with about one hour's community and private prayer in the chapel, followed by community Mass and a frugal breakfast. This was followed by lecture – a spiritual treatise read aloud to the assembled community (from the French *lecture*, meaning reading) – which lasted about 15 minutes. This exercise concluded, the Sisters dispersed for their various duties – in the house, the schools and the orphanage, in the hospital and with the sick of the local area – until midday. After lunch and a short period of prayer, duties were resumed as in the morning until the community met again for dinner at 4 p.m. Dinner was followed by about 45 minutes of recreation in common. At 5.15 p.m. all gathered in the chapel for the recitation of vespers, matins and compline – the Little Office of the Blessed Virgin Mary – in Latin. This was adopted in the Crumlin Road community on 8 September 1864. Originally, in Baggot Street Convent, the office was recited in English. However, in order to conform with the church at the time, the Latin form was adopted.[13] Next came a period of spiritual reading. Supper at 7.30 p.m. was followed by another period of recreation, again in common. This concluded with the bell for night prayers and, at last, bed at 9.30 p.m., with lights out at 10 p.m. The 'great silence' was observed from the night prayer bell at 9 p.m. until after breakfast the following morning. The atmosphere of quiet was supported by a general rule of silence in the convent throughout the day except for times of recreation and occasionally, on feast days, at meals. This horarium was, generally speaking, observed in the convent until the 1970s.[14]

The Sisters were not lacking in directives for their daily living. Besides the rule and constitutions and the *Guide* there were 'customs'. These regarded the details of community life and the apostolates and were usually particular to each community, while at the same time giving, through close similarities in content and style, a recognisable identity and spirit to the congregation as a whole. This is something the Sisters, though later spread worldwide, have always valued highly. The ideal was to capture and appropriate the charism and spirituality of the foundress in such a way that these would give inspiration to, and create a bonding among, her followers. Much has been written on the spirituality of Catherine McAuley (who was declared venerable, the first step towards canonisation, on 9 April 1990 and whose cause continues to be promoted) but it might be circumscribed in the concept of 'contemplation in action'.

Although at that time each Mercy community was autonomous and all followed a common lifestyle, there was regular communication between the communities which served to maintain the ethos and spirit of the congregation. Each community was open to learn from what had been found beneficial to another. An example of this occurred in 1884 when, during the annual retreat, Reverend Mother M. Magdalene Malone proposed to the Belfast community the adoption of customs either from the Baggot Street or the Kinsale community. The issue was not adequately clear to the Sisters and an agreement was not reached, so Bishop Dorrian was consulted. He rejected the introduction of either and declared that 'the Sisters should go according to the novitiate *Directory* as they were trained, and a horarium approved by the Ordinary'. He requested this directive to be recorded in the acts of chapter 'for the edification of future generations'.[15]

The quiet routine of community life was, from time to time, varied by special occasions. One of these was a visit on Sunday, 18 August 1887 from the papal envoy to Ireland, Monsignor Persico, when he came to visit Belfast. He arrived at the convent at 11 a.m., accompanied by his secretary, Father Gualdi, and Bishop McAlister. He was welcomed by the community and then brought to visit the national schools, where the children were assembled. The building had been appropriately prepared for the reception of the auspicious visitor:

> The several rooms were handsomely decorated with illuminated scrolls and evergreens, but the sweetest and gayest objects there were the hundreds of charmingly dressed children who, according to their classes, assembled in their classrooms to accord a welcome to the Papal Envoy.[16]

In the senior school the visitors were conducted to seats provided for them and a pretty little girl, Maggie Dillon, dressed in white and wearing a green sash, read a welcoming address on behalf of all the pupils, professing their loyalty to the holy father and their appreciation of his envoy's visit. When the script of the address was presented to his excellency he thanked the pupils appropriately for their kind reception, congratulated the Sisters on their fine schools and their work among the people and promised to convey their greetings and tokens of fidelity to the holy father. He concluded by bestowing on them the papal benediction. Needless to say, the Sisters and the children were delighted with the visit and treasured the memory of it for years.[17]

The close of the nineteenth century brought occasions for sadness as well as for celebration and joy. The year 1894 saw the death of the last surviving member of the founding community who had remained in Belfast. Sister M. Gonzaga Morrin had come to Belfast from Dublin for the occasion of the installation of Sister M. Philomene Maguire as superior of the new community. After an interlude of seven years in Downpatrick, she had resided in St Paul's for the remaining 32 years of her life. In fact, perhaps as a symbol of her new mission, she seems to have changed her name. Having been known in Dublin as Sister M. Aloysius (Gonzaga), in Belfast she was always called Sister M. Gonzaga.

She had been born Annie Morrin in the parish of Rathangan, County Kildare, on 3 December 1820. On 3 August 1849 she had entered the Convent of Mercy in Baggot Street. There she had received the religious

Golden Jubilee of the Mercy Order ~ December, 1881

Verses adapted from "Marie" by W.H.F.   Music by W.H.Flood.
Composed expressly for Mercy Convent, Belfast.

V. 1.   O   Mo-ther of   Mer-cy, blessed Mo-ther of   love, we   ask you be-seech thy Son, Mon-arch a-

V. 2.   If,   un-der thy   wing, in the fields of the   Lord,   those chap-lets shall bloss-om a   fade-less re-

-bove, and   deign our be-hest   to be min-gled with   thine,   as   chap-lets of   love   in the   king-dom di-

V. 2.

-ward, which the sis-ters of   Mer-cy the Spouses of   love   shall wear at the   Feet   of the Bride-groom a-

CHORUS

V. 1.   vine.   Mo-ther of Mercy, trans-cen-   den-tal,   Ma-ry sweet Mother of our   Lord.

V. 2.   bove

Altos:

Mo-ther of Mercy trans-cen-   den-tal,   Ma-ry sweet Mother of our

Mo-ther of Mercy, trans-cen-   den-tal,   Ma-ry sweet Mother of our   Lord.

Altos: Lord.   Mother of Mercy trans-cen-   den-tal sweet Mo-ther of our   Lord.

H. Freeman & Co.

Feast Day Hymn to Our Lady of Mercy

111

habit on 11 February 1850 and made her profession on 20 July 1852. She had joined the Belfast foundation on 17 March 1854 and six years later had become a founder member of the Downpatrick community, where she had been given charge of the schools. In 1862 she had been recalled to Belfast, where she had been appointed superior on the resignation of Mother M. Philomene Maguire. There she had remained, holding various offices in the community, until her death on 9 February 1894.

The requiem Mass and funeral service for Sister M. Gonzaga were held in the convent chapel two days later. The *Irish News*, reporting on the large assembly of mourners who participated in the obsequies, 'all eager, by their presence, to testify to the love and respect in which the deceased was held', paid her a moving tribute:

> Yesterday morning a very large number of priests and laity assembled in the neat little chapel attached to the Convent of Our Lady of Mercy, Crumlin Road, Belfast, to assist at the obsequies of Mother Mary Gonzaga Morrin. Mother Gonzaga was one of the oldest members of any of the religious sisterhoods in Belfast, and during the forty years she spent in the Crumlin Road establishment she was remarkable for the possession of all those qualities which contribute to the formation of the character of the true servant of God. Her charity and intense love for the poor and the suffering amounted almost to a passion with her, and she never lost an opportunity, either through the agency of her devoted and zealous Sisters in religion, or by herself, in seeking out and relieving those whom the hand of Providence had been heavy on. Only those who were most intimately associated with her, more especially the members of the community with whom she had been so long identified, can realise the loss that has been sustained by her demise. In losing her they have been deprived of the best of friends, the wisest and most judicious of counsellors. She had, at different times, held nearly every office in the community, and at the time of her death was Superioress of the House of Mercy.[18]

Bishop McAlister presided, assisted by a very large number of clergy, and accompanied the coffin to 'the picturesque and well-kept cemetery adjoining the convent'[19] where Mother M. Gonzaga was laid to rest.

Mother M. Gonzaga was outlived by only one member of the original group of Sisters who had brought the Mercy charism to Belfast more than 60 years before. This was Sister M. Ignatius Crolly. Lucy Crolly had been born in the parish of Loughfaughan, County Down, to John and Rosanna Crolly. She had entered Baggot Street Convent on 26 May 1850 and had made her religious profession there on 31 January 1853. One year later she had gone on the Belfast foundation. There she had served as the first mistress of novices, to which office she had been appointed in August 1858, and she had concurrently served as assistant superior to Mother M. Philomene Maguire. In June 1862 she had gone with Mother M. Philomene to make the foundation in Worcester and had returned to Ireland with her eight years later to take over the Ballyjamesduff foundation. In 1870 she had moved to Ballinasloe, County Galway, and her final years were lived out in Loughrea Convent, where she died on 10 March 1918 at the very advanced age of 88. She was buried in Loughrea. And so was laid to rest the last of the Sisters who had founded the Belfast community.

The 19 March 1894 witnessed the golden jubilee of the religious profession of Mother M. Juliana Delaney. At the time of her golden jubilee, Mother M. Juliana held the office of assistant superior, having previously served as superior for three terms (1868–71, 1871–4 and 1877–83) and as assistant superior and mistress of novices in the intervening years (1874–77). In her 12 years as superior and mistress of novices in St Paul's she had a great formative influence on the community during the important years of its growth and expansion. She was, as Sister M. Ligouri, the superior of the Dublin community, wrote in a letter to her shortly after her jubilee, 'the one who formed and spiritualised your community and made it what it is now'.[20] It would be interesting to have a record of the event of which the same writer said in her letter, 'The Account of your Golden Jubilee was balm to my heart,'[21] but unfortunately the preservation of correspondence was not a priority in the Crumlin Road community – except for the rare times when a point of order was made, to be noted and handed down to posterity.

The jubilee must have been an occasion for many congratulatory tributes from community, friends and ecclesiastics, but at the same time it must have been an unostentatious affair. Sister M. Ligouri implied that it was 'modest, not worldly, and in keeping with the spirit of simplicity of the Foundress'.[22]

Mother M. Juliana died not long afterwards, on 27 April 1900, having continued in office either as assistant or mistress of novices almost right up until the end of her life. She must have been in the eighth decade of her life. Unfortunately her obituary has not been preserved, but she remained in the living memory of many generations to follow. The precious treasure of the profession ring she had inherited from Catherine McAuley was a tangible link with the past and a token for the present of Catherine's dedication and charism.

Thus the first 50 years of the Sisters of Mercy's presence in Down and Connor drew to a close. There was a half century to look back upon with gratitude for what had been achieved and a new century pointing forward to challenges still to be met. The versatility of the first generation of Catherine's followers cannot but fill us with admiration as we see how they undertook, undaunted, missions and apostolates in conditions which appear heroic to their successors in a modern world. However, we cannot leave the first part of our story without introducing the last great project undertaken by these courageous Sisters before the end of the nineteenth century – the founding of the Mater Infirmorum Hospital, accompanied by an expansion of care for the sick and the dying, in particular those who most needed it, 'without distinction of class or creed'.

[1] Quoted in F. Heatley, *The story of St Patrick's, Belfast, 1815–1977* (Belfast: Diocese of Down and Connor, 1977), p. 57.

[2] A convent school, properly speaking, was attached to a convent, but often a parish school was so called if the nuns taught there.

[3] *Special reports of the Commissioners of National Education in Ireland on the convent schools*, HC 1864 (48) xlvi, p. 67.

[4] Ibid., p. 66 *et seq*.

[5] Royal Commission of Inquiry, Primary Education, Ireland, *Report of the commissioners* (Dublin: HMSO, 1870–71), vol. iii, Part 3, pp. 341–70.

[6] Ibid.

[7] *Special reports of the Commissioners of National Education in Ireland on the convent schools*, HC 1864 (48) xlvi, p. 66.

[8] Inglis, T., *Moral monopoly: the Catholic Church in modern Irish society* (Dublin: Gill and Macmillan, 1987), pp. 124–5.

[9] *Irish News*, 17 February 1880.

[10] Ibid.

[11] Sisters of Mercy, *op. cit.* (*Rule*), Chapter 15. The ordinary was the local bishop under whose jurisdiction the community lived.

[12] Sisters of Mercy, *op. cit.* (*Guide*), p. 213.

[13] Ibid, pp. 152–3; Acts of chapter, SPCMB.

[14] See Appendix to Chapter 11.

[15] Bolster, *op. cit.* (*Positio*), Chapter 23. See also McAuley, *op. cit.* and many modern works on the subject.

[16] *Belfast Morning News*, August 1887.

[17] Annals, SPCMB.

[18] *Irish News*, 10 February 1894.

[19] Ibid.

[20] Sister M. Ligouri, Convent of Mercy, Carysfort Park, to Mother M. Juliana (Archives, SPCMB, 1 November 1894).

[21] Ibid.

[22] Ibid.

12

THE MATER INFIRMORUM HOSPITAL

In the early 1870s a poor patient in Frederick Street Hospital asked to have a visit from Sister M. Magdalene Malone and Sister M. Vincent Byrne. They went and had a quiet talk with the girl (a factory worker and former pupil). Another patient in the ward called for the nuns, and while they were speaking to her the matron came along and was rather truculent in speech and manner to them. They left, feeling rather wounded at this uncivil treatment. The cause of this unpleasant incident was very likely the mistrust with which the nuns were still viewed by members of the Protestant population. For many of them, the very appearance of the nuns in their habits in the street seemed to pose the threat of proselytism. There were even stories that the nuns took advantage of the weakened state of the dying workhouse inmates to convert them to Rome. The *Belfast News Letter* suggested that this practice should be stopped by excluding the nuns from visiting the infirmary.[1] However, the outcome of Sister M. Magdalene's disconcerting experience that day was that she vowed that she would 'move heaven and earth' to get a hospital for Belfast that would be under Catholic management and in which all persons would be welcome.

Up until the beginning of the nineteenth century there was still little interest in or enthusiasm for providing hospitals or infirmaries. The care of the sick and infirm was seen as the concern of the family or local community. In the early 1800s there were regular fever epidemics, mainly due to very poor sanitation and overcrowding (the worse of these were in 1832 and 1837) and the mortality rate was high.[2] Among the most needy were the destitute, whose families and neighbours could not provide for them.

In many towns in Ireland the workhouse (or poorhouse) was the only and last resort of the abandoned, the elderly and the dying. In Belfast the workhouse and infirmary (Clifton House), opened on 24 December 1774, marked the beginnings of a medical service for the poor of that town. It had been set up by the Belfast Charitable Society, a voluntary organisation founded in 1752 which, until the opening of the infirmary, had made provision for visiting the sick poor in their homes and supplying them with medicines. When the infirmary was opened the sick patients were attended to for free by the physicians and surgeons for as long as this service could be maintained. But even these provisions were not adequate for the people of the growing town. In 1807 an act of parliament allocated public funds for hospital services and encouraged the building of fever hospitals in many parts of the country. One of the first of these was built in Belfast, on a site in Frederick Street, whose construction was funded entirely by voluntary subscriptions amounting to almost £5,000. It was Belfast's first purpose-built general hospital, with accommodation for one hundred patients.[3]

> In the year 1807 the representatives of the medical profession in Belfast – The Belfast Medical Society (19 persons) – gained a grant of a sum of £200 for the erection of a hospital. On 5 June 1815 the Marquis of Donegall laid the first stone of the General Hospital, Frederick Street.[4]

But this accommodation became totally inadequate at the time of the great outbreaks of cholera in the 1830s and had to overflow into property of the Royal Belfast Academical Institution in Barrack Street. The outcome of this situation was the setting up of a teaching hospital, in 1836, fulfilling the dream of Dr James McDonnell, a physician from the Glens of Antrim, who had co-founded and served in the Belfast Dispensary and Fever Hospital at the end of the 1790s and was founder of the Belfast Medical School, later to become the Royal Victoria Hospital (opened in 1903). In 1841 the Belfast Fever Hospital and Workhouse was opened on the Lisburn Road (later to become the Belfast City Hospital), not too soon for the many new outbreaks of fever consequent upon the famine in 1845–7.

It can be seen that provision for the care of the sick and dying poor was an urgent necessity in the growing industrial town of Belfast in the mid-nineteenth century. This did not escape the attention of the Sisters of Mercy, who, from their daily visitation in the mean streets that housed the factory and mill workers, the labourers and the destitute poor and abandoned, were only too aware of where the need lay. Because of the Sisters' experiences on their hospital and workhouse visitations they felt called to rise to the challenge and, trusting in divine providence, set about responding to it.

Fulfilling the vision

By the later 1800s the worst of the fever epidemics had passed. It was in the early 1870s that Sister M. Magdalene Malone paid her visit to Frederick Street General Hospital, an occasion that sparked off her determination to do all in her power to provide hospital care for the sick poor in Belfast. Sister M. Magdalene was, no doubt, inspired by the great work being done by the Sisters of Mercy in Dublin, who had undertaken the building of the Mater Misericordiae Hospital, which opened in 1861 to serve the needs of the poor and sick on the northside of that city. In doing this they were following the vision of their revered foundress, Catherine McAuley, whose great wish was that the sick, especially those in reduced circumstances, should have access to hospital and medical treatment and be cared for in their sickness with dignity and respect for the sacredness of human life. She herself, along with her first companions, had been called upon to nurse hundreds of cholera victims in a makeshift hospital in Townsend Street during the serious outbreak of Asiatic cholera in 1832. It is said that it was from this experience that Catherine conceived the idea of opening a voluntary hospital administered by the Sisters of Mercy.[5] The Sisters' care for the sick was carried to even more heroic heights when a little band of Sisters travelled to the Crimea to care for the sick, wounded and dying in the war of 1854. Soon afterwards, in 1857, Ireland's first Mercy hospital was opened in Cork.[6]

Dr Dorrian, bishop of Down and Connor, fully supported Sister M. Magdalene's plans and gave her every encouragement. On 25 March 1876, with the sanction of the bishop, a grotto in honour of the recent apparitions of Mary Immaculate at Lourdes (in 1858) was erected at the convent to implore Our Lady's help for the provision of a hospital for the sick poor in Belfast and in the province of Ulster. A donation box placed close by was generously contributed to. Sister M. Magdalene had also written a small booklet relating the story of Lourdes; this was published and sold by many booksellers over the country, the proceeds of the sales to be given to the hospital building fund.

Eventually a suitable place became available. In 1883 Bishop Dorrian purchased Bedeque House on the Crumlin Road. This was a property built in the early 1850s in the colonial style, on what was at the time the outskirts of the town, by Gordon A. 'Galloper' Thompson, a prosperous businessman whose son, a spendthrift, had put it on the market after his father's death. It was situated right next door to the new jail. In 1878 Frederick Kinehan, of Lyle and Kinehan, was in residence, and two years later it became the officers' mess for the Sixty-Third Regiment. The bishop acquired it for £2,300 and handed it over to the Sisters of Mercy, whose convent gardens adjoined those of the newly purchased house, so that they could begin a Catholic hospital.

The project entailed much expense but, as the community annals record:

> the Catholics, though poor in means were lavish in heart, and set to with a good will to begin a weekly penny collection and got, by dint of energetic labour, sufficient to cover the cost.[7]

So, with a further outlay of £1,000, Bedeque House was equipped and opened by Bishop Dorrian as the Mater Infirmorum Hospital on

Bedeque House, Crumlin Road, Belfast (1920) by Frank McKelvey (1895–1974) © Estate of Frank McKelvey RHA 2010
Photograph reproduced courtesy the Trustees of National Museums Northern Ireland

1 November 1883. The Sisters made the best use of the space available. The rooms upstairs were converted into small wards. The attics were occupied by the Sisters who were attending the sick. As well as the usual medical and surgical treatment for in-patients, a dispensary and external facilities had been fitted up in a cottage beside the main house. The hospital, despite its small beginnings, was to flourish for the next hundred years and more.

As has been mentioned, the prime mover of this project was Mother M. Magdalene Malone. She was born as Marianne Malone on 24 July 1840, the daughter of John and Mary Malone of Hayenstown, Dundalk, County Louth. She entered the Convent of Mercy, Belfast, on 27 May 1859 and received the religious habit on 8 December of that year. She made her profession on 23 December 1861. She was elected superior of St Paul's community, Crumlin Road, on 9 May 1883, which office she held for the next three years. It was during her first year of office that the Mater Infirmorum Hospital was opened. She placed Sister M. Aloysius Phelan and Sister M. Xavier Keegan in charge. Dr Magennis was the first house doctor. Mother M. Magdalene seems to have been quite a character. The story has passed down that once she was heard to say that she had two large pockets: into one of them went the pennies for the building fund and into the other went the insults she received.

Mother M. Magdalene's greatest collaborator in this venture was Dr Alexander Dempsey who, as the only medical professional, served the hospital alone as surgeon and medical officer for some years. He had been awarded an MD at the Royal University and the Diploma of the Royal College of Surgeons in 1874. Soon afterwards he set up a practice at 36 Clifton Street and quickly established himself as one of the leading medical men in Belfast. He was founder and president of the Ulster branch of the British Medical Association. He was also president of the Ulster Medical Association between 1880 and 1891 and contributed many important papers to the publications of both these prestigious societies. He was appointed a city magistrate in 1880, but his chief public service was founding and developing of the Mater Infirmorum Hospital. In 1911 the honour of knighthood was conferred on him in recognition of his work in the medical field.

Dr Dempsey took it upon himself to build up the staff of the hospital. He told the Sisters that he had brought a trained nurse from Dublin (a Derry girl, Nurse McCloskey) who, he claimed, was a great worker. Then he appointed Agnes, his own nurse assistant, trained by himself for his gynaecological cases in Clifton Street Infirmary,[8] to act as night nurse in Bedeque House as he did not always require her. Sister M. Rose Burke, from the Mater Hospital, Dublin, came to set the work afoot and train the Sisters into hospital routine. She stayed for over two years, giving every possible help, and then returned to her own work and community in Dublin.

A new hospital

No sooner was the small hospital in Bedeque House in operation than Mother M. Magdalene began planning for a larger and more permanent building. In June 1883 she consulted the community about the feasibility of purchasing Mountainview Terrace, a row of houses adjacent to Bedeque House, for the site of a new Mater Infirmorum Hospital. At this period the Sisters had cleared all their debts and held community funds, which came mostly from the dowers each young woman brought when she joined the community. Since there was no other source of income, the dowers normally provided both for the day-to-day upkeep of the community and also for their apostolic works. Other funds came from benefactors and bequests. Strict accounts were kept and the finances very well managed, as can be seen from the account books of the time. The funds were invested safely in case a fate similar to that of the early 1860s should befall the community.

A large majority of the community agreed to the proposal to buy Mountainview Terrace, as it was considered very suitable. It was purchased for the sum of £2,600. The Sisters raised the money, which Bishop McAlister later refunded from diocesan funds.

An amusing anecdote accompanies the chronicle of this period. It seems that there was a fine detached house called Mount View House, standing in its own grounds and adjoining Mountainview Terrace, which was occupied and owned by an old Protestant lady, Miss Officer, a descendant of Henry Joy McCracken.[9] She was favourably inclined towards Catholics. Her housekeeper, a Catholic, one of the first orphans to have been brought up in the convent orphanage, who had been a small child when Mother M. Magdalene had care of them, was a good and trusted friend – more than a servant – to Miss Officer. She told her employer that the nuns were buying the terrace to build a hospital. Why didn't Miss Officer sell her house to them and have a good work before her? 'They will not evict you,' she said, 'but, as you know, your days are numbered. Eventually they will get it but they might be charged exorbitantly, so do the best work quietly and God will reward it.'[10] Thus the house came into the hands of the Sisters, who used it for some time as a house of Mercy for the accommodation of young women until it was required for the building of the new hospital.

Immediately Mother M. Magdalene set about organising fund-raising schemes. The first benefactress of the proposed hospital was a Catherine

McMullan, who died in Bangor in 1882 and bequeathed the sum of £350 to the institution in accordance with a promise made six years earlier. Mother M. Magdalene had other contacts and friends, not only among the Catholic gentry of means, but also among businessmen, professionals and even politicians – and their wives, who played a very active part in fund-raising – right across the board of Belfast society. These were such people as Arthur Hamill, Bernard Hughes, J.F. McKenna, Henry Toner and many others.[11] Mother M. Magdalene had gained their respect and admiration through her courageous efforts to help the sick poor, irrespective of creed. Her policy in this regard is clearly spelt out in the prospectus of the hospital:

- This hospital is established for the relief of the sick WITHOUT DISTINCTION OF CREED.
- Clergymen of all denominations have free access to their co-religionists.
- Aid is denied to no one as far as the funds and accommodation permit.
- This Hospital receives no Government or Corporation grant. It is solely sponsored by voluntary contributions.
- Password to its wards – sickness.
- It is open at all hours for the reception of accidents and urgent cases.
- Subscribers have the right of recommending suitable cases.
- Gratuitous medical and surgical advice is given every morning (Sunday excepted) in the Dispensary attached to the Hospital. Doors open from 9 till 11 a.m.[12]

No one would have questioned the need for a greater hospital service at that time. In September 1893, a contributor to the (Belfast) *Evening Telegraph* stated:

> It is generally admitted that, for a city with a population like Belfast, hospital accommodation is grossly inadequate. Any attempt to remedy this state of things, which is admittedly deplorable, deserves the heartiest support of all classes and sections of the community.[13]

He asked his readers to respond generously to the appeal for financial help towards the building of the new Mater:

> The hospital is not so much in want of funds for maintenance; but its limited accommodation cramps its atmosphere of usefulness, and compels those who conduct it to turn many sufferers away.[14]

The writer's request was supported by a simultaneous article in the *Northern Whig*:

> Bedeque House, so long the handsome residence of Mr. Gordon Thompson, has been transformed into an excellent hospital, in the wards of which are to be found the suffering of all denominations. There they are treated in the most skilful manner by the medical and surgical staff. The institution, which is complete in every respect save as to accommodation, is conducted on the same principle as the Mater Misericordiae Hospital in Dublin. Everything seems well done, yet the strictest economy seems to prevail in its management throughout.[15]

The writer of this article then went on to give some statistics: in the previous year 4,051 persons had received treatment, either as intern patients in the hospital or at the dispensary attached to it. The total number treated since its opening was 37,030. No patient had ever been refused treatment for want of funds; only lack of accommodation limited the number who could be accepted and now attempts were being made to remedy the situation:

> A special effort is now being put forth for the purpose of securing the erection of a much more extensive Hospital. For the new edifice a very valuable site has been secured and the building, or rather range of buildings, will extend from the wall of the County Antrim Prison down the entire way to Elim Home for boys. The frontage will be 231 feet in length and, judging from the architectural sketch which we saw, it will be a really imposing structure. The cost is estimated as between £25,000 and £30,000, and the latter is the sum which is being aimed at by the promoters of the project.[16]

This, and other press coverage, was given on the occasion of the stepping up of the fund-raising drive in the early 1890s. Foremost among the fund-raisers, who gave so generously of their time and energy, were members of the Ladies' Hospital Co-operating Society, founded in 1895. It was organised and directed by Mother M. Magdalene Malone and in November 1896 already had 170 members. Their task was to arrange house-to-house penny collections and to organise entertainment and bazaars.

One scheme for a massive subscription drive was planned around the very popular railway network, which served the counties of the north of Ireland and extended to the Dublin routes. The plan was for a 'Great Railway Tour' whereby:

> a variety of Concerts, Drama Entertainments, Reunions, Garden Parties, Open-air Sports, Cyclists and Football Matches, etc. will be held at Bazaar Stations along the lines traversed by the Great Railway System and in all friendly districts for the benefit of the Building Fund of the New Mater Infirmorum Hospital.[17]

The County Down Railway Company voted £200 towards the project. In supporting this grant Thomas Andrews, chairman of the company, mentioned the benefit the Mater Hospital had given to the workmen of the company and emphasised the fact that Protestant clergymen were admitted to the bedside of the patients and that every facility was given them for any ministrations they thought right.

Many other voices also lent support to the project. For example, Reverend Eugene Canon McCartan, addressing the Board of Directors of the York Street Flax Spinning Company to appeal for donations, spoke with feeling about his confidence in the potential of the new establishment:

> The Sisters of Mercy will be the nurses, ladies of refinement and education, who will see in every sick person the image of Him to whom they have dedicated their lives, and for whose sake they left home and family and all the comforts and pleasures of the world. They will be tender, kind and sympathetic nurses, and good nursing does more to help and hasten recovery than medicine.[18]

The enthusiasm aroused for the fund-raising was obvious among those who supported the new project, but unfortunately it also met with considerable opposition from certain factions, antagonistic to the idea of a new Catholic hospital in the city. At this time the new Royal Victoria Hospital was being built and there was considerable competition between the supporting fund-raising parties to attract the major business concerns. However, nothing daunted, Mother M. Magdalene pursued her goal with unfailing vigour and dedication. Her efforts culminated in the Grand Bazaar, which ran, with great success, in the Ulster Hall on 22–7 November 1897. This event raised £20,000.

The building of the new hospital got under way. The architect was William John Fennell and the builders were H. Laverty and Sons. The work commenced in the last week of January 1895. During the building temporary arrangements had to be made in order that the usual care of the sick could continue as normally as possible. In the summer of 1889 an epidemic of typhoid broke out in the city and the bishop ordered that the newly completed wards of the Eastern Pavilion be opened for the reception of the victims of the fever. On the feast of the Immaculate Conception, 8 December 1898, in the presence of a representative assembly of the executive committee of the new Mater Hospital, Bishop Henry laid the foundation stone in the central corridor, Western Pavilion. On Thursday, 2 March of the following year, another important, but more private, ceremony took place. The bishop, attended by the members of the hospital committee, laid a memorial stone, a large block of grey limestone, ornamented with tracery work and bearing the emblem of a cross, near the western end of the great main corridor. In the heart of the stone were placed the records of the hospital to date, a copy of the *Irish News* of the day, 13 small silver medals and a statue of the Blessed Virgin Mary.

By 1900 work on the new Mater Infirmorum Hospital was completed and on 23 April of that year the lord mayor of Belfast, Sir Robert J. McConnell, performed the opening ceremony in the presence of a distinguished gathering. This included the marquis of Dufferin and Ava as guest speaker and Lady Pirrie who, along with her husband, was one of the most earnest supporters of the new hospital. Cardinal Logue occupied the chair. The event was given a full report the following day in the *Irish News* under the heading 'A great occasion':

> The Formal opening of the Mater Infirmorum Hospital yesterday must rank as a red-letter mark on the history of Belfast. Set apart as a crowning day of a great work, the elements seemed to combine to make it an occasion of rejoicing. The genial spring sunshine, smiling on the fine lines of the completed building in the early morn, was the harbinger of the memorable display that took place in the afternoon. It was a remarkable occasion in every sense, and the more so because it gave earnest of a closer relationship of Christian, and consequently charitable, feeling than has ever been witnessed in this hitherto divided community. The noble work, which has been a source of so much anxiety from its inception, was at length an accomplished fact, and compelled admiration from all sides; and the admirers were counted by the thousands. In anticipation of the formal opening, many sightseers congregated in front of the hospital to witness the arrival of the distinguished personages who were to take part in the consummation of the glorious work. Class and creed, sectarianism, and indeed every other 'ism', were forgotten in the tribute paid to the energy of the Sisters of Mercy and those who had assisted them to see their noble ideas crowned with success.[19]

It was indeed a day of joy and celebration for the Sisters of Mercy, especially for Mother M. Magdalene Malone, who happily lived to see her great ambition fulfilled. She died in 1902. We are told that with her last breath she asked God to bless and reward a hundredfold the benefactors whose kind generosity had enabled the hospital to be built and completed free of debt.

Since the hospital was a voluntary institution, funding was an ongoing problem. Most of the visiting consultants gave their services on a voluntary basis, among them Alexander Dempsey, Peter O'Connell, Daniel McDonnell, J.B. Moore, William M. Killen, R.J. Murray, W. McLorinan,

John McStay, and the resident physician, Sara L. McElderry. Likewise, the Sisters of Mercy, responsible for administration and most of the nursing in the wards, generously gave their services – not for any remuneration but, as Samuel Young MP, a contemporary witness, put it, because their soul is in their work and because they dedicate themselves to this in honour of God and for the glory of his kingdom.

The new hospital was an imposing structure. The official description from the architect's plans was as follows:

> The hospital is favourably situated for freedom of light and thoroughness of ventilation, and an uninterrupted enjoyment of sunlight … The site [has] a frontage of 230 feet to the Crumlin Road and altogether contains an area of slightly over one acre … [It] is designed on the 'pavilion' system, the object being as far as possible to obtain an isolation of the wards, and the principal portions may be said to consist of three distinct blocks facing the Crumlin Road, the centre one being the administration building, flanked by a pavilion block on each side, that on the east being for males, the west one for females. These pavilions present their gable ends to the Crumlin Road and extend backwards and parallel to the east and west boundaries about 146 feet and are connected on the ground floor only to the Administration Block by a wide corridor running east and west, the entire length of the frontage, forming the main artery, so to speak, through the establishment. Each pavilion [is] three storeys high and contains two large wards on each floor, each of these wards being provided with two sanitary chambers in towers, which branch off diagonally at the ends … The space formed outside the gable ends by the projection of these towers is utilised for verandas for the use of convalescents … The hospital is planned for 137 beds and 8 cots for children.[20]

Every effort was made to ensure that the hospital would be up to date in all the requirements of modern hospital planning of the time. A steam central-heating system was installed and electricity provided the lighting. An additional facility was the fine roof gardens on the flat roofs of the pavilions, intended for the benefit of convalescent patients and for the staff to relax in now and again.

The hospital became a landmark on the Crumlin Road. A Tudoresque building of red brick with stone facings, the frontage sits back 28 feet from the road. The intervening space was originally planted as a garden and railed off. The distinctive front entrance is in the centre of the main block connecting the east and west pavilions and is approached by a broad flight of stone steps. To the rear of the main block is a galleried chapel in late Gothic style, with a fine beamed ceiling and six stained-glass windows in the apse. The entrance to the chapel is on the ground floor and there are entrances to the galleries at first-floor level, so as to be accessible to patients in the wards. With minor additions, the main hospital kept this configuration until an extensive new building scheme was undertaken in the 1980s.

On 2 February 1899 a school of nursing was inaugurated, named St Philomene's Training School for Nurses, and on 18 August 1899 the Mater received recognition as a teaching hospital for medical degrees awarded by the Royal University of Ireland.

---

[1]   *Belfast News Letter*, 12 December 1857. See also Jordan, *op. cit.*, p. 194.

[2]   C. Dallat, *Caring by design: the archaeological heritage of the health and social services in Northern Ireland* (Belfast: Department of Health and Social Services, 1985).

[3]   Ibid.

[4]   O'Byrne, *op. cit.*, p. 218.

[5]   Bolster, *op. cit.* (*Positio*), p. 134. Mother Catherine did not live herself to see this achieved but her vision materialised in Mercy hospitals in many countries throughout the world.

[6]   E. Bolster, *The Sisters of Mercy in the Crimean War* (Cork: Mercier Press, 1964).

[7]   Annals, SPCMB.

[8]   Clifton Street Infirmary, a 'lying-in hospital for women', had been established in Donegall Street in 1794. It moved to Clifton Street in 1830, where a hospital with accommodation for 18 patients had been erected at a cost of £1,800. See Dallat, *op. cit.*, p. 31.

[9]   Henry Joy McCracken was a famous United Irishman inspired with one idea: a bond of brotherhood founded on true friendship and understanding between Catholics and Protestants, for which he pledged himself by oath. He was executed as a traitor at the Market House, High Street, Belfast, in 1798. His remains lie in the graveyard adjoining Clifton House (the old poorhouse) beside those of his devoted sister, Mary Ann McCracken. See O'Byrne, *op. cit.*, p. 206.

[10] Annals, SPCMB.

[11] 'List of subscriptions towards the building fund which have been paid or promised, ending 15th November 1894', *Mater Infirmorum Hospital publications* (Belfast: Mater Infirmorum Hospital, 1900).

[12] Mater Infirmorum Hospital, prospectus (MIHA, 1893).

[13] *Evening Telegraph*, September 1893.

[14] Ibid.

[15] *Northern Whig*, September 1893.

[16] Ibid.

[17] *Weekly Irish Times*, 10 December 1911.

[18] *Irish News*, 6 January 1897.

[19] *Irish News*, 24 April 1900.

[20] Dallat, *op. cit*, p. 25 *et seq.*

13

COUNTING THE BLESSINGS

> If any person in the remotest corner of the four provinces does a favour
> to the Sisters of Mercy or even speaks kindly of their Institute it must
> be noted in the Annals and all future generations of the Order must
> testify gratitude by daily prayers for the benefactor.[1]

The end of the nineteenth century was auspicious for the Sisters of Mercy
in the diocese of Down and Connor and they could look back on almost 50
years of achievement, though they also acknowledged sad times of failure,
bereavement and loss of one kind or another. By the first decade of the
1900s their schools were well established, the visitation of the sick and those
in prison was regularly attended to, the new hospital had been opened and
members of the community had gone to establish convents in Downpatrick,
England, County Cavan and even Australia.

It goes without saying that the Sisters could not have undertaken these
good works without the support of generous benefactors and it seems
appropriate that some mention should be made of them at this point in the
story. The first who comes to mind is Alexander O'Rorke. He was one of the
delegation of Catholic gentlemen who had invited the Sisters of Mercy to
Belfast. He was a prominent solicitor in the town, with residences at 14
Donegall Street and 4 College Square North. He was also a leading member
of a group of Catholic laymen – professionals and prosperous businessmen
– who founded the Catholic Institute, a study and recreation centre
established in the early 1850s for the benefit of the Catholic population.
These gentlemen were staunch supporters of the Sisters of Mercy and of the
Christian Brothers, who had been invited to the diocese in 1866 to take
responsibility for the education of boys. The bishop of the time, Dr Denvir,
felt threatened by this emerging Catholic middle class who were eager to
play an active role in the building up of Catholic life in the town.[2] However,
wishing to give the bishop reassurance of their good intentions, they
welcomed him with a congratulatory address on his return from the Vatican
Council in 1870. Alexander O'Rorke was chosen for this delicate task.

Another benefactor was Henry Loughran, a tea, wine and spirits
merchant and a wholesale and retail grocer with addresses at 41 York Street
and 1 Great Patrick Street. He was also a member of the delegation of

gentlemen who had invited the Sisters of Mercy to come north and who, along with Alexander O'Rorke, had received them on their arrival. It was in his home, warmly welcomed by his wife and her friends, that the Sisters had partaken of their first refreshments in Belfast. He and his family continued to support them in the early days of their establishment.

The name of Bernard Hughes also appears on the roll of the benefactors of the community. Records tell us that he was the proprietor of the extensive Railway and Model Bakeries, with businesses in Divis Street, Donegall Square West and Donegall Place. With his origins in Blackwaterstown, County Armagh, he had come to Belfast in 1827 to work as an apprentice baker. He became a highly successful and prosperous businessman, serving on the Belfast Town Council for several years, and was very active in promoting the influence of the expanding Catholic middle class in public life. He lived in College Square North, then a very fashionable quarter of the town, and owned Mount Charles Terrace on the Lisburn Road. It was said that he was a man whose great wealth was equalled only by his princely generosity to Catholic charities and he is best remembered as having acquired and presented to the diocese, in 1860, the site for St Peter's Church (later to become the cathedral) on the Falls Road. The community annals record that, over the years, Hughes regularly had bread delivered to the convent to be distributed among the poor. He was attended by the Sisters in his last illness and on his death his son sent the community a donation of £100. One of his daughters joined the community, receiving the religious name of Sister M. Teresa.

The Connor and McKenna families, related by marriage, are remembered as having given refuge to the Sisters at the time of the convent crisis of 1862. Both families were engaged in the wholesale spirit business, with shops on Royal Avenue, Academy Street and Donegall Place. James Connor was also engaged in building houses, docks and railways and, in spite of his success and prosperity, was described as 'an unpretentious man'. He was father-in-law of John McKenna, three of whose daughters entered religious life, two with the Sisters of Nazareth and one, Sister M. Gabriel, with the Sisters of Mercy in Belfast.

Mention has already been made of Matthew Bowen, who built schools to serve St Malachy's Parish, which became known as the Sussex Place Convent Schools. With his private residence at 1 Downshire Place, he owned the Royal Hotel and property on the Lisburn Road, which he bequeathed to the Sisters of Mercy for the upkeep of the convent in Sussex Place. His foresight in this matter was remembered with gratitude by the Sussex Place community as long as they lived there.

The Catholic women of Belfast were not to be outdone in generosity to the Sisters of Mercy. Miss Charlotte Stream of North Street gave the community an old oak chair said to have belonged to the martyr bishop St Oliver Plunkett, and on her death in 1875 she left a large bequest to the orphanage. Misses Mary and Charlotte Magill, sisters of Reverend Martin Magill, parish priest of Moneyglass (who lived with them until his death in 1877) also left a large bequest. It is recorded above how the Catholic women of Belfast were among the foremost supporters of Mother M. Magdalene Malone in her fund-raising efforts for the Mater Infirmorum Hospital. The bazaars and other events, so important for collecting funds for the charitable undertakings of the Sisters, could not have had such successful outcomes without these women at the helm.

The Hamills of Trench House

Needless to say, numerous anonymous benefactors of the early years deserve grateful remembrance from the community. But the list cannot be complete without the story of the most distinguished of the community's benefactors, the Hamill family of Trench House.

The Hamills of Trench House were, in their day, among the wealthiest families in Belfast and, without doubt, the wealthiest within the local Catholic community. The founder of the dynasty (if such it could be called, since it died out after two generations) was Michael Hamill (1752–1833), who was originally, research would seem to indicate, from Mallusk in County Antrim. The surname Hamill is possibly of Scottish origin, a derivation of the name Hamilton. Michael Hamill, though from modest beginnings, had an eye to business. Starting as a tradesman, he gradually built up his fortune by purchasing or leasing land and property in the environs of Belfast. The register of landowners in 1820 reveals that he had acquired lands, including the property named Trench House, from the marquis of Donegall.

History records that there were several occasions when Michael Hamill saved the unfortunate marquis from harassment and disgrace. The story goes that the marquis was once bankrupt, in the custody of the police and on his way to jail when he met, or sent for, his friend Michael Hamill, whom he asked to bail him out. Hamill enquired how much he owed his creditors, and there and then produced a handful of notes and cleared his lordship's debts. This second marquis of Donegall, George Augustus, Lord Belfast, a member of the Chichester family, to whom the borough of Belfast had been entrusted by royal charter in 1613, was an inveterate spendthrift and gambler, which unfortunate addictions had cost him a spell in a debtor's prison and, by the end of the eighteenth century, the sale or lease of most of the vast property inherited from his father.

By way of repayment the marquis granted Hamill an extensive tract of land on the western outskirts of Belfast, under the shadow of the Black Mountain and in the parish of Hannahstown. Michael Hamill gradually built up his holdings so that, when he died in 1833, the Hamill family were established landowners with extensive lands and property in the south and west of the town. Michael's third son, John, the only one to marry, inherited the property on the death of his two older brothers, Arthur and Thomas, and he in turn continued to add to the family estates. The Hamill estates extended from the Black Mountain in the north to the present site of the King's Hall, Balmoral, in the south, and into the heart of the town as far as Durham Street and Castle Place. John Hamill became a very prominent figure in Belfast public life and was elected as the only Catholic member of the town council at that time. John married Hannah Davies around 1830 and had nine children. Most of them lived to a ripe old age but none of them married. As the brothers died the estates and the family fortunes passed finally to the last two surviving daughters, Hannah and Teresa. Contemporary records portray these as rather formidable women and they administered the estates until their deaths, Hannah's in January 1918 and Teresa's in September of the same year. With Teresa's demise the Hamill line was ended.

The name Hamill was, and still is, associated with the family home, Trench House, on their west-Belfast estate. The family history indicates that Michael Hamill made Trench House his home around 1802 or even earlier (John Hamill was born there in 1802). When John Hamill died his son Arthur, who succeeded him, decided to build a much grander house on the same site as the original and completed it on 1 June 1880.[3] This gracious residence, situated on elevated ground at the foot of the Hannahstown Hills, commanded a unique view of the town, the lough and a wide sweep of the counties of Antrim and Down. It was made over in 1906 by deed of gift, 'with all its furniture, etc.', to the Sisters of Mercy 'for their own use, along with three fields adjoining the house, and the head rent of the Ulster Club to go for the upkeep of the same',[4] by Hannah and Teresa Hamill, the last surviving members of the family. Inevitably there was much legal wrangling over the sisters' will and it was not until 1926 that Trench House eventually came into the hands of the Mercy community.

Trench House was held in trust for the Sisters of Mercy. They had no express power to sell or lease any portion of the property, but the trustees were to safeguard it for them so long as they fulfilled certain conditions stated in the bequest. The convent archives hold the following record:

By deed of 20 December 1906, the Misses Hamill conveyed to the late Most Rev. Henry, D.D., the Rev. James Hamill and the Rev. Murtagh Hamill the property known as Trench House, and the gardens, buildings and lands used in connection therewith and containing as acreage of 39 acres, 1 rood and 3 perches Statute measures, free of rent, together with the furniture, etc. in said house.[5]

The chief condition of the trust was that the Sisters should be responsible for the upkeep of the Hamill family vault, with its memorial chapel, in the graveyard of Hannahstown. This was a charge that was willingly undertaken and faithfully observed until any interest in the property passed out of the hands of the Sisters of Mercy.

It is believed that Teresa Hamill envisioned that on her death the Sisters of Mercy would occupy Trench House and use it as a convalescent home for the community or a place where aged Sisters might spend their declining years. For that reason comprehensive powers were not given to the trustees. This, unfortunately, precluded the use of Trench House for charitable purposes associated with the apostolates of the community, and its distance from the city and the convent on the Crumlin Road made the house's use as a residence for elderly Sisters unfeasible at a time when transport was very inconvenient. However, it was used for a few years as a holiday house until the community leased it, in 1920, to Dr McRory, the bishop of the time, as his residence, and to his successor, Bishop Mageean. It remained the episcopal residence until 1938 and, except for a period of military occupation during World War II, it lay vacant until the diocese made a request in 1948 for its use as a teacher-training college. The house and 21 acres of land were sold in 1955 by the trustees (Dr Mageean, Very Reverend J. McMullan, Reverend P. McGouran and Reverend M.J. Blaney) for £13,000 to St Mary's Training College. Later this became a separate establishment, a teacher-training college for men (St Joseph's). Some 30 years later, in 1992, owing to cuts in teacher training and legislation from the Department of Education St Joseph's merged with St Mary's and the process of vacating Trench House took place. The year 1996 saw the demolition of the tutorial blocks. Efforts were made to preserve Trench House itself but sadly vandalism reduced the former gracious residence to an empty shell within a short time.

The Sisters of Mercy were not the only beneficiaries of the Hamill fortunes. The family gave lavishly to many Catholic charities and good causes. They built St Teresa's Church, schools and parochial residence on the Glen Road, which opened in 1911 and were named in memory of Teresa Hamill. They also donated the pulpit of Clonard Monastery Church and the baptismal font of St Joseph's Church in Hannahstown, their own parish. Each member of the family who died after 1830 was buried in a vault in Hannahstown cemetery, over which a memorial chapel was erected in 1905. The same vault and chapel had been entered into the codicil relating to the Hamill bequest to the Sisters of Mercy. However, of all the laudable charities bestowed by the Hamill family the most memorable to the Mercy community was the donation of the beautiful convent chapel.

Saint Anthony's Oratory

St Anthony's Oratory at St Paul's Convent, Crumlin Road, was built by Hannah and Teresa Hamill and dedicated to the memory of their brother Arthur. This graceful place of prayer and worship was blessed on the feast of St Anthony of Padua in 1910. The bishop's address on the occasion, reported in the *Irish News* the following day, sums up the significance of the event. In the report, the address is prefaced as follows:

> The Misses Hamill, of Trench House, Belfast, have done many noble works for the greater glory of God, and their latest benefaction is one that may well challenge the admiration of all creeds and classes, and further establish the claim of these ladies to the gratitude of their co-religionists for the munificent generosity of their latest gift. Yesterday witnessed the solemn dedication of the new chapel of St Anthony of Padua at the Convent of Mercy, Crumlin Road. The chapel and cloisters, which are the gift of the Misses Hamill to the community, were erected at the cost of about ten thousand pounds, and yesterday witnessed the handing over of this regal offering to God through the hands of the Most Rev. Dr Tohill, Lord Bishop of Down and Connor. The Hamill Family have all along been sincere friends of the Sisters of Mercy who, it is well known, devote their lives to God and their unselfish services to visiting, comforting, consoling and educating the poor.[6]

The origins of St Anthony's Oratory make an interesting story. By the end of the century the community was badly in need of a larger chapel, and in the early 1900s the Misses Hamill offered to have a convent chapel built if a suitable site could be found. Needless to say, countless novenas were made and the Sisters engaged in a campaign of 'storming heaven' for a solution to their need.

At this time there were two houses flanking Convent Avenue, with gardens reaching to the Crumlin Road and large yards at the rear adjoining the convent itself. One of these houses was known as the Bird's Nest and was owned by a Protestant charitable agency that gave food and clothing to poor children. It was strongly suspected of proselytising by attracting poor

Catholic children, through charity, to the Protestant faith. Early in 1909 this institution had to close because of financial difficulties and the property came up for sale. Through solicitors it was purchased for the community and paid for by the Hamill sisters. The second house was also acquired and on this site the new convent chapel was built.

In the summer of 1910, the chapel, constructed and adorned at a cost of £14,000 by the Hamill sisters, was handed over to the community with a request that it should be dedicated to St Anthony in memory of their brother, Arthur Hamill. Before the ceremony of dedication, on 13 June 1910, Miss Teresa Hamill, accompanied by members of the community, had unveiled a statue of St Anthony of Padua at the inside entrance door, and formally declared open the new upper and lower cloisters leading to the chapel. At the close of the dedication ceremonies the Misses Hamill entertained their guests to a sumptuous luncheon in the convent parlours.[7]

When the building was completed, a railed-off garden with flower beds, trees and shrubs between the apse of the chapel and the Crumlin Road was named Hamill Park in honour of the benefactors, and formed an oasis of green lawn and leafy foliage providing relief amidst the red brick of the surrounding hospital and convent buildings. This little park, sometimes used by the patients and nurses from the hospital on summer days and occasionally functioning as a 'nature trail' for the schoolchildren, was carefully tended until the chapel was demolished for hospital extension.

The beautiful, spacious convent chapel, a place of prayer and devotion for generations of Sisters, witnessed many joyous ceremonies of religious reception and profession and many solemn requiem liturgies over the next 70 years. In the 1970s a heart-rending decision was made by the community to release the chapel site for an essential extension of the Mater Hospital. The decision was not taken lightly, but the community considered that if the service of the sick and needy, for which they had originally come to Down and Connor, required sacrifice, even of their dearest possessions, then this was the right thing to do. St Anthony's Oratory was closed for worship in May 1983 and demolished in 1984. Thus ended a beautiful phase in the history of St Paul's community.

[1] Catherine McAuley, quoted in M.A. Carroll, *Life of Catherine McAuley, foundress and first superior of the Institute of Religious Sisters of Mercy* (New York: D. & J. Sadlier, 1871).

[2] This insecurity is referred to in biographical records of Bishop Denvir's later years. See Macaulay, *op. cit.*, pp. 88–9.

[3] For description see *Irish Builder*, 1880, and 'Some notes on the Hamills of Trench House' (Belfast: Resources Centre, St Joseph's College of Education, 1978).

[4] 'Codicil, 22 July 1918', legal documents (Archives, SPCMB).

[5] F. Kerr to Reverend Mother M. Imelda, referred to by R. Murphy, solicitor (Archives, SPCMB, 11 November 1938).

[6] *Irish News*, 14 June 1910.

[7] *Irish News*, 14 June 1910.

14

INTO THE TWENTIETH CENTURY

For Belfast, the nineteenth century ended on a high note of prosperity and peace.[1]

Such was the verdict of the historian Jonathan Bardon. The population had soared to almost 350,000 and Belfast had been granted city status in 1888. In the first decade of the twentieth century this growth in prosperity continued and the years of World War I brought a minor economic boom. Linen, a primary product of the Belfast mills, was much in demand for military purposes – for tents, haversacks, hospital equipment and aeroplane fabric – and after the war the demand for linen for clothing and household goods remained high. The Belfast shipyards which, by 1912, were the largest in the world, achieved their maximum production level in the war years with the need to replace naval vessels lost in combat. For this work, Belfast harbour was strategically in an ideal position. The food industry likewise prospered because of the demands of the wartime British market. As a consequence, during the opening decades of the new century employment in the north of Ireland, and especially around Belfast, was, in general, of a satisfactorily high level.

Sadly, the euphoria was short lived. The economic fringe benefits of the war years, it could be argued, were far outweighed by the tragic losses. The Great War had taken its toll on the youth of Ireland, north and south. The city of Belfast will never forget that thousands of its young men were slaughtered in the futile battle of the Somme in 1916. However, even though young men from both unionist and nationalist sections of the community had fought and died side by side in the bloody misery of the trenches, true to the unfortunate heritage of centuries of conflict in Irish history, at the conclusion of the European hostilities attention in the north-east of the island turned once again to the deep divisions created by sectarian and political differences. Even an incipient Labour movement, at first encouraging, could not unite the province's working class. Political upheavals shook the whole of Ireland in the second decade of the twentieth century – the Easter Rising and the Anglo-Irish conflicts.

Vicious rioting broke out again in the north of Ireland in the early 1920s as a response to partition. As one writer enumerated, 'In just under two years, from July 21, 1920, to June 24, 1922, 455 people, 268 Catholics and

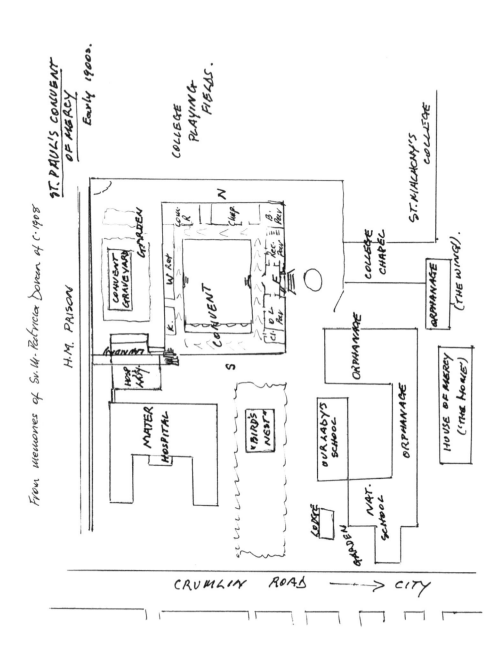

Site plan of St Paul's Convent of Mercy, Crumlin Road, Belfast, in the early 1900s

187 Protestants, are listed as having died in the streets or in the homes of Belfast at the hands of gunmen.'[2] The state of Northern Ireland was constituted in the years 1920–1 with the Government of Ireland Act of November 1920. The state of Northern Ireland was born of the conflict and suffering that had become part of the life of the population of these few small counties with their divided loyalties. As the historian J.J. Campbell put it:

> The state was born in turmoil and terror. Every account of those terrible years, 1920–1922, in Belfast, tells the same story in terms of human suffering; in the numbers killed and wounded; in the destruction of property; in evictions and victimisation; in loss of livelihood; in the poverty and the queues for relief from public and voluntary sources; in the terrors of the curfew nights and the dread of the sniper, the bomb and the beating by day; in the dread of reprisals.[3]

An uneasy peace was restored in 1923 but the Catholic population was now a subdued minority, mainly channelled into nationalist ghettos, bearing much of the brunt of the economic recessions and chronic unemployment of the early 1920s. They suffered all the more because of their policy of non-cooperation in the new state of affairs, a province dominated by 'a Protestant Parliament and Protestant State'.[4]

Such a social and political setting constituted the background for the life and work of the Sisters of Mercy in Northern Ireland in the opening decades of the new century and, in fact, for the following 60 years and more. Their communities were affected, more or less immediately, by these events, particularly by the periodic outbreaks of rioting in Belfast. Also, when the Government of Ireland Act came into effect, separating six of the northern counties from the rest of the island and leaving Northern Ireland under the jurisdiction of Britain (though with a degree of self-government), this occasioned for the Sisters a break with the great majority of the communities of the Mercy Congregation in the south.

However, the turn of the century brought a milestone in the history of the Sisters of Mercy in Down and Connor. On 25 January 1904, the feast of the conversion of St Paul, the golden jubilee of the foundation was celebrated with a *missa cantata* in the convent chapel. There was an augmented choir from St Patrick's Church, with Hayden Mulholland at the organ. Bishop Henry, the priests and a large number of friends of the community were afterwards entertained to lunch in the refectory. Sisters from the branch houses and other communities came to share in the celebrations.

At this time the community in St Paul's numbered 57 Sisters. That in St Patrick's, Downpatrick, numbered 21, most of whom were engaged in the schools, the orphanages, the hospital and the various other Mercy apostolates. As the work of the hospital expanded, the bishop advised the community in St Paul's to welcome young women with a religious vocation who would not, perhaps, be prepared to work in the schools but who could undertake duties in the hospital and ancillary roles in the convents. Several generous young women responded to this vocation, the first of whom were Kate Corcoran (Sister Martha), Annie O'Donnell (Sister Gerard), Annie Fox (Sister Ann), Catherine Cawley (Sister Bernadette) and Brigid O'Donnell (Sister Zita). These were the first lay Sisters for St Paul's community, Crumlin Road. Generally speaking, the lay Sisters were responsible for housekeeping in the convent and in the schools where there were boarders and usually for catering in the hospital and its departments. The role of lay Sister was discontinued in the 1960s. Sister Martha entered St Paul's in January 1903; Sisters Bernadette and Zita entered in October 1904. The date of Sister Gerard's entry into the community is not known.

Around this time the Mater Hospital trustees purchased a large mansion near Carrickfergus, County Antrim, to be used as a sanatorium. When it opened Sisters Martha, Zita, Gerard and Bernadette went to work there. Later they returned to the hospital and the convents in Belfast, where they were highly valued members of the communities, most of them living to a ripe old age. Sister Zita died in 1948 at 66 years of age; Sister Martha in 1966 at 86 and Sister Bernadette in 1978 at 83. Sisters Ann Fox and Gerard O'Donnell appear to have left the congregation at some stage.

The year 1904 also saw the first extension added to Crumlin Road Convent, necessitated by the expanding community. Between 1900 and 1910 16 young women sought admission, all of whom except two persevered. In that decade 13 Sisters died. Between 1910 and 1920, 20 joined (a steady average of two each year), 6 left and there were 12 deaths. Between the years 1920 and 1930, 20 entered, 9 of whom left; there were 20 deaths. In short, the Down and Connor communities went through the normal human process of expansion and contraction. Between the years 1900 and 1930 56 young women had joined the community in Crumlin Road, 39 of whom had persevered. In the same three decades there had been 32 deaths. At the time of the celebrations of the centenary of the founding of the Mercy Congregation (1931) it was reported in the local newspaper that St Paul's community 'numbers close to eighty members'.[5] We can add to this four young women who entered St Patrick's community, Downpatrick, between 1900 and 1911. Three died during the same period. There were 22 Sisters in Downpatrick at the time of the amalgamation of the two communities.

An experiment in reunion

In 1911 the Downpatrick community reunited with St Paul's in Belfast. The annals record that:

> Dr Tohill [bishop of Down and Connor] thought it would be advisable, in compliance with the directions of the Holy See, to amalgamate the Sisters of Mercy in the diocese.[6]

This he put to both communities on 9 March 1911. Chapters were held on the issue simultaneously in both convents and the vote was in favour of amalgamation. The amalgamation took place on 23 December 1911 and chapters were held, again simultaneously in both communities, 'for the purpose of electing a Superior for all the Sisters of Mercy in the Diocese of Down and Connor'.[7] Sister M. Xavier Keegan was elected superior, with Sister M. Gertrude McAuley as her assistant. Sister M. Benignus Doey was elected bursar and Sister M. Emilian McCartan novice mistress.

With the new united community, some adjustments had to be made. It was decided to keep the novitiate in St Paul's (there were no novices in Downpatrick at that time) and the Belfast convent was recognised as motherhouse. On 9 March 1916 an election chapter was held but there was no majority vote.[8] In this impasse Bishop McRory (who had succeeded Bishop Tohill), appointed Sister M. Ethna Grene superior, an office she held until 1922. Her assistant was Sister M. Benignus Doey. Sister M. Magdalen Toner was elected bursar and Sister M. Emilian McCartan continued as novice mistress.

On 1 June 1922 Mother M. Ethna Grene had completed her six years in office and Sister M. Benignus Doey was elected superior. About a year later she represented to the bishop that the amalgamation was not working. There is no clear indication of what the hindrances were, but such things as the difficulty of organising chapters and elections come to mind, with the two main convents relatively far apart at a time when transport and communications were less advanced than they are today. The election chapters of the Sisters of Mercy were 'open' chapters – that is, all finally professed Sisters had the right to vote (were 'vocals'). They had to be held on consecutive days or, if they took place simultaneously, the votes were conveyed post haste from one town to the other. One can imagine the inconvenience when second and third scrutinies were required. In the light of the information submitted to him the bishop gave the matter serious consideration and held interviews with all the members of both communities. Then, on 25 June 1923, a chapter of the vocals in St Paul's and in St Patrick's was held to ascertain their views with regard to the amalgamation. Bishop McRory presided at both chapters. By a very large majority both communities voted for separation.[9]

Mother M. Ethna Grene returned to Downpatrick to be superior of that community and, the following August, Sister M. Anthony Crangle, who had been mistress of novices in Crumlin Road Convent, was recalled there also. She was accompanied by a novice, Sister M. Kieran O'Carroll (who had entered the community in Belfast on 8 December 1922), who had volunteered to go and was given the bishop's consent. Her dower of £200 was given over to the superior of the Downpatrick community. Sister M. Kieran made her profession in Downpatrick on 24 June 1925 and became a very influential member of the community there in later years.

Expansion of the education apostolate
The turn of the century saw the Sisters of Mercy in the diocese of Down and Connor at the helm of a well-developed education system. In the late 1800s the education apostolate in Belfast and Downpatrick had expanded to meet the apparent needs of their locations. This included: the education of young children in the national schools; pension schools for young ladies who wished to further their education; the training of monitresses and later teachers, work which was associated with the national schools; evening classes for young women employed in the mills, the factories and in service; and, in Belfast, an industrial school for children of school age who, for one reason or another, had been admitted to residential care.

The elementary schools conducted by the Sisters of Mercy were: Crumlin Road Convent National Schools; St Malachy's Convent National Schools (Sussex Place); Star of the Sea Convent National Schools (Halliday's Road); and Mount St Patrick Convent National Schools (Downpatrick).[10] The convent national schools taught both girls and boys of school age – that is, between 6 and 14 years – in infant and senior classes.

School attendance was an important factor, particularly in relation to finance. In 1884 the National Education in Ireland Bill introduced a ban on the employment of children who were not being educated and this ruling was overseen by attendance officers. Attendance rolls were made obligatory for all schools. (The same bill also provided some financial help for non-vested schools.) For the Sisters of Mercy, numbers fluctuated. For example, in Crumlin Road Convent National Schools daily attendance in the last decades of the nineteenth century was high. The years between 1884 and 1889 saw an increase from 283 to 325. This decreased slightly in 1890 to 289 but by 1892 it had dropped to 143. Several factors were accountable for this rather noticeable fall-off. The opening of the Star of the Sea Convent National Schools (in 1889) and the expansion of the schools in Sussex Place would have played a significant part. Numbers picked up again in the early years of the new century (in 1901 there were 221; in 1903, 239; and in 1910, 262). It is interesting to note also that the school still catered for children of all denominations (for example, in 1910, 40 per cent of the pupils were non-Catholics).[11]

In the convent schools there was an imbalance in financial support in comparison with that given to non-religious schools. The convent-school teachers, lay and religious, received a grant each year from the National Education Board, with a certain allowance for the monitresses, but this grant was still lower than the amount the state schools received.[12] To make up the deficit the schools depended much on fundraising through concerts, raffles, bazaars and so on and on a minimal contribution (one penny a week) from the children who could afford it. These voluntary contributions accounted for approximately 35 per cent of the funding at that time.[13] Welcome help was given over some years (from 1894 to 1921) by the York Street Spinning Company. The York Street Mill was founded by Alexander Mulholland and was the first of its kind in Ireland. The company had the biggest spinning mill and the largest weaving factory in the world. It employed over 4,000 people, not counting outworkers, and was the main source of employment, particularly for women, in north Belfast. In 1894 the company began to subscribe some money to the Crumlin Road Convent Schools to subsidise the education of the mill girls at evening classes. They began with the sum of £25, which remained at around £24 until 1903, after which the contribution dropped and ended in 1921 with a £4 donation. The mill was badly bombed during World War II (on 4–5 May 1941). As one writer puts it, 'In many ways the destruction of the York Street Mill was symbolic of the end of an era for an industry and a city that had already passed their growth.'[14]

Numbers on roll were important because the capitation system was in operation as the criterion for the allocation of grants, and in 1872 a further measure had been introduced (an outcome of the Powis Commission) – payment by results. This meant that an additional sum was paid to the teacher for each pupil who made 100 attendances during the year and reached a prescribed standard for his/her class in compulsory and optional subjects. These results fees were paid annually, in one lump sum, and added considerably to the income of a successful teacher. However, the scheme was very unpopular. It was abolished in 1900 and replaced by another system of teacher remuneration.

'Half-timers'

A notable proportion of children attending the convent schools were those known as 'half-timers'. These were children of school age who were employed in the mills and factories and for whom partial attendance at school was compulsory under the 'half-time system' enforced by law as of 1844. These were the only children for whom school was compulsory up until 1892, at which date full-time attendance for all school-age children began to be implemented under law. In 1819 the school-leaving age had been set at nine years. (The Factory Act applied, until 1876, only to children working in factories, not in agriculture.) In 1874 the minimum age for employment was raised to ten years and in 1891 to 11 years. Those children who had not attained a certain standard (or 'book') by the age of 13 were required to continue with school for another year.

Under the half-time system all mill and factory owners had to ensure that children working in their establishments also attended school. Sometimes the employers provided for this by setting aside a room as a classroom, or by renting an outside building and appointing a teacher. However, it was usually found to be more satisfactory to release the children to attend school in their own locality. This was arranged on a half-time basis. It is recorded that in 1902 there were 2,300 half-timers in Belfast.

For some the arrangement was that the children worked on either morning or afternoon shifts and went to school when not working. These shifts changed on alternate weeks. For example, week one: work, 6 a.m. to 12.30 p.m.; break for dinner; school, 2 p.m. to 3 p.m; week two: school, 10 a.m. to 12.30 p.m.; dinner; work, 1.30 p.m. to 6 p.m. For others schooling varied on a weekly basis: for example, they attended for three full days one week and two full days the next (five days out of ten).

Half-timers had to attend school for a minimum of 200 half days over 12 months for promotion through the standards or grades. (Full-timers had to attend for 100 days). Obviously it was not easy for them and they usually dropped out of school after the fourth or fifth book (first year). The very fact that they were half-timers confirms that their parents needed their wages. The children, for their part, were aware of the importance of their contributions to the family income and took pride in this knowledge. They were reluctant to give up earning time – or, indeed, well-deserved recreation time – for school. Thus the half-timers present in the upper level of the fifth book (second year) were a minority whose parents sacrificed the increase in household income for the sake of their children's schooling.

Records show that half-timers were also consistently one to three years older than full-timers, except in the upper-level classes. This suggests that they indeed took more time to pass promotional tests because they failed or did not attend for the required number of days. Non-attendance, in not a few cases, occurred because the children were too poor to afford suitable clothes for attending school. In the convent schools clothing was provided for children who needed it. Many also had to repeat grades because they were absent on the day of the tests. Consequently they were held back and were older than the full-timers in their class group.[15] The half-time system was not easy for the often reluctant working children. Neither was it easy for the schools to keep up a consistent quality of education which combined both full-time and half-time pupils. The schools were paid, by the National Education Board, only a 50-per-cent allowance for half-timers.

The majority of children – 88 per cent – attending the convent schools came from working-class backgrounds. From an early register we can see, for example, the occupations of their fathers: artisan, carpenter, labourer, printer, cooper, boatman, barber, reporter, policeman, hairdresser, shopkeeper, paver, sea-captain, coachman.[16]

Some children were orphans or had been deprived of one parent through death or because their fathers had gone to seek work elsewhere. One note accompanying an early school photograph informs us:

> Some of the children sitting in the front row, whose mother had died during childbirth, were extremely poor. Their father, who was in America at the time, returned to Ireland, removed the children from the school and took them to America.[17]

This would not have been an atypical story – and lucky were those who could escape the poverty of Belfast for a better life elsewhere.

As far as parents were concerned, there were different levels of motivation for sending their children to school:

> For most of the working class, schooling was neither a means of upward mobility nor of future prosperity. As a rule, all the parents wanted for their children was basic reading, some arithmetic and, in some cases, writing.[18]

Writing was considered a job-related skill and therefore male. Girls were trained not to hold jobs but to become homemakers. These children usually began school at five or six years of age and left at twelve or thirteen. However, with irregular attendance, most only got an average of three and a half years' schooling. On the other hand, many children made the most of their opportunity and moved into the professions and the arts. Most, we would hope, became good parents; they certainly passed down the tradition of convent education to their families. Recurring family names appear over generations of children who attended the Mercy convent schools. Stories of teachers and Sisters were passed down and kept the memories alive. Jubilee and centenary publications ensured faithful records. However, many changes were to take place as the century unfolded, some much more radical than the first generations of Sisters could ever have dreamed of.

In the early 1900s the Sisters continued with their evening schools for the many young women who had not received adequate schooling before they were obliged, because of circumstances, to take up full-time employment. In the period prior to World War I children could stay on at school until the age of 14 or 15 years, but the average attendance for full-time schooling was 7.4 years. Though many, if they had continued at school, could have attained the second year of the seventh standard, the majority left in the fifth in order to become wage-earners. Some of these young people, however, returned for evening classes, having a sense of the value of education for the possible betterment of their position in life. The Sisters of Mercy gave every encouragement to the young women to continue their education, and even went to their homes when on visitation to urge their parents to send them.

The young women who attended the evening classes were a colourful group. Those who worked in the mills were called 'doffers', or often 'shawlies' because of the traditional black drugget or crocheted shawl worn over a long, dark frock (ankle to neck). Around the waist was tied a crisp, bleached apron, meticulously pleated, on which hung the tools of their trade – 'hackle pins', 'scrapers' and 'pickers'. Great care was taken to keep these aprons smart. The doffers went barefoot, but they had gusset boots for Sundays and special occasions. As Peter Collins explains:

> It was the doffer's job to see that the spinning frames were stopped at the appropriate time. The filled bobbins were removed and thrown into boxes and empty bobbins were put into the spindles. The spinning frame was set ready for motion again. The full bobbins were then taken to the reeling room.[19]

They went and returned from work in large groups and were a familiar sight on the streets of Belfast, such as the New Lodge, Crumlin, Shankill and Falls Roads. They emerged *en masse* from the mills when the horn for the end of work sounded and enlivened the area with laughter and banter, playing mouth organs and singing, exuding a sense of freedom after a long, hard day's work.

Mill girls were not the only pupils of the evening schools. The registers show also dressmakers, capemakers, milliners, machinists and even a book-gilder.

Paying for teachers for the evening schools had always been a problem. As has been noted, some help came from business concerns such as the York Street Spinning Company. However, though financially constrained, the Sisters saw this field of education as very important as long as the need for it was there, believing that:

> no work of charity can be more productive of good society, nor more conducive to the happiness of the poor than the careful instruction of women; because, whatever be the station they are destined to fill, their example and their advice will always have great influence.[20]

When school attendance up to the age of 14 years became compulsory, circumstances changed. However, evening classes in one form or another continued intermittently as different needs arose and the young working women were always welcome at the convent. Many joined the Children of Mary, the Pioneer Association and other religious confraternities, which gave nourishment and support to the spiritual and social dimensions of their lives.

The pension school

Though the education of the poor was given priority, the pension school – Our Lady's Collegiate School – continued to do well and was recognised for the high standard of education it provided. This was acknowledged in a report in the *Irish News*:

> Our Lady's Collegiate School, Crumlin Road, Belfast, enjoys a well-merited reputation as an educational establishment not only in the city but throughout Ulster and other parts of Ireland. The successes obtained at the last Intermediate Examination and published in our advertising columns today are a striking tribute to the value of the tuition imparted by the Sisters of Mercy under whose management and supervision the school is conducted. The curriculum of the 1923 examinations were in the middle, junior and intermediate grades and included passes in French, Irish, arithmetic, algebra, geometry and history. In all these subjects numerous passes have been obtained. Prizes have been secured by the pupils in painting and Irish dancing.[21]

Several of the young ladies who had attended this school in the early decades of the century joined the community, for example Mother M. Magdalen

Toner, Mother M. Dominic McSorley and Mother M. Ursula McGeown. They brought with them the high standards of learning and social graces that had been imparted to them by their teachers. These women were to be very influential with the generations that followed them. However, in the 1930s the pension school was closed as the community – and principally the superior, Mother M. Magdalen (herself a past pupil) – did not consider it the proper work of the Sisters of Mercy, especially when there was now provision for such a school in Belfast. The Dominican Sisters had come to Belfast in 1870 and had opened a boarding school at their convent on the Falls Road so that young ladies could further their education there. At the Convent of Mercy and Sussex Place schools, those who wished to become monitresses could stay on in the elementary schools until they were 18 years old.

[1] J. Bardon and H.V. Bell, *Belfast: an illustrated history* (Belfast: Blackstaff Press, 1982), p. 156.

[2] Heatley, *op. cit.*, p. 63. For fuller details of these years of sectarian conflict see p. 63 *et seq.*

[3] Beckett and Glasscock, *op. cit.*, p. 146.

[4] Sir James Craig (Lord Craigavon), the first prime minister of Northern Ireland (1921–40), said this in 1934.

[5] *Irish News*, 12 December 1931.

[6] Annals, SPCMB, 1911.

[7] Ibid.

[8] There is no record in the acts of chapter of an election in 1914 of a new superior and council. Canon law required that such an election be held every three years. The diocesan bishop could modify this law if circumstances required it.

[9] Acts of chapter, SPCMB, 25 June 1923.

[10] See registers of inspectors' observation books (PRONI, Education section, 6/1/3/3, 1,840 *et seq.*).

[11] See school register (PRONI, Education section, 6/1/3/3, 1,840 *et seq.*).

[12] See O'Connell, *op. cit.*, Chapter 3.

[13] See convent account books (Archives, SMD, early 1900s).

[14] P. Collins, *The making of Irish linen: historic photographs of an Ulster industry* (Belfast: Friar's Bush Press, 1994), pp. 74, 75.

[15] I am indebted for much of this information to M. Cohen, 'Paternalism and poverty: contradictions in the schooling of working-class children in Tullylish, County Down, 1825–1914', *History of Education: Journal of the History of Education Society*, vol. xxi, no. 3 (September 1992). See also A. McEwen, 'Half-timing in Belfast', *Northern Teacher*, vol. xiv, no. 1 (autumn 1983).

[16] Early register (Star of the Sea School, Belfast).

[17] Archives, SPCMB.

[18] Cohen, *op. cit.*

[19] Collins, *op. cit.*, p. 19.

[20] Sisters of Mercy, *op. cit.* (*Rule*), Chapter 2, Section 7.

[21] *Irish News*, 8 September 1923.

15

THE NEW MATER INFIRMORUM HOSPITAL AND THE EXPANSION OF HEALTHCARE, 1900–50S

The new Mater Infirmorum Hospital had officially opened on Monday 23 April 1900. The ensuing decades were to witness a process of steady expansion of the healthcare it provided.

At this time it was necessary to upgrade hospital services in Belfast and the Board of Management of the Mater Hospital believed that a Catholic teaching hospital was needed. A school of nursing had been in operation since 1899. Now there was a need for recognition of the medical training. Following the Irish Universities Act 1908, the Mater in Belfast, already approved by the Royal University of Ireland as a teaching institution, received recognition as such by Queen's University. This was a source of deep satisfaction to the medical staff of the hospital, who had struggled for this status since the opening of the hospital. Medical training began on 9 October 1908 with the opening of a clinical school and the staff threw themselves into the job of teaching with energy, enthusiasm and very considerable success, as we learn from a letter of 13 June 1910 to the commissioner from J.B. Moore, then secretary of staff, commenting on the clinical school of Queen's University:

> The [Mater Infirmorum] Hospital has now had a clinical class for two winter and two summer sessions, and the efficiency of the teaching given in its wards is strikingly demonstrated by the attached list of prizes for the fourth year students of the University at the sessional examinations at the end of the winter session, 1909–1910.[1]

This was a reference to the fact that out of the overall prizewinners in the fourth-year group seven were Mater students, and that in medicine and surgery all four prizes were awarded to the students of the same hospital.

The school of nursing – St Philomene's Training School for Nurses – which had opened in February 1899, was also flourishing. It was first under the supervision of a Miss Pringle, a Nightingale nurse and friend of Florence

Nightingale. She was a lady of unusual ability and talents whom Miss Nightingale once called 'a regular general'. Miss Pringle gave five years' service to the hospital and was succeeded by another Englishwoman, Miss May, who followed her predecessor's methods. In 1909 Miss Hannon, an Irish-trained nurse from St Vincent's Hospital, Dublin, was appointed matron. She was a very progressive woman, an advocate of a three-year nurse-training course and in favour of state registration.

Nurse-training was, at the beginning, a two-year course. The age intake was 22 or 23 years – only mature young women were considered. They paid a yearly fee of £20 and were also required to provide their own uniforms: dresses, aprons, caps, long over-sleeves and cuffs. The outdoor uniform was a brown coat, hat and gloves. The daily timetable was exacting. The trainee nurses arose at 6 a.m. and had breakfast at 6.30 a.m. They then set fires in the wards, carried coal, mopped floors and applied poultices every four hours. The nurses dined together at a long table at which matron presided and carved. Supper was from 6 p.m. to 6.20 p.m. and was followed by the rosary. Lectures were given to the nurses after 8 p.m. when they came off duty in the wards, and all had to be indoors at 9 p.m. Discipline was strict – the students had a day off perhaps once a month and two weeks' leave for holidays. The home-nursing training period, which followed general training, was four years. With legislation in 1919, things improved. The general training was lengthened to four years and the required period of home nursing ended.[2]

Orlands, St John's and Beechmount

Not long after the opening of the new hospital the trustees, under the chairmanship of Bishop Henry, saw the need for additional accommodation in the form of a sanatorium and a private nursing home. For the first a mansion named Orlands, situated between Carrickfergus and Whitehead on the Antrim coast, was bought. This was also staffed by the Sisters of Mercy. The first Sisters who worked there were Sister M. Martha Corcoran, Sister M. Zita O'Donnell, Sister M. Gerard O'Donnell and Sister M. Bernadette Cawley. However, Orlands was too distant from Belfast and too inconvenient to manage, so after four years it had to be given up.

A few years later St John's Private Nursing Home opened. Because of the great demand for beds in the hospital and the particular needs of poor patients, to whom the hospital was pledged to give priority, it was decided to open a nursing home attached to the Mater for private paying patients who were admitted upon the recommendation of, and for treatment by, members of the hospital's medical staff. Furthermore, there was an understanding with the management that if, after paying the expenses of staff and servants, any surplus remained it was to go to the hospital to help the work there. In 1912 a block of large residential houses adjoining Florence Place and opposite the hospital, 72–86 Crumlin Road, was purchased. It was suitably renovated and equipped and opened in that same year. There, also, beds were in great demand and the home was extended in 1914 with the purchase of an adjoining house. In all there was accommodation for 30 patients. Later lifts and an operating theatre were installed, with all the necessary requirements.

Care of the dying has always had priority of place in the Mercy apostolate. This was the next service for which suitable provision was sought. In 1913 the hospital acquired two houses in Lonsdale Terrace, also on the Crumlin Road, and there the Sisters established Our Lady's Hospice for the Dying. It was opened by Bishop Tohill that same year. This was the first hospice in Belfast. The first in Ireland was opened by the Irish Sisters of Charity in Harold's Cross, Dublin, in 1879. John F. Fleetwood writes that 'The concept of a special unit for terminally ill patients is sometimes thought to be of very recent origin. In fact religious orders and benevolent individuals had looked after such cases for centuries.'[3] Other hospices were established in Dublin and Limerick in the early twentieth century.

As the years went by it became clear that there was a need for care not only for the dying, but also for a very deserving section of the community that had not been adequately provided for previously – that is, for those aged and infirm persons, both women and men, who were suffering from incurable illnesses and who had no relatives to look after them. These patients were often ineligible for admission to the general hospital, where priority of space and attention had to be given to the care of patients with a view to rehabilitation. The hospice in Lonsdale Terrace could not cater for all those who requested admission so Mother M. Imelda Laverty, superior at the time, sought alternative accommodation, believing that care of the elderly, infirm and dying was a primary work of mercy. In 1932 a large property on the Falls Road known as Riddell's Demesne (it was formerly owned by a James Riddell, a Belfast businessman) came on the market and Mother M. Imelda approached Bishop Mageean. She proposed that the house and land be purchased with a view to opening a new hospice. The bishop agreed and this valuable property, which comprised 31 acres, was acquired.

Beechmount, as the residence was known, a two-storey house, is beautifully situated on a piece of rising ground commanding an extensive view over the city to the south, with the Castlereagh Hills on the horizon.

To the rear rises the Black Mountain and the house itself is approached from the Falls Road by a long avenue. The Sisters of Mercy opened the new hospice there on the feast of Our Lady of Dolours, 15 September 1932, and it became known as Our Lady's Hospital, Beechmount. It was advertised in the annual report of the Mater Hospital as follows:

> OUR LADY'S HOSPITAL, BEECHMOUNT
> The above Hospital is for the reception of patients the treatment of whose complaints is of too prolonged duration for their reception in an ordinary hospital. This noble service was carried on for many years in the old Hospice on the Crumlin Road. As the accommodation there was found entirely inadequate, His Lordship, the Most Rev. Dr Mageean, acquired the present Hospital which was formerly the residence of the Riddell family.[4]

It was evident from the opening of Beechmount that the house itself was inadequate to accommodate all who were seeking admission. It was necessary to extend the accommodation and plans were made for a purpose-built hospital to be constructed adjoining the original house. Funds were appealed for, people were generous in their response for this worthy cause and by 1935 the new building was completed. This provided accommodation for 100 elderly patients, male and female.

The new hospital, of warm red brick, was built on a E-shaped plan similar to the Mater, though on a smaller scale. This ensured maximum light, sunshine and air and gave a bright and open atmosphere to the whole building, such as might create a cheerful environment for the elderly and infirm for whom it provided a home. The building also had several small semi-private wards for those who wished to avail of them. These also were in great demand.

A particular feature of the new hospital was the beautiful chapel, all the appointments of which were gifts from generous donors. Among the donors were the Kerr family, the McSorley family, Mary E. McAlister, F. McArdle, architect, Mr McAufield, W. O'Neill and Mary McCartan. The community of St Paul's Convent, Crumlin Road, contributed £3,000.[5] It was built between the original house (which became the residence for the Sisters and staff) and the new hospital building. It was blessed on the feast of Christ the King, 1935, and dedicated to Our Lady of Lourdes. There the residents of the hospital could attend Mass every day and this beautiful oratory was a haven for the elderly and disabled in their declining years.

The Mater Hospital, at this time foremost in nursing care in the city, kept up with advances in medical technology. In 1929 a new radiology department was built and staffed, adding greatly to the efficiency of the treatment of patients. In 1936 the hospital complex was augmented by the construction of an extern (casualty and outpatients) department. This was built specifically to cater for the hundreds of casualty and day-patients who sought medical attention there annually. It is interesting to note that, since the site chosen for this new department bordered upon the property of the Crumlin Road Jail, an act of parliament was required for permission to build. This proximity to the prison caused no inconvenience whatsoever to the Extern Department, nor in any way hindered its efficiency.

Each year many thousands of patients passed through the hands of Mater Hospital staff. To take one example, the hospital records for the year 1933 show 2,640 inpatients, 58,628 outpatients and 14,798 accidents. While the main hospital was coping with its full complement of long-term patients it is very obvious that the services of the Extern Department were in constant demand. The variety and complexity of the emergency and accident cases provided an excellent training ground for the young medical and nursing staff.

As we have noted, the Mater was an established training school for nurses, attracting many young women who felt themselves called to the nursing vocation. For them, new up-to-date accommodation was needed and in 1931 a suitable site, formerly a terrace of houses with spacious gardens front and back, next to the convent schools and adjacent to the hospital, was acquired. Here the new nurses' home was built and opened in 1934. It was designed by Frank McArdle, architect, in the same architectural style as the hospital itself, both establishments creating a pleasing complex fronting the Crumlin Road. The handsome red-brick buildings of the Mater Infirmorum Hospital were to provide a very familiar landmark for generations of local people travelling up and down the Crumlin Road, right up until the present time.

The war years
During the years of the Great War (1914–18) many of the wounded from the battlefront were brought to the Mater in Belfast and later praised highly the treatment they had received. But there was also war at home to contend with. Regular outbreaks of sectarian rioting in the city in the 1920s and 1930s brought their own share of casualties to the hospital and even endangered the hospital itself. However, some incidents were not without their own brand of wry humour. According to one story, on the night of 7 June 1922, the hospital came under machine-gun and rifle fire for 45 minutes during the hours of darkness. It continues:

> On the following day the staff drafted a telegram of protest and demanded immediate military protection. They sent it – with admirable impartiality – to His Majesty the King; The Right Honourable Lloyd George; The Right Honourable Winston Churchill; and to Mr. Michael Collins of the Irish Republican Army. Presumably someone sent help. The attack was not repeated.[6]

The threat arose again during the 1935 riots. The hospital had to be guarded day and night by both police and the military while the Catholic homes in the streets opposite – Twickenham, Bedeque and Fairview Streets – were wrecked by gangs who turned out the street lights after having marked the doors of their intended victims with chalk or painted crosses.[7] Relatively undaunted by threats and attacks, the Mater carried on with its work.

The next great crisis came with World War II and the Blitz attacks, which took place on the nights of 7 April, 15 April and 4 May 1941. During those nights the German bombers dropped over 1,000 tonnes of explosives on Belfast. Around 95,000 incendiaries were dropped during the third raid alone. At that time the Belfast shipyards Harland and Wolff and Workman Clark were two of the largest in the world and, along with the Short and Harland aircraft factory, contributed more than any other such industries in Great Britain to the war effort. Brian Barton tells us that Harland and Wolff was, at the time of the Blitz, completing contract work for five different Westminster government departments – the Admiralty and the Ministries of War, Supply, Transport and Aircraft Production.[8] The yards and factories were foremost in producing vessels for the British naval campaign against the enemy and fighter planes for the Royal Air Force. They were, then, obvious and easy targets for Nazi bombers.

The irony was that, even with this high production profile, everyone assumed that Ulster was beyond the reach of the Luftwaffe. Belfast was one of the least protected cities in the United Kingdom. Minimal precautions had been taken to provide anti-aircraft protection and blackout and Belfast city and harbour were easily identifiable from the coast. Belfast had no fighter squadron, no barrage balloons, few searchlights, only 20 anti-aircraft guns and no air-raid shelters. The city was totally unprepared.

The first bombing was a novelty to people – even a spectacle. Even though it caused considerable damage and 13 deaths it gave the citizens of Belfast no idea of the devastation to come. The second attack, on the night of Easter Tuesday, 15 April 1941, was the most severe. Around 200 German bombers blitzed the city for six hours, from midnight until 5 a.m. Over 200 tonnes of explosives and 800 fire canisters were dropped. North Belfast suffered the worst of the damage as the bomber pilots mistook, in the bright moonlight of that night, the waterworks at Queen Mary's Gardens on the Antrim Road for a basin in the shipyards, which were their target. Many bombs fell on the surrounding area – the Antrim, Oldpark and Crumlin Roads. York Street Mill was completely razed; 63 houses in two of the adjacent streets were flattened and 35 people killed in the process. Altogether on that terrible night 900 people died and another 1,500 were injured.

The morning after the raid 100,000 people fled Belfast for the safety of the countryside and another 10,000 walked into the hills each night to sleep in the fields. The final raids came on 4–5 May and, even though on this occasion the bombs were on target, once again civilian areas also suffered. Besides the bombing there was a massive incendiary attack, turning the city into a sheet of flames. Belfast appealed for help from across the border and 13 fire brigades from Dublin, Dundalk and Dún Laoghaire came to the aid of the beleaguered city.

Much has been written about these terrible weeks and much remains indelibly printed in the memories of those who endured them, but our specific interest here is in the role played by the Mater Hospital. The raids caused hundreds of casualties and all the hospitals were stretched even beyond their limits. During the night of 15 April the Mater, which was the hospital nearest to the areas bombed, was so overwhelmed by the incoming casualties that, even at an early stage, it found itself unable to accept more stretcher cases. These had to be diverted elsewhere, mostly to temporary first-aid shelters which had quickly been erected. The scene in the hospital was described in a one-sheet edition of the *Irish News* (its offices in Donegall Street had been badly damaged by the raid and the *Belfast News Letter* offered the use of their printing facilities):

> Ghostly white figures of doctors and nurses flitting about examining stretcher cases, the seemingly endless night filled with the roar of guns, crump of heavy bombs and the crash of falling masonry, pierced with the agonizing cries of the injured; such was the scene of the Mater Hospital, Belfast, during a recent blitz in the city.[9]

The nurses' home had been hit by incendiary bombs and severely damaged. The *Irish News* reported:

> The Mater Nurses' Home was one of the first buildings to fall victim to the indiscriminate bombing of the Nazi raiders, and was soon a mass of crackling flames. But there was not one person in the building. All the nurses had answered the call of duty and had immediately reported to the hospital as soon as the alarm was sounded. The total staff worked through the night.[10]

While the raids were going on, casualties who had received treatment and were sufficiently mobile huddled into the air-raid shelters in the hospital grounds. The hospital's morgue capacity was exhausted. Joseph Crilly, then a medical student, recalled:

> at the Mater hospital, within two or three days, the number of corpses had risen to about eighty. In the later stages they were arriving in an extremely mutilated condition – dismembered limbs and fragments of human remains. They over-spilled from the morgue into an open back yard at the rear of the hospital, and into an area around the boiler house … A steady stream of people came to the hospital desperately hoping to identify missing friends and relatives.[11]

Over the days following the Blitz hundreds of bodies were laid out for identification in hospital morgues throughout the city. St George's Market and the Falls Road Baths also had to be used as mortuaries. Many bodies remained unidentified because whole families had been wiped out. The hospitals' lists of dead and injured make tragic and horrifying reading. An eyewitness recorded later:

> One recalls very vividly one of the nights when the city was heavily bombed and a landmine exploded no more than a hundred yards away from the hospital; when the nurses' home was in flames; and when, at one point, bodies were stacked high against the wall of the jail which runs towards the mortuary because there was nowhere else to put them.[12]

After the bombings of 1941, although the city held itself in readiness, the Belfast Blitz was not repeated. In the following years the population had to pick up the threads of normal life and begin to rebuild for future generations. The staff of the Mater Hospital (like those of other hospitals) had responded magnificently to the gargantuan demands made upon them during the horrifying weeks of slaughter. The hospital itself had, mercifully, not suffered structural damage. The damage done to the nurses' home was repaired and soon new expansion was under way.

During the stressful post-war years the superior of the hospital was Sister M. Xavier Larkin. Sister M. Xavier was reputedly a strong woman who, during her term as superior (1945–57), contributed considerably through her leadership to a progressive policy of upgrading the hospital. In this she was loyally supported by the Sisters who headed the main departments: Sister M. Eugene Murphy, matron, Sister M. Camillus O'Doherty, Sister-in-charge of the Extern Department, Sister M. Benedict Monan, Sister-in-charge of St John's Private Nursing Home, Sister M. Gerard Laverty,

Sister-in-charge of the Maternity Unit, Sister M. Genevieve Martin, principal tutor of the School of Nursing.

The Mater Maternity Unit

On 2 July 1945 the Mater Maternity Unit was opened. It would appear, from old records, that this was not the first, but that in 1912 a maternity hospital, St Mary's, had actually been in operation in Lonsdale Terrace. This had been taken over, a few years after its opening, for the overflow from the main hospital of the casualties of World War I, who had been brought to the Mater from the battlefront where so many young men had fallen.

The new unit was an adaptation initially of two, and later of three, terraced houses on the Crumlin Road, facing the nurses' home. The purchase and furnishing of the unit cost about £20,000 and when it was ready it provided for a 24-bed obstetric department.[13] In 1948 it was inspected and approved as a training centre for the first part of the required training in midwifery. In 1952 the unit was recognised by the Royal College of Obstetricians and Gynaecologists for training for the Diploma of Obstetrics examination.

The unit was never intended as a maternity hospital. It was considered temporary, fulfilling a need for a Catholic maternity facility in Northern Ireland until a new maternity department could be built for the Mater. In fact, it continued to serve for the next 46 years, the provisional character of the accommodation creating a homely atmosphere for the mothers and the generations of babies born there. No doubt it had many shortcomings, and it was certainly difficult to run, but that did not limit the service it gave. For example, it dealt with an average of 300 births per year in the 1940s; the number increased to 642 in 1964.

The Welfare State

During the years 1946 to 1948 new health acts were introduced for England and Wales, Scotland and Northern Ireland. In the summer of 1947 steps were being taken for the implementation of an act for Northern Ireland and this, unfortunately, introduced a long period of controversy and negotiations between the Board of Management of the Mater Infirmorum Hospital and the Northern Ireland Government.

On 5 July 1948 the Northern Ireland Health Act came into force. The Mater, as a voluntary hospital, had to be self-supporting and could have done with funding and other benefits from the government. However, the hospital's governing body made a decision to remain outside the health scheme as it wished to remain independent of the Hospitals' Authority's jurisdiction. There were good reasons for taking this option. The most important was the government's decision not to implement a clause in the original act which would enable hospitals in the National Health Service to preserve their religious affiliation. Consequently, the Board of Management of the Mater Hospital believed they lacked the necessary assurance that under the new scheme the hospital's religious character could be retained intact.[14] Moreover, the adoption of the act in Northern Ireland differed in some points from its implementation in other parts of the United Kingdom, specifically with regard to the appointment of the members of the boards of the Northern Ireland hospitals. Another point of contention was that, whereas the English and Scottish acts contained a clause that permitted voluntary hospitals that were unwilling to come under the state scheme to remain outside it and yet receive payment for services rendered, no such provision was made in the Northern Ireland act.

Despite these serious difficulties, the Board of Management of the Mater Hospital tried in every way to cooperate and negotiate with the Minister of Health in order to qualify for the financial benefits available, but it was told quite bluntly that in order to do so it would have to be 100 per cent inside the state scheme. To have entered the scheme would have been to sacrifice the prerogatives of the Mater as a Catholic voluntary hospital, with its own particular ethos, and this the Board of Management felt it could not do. After considerable negotiation the Mater was permitted to opt out of the scheme, with the penalty that it would receive no public funds whatsoever.

These years, when the hospital had no government funding, were years of considerable hardship for those involved in running it. Money for equipment was hard to come by. As well as this, each member of staff was stretched to cover the duties of at least one other person in order to save the cost of salaries. The nurses were paid but the Sisters of Mercy working in the hospital, both in nursing and in auxiliary capacities, gave their services free. For the healthcare provided the hospital had to depend almost entirely on voluntary contributions. These were organised by a body of young men and women known as the Young Philanthropists, who initiated annual collections and many fund-raising schemes, the best-known of which being the Y.P. football pools. These contributions provided the backbone of income for the day-to-day upkeep of the hospital for several decades.[15]

In spite of all these problems the hospital continued to expand. The year 1948 saw the opening of a new lecture theatre in the main hospital, fully equipped for teaching purposes. In the same year Fatima House, a residence on the Crumlin Road for student Sisters of various religious congregations in Ireland and abroad who were pursuing their studies as nursing trainees in

Mater Infirmorum Hospital,

BELFAST.

———◆———

This Hospital is established for the relief of the sick **without distinction of creed.**

Clergymen of all denominations have free access to their co-religionists.

Aid is denied to no one as far as the funds and accommodation permit.

This Hospital receives no Government or Corporation grant—is supported solely by voluntary contributions

Passport to its Wards—Sickness.

It is open at all hours for the reception of accidents and urgent cases.

Subscribers have the right of recommending suitable cases.

Gratuitous medical and surgical advice is given every morning (Sunday excepted) in the Dispensary attached to Hospital. Doors open from 9 till 11 a.m.

Mission statement of the Mater Infirmorum Hospital, Belfast, 1883 the Mater, was opened. In 1950 Bedeque House, also on the Crumlin Road (and named after the original house in which the Mater Hospital was founded) was opened as a residence for medical officers and students at the hospital.

In 1952 a neuropsychiatric unit was opened in the main hospital, in Flat 4. The Belfast Mater was the first general hospital to include a department dealing with psychiatric disorders. The opening of the Maternity Unit and Psychiatric Department in the Mater was a deliberate policy on the part of Bishop Mageean and the hospital trustees to make sure that Catholic ethical standards in these two fields of medical care be preserved.

Professional training had always been an important part of the services provided by the Mater and by the 1940s the hospital was engaged in training on several levels: medicine, nursing and radiography. Not least among the other services provided, as befitted a hospital run by religious Sisters, was that of pastoral care. A former senior nursing tutor, Sister M. Genevieve Martin, recalls that an important aim in the minds of the Sisters working in the hospital, in keeping with the charism of the Mercy Institute, was always to treat the patients with tenderness and respect and to show compassion for them in their illness. Besides their physical healing and well-being, the spiritual welfare of the patients was also considered of great importance and this care was an essential part of the Catholic ethos of the hospital. Ministers of the various Protestant churches and denominations were made welcome when they came to visit members of their congregations. For Catholics, the priest chaplain came each day to check about all new admissions and visited the Catholic patients in each ward in turn. Where necessary he administered the sacraments and often had the privilege of reconciling to God and bringing to peace some who had strayed from their faith over the years. Sister M. Genevieve remarks that 'Many, many patients were reconciled with God; many received the sacrament of extreme unction, some baptism, and in some cases even the sacrament of matrimony.'[16]

The hospital Mercy community

The presence of the Sisters, Sister M. Genevieve believes, was an 'incentive to spiritual living'.[17] Up until the late 1960s all the Sisters engaged in the hospital in various capacities resided there and, as far as their nursing, administrative and ancillary duties allowed, followed the regular routine of community life. They lived in the so-called 'convent portion' – the floors above the main entrance. Several times each day they gathered in the hospital chapel for their spiritual exercises. There was Mass each morning, to which patients and staff were always welcome, and they recited the Little

Office of Our Lady (later replaced by the Divine Office) at appropriate times during the day. Spiritual reading, community lecture and personal prayer were all also part of the daily horarium. The rosary of Our Lady was recited every day in the wards by the Sisters-in-charge and again each evening in the chapel when all the nurses who could attend were present. The Sisters saw their nursing vocation as a way of living out their Christian faith and of a particular charism of the Mercy apostolate. The nurses were encouraged to join the Sodality of Our Lady, which had weekly meetings and annual retreats. They also formed the choir for Sunday Mass in the chapel.

The vital Catholic ethos of the hospital was appreciated even by the many patients who were not of the same faith and the chapel was a haven of comfort and prayer for many patients and their anxious relatives.

1   Quoted in R.S. Casement, 'History of the Mater Infirmorum Hospital', address to Obstetrical Society (MIHA, 1968).
2   Sister M. Genevieve Martin, pers. comm., 1992. Sister M. Genevieve was on the staff of the hospital, first as a trainee nurse and then as a member of staff. She became a nurse tutor and later principal tutor and head of the School of Nursing there. For further biographical details see Chapter 23.
3   J.F. Fleetwood, *The history of medicine in Ireland* (2nd ed., Dublin: Skellig Press, 1983), p. 232 *et seq.*
4   Mater Infirmorum Hospital, annual report (MIHA and SPCMB, 1932).
5   Mother M.M. Toner to bishop (Archives, SPCMB, 13 September 1933). See also report on the chapel opening ceremony, *Irish News*, 28 October 1935.
6   Casement, *op. cit.*, p. 16.
7   Heatley, *op. cit.*, p. 65.
8   B. Barton, *The Blitz: Belfast in the war years* (Belfast: Blackstaff Press, 1989), p. 146. Barton refers also to Brian Moore's description in his book, *The emperor of ice-cream* (London: Mayflower, 1970). Moore was an air-raid warden at the hospital at the time of the Blitz. See also reports about the Blitzes in Northern Ireland in the local newspapers of the time.
9   *Irish News,* 16 April 1941.
10 Ibid.
11 Quoted in Casement, *op. cit.*
12 Sister M. Genevieve Martin, pers. comm., 1992.
13 Mater Infirmorum Hospital annual report (MIHA, 1965).
14 For information on these issues see Fleetwood, *op. cit.*, p. 180.
15 For details of the early negotiations with the Northern Ireland Ministry of Health see the article by Reverend M. Kelly in Sisters of Mercy, 'Convent of Our Lady of Mercy, St Paul's, Belfast: centenary souvenir, 1854–1954' (MCA), p. 24 *et seq.*
16 Sister M. Genevieve Martin, pers. comm., 1992.
17 Ibid.

16

THE MERCY COMMUNITY, 1920s–40s

In 1904, the Sisters of Mercy of Down and Connor had marked 50 years of growth and achievement by the celebration of the golden jubilee of their arrival in Belfast.

What was the convent like in those early years of the twentieth century, when the foundation had been stabilised and the apostolate established? Some description of this has been left to us by a Sister who entered the community in 1908 and led a very full and fruitful life, passing away in 1978 after 70 years' service. She was Sister M. Patricia Doran, a strong and valiant woman like so many of her contemporaries in the community.

In an interview with the present writer in the mid-1960s, she described St Paul's Convent as she remembered it in the first decades of the twentieth century (see early plan p. 136). Now that the convent is no more, it may be of interest to our readers to visualise it as it was then, when religious life was at a high point of vitality and the community was expanding and building and planning for the future, stretching its capacities to meet the many demands, both internal and external, on its resources.

By the end of the first decade of the twentieth century, St Paul's Convent, whose construction had begun with a three-storey east-facing facade, now formed a complete square. The original block contained, on the ground floor, a spacious entrance hall with a large and bright reception room and a community room on either side, along with a refectory, a kitchen and other offices. On the first floor, over the hall, was Our Lady's Oratory, with 'cells', as the Sisters' bedrooms were called (in monastic style), the noviceship and the room of the mistress of novices. On the second floor was another corridor of cells and an infirmary. The front hallway on the ground floor opened onto a wide tiled and arched Gothic-style enclosed cloister, which ran the length of the building.

Over the ensuing years extensions to the main building were added gradually. A ground-floor north wing provided for a large new community room, with a superior's office adjoining a community chapel and a sacristy. These also opened onto an internal cloister at right angles to the cloister of the main building. Then a west wing was added, which accommodated on the ground floor the refectory, kitchen and services area, and above that a corridor of cells. Along the ground floor of the west wing the cloister was extended and some years later the square was completed by the addition of a south-facing wing of enclosed and open cloisters. The building now surrounded a large central quadrangle, a sort of cloister garth, which became known as Calvary when a life-sized Calvary group was mounted in the centre of this area. This was a calm and peaceful 'garden enclosed' into which the four cloisters gave view through mullioned Gothic windows and where shrubs and flowers abounded in season.

Behind the west wing of the convent were quite a spacious garden and a little community cemetery. Beyond its walls rose the Crumlin Road Jail, but this imposing edifice did not spoil the serenity and peace of the flower-filled space.

Before 1910, between the convent and the Crumlin Road and alongside the Convent Avenue schools and orphanage, was sited the Birds' Nest, a house sponsored by a Protestant charitable body to give accommodation to homeless children and provide soup daily to others who came in off the street. However, by the turn of the century it had run out of resources and the community bought the site to build a new convent chapel through the benevolence of the Hamill sisters of Trench House.

Across from the convent were the orphanage and schools. The main school building was three storeyed, providing a baby room, a kindergarten (boys' and girls') and classrooms for the national school, facing the Crumlin Road. Adjoining it, and alongside Convent Avenue, was Our Lady's Private School for Young Ladies, a two-storey building with its entrance from the garden on the Crumlin Road. On the first floor of this were two classrooms, one the 'doffers' room', where the mill girls were given lessons, and the other the 'sixth book'.

As the years went by and the community grew in numbers, additional accommodation was needed in the convent. In 1925 a third storey was built over the north wing with cells for the choir novices (St Joseph's corridor). Immediately afterwards the building of a new corridor on the west side was begun, with cells and facilities for the lay novices. After completion it was blessed on 8 December 1926. In 1935 a new storey, to give additional accommodation for the professed Sisters, was erected over the station corridor (south wing). These upper floors, now added to the north, west and south wings, completed the enclosure of the central quadrangle and gave this very monastic-looking building an appearance of completeness and permanence. Finally, to the rear of the convent, in the garden area, a new refectory was built for the lay Sisters (in 1927). This gave them the facilities to have their meals independently of the main refectory at the times that suited them best. The refectory was further extended in 1953.

The 1920s brought some constitutional changes for the community. In recommendations from the Congregation for Religious in Rome the community were informed that all the Sisters would no longer make annual vows, as was the custom, but from then on would make both triennial vows (that is, for three years at first profession) and then final vows. The making of the first (triennial) vows would be a private ceremony. The public profession ceremony would take place at the time of final vows.[1]

Also in the early 1920s, the constitutions of the Sisters of Mercy were revised in accordance with the new Code of Canon Law, and received approbation from Rome in January 1926. This revision was careful to preserve the spirit of the foundress, Catherine McAuley, while at the same time allowing for whatever adaptations were necessary to meet the particular needs and widely varying circumstances of the many Mercy communities spread throughout the world. It is also interesting to note that, while each Mercy motherhouse was autonomous – that is, independent in organisation and administration and not under an international Superior General – this revision, initiated by the Sisters of Mercy in Carysfort Park, Dublin,[2] was accepted by the universal congregation. At this time also the Holy See recognised the Mercy Congregation to be of pontifical rite. From then on it was fully recognised by the universal Catholic Church as a religious congregation and was answerable only to the pope (pontiff) in Rome.

Educational reforms

The new political regime in Northern Ireland naturally affected the apostolates of the Sisters of Mercy in the six northern counties. The partitioning of Ireland in 1921 brought two systems of education for the island, one for the south and one for the north. In February 1922 the northern schools were formally transferred to the new Northern Ireland Ministry of Education in Belfast. The first minister of education was Lord Londonderry and he found that education in the new state needed urgent attention, there being a marked inadequacy of school places and a need for the replacement of many of the existing decrepit school buildings. He appointed the Lynn Commission to look into the matter and make recommendations.

The recommendations of the Lynn Commission resulted in the Education Act (Northern Ireland) of 1923, which recognised three classes of schools according to the form of management and the manner of financing of each.[3] Notably, the national-school system was abandoned in

Northern Ireland; local education authorities (LEAs) took over the former national schools, which became known as public elementary schools.

In the event, the 1923 Education Act was unacceptable to all the churches (many of the schools were owned by church or religious bodies). Amendments in 1925 and 1930 made it fully acceptable to Protestants but the majority of the Catholic school managers (and the bishops) wished their schools to remain entirely independent of the local education authorities – that is, they opted for class 3 status, which qualified them to receive only minimal financial assistance from the government.[4] However, a compromise was reached and in 1930 grants made available for the building of voluntary schools eased their burden somewhat.

With the new education legislation the building of primary schools was undertaken as a matter of urgency. In addition, a scholarship scheme to facilitate the admission of selected children from lower-income homes to secondary and further education was introduced on a small scale. Obviously this benefited the poorer Catholic population, whose expectations of advancement in the new state were pretty low. Around Northern Ireland many convent schools (and also those run by the Christian Brothers) expanded their provision for secondary-level education. The Dominican Sisters, for example, opened two grammar schools in Belfast. The Sisters of Mercy in Belfast took the option of concentrating on elementary education. There, they believed, lay the greatest need in the city. A specific indication of this was the closing of the pension school at the convent. A further reform in the education system came in 1932 with the introduction of a new curriculum. This was timely and was welcomed by teachers, managers, administrators and school inspectors alike.

Some years later further steps were taken in the process aimed at upgrading the teaching profession. In 1937 new regulations were issued from the Ministry of Education, making the certification of teachers obligatory. As far as religious communities engaged in education were concerned, this was scarcely anything new. The importance of training for the teaching profession had already been emphasised more than 30 years previously (on 7 December 1894) when a synod of the Catholic bishops in Maynooth issued a statement addressed to all religious communities involved with education. The meeting laid down that 'all Religious who are engaged in the work of teaching in schools should receive a special training for that work and bishops are asked to exercise the utmost vigilance in this matter which is declared by the meeting to be of the highest importance'.[5]

The implications of the 1937 legislation for the Sisters of Mercy in the schools in Belfast and Bangor is noted in the community acts of chapter of this time. Here we read that the superior (Mother M. Magdalen Toner) informed the Sisters that, according to the new legislation issued by the Ministry of Education:

> From the present date (1 January 1937) the Sisters on the teaching staffs must retire at the age of sixty-five and in the future no new members of the community will be allowed to teach in the schools unless certified by the Ministry or who have at least passed the King's Scholarship Examination. In the latter case the Sisters will be allowed four years to teach at the end of which period they must leave the school and enter for a course of training, otherwise they will not be recognised as members of the teaching staff.[6]

The Mercy communities took seriously their teaching vocation. In the community horarium for each school day, time was set aside for the preparation of lessons, usually the hour and a half between vespers and supper, and the Sisters with experience in teaching, and in particular subjects, were expected to help the neophytes. Particular attention was given to pedagogy (the art of teaching) and classroom management and discipline. Good teamwork was valued and was evident in a successful and happy school. The harmony and stability the school provided was an ethos the Sisters considered very important, endeavouring to realise the dictum of the foundress, which said, 'Wherever a religious woman presides, there peace and good order are generally to be found.'[7]

Saint Brigid's Club for Girls

The Mercy apostolate was ever expanding at the convent, Crumlin Road. Sister M. Dympna Fegan's zeal had been directed not only towards founding the home and a school for the blind[8] but also towards caring for poor women 'of good character' who, coming into the city for employment, had found themselves jobless and homeless among strangers.

When the children had vacated the orphanage premises on Convent Avenue, and a small group of blind women and children was established there, there was still room to spare. Part of the industrial-school building had been incorporated into the national school as classrooms. Sister M. Dympna opened St Brigid's Club for Girls on the feast of St Brigid, 1 February 1921. This succeeded the first House of Mercy, which had been on Royal Terrace and had been absorbed into the site for the new Mater Infirmorum Hospital at the end of 1898. As the club became well known there was such a demand for admission that, a few years later, another house had to be rented, 37 Crumlin Road. This was opened by Bishop McRory on 27 June 1927.

An interesting letter from Sister M. Dympna to the bishop, written on 23 January 1930, gives us a little insight into the trouble taken to stretch the meagre finances available in order not to have to turn away any young woman in need:

> The house [37 Crumlin Road] was in bad order and had to be cleaned and patched up before we could go into it. The painting, plumbing and carpenter's work cost roughly £65. Extra cash for structural alterations, etc., was £17-5d. Rev. Mother paid the £65 and perhaps a little more as I had very little money for the Club at the time except what I got to get furniture.[9]

The owner, Mr McGann, had written demanding payment of arrears in rent he claimed was due for the previous two and three-quarter years (in fact, Sister M. Dympna had not received the key of the house until May 1927). Sister M. Dympna begged that the bishop 'would give this great charity a favourable consideration regarding the amount of rent to be paid at present – £110'.[10] There is no record to tell us if the bishop concurred. However that may have been, the club continued its good service of giving a temporary home to girls coming to seek work in the city and also providing hostel accommodation for servant girls and others, who were only charged a nominal sum for their maintenance.

There was always great demand for accommodation in the club and hostel so, when the women and children of St Brigid's Home and School for the Blind moved to Abbeyville in March 1934, the building did not lie idle. The young women from 37 Crumlin Road moved in to join their companions on Convent Avenue and a more permanent St Brigid's Club and Hostel was established. Thus flourished the work of hospitality started by Sister M. Dympna in response to a genuine need of the times.

Sister M. Dympna went to Abbeyville (see Chapter 18) when the blind children and women moved there in February 1934. She remained there for about 15 years (that is, as long as she was able to work) and then returned to St Paul's Convent for the declining years of her life. An obituary pays tribute to this very enterprising woman:

> In the late 1940s Sr. M. Dympna, then in her 80s, returned to St Paul's Convent, Crumlin Road, and well-deserved retirement. She went to her eternal reward on 9 September 1953 (Feast of the Holy Name of Mary), but not before she endured the painful experience of hearing that the upper floor of her beloved Home and School in Abbeyville had gone up in smoke when a disastrous fire broke out on the night of 9 May 1953. Fortunately no lives were lost, but virtually it was the 'death

knell' for Abbeyville Home and School for the Blind. However, as far
as Sr. M. Dympna was concerned, her life's work was accomplished,
and as long as Abbeyville remains Sr. M. Dympna's name will always be
remembered.[11]

Sister M. Dympna was the last Sister to be buried in the little convent
graveyard at Crumlin Road.

The club on Convent Avenue continued to function for more than 50
years and many young women experienced the solicitous care of the various
Sisters in charge there. Besides the young women who came to the club of
their own accord, charitable organisations – St Vincent de Paul, the Legion
of Mary, the Salvation Army and occasionally even the police – made
frequent requests for decent young women, newly arrived in the city and in
need of a temporary home, to be accepted. Not only were these young
women housed, but they were also helped to find employment and their
own private accommodation elsewhere before they left the Sisters' care. The
Sisters never refused any girl admission to the hostel, no matter how late
the hour of arrival on the doorstep. When necessary they went to the trains
bringing the young girls coming to the city from rural areas, and especially
provided shelter during the war years when accommodation was scarce and
work had to go on.

Over the years many wonderful Sisters took a motherly interest in, and
gave wise counsel to, the many young women who passed through the
hostel's welcoming doors. This good work continued beside the convent
until the building was demolished, along with the school, in the late 1960s,
in view of plans to build a more spacious and modern school on the site.
Sadly, at this time, the familiar Angelus bell tolled from the tower of the
club for the last time. The bell was given to St Michael's Church,
Andersonstown, when it opened in 1972.

New accommodation was found for the hostel not far away when two
adjoining three-storey houses were purchased in Thorndale Avenue, off the
Antrim Road. The new hostel was named Villa Maria. The Sisters-in-charge
at the club and hostel were: Sisters M. Dympna Fegan, M. Raphael
Kennedy, M. Philomena McMullan (on Convent Avenue) and Sisters
M. Mercy Cummins, M. Majella McAlinden and Briege O'Callaghan
(Villa Maria).

By the third decade of the twentieth century the Sisters of the Belfast
community were engaged in schools, hospitals, a hospice for the dying, a
home and school for the blind, an industrial school, a club for working girls
and visitation of the poor and the sick. In the three convent public
elementary schools in Belfast (Crumlin Road, Star of the Sea and Sussex

Place) there were upwards of 1,400 children. The Mater Infirmorum Hospital had attached to it a private nursing home (St John's). The community, at the beginning of the 1930s, numbered over 70 Sisters: 55 of them were professed, 12 of them were novices and there were several postulants. It would continue to grow and flourish for the next 20 years or more.

Celebrations

The Belfast Sisters of Mercy could, then, join wholeheartedly in the great celebration of the centenary of the founding of the Mercy Institute by Mother Catherine McAuley on 12 December 1831. The centenary was celebrated by all the Sisters of Mercy in Ireland, England, Scotland, America, Australia and New Zealand and in all the far-flung mission lands. On the feast of Our Lady of Mercy, 24 September 1931, the celebration took place at St Paul's Convent, Crumlin Road. This lacked nothing in splendour, as we gather from the report published in the local newspaper:

> The ceremonies commenced with the Missa Cantata 'Kyrie Magnae Deus Potentiae' sung by Very Rev J. Hendley, D.D., in the convent chapel, the choir being composed of members of the community, and afterwards the Blessed Sacrament was exposed for adoration. In the afternoon a procession in honour of the Blessed Sacrament took place throughout the convent grounds, which had been tastefully decorated for the occasion with garlands of bay, shields bearing sacred inscriptions and representations surmounted by the Papal colours, and many coloured candle lights.
>
> The procession was composed of members of the community, children from the various schools and from the Home for the Blind, nurses from the hospital and students from St Malachy's College. The music was the age-old plain chant hymns of the Church sung by the College boys under the direction of Very Rev Dr Hendley: the Ave Verum, Adoro Te, Pange Lingua, Salve Regina and Ave Regina Caelorum. At a beautiful open-air altar Benediction of the Most Blessed Sacrament was given, and afterwards the procession returned to the chapel where solemn Benediction was given and the Te Deum chanted.
>
> Thus was brought to a close the preliminary celebrations of the Centenary of the founding of the Order of Mercy [sic], which will have their culmination on 12 December next.[12]

The 1940s opened with yet another congregation celebration, the centenary of the death of Catherine McAuley on 11 November 1941. This celebration was called for by the Sisters of Mercy in the United States and introduced the issue of the cause for Catherine McAuley's canonisation. In a letter of 11

November 1935 Sister M. Carmelita, mother general of the Sisters of Mercy, Bethesda, Maryland, USA, sent a circular letter to the superiors of all the Mercy communities throughout the world reminding them of the anniversary to come in 1941 and raising the issue:

> My dear Reverend Mother,
> On November 11, 1941, the centenary of the death of our revered Foundress, every Sister of Mercy in the world will rejoice in spirit with our loved Mother, and will praise God for the good that has been wrought through the Institute she founded. But will there not be a note of sadness in our joy? Will we not feel that we have failed in our love for Mother Catherine McAuley if, by November 11, 1941, we have not so much as raised our voices to plead for her canonisation?[13]

She went on to urge 'every Sister of Mercy in the world to ask the Archbishop of Dublin to begin the process'[14] and to encourage relations, friends and associates of the congregation to join in the petition for the cause's introduction. When the superior of the Carysfort Park Sisters of Mercy forwarded the petition to the archbishop, Most Reverend Edward J. Byrne, she received a favourable response. The matter was put into the hands of Reverend John McErlean, S.J., of Milltown Park, Dublin, as the named vice-postulator, and this put in train the long process which is still under way.

As we have seen, many changes and developments had taken place for the Belfast Mercy community during the first 30 years of the twentieth century. The beginning of the fourth decade was to bring entirely new challenges, in particular with the outbreak of World War II, an event that was to affect the lives of millions of people and even to touch tragically and disastrously the city of Belfast and other locations in the remote province of Northern Ireland. The story of the war has already been introduced in the history of the Mater Hospital. Its effects and consequences were wide ranging for all who lived in Northern Ireland at the time – and, in fact, for the whole of Ireland, though the republic remained technically neutral. The story deserves fuller telling.

---

[1]   In a Mercy community, at first profession a Sister was given a brass crucifix, worn in the cincture; at final profession she was given the profession ring, the traditional seal of life commitment.

[2]   Correspondence, Rome to Carysfort, (MCA, January and February 1926). Carysfort Park, Blackrock, was an extension of the Baggot Street Mercy Convent and became the motherhouse in Dublin.

3   See Chapter 19 for details about this system.
4   Ibid.
5   Meeting of Catholic bishops in Maynooth (SPCMB, December 1894); *Belfast Telegraph*, November/December 1894.
6   Acts of chapter, SPCMB, 1937.
7   Sisters of Mercy, *op. cit.* (*Rule*), Chapter 11, Section 7.
8   See Chapter 18.
9   Sister M. Dympna Fegan to Bishop McRory (Archives, SPCMB, 23 January 1930).
10 Ibid.
11 *Irish News*, 16 September 1953.
12 *Irish News*, September 1931.
13 Sister M. Carmelita to superiors of Mercy communities (Archives, SPCMB, 11 November 1935).
14 Ibid.

17

WORLD WAR II
AND THE POST-WAR YEARS

In the summer of 1939 war clouds were threatening western Europe. Even before Great Britain was actively engaged in the hostilities of what was to become World War II it was suspected that if Britain came under attack from the air, Belfast, with its harbour, shipyards, aircraft factories and engineering works, would be a probable target for enemy bombardment. Consequently there were discussions about precautionary measures, but these were only half hearted as most members of the Stormont government did not seriously believe that the city would be attacked. Nevertheless, in June 1939, the Education (Evacuated Children) Act (Northern Ireland) was passed, providing for the evacuation of 70,000 children, in particular from the urban areas. In July 1940 the scheme was put into operation but in the event fewer than 18,000 children registered. In Belfast itself it was intended that 17,000 children be evacuated but very few children actually left. On evacuation day only 7,000 children turned up and by the spring of 1941 more than half of these had returned to the city, to be caught, unfortunately, in the terrible Blitzes of April and May of that year.

When the first Belfast Blitz took place that Easter week much of the bombing was concentrated on a small area of north Belfast: the lower Antrim Road, New Lodge, Duncairn, North Queen Street and Peter's Hill areas were devastated. Most of the Crumlin Road Convent School children came from these districts and many lost their lives. Two schools in St Patrick's Parish, St Malachy's Boys' School and St Malachy's Girls' School were completely destroyed and the Star of the Sea Schools on Halliday's Road were badly damaged. As has been mentioned in a previous chapter, it is believed that the waterworks – two large reservoirs in Alexandra Park on the Antrim Road – were mistaken for the Belfast docks, while the large industrial complexes, Gallagher's Factory and the York Street Flax Spinning Mills were intentionally targeted. The huge York Street Mill collapsed on top of the streets of small workers' houses nearby, burying them completely under steel, machinery and rubble, at the cost of many lives. Many of the people who escaped this devastation left the district, never to return.

The buildings of the Crumlin Road Convent were not spared.

Incendiary bombs dropped on the south-east wing of the school, burning the top storey, and much of the school furniture and equipment was destroyed. The school principal, Sister M. de Sales, and the other Sisters made heroic attempts to stem the conflagration but only by the arrival of the Dublin firefighting services was the blaze brought under control.

After these attacks upon Belfast evacuation became a very serious matter, but it did not happen in the orderly manner that had been envisaged. The horrific experience of the Easter-week Blitz triggered off a mass exodus of tens of thousands of citizens. The following days and nights saw masses of men, women and children on the move, seeking refuge in the countryside either on a temporary or long-term basis.[1] The official estimate is that, in the weeks following the Blitz, around 26,000 people fled Belfast. Many others moved out to the hills each night, returning home with the dawn when it was thought that the danger had passed. The bombings, with their consequent death and destruction, were terrifying events, a small sample of the horrendous bombings that were searing London, Birmingham and some European cities at this time.

Evacuation

After the first Blitz evacuation became virtually mandatory. The Sisters of Mercy in the Belfast schools were called upon to help coordinate the evacuation of the children who attended their own schools. Some Sisters were requested to go with the children and were assigned to the convent schools in Newry, Lurgan, Warrenpoint, Dungannon, Cookstown and Bessbrook – a great dispersal of both pupils and their teachers. Others remained in Belfast with the children who refused to be evacuated, and the convent schools continued with very small classes for the rest of that year.

From the annals of the Sisters of Mercy, Newry, we learn that on Easter Tuesday, the day after the first bombing:

> refugees poured into Newry where they were fed and comforted in the elementary schools. The Superior of the Lurgan community sent word to the Sisters of Mercy, Belfast. About twenty Sisters arrived, all very shocked after their terrible ordeal. (Some stayed on for two years.)[2]

After the second bombing, in May, refugees from Belfast streamed to Lurgan. They were given shelter in the convent and school buildings and cared for by the community and many willing helpers. About 200 children from Belfast were boarded in various houses in the town, and classes were organised for them in St Joseph's Hall and taught by the Belfast Sisters who had accompanied them.[3]

As far as the Crumlin Road Convent was concerned, the stresses and strains of those war years fell ultimately on the shoulders of Mother M. Magdalen Toner, who was superior from 1940 to 1946. A native of Belfast, Ellen Toner had entered the community in 1905. She was 46 years of age when she assumed a leadership role, a position which she held for 15 years in all: she was superior from 1931 to 1937, assistant from 1937 to 1940 and superior again from 1940 to 1946. After her retirement from the office of superior in 1946 she served as mistress of novices for most of the remainder of her active life. Mother Magdalen was a very active and able woman, a woman of great faith and prayer, and her courage and leadership supported the community through the very difficult war years. Apart from dealing with emergencies on the spot, she saw fit to rent a house in Ballygalgath, County Down in 1941, to which Sisters could go, if necessary, in times of danger.[4]

Gradually, as the danger of another Blitz seemed to have passed, the children filtered back to Belfast and by the following Christmas (1941) most had returned and an attempt was made to repair the damage done and resume normal life and schooling.

The hospitality and care given so generously during this time of great need created close bonds of gratitude and friendship between the Belfast Sisters of Mercy and their host communities in Newry, Lurgan, Dungannon, Cookstown and Bessbrook, which continued throughout the years. Regular visits between the communities sustained friendships which were valued by all.

Precautionary measures had also been taken for the Mater Hospital. After the April Blitz, which had so nearly caused serious damage to the hospital, a scheme for partial evacuation for the duration was proposed, both in order to safeguard the patients and to increase the hospital's capacity for emergency services in the event of further attacks.

This foresight was inspired, as the raid of 4–5 May quickly followed. The nurses' home had been bombed and now the top floor of Flat 3 was used as a nurses' dormitory. Patients and Sisters from St John's Nursing Home were evacuated to Lurgan and accommodated in St Michael's Boarding School until it was considered safe to return to Belfast. Mother M. Gonzaga O'Kane, then assistant superior in St Paul's Convent, resigned her office in order to take up duty as superior of the hospital and oversee the necessary changes. At this time Miss Earley was matron and Sister M. Eugene Murphy was in charge of the Extern Department.

Conditions for running a hospital were far from easy at this time. As a precaution in times of air-raids water and gas were turned off at the mains. Water carts came each day and the water had to be boiled before use.

Blackout was enforced after dark and all the windows had to be covered with blackout blinds or dark-brown paper. Food was rationed and patients had to bring their ration books. This requirement continued even for several years after the war.

Convent under fire

Sisters M. Genevieve Martin, M. Kevin Drain and M. Finbarr Maloney left us accounts of what life was like during these traumatic war years. The food rationing posed considerable difficulties for the Sisters who had to provide the meals for the community (and, though the war ended in 1945, rationing continued for another five years). At times, when there was serious threat of air-raids, there was no sleep, no hot water, no gas. When the siren went during the night all had to rise and go immediately to the air-raid shelter that had been constructed in the garden. Water was turned off at the mains and, as in the hospital, everyone was dependent on the water carts that delivered supplies. After the first raid, when the danger from incendiary bombs was realised, Sisters had to take turns as firewatchers on the top corridors and all the baths and basins had to be filled with water in case of fire. However, amidst all this surrounding disruption, regular life went on as usual in the convent. After one of the raids and a night in the shelter, Father McMullan, convent chaplain (and president of St Malachy's College) celebrated Mass at 5.30 a.m. – and permission was given to talk at breakfast.

At this time, when Belfast was under threat of bombing, the novices were offered the opportunity to return to their homes. Most were from the Republic of Ireland, which was neutral during the war. None elected to go, though their living in Belfast must have been a cause for considerable concern to their families. However, everyone trusted in God's protection and no one in the community suffered harm.

During the war years the community prayed fervently for the safety of the schoolchildren and all others under their care. When the war ended there was a procession of the Blessed Sacrament around St Paul's Convent in thanksgiving for the safety of the Sisters and the convent, the hospital and all those who had contributed so fearlessly and generously to the care of the afflicted in these times of terrible crisis.

The post-war years – changes in education

When the war ended the slow climb to recovery began, with a Labour government in Britain, the inauguration of the Welfare State and major education reforms. The Education Act of 1947, which extended to Northern Ireland, discontinued the existing system of elementary schools. These schools had catered for children up to the school-leaving age of 14 years.

There was now a new system of primary schools for children up to the age of 11 years and compulsory secondary schooling between the ages of 11 and 15. Post-primary education was of three types. The first was the grammar school. This would cater for the most academically gifted children and was a continuation of the old grammar-school system. Entrance to the grammar schools would be by means of a test at the age of 11 and the pupils could continue there until they went to university. The second type was the secondary intermediate school. This was a new type of school designed to provide an education after the age of 11 years for those children for whom the more academic courses were not suitable. The third type was the technical school. This type of school continued as before and provided vocational training courses. Pupils had the option to transfer to a technical school at the age of 13. The test the children did at the age of 11 – an examination in arithmetic, English and general intelligence – became known as the 'qualifying examination' or the '11 plus'. The first qualifying examination, for primary-seven pupils, was held in 1948. In Northern Ireland it was to become an important feature of primary schools for the next 50 years and more.

The Northern Ireland Education Act of 1947 provided free post-primary education for all children and generous grants made the possibility of university education available to able young people who otherwise could not have afforded it. The act made further provision in terms of financial aid to the voluntary schools, increasing this from 50 per cent to 65 per cent (a figure raised to 80 per cent in 1969). Also, the salaries of teachers in these voluntary schools were at last paid in full by the Ministry of Education according to qualifications and length of service. With the new legislation, the voluntary (including the convent) schools had more money to spend on equipment, meals, classroom maintenance and the replacement of out-of-date books.

The rising birth rate of the post-war years meant that more children than ever before were attending primary schools, as is reflected in the statistics for the Belfast Mercy primary schools:[5]

Name of school	No. of children on roll	No. under 11½ years	No. over 11½ years
St Paul's Convent P.E.S., Crumlin Road	690	480	210
St Malachy's Convent P.E.S., Sussex Place	454	344	110
Star of the Sea Convent P.E.S.	250	183	67

From the Crumlin Road Convent School the boys were transferred, in 1947, to other schools in the district in order to provide additional accommodation for the girls. By 1954 there was an average of 800 girls attending the school. The classrooms that had been destroyed during the air-raids were reconstructed on modern lines and new, up-to-date equipment was installed. The schools maintained high standards in their curriculum. Besides the required school subjects the pupils were taught speech and drama and Irish language, history and music. As always, pride of place was given to religious and moral education and all the teachers collaborated to maintain an ethos of truthfulness, generosity, responsibility and punctuality among the pupils.

The setting up of the free secondary intermediate-school system posed financial difficulties for the voluntary schools. Most of the Protestant schools had transferred to the local education authorities and therefore were fully financed. The Catholic schools, still voluntary, could only with difficulty raise the funds to build secondary schools. When the school-leaving age was raised they were permitted to allow their pupils to stay on in the primary schools with senior classes for the 11–15-year-olds. These schools were known as 'unreorganised primary schools' and permission for these was short-term, pending the building of the secondary intermediate schools which would be largely funded by the Catholic owners. From 1970 on the Catholic voluntary schools gradually joined the 'four-and-two' system – in which management committees were made up of four representatives of the former managers and two of the local government authorities – so that they could financially be maintained in full independence.

As we know, the Belfast Sisters of Mercy did not conduct grammar schools but they did feel an obligation to provide secondary intermediate education for the pupils of their primary schools until they reached the new school-leaving age of 15. At first the community proposed to integrate a secondary intermediate school into the existing Crumlin Road Primary School, with an extension on Twickenham Street across the road. This idea was put to the Ministry of Education, as we read from a report submitted to the ministry from a senior inspector who was asked to look into the matter:

> The scheme submitted provides for the establishment of an Intermediate School for girls by the division of the existing Crumlin Road Convent Primary School building into two self-contained schools, one to continue as a primary school and the other to serve as an intermediate school for the senior pupils of the Crumlin Road and Star of the Sea (Halliday's Road) Convent Schools.[6]

His summary of the plan was followed by a description of the restructuring that would have to be carried out and the pros and cons of the project. The inspector's response was that, in the very limited space available in the present school premises, the plan submitted was not feasible:

> For the reasons stated, it appears to me impossible to accommodate a primary school and an intermediate school for the present and prospective enrolments in the existing buildings; and the Twickenham Street site provides no solution. In the circumstances, therefore, I recommend that the application in its present form be refused. Knowing the anxiety of the community to continue and develop its long and honourable educational tradition by the establishment of an intermediate school, I deeply regret the necessity of having to make this recommendation.[7]

While the proposal was turned down, the community considered it important that the new secondary intermediate school should be in a place accessible to the convent-school pupils, mostly from St Patrick's Parish and north Belfast. In the summer of 1949 a suitable plot of land was purchased on the Ballysillan Road, on the outskirts of north Belfast, near the village of Ligoniel and two and a half miles away from the convent on Crumlin Road. It was a very fine site, on the foothills of Divis Mountain, with a sweeping vista to the south of the city, Belfast Lough and the Castlereagh Hills in County Down.

The plan was for a school for 400 pupils, priority to be given to the girls from the Crumlin Road and Star of the Sea Convent Schools. There were some preliminary problems with drainage of the site, since it was discovered to be on the springline of the mountain, but these were largely overcome and on 3 August 1954 Bishop Mageean cut the first sod of what was to be Our Lady of Mercy Secondary Intermediate School (afterwards popularly called Ballysillan).

The older pupils of Sussex Place Convent School (which was in St Malachy's Parish) went St Monica's Secondary Intermediate School on the Ravenhill Road.

A second spring: a new vitality in religious life

Most Catholics will agree that the 1950s was a decade of notable growth and vitality for religious life in the western world. Large numbers of young people entered the seminaries, monasteries and active religious congregations, and missions as well as apostolic works at home were expanded with enthusiasm and zeal.

The Belfast community shared in this new vitality. At the beginning of the 1950s the community numbered almost a hundred; this included four Sisters in simple vows (that is, temporary profession), four novices and five postulants. At that time the Sisters in simple vows, while mostly pursuing studies, remained part of the noviceship community.

To the postulants and novices, for whom all was new, the year seemed a round of receptions, professions, jubilees, holy days and feast days – 'big days', in convent parlance. There were also the annual retreats and, of course, an occasional funeral – not necessarily a sad event in a religious community if a Sister had lived to the fullness of her years. There were also joyous school events such as first communion day, which was also a general communion day for all the pupils, when the children came back to the convent school for a celebratory breakfast and all the novices and postulants were recruited to help and joined in the general rejoicing. Mother M. Eugene Murphy was reverend mother at this time, Mother M. Bernard McKillop was assistant and Mother M. Magdalen Toner was mistress of novices.

In those days religious life was very structured, with emphasis on traditional values and customs as embodied in the 'Common Life'. Those who entered the congregation embarked on a lengthy process of training, or novitiate formation, lasting approximately six years. When a young woman was accepted as a postulant (at anything from 16 years of age) her separation from the world was marked not only by a change of lifestyle but also by a change of dress. On the first day of entrance she donned a calf-length black serge dress over a black serge petticoat and a black serge elbow-length cape. The dress had a white starched collar with a stud. On her head she wore a white net cap with a stiff frill and a black net shoulder-length veil. To the headdress was attached a large black silk ribbon bow at the chin. Black woollen stockings and 'sensible' shoes completed the outfit. Those candidates who entered as lay postulants wore a slightly different version of this dress.

The postulancy period lasted for six months. After about four months the postulant asked for her 'white veil' at supper time in the refectory. (The community celebrated the event with jam for tea.) Then, a short time later, a community chapter was held to give the postulant the opportunity to make her request to be received into the congregation. If all went well she then entered a period of preparation for reception. This began with a distant retreat of one month, followed by eight days' silent retreat immediately preceding the ceremony. Apart from the spiritual exercises of these weeks, time was given to preparing the white bridal dress (high necked, second hand and adjusted to size). Along with this she would wear a bridal veil and wreath with white stockings, shoes and gloves and carry a bouquet of flowers. She also had to make her new religious habit, white veils, coifs, guimps and dimities (traditional head coverings). All except the habit was hand sewn, although, with multiple pleats to be stitched, quite a lot of hand sewing was required for that too. The habit had a long train which, except in the chapel and on very formal occasions, was worn hooked up behind. The crowning glory of a young nun's dress was the beautiful, full-length, cream serge church cloak, worn on high, holy days and said to have been chosen by Catherine McAuley as a tribute to the Carmelite fathers (of Clarendon Street, Dublin) to whom she owed so much for the establishment of the Mercy Institute. This dressmaking time was usually a very enjoyable interlude in the noviceship routine. All joined in on the jobs to be done, especially if there were two or three postulants for reception at once. All hands were needed if everything was to be ready in time. Besides the new trousseau the new novice was given a second (second-hand) habit – usually that of some Sister who had died. It was adjusted to size. However, as each Sister was buried in her church cloak, each novice got a brand new one of these.

The reception day was a great occasion. The postulant entered the chapel, which was already filled with community, family and friends, in full bridal dress and to the strains of a solemn march played on the great pipe organ. The sanctuary was beautifully adorned with flowers and lights and the presiding cleric awaited in full pontificals. The ceremony proceeded solemnly until at one point the 'bride' withdrew from the chapel, had her hair symbolically cut and returned dressed in religious habit, white veil and church cloak. A 'Te Deum' was sung and the ceremony ended to the beautiful strains of 'Ecce quam bonum' while each Sister in the community embraced the new religious.[8]

In the daily horarium of a novice, emphasis was on the rule and constitutions and 'Common Life' – that is, conformity. The novitiate period lasted for two years, called 'spiritual years'. The first was spent solely in the study and practice of religious life and spirituality (with plenty of manual work thrown in for a healthy balance). In addition to the usual community religious exercises, there was a second meditation period each day, in the afternoon, after lunch and 'catechism' (that is, spiritual instruction mainly on the catechism of the vows and the rule and constitutions of the congregation). Each morning also there was a lecture by the mistress of novices, with 'notes of lecture' to be written up each evening before supper. Personal spiritual reading had an important place, a required text being the manuals of Alphonse Rodriguez, S.J. Contact with the secular world was strictly curtailed and visits from family were allowed only twice in the year.

The second novitiate year allowed for some secular reading in preparation for future professional studies and training, which would be taken up or resumed after profession. Sometimes the second-year novices were asked to help out in school. They were also appointed regularly to accompany a professed Sister on visitation on Sundays. After 18 months as a novice, if she had been found satisfactory and felt herself suited to religious life, the young woman would ask the community to accept her for profession. This was a formal request, on one's knees, before the assembled community in chapter – quite intimidating and awe inspiring. After all, taking religious vows is a serious matter.

The first profession (the taking of triennial vows) was a private ceremony, carried out in the presence of the community only. It was preceded by two months' strict distant retreat and eight days' immediate retreat in total silence. On her profession day the candidate made a commitment for three years to the vows of religion (poverty, chastity and obedience), and the specific Mercy dedication to the service of the poor, the sick and the ignorant, and fidelity to the rule and constitutions of the congregation for the period of her temporary vows. She received the black veil of a professed Sister and a brass crucifix which would be worn in her cincture, a daily reminder of her personal dedication to Christ.

After first profession, the newly professed remained a member of the novitiate community for three years. At this stage she was familiarly called a 'black veil'. During this time she took up her studies, sometimes away from the convent at college, university or nursing school. Six months before the expiration of her triennial vows, all being well, she made a request to be admitted to final profession – to take perpetual vows. The date of final vows sometimes had to be postponed because of the requirement to make two months' distant retreat, which could not be done in the middle of studies. In this case, the junior professed renewed her vows for a further temporary period.

The taking of final vows was a big and public ceremony. The candidate made perpetual commitment to the vows already taken at first profession and to perseverance for life in the congregation. As a seal of her commitment she received a profession ring. Having made her final profession the Sister graduated from the novitiate community to that of the professed. The inauguration into the community room was quite a formal occasion, and rather daunting to a Sister who may always have looked up with awe to her seniors as the paragons of perfection. It was also lonely for some, moving away from noviceship companions with whom so much had been shared. But this separation was only temporary as all would eventually move on to full community status. At this stage the newly professed was usually now ready to be launched into her full time apostolate – a big step.

Life in the community

After final profession and the completion of preliminary secular professional training the Sisters were assigned to the various apostolates in which the community was engaged – at that time, chiefly to the schools and the hospitals. This would mean for some Sisters a transfer to one or other of the branch houses – Abbeyville, Sussex Place, Bangor, the Mater Hospital or Beechmount. Close contact was always kept with the motherhouse (Crumlin Road Convent), with regular visits and return for retreats and special feasts. Likewise there were exchange visits to the branch houses, especially at holiday times.

According to the 'customs' (the details of practices of the community) the Sisters' appointments to any of the community apostolates were of three years' duration, after which changes were made unless it was deemed appropriate to do otherwise. So there could be a considerable amount of movement each year after the changes had been posted up, with many Sisters moving into new communities. Naturally there was much to be said for and against this practice but, whatever their personal feelings, obedience always dictated the response and generally things worked out well.

Essential to the smooth functioning of the apostolates and works of the community was the part played by the lay Sisters, who saw to the material needs of the community in each convent – housekeeping, cooking, laundry, infirmary duties and whatever else was needed. They also had similar roles in the hospital and homes and each Sister had her own area of expertise. In a quiet way they had a very special influence on all who came in contact with them. They were also moved around frequently, as the need arose. The curriculum vitae of one Sister gives an interesting example of this:

> Crumlin Road Convent: 6 years (postulancy and novitiate); Bangor Convent: 1 year; Crumlin Road Convent: 1 year; St John's Private Nursing Home: 6 years; Mater Hospital: 6 months; St Malachy's College[9] : 4 years; Immaculata School (Abbeyville): 12 years; Bangor Convent: 2 years; Immaculata School: 2 years; St Malachy's College: 8 years; Crumlin Road Convent: 10 years.[10]

Finally, this Sister retired to a well-earned (but certainly not inactive) rest in Beechmount Convent after 46 fruitful years 'on mission'.

This fairly typical example shows very well the availability of the lay (later known as 'house') Sisters wherever their services were needed, an availability

Saint Joseph's cloister, Downpatrick Convent

Community group, 1850s. Centre, seated, Mother M. Aloysius Brady

Mother M. Aloysius Brady and Mother M. Borgia Fortune (1850s)

Sisters in visitation dress, mid-1800s

John Street School – first Mercy school in Downpatrick

Senior classes, John Street School. Principal, Sr M. Vincent O'Hara

Former Mercy Convent School, Stream Street, Downpatrick
(opened 6 June 1876), adjoining the convent

Class of monitresses, St Michael's, 1868

St Anne's Convent of Mercy, Warrnambool, Australia in 1972

Early photo of St Anne's shows front garden with Sisters and their pupils
relaxing on the lawn, 1880s

Mater Infirmorum Hospital, Belfast

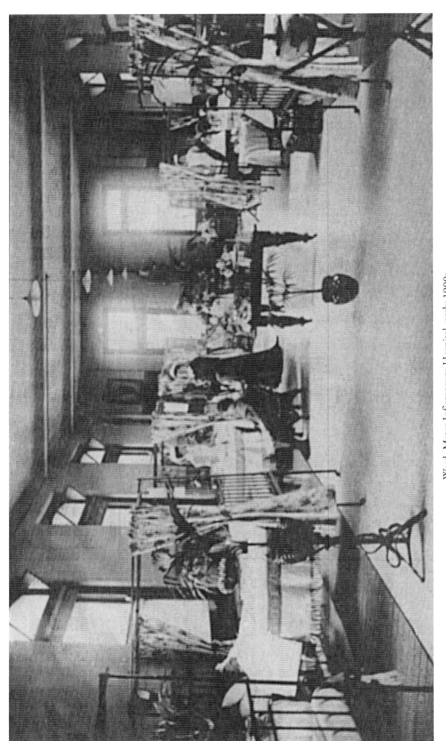

Ward, Mater Infirmorum Hospital, early 1900s

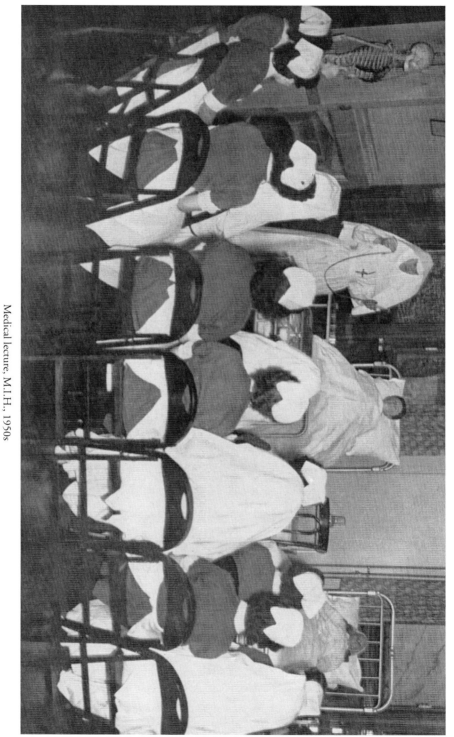

Medical lecture, M.I.H., 1950s

which also required great adaptability and generosity on the part of each. Also their apostolate of prayer for the Sisters engaged in the external works of the community (and in studies) was well known and much appreciated.

The community still followed a regular daily horarium. A typical horarium up until the end of the 1960s was as follows. The Sisters arose at the sound of a bell at 5.30 a.m. for meditation, morning office and Mass. This was followed by breakfast, some small household chores and lecture. After this the day was a well-organised routine of work and prayer. Shortly after 8 a.m. the Sisters went out to the schools or the hospital, or engaged in their various duties in the convent. The novices and postulants had their studies and work allocated to them in the house. On Sunday mornings many Sisters went out to visit the sick in the local area. The Sisters had lunch at liberty between 11 a.m. and 12.30 p.m., according to their personal timetables. Those in the house assembled in the chapel for the Angelus at midday. This was followed by a time of private prayer, after which they returned to their various activities. Dinner was at 4 p.m., when the Sisters had come in from the schools. A period of community recreation followed and at 5.15 p.m. the community assembled again in the chapel for vespers and other offices and some private spiritual reading. Before supper at 7.30 p.m. the school Sisters prepared their schoolwork for the next day. After supper there was another period of community recreation and at 9 p.m. the bell rang for night prayers and the beginning of the period of silence which would last until after breakfast the following morning. A general rule of quiet and silence (when appropriate) was maintained in the convent, as this was considered conducive to inner recollection and the spiritual life. After night prayers all retired and the lights-out hour was 10 p.m. Of course, this horarium could be rearranged for feast days and special occasions and the annual holiday times allowed a little relaxation, though the ongoing community prayer was an integral part of even those weeks.

The convent on the Crumlin Road

Since St Paul's Convent is now no more, the Sisters having vacated it in 1992, it is useful to retain a mental image of it as it was in the years of its flowering. As one approached the convent along the wide avenue from the Crumlin Road, inside the entrance gates on the right was the lodge where the Quinn family lived, caretakers for a couple of generations. Beyond that were the convent school and St Brigid's Club for Girls, overlooked by the bell tower. On the left of the avenue were Hamill Park and the convent chapel, with the porch door linking to the main convent building. The avenue led to the front entrance, approached by a short circular drive surrounded by a small garden of lawns, shrubs and flowerbeds. Beyond the garden wall were the buildings of St Malachy's College. At the rear of the convent was a larger garden and in it the small community graveyard, which faced the refectory, kitchen area and laundry. Behind the laundry were the rear buildings of the Mater Hospital.

Here it is worth giving an extract from the reminiscences of Frank Quinn, who grew up in the lodge. Frank Quinn remembered convent life as he saw it, from the outside, in the 1940s and 1950s:

> My father's first duty was to ring the Angelus bell at 6.00 am. Then the gates (to the road) were opened and remained open until 9 o'clock at night. The nuns arose at 5.30 each morning, said prayers, went to Mass and then had breakfast. The nursing Sisters then left for the hospital at 8 o'clock, followed by the teaching nuns who went to the Convent School and the Star of the Sea School, and the Matron of St Malachy's College where she cared for the boarders. This left the novices to study. The Lay Sisters prepared dinner for the evening time (4.00 pm) and worked in the laundry.
>
> In the summer evenings the nuns sat around a large table which was situated between the summer-house and the green-house, where they did embroidery, repaired vestments and altar cloths and made 'Sacred Heart Badges' …
>
> On Sunday mornings they left [the convent] at 9.45 am to supervise the schoolgirls at 10 o'clock Mass [in St Patrick's Church] where the Christian Brothers and teachers also supervised the boys. Towards 12 o'clock they left the convent in pairs to visit the sick and the poor in the parish.[11]

Frank was the brother of the late Joseph Quinn, who is fondly remembered by the present senior Sisters of the community. He succeeded his father as gardener, bell-ringer, later car-driver and general factotum and indispensable caretaker of the convent and grounds. He lived with his sister Jeanie in the lodge until it was demolished in the late 1960s; then they moved to a house provided for them by the community in Thorndale Avenue.

Mention has been made of St Malachy's (Diocesan) College on the Antrim Road. St Malachy's, a grammar school for boys and residence for seminarians who are following courses in Queen's University before going on to a major seminary, is situated on a site adjoining that of the former St Paul's Convent and of the present Mater Hospital. The college enjoyed a strong and beneficial association with the convent over many years – since at least 1918, when the Sisters were asked to provide nursing care for the seminarians during a severe flu epidemic. In the ensuing years the Sisters served there as matrons and supervisors of catering, sometimes in residence (if any of the students were ill) until the community could no longer provide this very valuable – and much appreciated – service. The last Sister serving there, Sister M. Augustine O'Neill, retired in 1991 after 11 years' service as college matron. Other Sisters who served in St Malachy's College in recent decades were: Sister M. Attracta Byrne, Sister M. Kevin Drain, Sister Kathleen Gill, Sister M. Ignatius McAvoy, Sister M. Gemma Thompson and Sister M. Aidan Mullarkey.

Holidays were another important part of convent life. At that time Abbeyville was the holiday house and in the summer months the professed Sisters and the novices took their turns at having a couple of weeks' vacation there. Abbeyville garden stretched down to the shore of Belfast Lough and bathing was one of the delightful exercises in which those who chose to could indulge. There were quite extensive gardens and orchards where one could find paths for walking or quiet spots for reading, and 'the corner' at the bottom of the garden was a sun trap where the Sisters could sit to capture the best part of a summer's day. During the vacation weeks the rule of silence and the strict horarium were relaxed somewhat, and some Sisters who had been scattered during the year in the various branch houses got together to renew friendships and enjoy each other's companionship.

The holidays, though short, were naturally much enjoyed by the novices. Their holiday accommodation was in comfortable cubicles in the spacious dormitory at the top of the school. Not much time was spent indoors, however, and the greatest possible advantage was taken of those precious days by the sea.

So the tide of convent life flowed smoothly from day to day, from year to year. But already in 1953 a whiff of change was beginning to drift over the Mercy Congregation. It was a harbinger of things to come, though at that time the Sisters were blissfully unaware of how far reaching these changes would be. On 1 January 1953, at a general chapter of the community, a correspondence from the Mercy Generalate, Carysfort Park, Dublin, was read. This related to proposed alterations in the dress of the Sisters of Mercy. As a consequence it was announced that the Sisters should have their habits remodelled for Easter Sunday, 5 April, of that year. It also stipulated that all members of the community were to be present on that day at St Paul's Convent, Crumlin Road, for the community Mass, at the 'warning bell' of which all professed Sisters should be prepared to move their rings from the left hand to the third finger of the right hand. There was no special significance in this change, except that it would bring the St Paul's community into line with what was customary in most Mercy communities in Ireland. The bishop had been consulted prior to the chapter and had given his written approval for the changes.

It was also announced on this occasion that the centenary of the coming of the Sisters of Mercy to Belfast would be celebrated in January 1954. This would be a big event and necessary preparations would be made during the course of the coming year.

[1] Barton, *op. cit.*, p. 243.
[2] Sister Evelyn Kenny, RSM, 'Annals of the Dromore Sisters of Mercy' (MCA).
[3] Ibid.
[4] After some years of illness Mother M. Magdalen Toner died in 1969 at the age of 84.
[5] Report to the bishop from Mother M. Ethna McAuley, superior of St Paul's Convent (Archives, SPCMB, 17 October 1946).
[6] Report of A.J. Tulip, H.M. inspector (Archives, SPCMB, 14 September 1948).
[7] Ibid.
[8] The full ritual can be seen in the 'Ceremony book' (MCA).
[9] At St Malachy's College this Sister was household administrator and matron to the student boarders and resident college staff.
[10] Sister M. Kevin Drain (Archives, SPCMB, 1993).
[11] F. Quinn, *The Collegian* (yearbook of St Malachy's College) (1992).

18

ABBEYVILLE: ORIGINS TO 1953

The house and property known as Abbeyville was a place dear to many generations of the Sisters of Mercy from St Paul's community from 1890 to the present time. Although chiefly remembered by most of the Sisters as a holiday home, the property was acquired for a much more pragmatic purpose – to accommodate an industrial school.

The Sisters of Mercy had run St Patrick's Orphanage, situated beside the convent on the Crumlin Road, since 1859. When the government had undertaken to give grants to industrial schools the Sisters had made an application. In 1869 they had received recognition and funding for first of all 80, and a short time later 100, children. The school flourished and, in order to provide more accommodation for this important work, the diocese purchased Abbeyville in 1890. Abbeyville was an estate on the north shore of Belfast Lough, near the village of Whiteabbey. The administrator of the sale was Reverend James Hamill, then parish priest of Greencastle and Whitehouse. He was brother of Sister M. Malachy Hamill of the Belfast Mercy community, then Sister-in-charge of the orphanage and industrial school in Belfast. The purchase was made possible from funds reserved from the existing institutions. The property was acquired in January 1890 and Mass was celebrated in the house for the first time on 2 February, when the Sisters took charge of the place. A short time later a fine residential school was built beside the original house (the architect was G. Byrne and the builder was J. Fegan), which was itself reserved as a convent for the Sisters engaged in the school. The new school, which opened in 1894, was certified for 200 pupils.

Abbeyville, a property of about six acres, is a picturesque spot close to the village of Whiteabbey and in the parish of Whitehouse. The prefixes 'white' of both names are said to be associated both with the white oaks indigenous to the area in the early days, and the so-called White House, built of the same white oaks in the late sixteenth century by a soldier who had seen active service under the earl of Essex. This White House was a landmark on the northern shore of the lough, then known as Carrickfergus Bay. In the early seventeenth century the White House was occupied by a tenant of Sir Arthur Chichester. Later the house fell into ruin but the name lived on in the parish of Whitehouse.

Close to the site of the White House were the ruins of an ancient abbey, which appears to have fallen into decay before the dissolution of the Irish monasteries and which, according to one tradition, could be traced back to the order of St John of Jerusalem. This order reputedly had a monastery there known as the White Abbey. Another tradition claims the site as that of the Premonstratensian 'white' canons, whose abbey was a daughterhouse of Drieburg Abbey in Scotland.[1] Even as late as the mid-nineteenth century there were still extensive ruins on the spot. It is recorded that the stones from these ruins were used to build a neighbouring house, Abbotscroft. In the grounds of Abbeyville there is to be found an old covered well traditionally associated with the monastic foundations.

There is also a reference to Abbeyville in C.E.B. Brett's *Buildings of County Antrim*:

> Thomas McTear, born in 1800, says that next to Abbeylands and Woodbank [mansions in Whitehouse Parish] was Abbeyville, the residence of Maxwell Leper, who sold it to the widow of Thomas Sinclaire, who left it to her nephew, Rev R.W. Bland of St George's Church, and then occupied by his son, General Bland, R.E. ... The original Abbeyville may have been Elizabethan in style. It was knocked down to make way for the late-Victorian house [which became the convent].[2]

Whatever the derivation of the various names of the house, village and parish, the site and hinterland of Abbeyville have a long and interesting history. It may well be said that with its historical religious associations it was not inappropriate that this spot should house yet another religious community in the twentieth century.

For 20 years the Sacred Heart Industrial School flourished independently in Abbeyville, while the earlier-founded St Patrick's Orphanage and Industrial School continued on the Crumlin Road. There was regular interchange between the two industrial schools as the government developed its policy with regard to these institutions. For example, in June 1903, 39 children were transferred from Crumlin Road to Abbeyville and 39 from Abbeyville to Crumlin Road, a measure to regulate the age groups of the pupils and their educational needs.[3] In January 1921 funding for the Crumlin Road Industrial School was discontinued because of a fall in the number of pupils. Consequently the school closed and the remaining children, both from St Patrick's Industrial School and the Orphanage, were sent to Abbeyville.

The first Sister-in-charge of the new Sacred Heart Industrial School in Abbeyville was Sister M. Malachy Hamill. She moved there from the orphanage and industrial school on the Crumlin Road, of which she had been in charge since the 1880s, assisted by her niece, Sister M. Ligouri Neeson.[4] When she died at the ripe old age of 87 on 23 December 1939, in the sixty-ninth year of her religious life, her obituary in the *Irish News* paid her the following tribute:

> For many years Sr. M. Malachy devoted herself to the care of the children in the Industrial School, Crumlin Road and also in the Sacred Heart Orphanage, Whiteabbey. The widespread grief occasioned by her death among her 'old children' and the many messages of sympathy received prove that the deceased is still kindly remembered by those who were the objects of her care.[5]

Many other Sisters, teachers and workmistresses devoted their talents to the education and care of these dependent children and young women in the orphanage and school over the ensuing years. The industrial school cultivated the talents and developed the skills of the young women with a view to preparing them to take up the various work opportunities that would come their way as they moved into adult life. Most of all it endeavoured to prepare them for the responsibilities of family life and of constructive citizenship as they moved out of school to face the many challenges of the wider world. It is recorded in the school's register that many of the young women who had been trained there, and indeed those who had come as children to the orphanage and who had subsequently obtained employment in or around the city, came back regularly, or even each week, to visit. There was already a train from Belfast to Whiteabbey at that time and one can imagine the young women, on their day off from factory, mill or service, enjoying a day's outing to their former home by the sea. The Sisters, for their part, delighted in hearing from employers that their former pupils were giving every satisfaction.[6]

Abbeyville, synonymous in the first place with the Sacred Heart Industrial School and Orphanage, was to house various other educational enterprises over the next 80 years as changing circumstances dictated adaptations in apostolate. Meanwhile, what of the premises of the former orphanage and industrial school on the Crumlin Road?

St Brigid's Home for the Blind

The children of the orphanage and industrial school on Convent Avenue had been transferred to Abbeyville in January 1921 and the orphanage building was taken soon afterwards to become St Brigid's Home for the Blind. It was blessed as such on 1 February 1921 under the special patronage of Bishop McRory.

This new home, which was to provide care for blind women and for children, girls and boys from the age of three years, had long been needed in Belfast. The only other Catholic home for the blind was at Merrion, in Dublin. Its founder was Sister M. Dympna Fegan, who had for some years been visiting Catholic blind women and children in non-Catholic homes around the city. The former orphanage building needed adaptation in preparation for the new residents and, when it was eventually opened on 29 June 1921 the first resident was 'Agnes O'Neill, 38 years'. A diary kept from 29 June 1921 to 18 December 1924 (most likely by Sister M. Dympna) records that Agnes came 'in a dying state' from a house in Cliftonville Avenue where she had lived for eight years. A later diary entry tells us that Agnes O'Neill died on 2 February 1923.[7] A touching tribute to this lady was published anonymously in a local newspaper about a month later under the title 'Blind Agnes':

> Recently I came across a little booklet of the past generation bearing the above title, and its perusal gave me a sad feeling of intense sympathy for one whom God had sorely tried by depriving her of one of the greatest blessings we poor mortals enjoy. Bearing bravely her sore affliction, the life of the young girl was a model of patient resignation to God's holy will, and was filled with a multitude of good works which will have their due reward on the great Accounting Day. Moreover it recalled to me the holy, hidden life of one who had just passed away in Belfast, one who also bore the name 'Agnes' and who 'sat in the shadow' and suffered and prayed like her sainted prototype.[8]

The author goes on to tell us that Agnes, who had come from a Leinster farmstead, had spent many years in the Belfast Home for the Blind, where her many accomplishments were the wonder of those who had the pleasure of knowing the stricken girl. She bore patiently with her affliction but one temporal matter often engrossed her thoughts, the institution of a Home for the Catholic Blind in Belfast and district:

> For years she pondered on the possible means of accomplishing this idea, and her joy was intense when, a little over a twelvemonth ago, state provision was made for the support of all blind persons. In haste she sped to the bishop of Down and Connor, Most Rev. Dr McRory, and besought him to open a home for blind Catholics. The kind bishop was moved by the eloquence of poor Agnes and willingly promised her his support. Then a difficulty arose over a suitable domicile in congested Belfast. But God's ways are wonderful, and about this time the Orphanage, Crumlin Road, under the care of the Sisters of Mercy, had been transferred to Whiteabbey, leaving spacious quarters vacant.

The good Sisters were earnestly praying for divine direction as to the utilisation of the rooms. When lo! the bishop speaks of his quandary and at once the solution comes. St Brigid's Home for the Blind was immediately established, and today it shelters twelve blind women and girls. God's blessing was on the tiny seed sown by Blind Agnes. Her life work was crowned with the success she had striven and prayed for, and now her time was come to part with loving friends and go home to God.[9]

Sister M. Dympna had worked in the orphanage and now remained as the first Sister-in-charge of the home for the blind. It is recorded that she maintained a great devotion and enthusiasm for her charges. In the home a school was formed, equipped with all the requisites for teaching blind children. The curriculum, which was conducted in the Braille system, included all the subjects taught in the ordinary primary school. The boys (who also were accepted into the home as small children) remained there until they reached the age of nine; the girls stayed until school-leaving age. This school was the first of its kind in Northern Ireland certified by the Ministry of Education.

Academically, the school ensured the best education possible for the children within the limits of their abilities. In September 1923 an inspector, Councillor Harper, visited on behalf of the Belfast Corporation and pronounced himself 'highly pleased with everything'. A cheque for £200 from the corporation towards the expenses of setting up the home followed in November – a very welcome contribution.[10]

Though St Brigid's Home for the Blind was providing an invaluable service, as time passed it was realised that the location near the Crumlin Road was far from ideal for such an institution. It had limited accommodation, lacked sufficient recreation ground and there was a busy road nearby. Before long an opportunity for relocating arose. By the 1930s the numbers in the Sacred Heart Industrial School in Abbeyville had declined. In August 1933 the Mercy community decided that the school was no longer viable and that the children in it could be transferred to similar institutions in Middletown and Strabane. This, in turn, would allow for the removal of St Brigid's Home and School for the Blind to Abbeyville.

On 7 October 1933 the industrial school closed and steps were taken to adapt the school building for the accommodation of the new occupants. This was done under the direction of J.V. Brennan, architect, in conformity with Home Office requirements respecting the housing and training of the blind. It entailed a considerable financial outlay on the Sisters' part and they counted on the support of various generous benefactors. The result was a building fully furnished for the accommodation of the blind and among the first of its class in the whole country.

Eventually the great day arrived for the move from Belfast to Whiteabbey. One can imagine the excitement and anticipation – and perhaps no little confusion and anxiety – as the women and children of the Crumlin Road prepared to depart for their new residence in unfamiliar surroundings. The event was noteworthy enough to be reported in the local newspaper on 1 March 1934:

> The inmates of St Brigid's Home for the Blind, Crumlin Road, have arrived in their new residence at 'Abbeyville', Whiteabbey. The parting and journey from their dear old Alma Mater, which they expected would have been a sad one, was made very pleasurable.
>
> His Lordship, Most Rev Dr Mageean, very kindly visited the Home for a short time previous to their departure to wish all the inmates many long years of health and happiness in their spacious new abode, where everything had been provided for their comfort. His Lordship then imparted his blessing to them.
>
> Many kind friends provided motor-cars, eighteen in all, to convey the inmates to their destination, and the Reverend Fr McMullan, Reverend Fr Crossin and Reverend Fr Armstrong, as well as Reverend Mother and a number of the Sisters of the Community, very kindly accompanied them to help, an action that was appreciated very much by the inmates. Some of the Ladies of Charity also gave valuable assistance.
>
> On arrival at Abbeyville they were met and heartily welcomed by the Community there, and also by the Very Reverend J. O'Neill, P.P., V.F., who gave Benediction of the Most Holy Sacrament in the Convent Choir, the singing of which was rendered by the blind children, one of whom presided at the organ.
>
> When they entered their new dwelling a most enjoyable feast was awaiting them, to which they were helped by the kind visitors who were afterwards entertained to tea. An impromptu concert followed. It was given by the blind children, and consisted of pianoforte solos, duets, singing and recitations.
>
> The Sister-in-charge thanked the very many kind friends of the blind who rendered such valuable assistance in the task of conveying them to their present home. The address in future will be – St Brigid's Home and School for the Blind, 'Abbeyville', Whiteabbey, near Belfast.[11]

Everything had been done to make the new home comfortable and convenient for the new residents. The most modern household facilities, heating and lighting had been installed. On the ground floor there was a large, bright parlour for the older folk, pleasant work and recreation rooms for the younger adults and a classroom for the children. The latter rooms were separated by soundproof folding partitions which could be opened between them when a larger space was needed. Large windows facing south-east and with an unimpeded view of the lough ensured an abundance of light and sunshine. A communicating corridor ran alongside the class and work rooms to a large apartment, which could be used for music, recreation and visitors. Many a concert was given in this room for the entertainment of guests and friends. Soon the new inhabitants settled down very happily, it would appear, from the impressions of a visitor of the time:

> Apart from the fine building … what strikes the ordinary visitor most of all is the air of supreme content visible everywhere on the faces of the inmates – young and old. In every section and in every room of the building happiness and cheerfulness seem to be the keynote; indeed, to those most happily endowed with that most precious of all gifts – sight – the look of supreme content and happiness in the faces of the inmates is something he might very well envy. Situated where it is, directly on the sea, amidst pure, sea-borne air and far from the smoke and grime of the city, brightened and heartened by the unremitting care and attention of the Sisters of Mercy, whose only thought day after day is the well-being of the afflicted ones committed to their charge, it is little wonder they are cheerful and happy.[12]

The same writer went on to report that, in the fine workroom, the young, and those adults capable of working, were encouraged to develop skills in needlework and handcrafts, and he was greatly impressed by 'the wonderful skill and dexterity with which these blind inmates carry out their beautiful work'. Music, of course, was rated very high in the accomplishments of the pupils:

> [I] was greatly interested in watching a girl at the piano studying music through the medium of the Braille system. From an adjoining room was heard an extract from one of the classics, faultlessly played, and was astonished when told that the player was sightless. Moving her hands rapidly along the Braille script, duly memorising it, the hands are then transferred quickly to the keyboard and the piece is played in a manner, and with a touch that many gifted with sight could not achieve.[13]

The musical skill which was an outstanding mark of St Brigid's Home and School for the Blind was cultivated from the earliest days when the talent of any particular child was recognised. Much was due to an exceptional teacher of music, Mr H. Walls, who had been invited to give lessons while the home was still in Crumlin Road. Mr Walls had come to give the first lessons on the piano to six residents.[14] He was fondly and gratefully remembered by several generations of pupils. The musical entertainment was the highlight of every occasion, official or purely for pleasure. A year or so after the move to Abbeyville similar impressions were recorded of an evening spent at the home, when not only the musical, but also the dramatic, skills of the children provided great enjoyment for all:

> One of the charms of blind children is their freedom from an awkward shyness; they are unconscious of the hundreds of eyes directed towards them. The performers the other evening, who showed their skill in piano and violin playing, solo and choral songs and recitations, as well as in their sketch (The Crazy Fiddler), included the Misses Rose Keenan, Annie and Alice Kelly, Catherine McMonagle, Mary and Josie Clarke, Vera Keenan and little 'Baby Lila'. The pleasure they gave was only equalled by the pleasure and benefit they themselves derived by such careful and skilled training, credit for which is due to Sister Dympna and her colleagues.[15]

In the classrooms the teachers were highly skilled in the use of Braille, through which all the usual primary school subjects were taught. As we have seen, music and drama also held prominent places in the curriculum. In addition, particular attention was given to teaching the pupils the practical skills that would help them to earn their living and carry out the normal duties of a household.

There was plenty of opportunity for recreation other than through cultural pastimes. A wide lawn and playing area graced the front of the school and the grounds extended further to cover an area of six acres, 'replete with lovely gardens, beautifully laid out and kept, and complete with shelters for wet weather'.[16] Protective fences and guide rails ensured the safety of movement so necessary for those without sight. The gardens and orchard extended to the sea wall and expeditions to the shore were a favourite treat. The children were well supervised when outdoors so that they could play with perfect safety and yet experience a freedom of movement of which the blind often unfortunately feel deprived.

Sister M. Malachy Hamill and Sister M. Ligouri Neeson remained in Abbeyville after the industrial school closed. Sister M. Attracta Byrne served as matron, assisted by Sister Monica Mulligan. Sister M. Philomena McMullan trained for the teaching of Braille and later joined the staff. Other teachers were Miss Brady ('who always wore a hat'),[17] Miss Brogan, Mrs O'Prey and Miss Rose Keenan, a former pupil. Rose Keenan was an inspiring teacher and friend to the blind children. The poet Seamus Heaney, a young neighbour of hers in their homeplace in County Derry, found her an inspiration and wrote a poem about her, 'At the wellhead'.[18]

Under their guidance the school achieved a high standard and was classed by the Ministry of Education as 'highly efficient'. Many of the pupils earned high awards, particularly in music.

The school could not have prospered without the help of generous benefactors. Among these were Mrs Jim Rice, Mrs Godfrey and Mrs McGouran, who arranged whist and bridge drives, raffles and bazaars. Not to be outdone by the women, their husbands also played an active part. Those mentioned are Gerard McGouran, Mr Dunahue, Mr McMullan and Mr McParland, to name just a few. The Ulster Sports Club supported the fund-raising and the owners of the Avenue Hotel, the Misses Burke, provided a venue for events. This sponsorship raised necessary funds for the equipping of the new home and also made possible outings and celebrations on many occasions.

The Little Flower Oratory

Now that the home and school for the blind were functioning smoothly, there was just one other matter that was a cause of concern for Sister M. Dympna. This was the absence of a proper oratory where her charges, old and young, could gather for prayer and for visits to the Blessed Sacrament. There was, of course, a small chapel in the convent where the Blessed Sacrament was reserved and where daily Mass was celebrated. When any of the blind residents came to Mass there was insufficient space so on Sundays Mass was celebrated in a large room upstairs in the school. Within a couple of years the insufficiency was made good when the Mercy community financed the building of a chapel adjoining the convent and linked by a corridor to St Brigid's Home. Dr Mageean laid the foundation stone on the feast of St Mary Magdalene, 22 July 1934. At that time Mother M. Magdalen Toner was superior in Crumlin Road Convent and had advocated the building of the new oratory.

The oratory was built on the south-west side of the school and linked with both school and convent. It was designed by J.V. Brennan and built of red Laganvale facing brick; the buttresses, apex crosses, door and window copings were made of pre-cast stone. Thus it harmonised with the adjacent buildings and fitted comfortably into the school and convent complex. The interior was furnished with oak choir stalls for the community and pews of different sizes for the adults and children of the home. The sanctuary, with its marble altar, was graced with beautiful stained-glass windows through which the evening setting sun flooded the interior space with colour. The floor of the sanctuary and choir was of coloured mosaic and the nave of polished oak. At a later date a tall statue of St Thérèse of the Child Jesus (the

'Little Flower') graced the entrance from the convent, and a statue of St Michael the Protector could be seen in the entrance from the Home.

On the feast of the Immaculate Conception, 8 December 1935, the bishop opened the new house of prayer and named it the Little Flower Oratory. The preacher for the occasion, Reverend Father Richard, C.P., spoke of how meaningful this new sanctuary would be to the residents, young and old, of St Brigid's Home, who would join their voices with all those assembled for the occasion 'in congratulating the Sisters of Our Lady of Mercy upon the accomplishment of another labour of love', and as a token of their gratitude would promise their kind benefactors daily remembrance in prayer 'when assembled before the all holy presence of the Great God who deigns to take up His abode in their midst'.[19] Besides the resident community the oratory welcomed many people from the district who, for one reason or another, could not make the journey to their parish church for Mass.

In the course of the previous year (1934) Reverend Mother M. Magdalen Toner had the old mansion completely renovated and made into a fine convent for Sisters requiring convalescence or a change of air from the city. It had the amenities and comforts that were appropriate at the time to provide an ideal holiday and rest house for the Belfast community. Also, since the home and school for the blind did not require the whole of the former industrial-school building it was decided to set apart the top floor as holiday accommodation for the Sisters. This was a decision much appreciated by the community in the years that followed. Many happy holidays were spent on the shores of Belfast Lough. The extensive gardens, lawns and orchards and the sandy lough shore provided welcome relaxation for the Sisters – and especially the novices – for the next 20 years.

St Brigid's Home and School for the Blind continued to flourish until the early 1950s.[20] But on Saturday, 9 May 1953, tragedy struck. Workmen on the roof of the home were using a blowtorch near a ventilator when the flame set fire to birds' nests. It was a dry and sunny day and the fire spread rapidly. Six fire-brigade vehicles quickly reached the scene but it was quite a while before the fire was brought under control. The dormitory and one of the classrooms were destroyed but fortunately no one was hurt. The children were put up for the night in Whiteabbey Hospital and the older women were moved to Beechmount, where they remained for good. In a short time the school was reopened and the undamaged rooms were used as dormitories and classrooms. However, as there were now only seven pupils (the others having transferred to a school for blind in Dublin) the school's continuation was not feasible. It was decided, in 1956, that the children could be accommodated in a similar school in Dublin, and so St Brigid's closed as a school for the blind. New plans were made for Abbeyville, but we shall take up this story in a later chapter.

[1] The Premonstratensians are a clerical order of canons regular of the Catholic Church, founded by St Norbert in 1119 at Prémontré, near Laon, France. They wear white robes. See the *Itinerary* of Father E. McCans, superior of the Franciscan convent at Carrickfergus, written in the early seventeenth century, and W. Reeves, *Ecclesiastical antiquities of Down, Connor and Dromore* (vol. i, Dublin: Hodges and Smith, 1847).

[2] C.E.B. Brett, 'Abbeylands, Woodbank and Abbeyville' in idem and M. O'Connell, *Buildings of County Antrim* (Belfast: Ulster Architectural Heritage Society and Ulster Historical Foundation, 1996), p. 194.

[3] See registers of Sacred Heart Industrial School, Mercy Northern Province Archives (MCA).

[4] Sister M. Malachy had a sister in St Paul's community, Sister M. Ligouri Hamill, who had died on 25 April 1884. They came from a distinguished Belfast family and their two brothers were Right Reverend Monsignor Dean Hamill, P.P., V.G., Whitehouse, and Right Reverend Murtagh Hamill, P.P., V.F., Kilkeel.

[5] *Irish News*, 27 December 1939.

[6] See registers of Sacred Heart Industrial School, Mercy Northern Province Archives (MCA).

[7] Sister M. Dympna, 'Diary 1921–4' (SPCMB, 1930s).

[8] Quoted in ibid.

[9] Ibid.

[10] M.D. Fegan (attributed), 'St Brigid's Home and School for the Blind, Abbeyville: diary' (Archives, SPCMB, January 1921–24).

[11] *Irish News*, 1 March 1934.

[12] *Irish News*, 8 December 1935.

[13] Ibid.

[14] The importance of this engagement in the minds of those conducting the blind school is indicated in the several entries in Sister M. Dympna's diary: '17 November 1923: Mr. Walls was appointed to teach the piano to six inmates. 19 March 1924: Mr. H. Walls, Mulholland Terrace, Belfast, was accepted [by the corporation] as Musical Instructor to the blind inmates of St. Brigid's Home – for six months.'

[15] Ibid.

[16] Abbeyville (Archives, SPCMB, 1930s).

[17] Ibid.

[18] 'At the wellhead', *The spirit level* (London: Faber and Faber, 1996). He also speaks of her in D. O'Driscoll, *Stepping stones: interviews with Seamus Heaney* (London: Faber and Faber, 2008), pp. 366–7.

[19] *Irish News*, 9 December 1935.

[20] Many reminiscences have been passed down by former pupils who give us an insight into the activities and personalities of the residents, teachers and Sisters who shared life in the school for the blind, Abbeyville (see Archives, SPCMB).

19

BANGOR 1930s–60s

In the early 1930s the Sisters of Mercy in Belfast were asked to open a new foundation in Bangor. The town of Bangor, picturesquely situated on the north-east coast of County Down at the mouth of Belfast Lough, has a long history associated particularly with its position as one of the nearest points on the coast of Ireland to Britain. It has therefore been considered a stepping-stone to the neighbouring island and thence to continental Europe. This strategic location was important for Irish missionaries whose zeal attracted them to the challenge of bringing the gospel to the people of northern Europe.

Most prominent among these monk-missionaries was St Comgall – 'Comgall of Bangor' – who founded a monastery there in 559 CE which became a great seat of learning and a training ground for future monks, many of whom would follow in Comgall's footsteps to bring the Christian faith to the Germanic peoples and as far as northern Italy. The original Bangor Abbey was a huge establishment. We read in St Bernard's *Life of Malachy*:

> [In] Bangor … there had been a very celebrated monastery under the first Abbot, Comgall, which produced thousands of monks and was head of many monasteries. A truly holy place it was, and prolific of saints … Into foreign lands these swarms of saints poured as though a flood had arisen.[1]

One of the most illustrious of the disciples of Comgall was Columbanus (d. 615), who journeyed to central Gaul and built the monastery of Luxeuil, which was 'recognised as the monastic capital of all the countries under Frank government.'[2] Comgall's name and legacy remains in the present abbey church at Bangor and other sites dedicated to his memory.

However, Bangor's name comes from an even earlier tradition, the legend that St Patrick, on his return to Ireland, rested on a hill set in a valley in this area. While he was there the valley was filled with heavenly light and the voices of choirs of angels. It became a holy place and was named Banchoir – vale of the angels.[3]

We cannot leave the early history of Bangor without mentioning the great St Malachy, patron both of the diocese of Down and Connor and of the archdiocese of Armagh. In the Middle Ages the Bangor community held the right to elect the bishops of the diocese and, when the united diocese of Down and Connor was formed in 1124, Malachy was called to assume the role of bishop. The monastery of Bangor, of which he was also abbot, became the centre of his episcopal administration. Ten years later he became archbishop of Armagh, but after three years he resigned his see to return to his beloved Bangor.

It was to this illustrious centre of the Irish Christian faith that the Sisters of Mercy were called in 1932, but by then it was a town greatly depleted of its ancient clerical heritage. Monastic life in Bangor had ended with the dissolution of the monasteries under Henry VIII of England (in the mid-sixteenth century), when the abbey's vast possessions were confiscated and its community dispersed. Following this came a wave of planters, who forced out the Catholic population. By the end of the eighteenth century there were no Catholic families in the Bangor area. A 1766 letter from a Bangor minister to the clerk of parliament states:

> SIR, I sent you the number of families in the parish – eight hundred Protestant families; no Popish families, and no reputed Popish priests; no friar. I am your humble servant, Peter Winder, Minister of Bangor.[4]

Needless to say, there was no Catholic church and no Catholic school.

With the ending of the Penal Laws in the middle of the nineteenth century the Catholic population of Bangor began to revive and in 1851 a small chapel was built on the outskirts of the town and dedicated to St Comgall. About 35 years later a larger church was needed. This was built in 1889, leaving the old church vacant to serve as a schoolhouse. Bangor, which had been part of the parish of Newtownards, became a separate parish in 1903.

Schooling

Life was never easy for the Catholics in Bangor in the early days of the twentieth century but their numbers were steadily increasing. As a result, the school accommodation was totally inadequate both in size and condition and it fell to the new parish priest, Reverend Patrick Scally, who arrived in 1916, to deal with this situation. Fortunately he was a man with a great gift for organising and fund-raising. He was also skilled at making friends and in time he became socially accepted (to the advantage of his parish) among those in power and authority in this predominantly Protestant town.

The Catholic parish of Bangor was blessed in having a good tradition of very dedicated and capable teachers from the earliest days, as the inspectors' reports show, making the most of the cramped and inadequate conditions in which they had to work. It was observed that the children were quiet, orderly, well behaved and nicely mannered and their discipline, order and appearance were highly commended. There was a boys' and a girls' national school (St Comgall's) and the numbers in both were steadily increasing. By 1926 the numbers in both schools had increased so much as to cause serious overcrowding and health hazards to both children and teachers. Consequently Father Scally saw an urgent need to do something about the matter of accommodation. And in the steps he took he made controversial history.

A new school was needed but the funds were not available. Besides the schools, the parish had other financial commitments and the Bangor Catholic congregation was by no means wealthy. So Father Scally turned to an obvious source of funds, the Ministry of Education for Northern Ireland. The new ministry had been set up in Belfast when, after 1921, responsibility for education in the new state of Northern Ireland had moved from Dublin. The first minister of education was Lord Londonderry. He appointed a committee to look into the state of education in the province and make recommendations. The committee recommended three types of elementary schools. Class 1 would be those built by local authorities or the ministry or those handed over to the ministry by previous managers. This type of school, called 'provided' or 'transferred', was to receive a grant of 100 per cent for both capital expenditure and maintenance. Class-2 schools would be those with special management committees composed of four representatives of the former managers and two of the local government authorities. This type of school was to receive a grant of around 82 per cent for capital expenditure and 50 per cent for maintenance. The committee was termed by most people as a 'four-and-two' committee. Class-3 schools would be those whose managers wished to remain entirely independent of the local government authorities. This type of school was to receive a grant only for heating and lighting.

This new legislation raised suspicion in the minds of the Catholic hierarchy in Northern Ireland. They resisted anything that threatened the independence of Catholic education and saw these new financial offers as opening the possibility of a gradual takeover of the Catholic schools by the state. Most Catholic schools opted for Class-3 status. (It seems that at this time only two opted for Class-2 status.) For the first nine years of the Northern Ireland state, Catholic schools received no money for capital expenditure or maintenance. (Later, in 1930, another education act gave

Class-3 schools a 50-per-cent grant for both capital expenditure and maintenance. At this time the schools were called public elementary schools.)

With an urgent need for a new school and no source of funding for such, after 1926 Father Scally stepped aside from church policy and made application for funding for his new school under the 'four-and-two' scheme. The reason he gave for this was that he wanted the best for the children of the parish and found it difficult (well-nigh impossible) to provide this without any financial help from the state. When he made application to the Regional Education Committee the option he was offered was that his schools should apply for Class-2 status. Father Scally proceeded to do this, in spite of Bishop Mageean's opposition. Father Scally agreed with the concept of the 'four-and-two' system and he believed that the new Northern Ireland Ministry of Education had a progressive policy to bring Northern Ireland schools up to the highest standards.

The parish priest found that his application was facilitated by the fact that he was of high standing among the important and influential men in the town. So, in 1928, St Comgall's Boys' and Girls' Schools were both granted Class-2 status. The new arrangement meant that the parish trustees could nominate four members to the management committee and the Regional Education Committee two members. This having been achieved, plans were made right away for the erection of a new school, based on the hope of obtaining a loan for the capital expenditure.

A new mission
The foregoing story has been told because it would, later on, have a bearing on the establishment of the Sisters of Mercy in Bangor. When the new status of the schools had been fixed, in 1930, Father Scally asked the Sisters of Mercy in Belfast to consider coming to Bangor to take charge of the girls' school. The then principal, Mary Conway, resigned. Although she had been a very successful principal of the school for 20 years, Mary Conway believed she had a religious vocation. As an only child she had taken care of her mother until she died in 1930. Now free, she intended to resign from her teaching post. She entered the Congregation of the Cross and Passion in 1932. Her religious name was Sister Francis.

Father Scally had a cousin in the Belfast Mercy community, Sister M. Ligouri Neeson, and he knew something of the Mercy apostolate. The special reason for his request was 'to have Sisters for looking after the girls who had left school, to prevent them from falling away from the practice of their religion and falling into the dangers attendant on low company'. He also gave the assurance that 'the coming of the Sisters would not interfere with anyone's (specifically the teachers') rights' – that is, their posts in the schools.[5] It seemed that even some years earlier he had broached the subject with the bishop and got his approval. When Mary Conway tendered her resignation in 1931, making known her intention of leaving the school at the end of the year, the time for renewing a request for the Sisters was ripe.

On 24 April 1932 Mother M. Magdalen Toner, the superior in Crumlin Road Convent, informed the community that she had received a request from the parish priest of Bangor (now Canon Scally) to establish a branch convent in the town when it would be convenient for the Sisters to take control of the parish girls' elementary school and a select (private) school there. The community agreed that this was a worthwhile apostolate in view of the fact that the Catholics in Bangor were a minority group and struggling to establish themselves. There were many mixed marriages (a fact which was looked upon with regret in those days) and many Catholic children were already attending the Protestant schools. The hope was that the Sisters might be able to attract them back to their own schools.

On 1 September 1932 the Sisters went to Bangor. The first were Sister M. Ligouri Neeson, who was appointed local superior, Sister M. Paul McCarthy, school principal and Sister M. Joseph O'Hare, assistant teacher. In October they were joined by Sister M. Peter Cassidy and Sister M. Alphonsus McKernan for the school and Sister Laurence McCann as housekeeper. Their first home was a small rented house at the corner of Brunswick Road and Brunswick Park, which the Sisters familiarly called 'the lean-to'. As the accommodation was inadequate when the other Sisters joined them, they made two further moves over the next seven years, first to Farnham Road and then to Osborne Drive, before they eventually acquired their own convent home.

During those years the composition of the community varied. Between 1933 and 1936 Sisters M. Gerard Laverty, M. Berchmans Donegan, M. Philomena McMullan, M. Mechtilde McKay, M. Raphael Kennedy, Ann Gallagher and Brigid McDermott spent some time there. In 1937 Sister M. Austin Murray arrived, and in 1938 Sisters Marie Thérèse Laverty, M. Mercy Cummins and M. Augustine O'Neill came. (As was the custom in Mercy communities then, appointments usually changed every three years.)

The first Sisters quickly settled into their new school and parish duties. As Canon Scally had promised, the former teachers of the girls' school were not ousted. Miss Black was retained as an assistant teacher and the other two teachers, Miss Short and Miss McAlinden, were found posts that suited them in the Belfast convent schools. The Sisters took it upon themselves to maintain the high standards set by the former principal, Miss Conway. They were teachers who were highly qualified and well experienced. Apart from the academic subjects, home crafts and needlework, music and elocution figured prominently on the curriculum. Of course, religious education took pride of place and, in the first year after the Sisters came to Bangor, the school grading for this subject was 98.5 per cent.

The Sisters were warmly welcomed by the people of the parish and, over the ensuing years, found themselves involved in many additional apostolates besides teaching.

Bangor Convent

After seven years of wandering, a suitable place was finally found for a permanent convent in Bangor. There is an interesting story associated with the acquisition of the site. A very devout Catholic woman of the parish, Margaret Mulholland, who lived in a house next to the Catholic parish church and schools, had a great desire, as the end of her life approached, to bequeath her house and the surrounding land to the parish as a site for a future convent. By the 1930s Margaret Mulholland was a widow and her son and his family had their home in England. Her granddaughter Mary stayed with Mrs Mulholland as a child in the 1930s and had often heard her express her wish, saying, 'This house I am in will be demolished some day and a convent will stand in its place. The grounds around will be convent grounds.' She made her bequest and knew, before she died, that her dream would be realised.[6]

The site of the Mulholland home was not very extensive but it was very suitable because of its proximity to the church and schools. In addition, it was the only available building land in the area whose deeds did not contain a restrictive clause prohibiting the erection of a church, convent or school. However, it still took some years to release the property and when the house was demolished plans were drawn up for the new convent. On 11 February 1939 Canon Scally laid the foundation stone.

The building proceeded rapidly (the architect was Frank McArdle of Belfast) and, though the new convent was not quite ready for occupation, on 8 September 1939 the Sisters moved in. The official opening took place on 15 September. Besides the first community (Sisters M. Ligouri Neeson, M. Paul McCarthy and M. Joseph O'Hare), present at the occasion were Mother M. Magdalen Toner (superior of the Crumlin Road Convent), Mother M. Imelda Laverty, Sister M. Anthony Ward (from the Mater Hospital) and Sister M. Martha Corcoran. The convent was blessed and Canon Scally celebrated the first Mass in the beautifully appointed convent chapel 'and, as the rumbling of war gained momentum over Europe, a new sanctuary lamp shed its rays over what was once known as the Valley of the Angels'.[7]

It seems that the opening of the new convent had not gone without a hitch. When the building had been decided upon, complications arose. The story goes that Bishop Mageean, who had been opposed to Canon Scally's move to place the Bangor parish schools under the 'four-and-two' system, did not approve of the Sisters teaching in such schools. He considered them under the jurisdiction of the Northern Ireland government. He confirmed his disapproval by refusing to give permission for the new foundation to be set up canonically as a religious community in Bangor until the school in which the Sisters taught was withdrawn from the 'four-and-two' system.[8] After a long controversy Canon Scally conceded. The girls' school reverted to Class-3 status, fortunately without incurring any financial penalties from the government, and was placed under the control of a diocesan committee: the bishop, Canon Scally, Reverend T.J. O'Neill, Reverend J. Blacker and Reverend J. Murphy. It was renamed St Comgall's Convent School.

The convent school flourished steadily. The pupils came from a wide range of backgrounds. Most of their fathers were in service occupations, since the businesses in Bangor (except for the main hotel) were owned by their Protestant neighbours. The school register for 1932 lists the pupils' fathers as, for example, shopkeepers, hairdressers, publicans, salesmen, mechanics and carriers.

The year 1939 was notable not only for opening of the new Mercy convent in Bangor but also for the outbreak of World War II. One Sister who lived in Bangor at the time recorded, in retrospect, her reaction to this disastrous event:

> On 3 September 1939 war was declared between Britain and Germany. It was Retreat Sunday.[9] There was torrential rain accompanied by thunder and lightning and the day was dark and miserable. Everyone was frightened at the thought of war and conscription. [Later] air raid shelters were being built everywhere in the North. Our laundry window was bricked up and we used [the laundry] as a shelter. The Blessed Sacrament was brought there and placed in a safe every time the sirens were sounded foretelling an air raid.[10]

Frequent sirens would have been heard in Bangor as the German planes passed up along the lough, making for the Belfast docks. About the Belfast Blitzes, which followed a year and a half after the declaration of war, our witness continues:

On Easter Tuesday night, 1941, Belfast was showered with bombs, especially around the docks and the Ardoyne area. Many people were made homeless and quite a number came to Bangor. Eight were lodged in a house opposite the convent. It is now the curate's residence. The Catholic ladies came round daily to what was then the [school] cookery kitchen. They made a good meal for the refugees and then took the small children to their homes and bathed them. Miss Stewart, who had taught in Ardoyne school, was in constant attendance. The Sisters had been up in Crumlin Road convent [for Easter] but as soon as the news arrived that refugees were in Bangor they returned to give as much help as possible. Thank God the planes did not drop any bombs over Bangor as they passed on to Belfast. Scrabo monument seemed to be a landmark for them as they came up Strangford Lough.[11]

Bangor was considered a safe place to which to evacuate children, who could be conveyed by train from the County Down Railway Station in Quay Street. Teachers went with them, equipped with the basic necessities. The major grocery stores in Bangor provided much-needed food supplies. Evacuees continued to arrive through May and June and there were even refugees from Belgium. As the emergency continued, the school numbers were also increased by children whose parents were stationed in Bangor as members of the armed forces, but they did not stay long and by 1942 most had departed.

Canon Scally

On 21 February 1940 the Mercy community, along with the whole parish, suffered a great loss with the death of Canon Scally. The canon had been a great character in his day. He enjoyed nothing more than his daily horse ride and he occasionally rode to hounds with the local gentry. Later he acquired a car, as his parish had a radius of nine miles. As he did not learn to drive himself, his sexton, school caretaker and general factotum, Pat Vallely, drove him around. A contemporary member of the congregation recorded:

the Canon, with his caretaker driving his car, went around to collect the junior children who lived at a distance from the schools and drove them to school, especially in inclement weather.[12]

But this generosity was not wholly disinterested. The fact was:

to have the schools recognised by the Ministry of Education, sixty pupils must be on the rolls. Even if the Canon was not available every day Mr. Vallely went along.[13]

Canon Scally sometimes went riding with a young friend, Mon (Mr, later Dr, Edmund) O'Driscoll. One day, while they were riding, the canon's horse was very agitated. Just outside Crawfordsburn he and Mon swapped horses. While the canon held Mon's horse (which was not strange to him), Mon took the restless horse for a thorough gallop to quieten him down. By the time he came back Mon found the canon lying on the ground. He had died of a heart attack.

An account of what, on hindsight, looks like a premonition the canon had of his sudden death has been left to us by a parishioner of the time. She relates:

> It was rather prophetic that Canon Scally, in what was to be his last sermon at his celebration of Holy Mass on Sunday, 18 February, preached on 'Sudden Death'. He mentioned that there was only one pound five shillings debt on the parish, and that for the Ballyholme side of it. 'I think I'll leave that to the next man,' he said. The church had been redecorated for the Canon's Golden Jubilee, June 1939 ... The Canon had celebrated Holy Mass and heard Confessions as usual on [the morning of] Wednesday, 21 February ... He had kept active at his priestly duties to the end.[14]

St Sillan's

On 12 September 1946 the Sisters opened a kindergarten in Ballyholme. This village is a seaside suburb of Bangor and because of the influx of visitors during the summer (Bangor and Ballyholme were popular seaside resorts for Belfast people; they could be reached by a short scenic train journey along the north-Down coast) a chapel of ease was built there as an extension of Bangor parish. As the nearest Catholic school was in Bangor itself a need was seen for some provision in Ballyholme for the youngest children. So the parish priest, Father McGowan, invited the Sisters to open a small fee-paying kindergarten, called St Sillan's (after the third abbot of Bangor), in a house on Ballyholme esplanade. This house had been left to the church by Mary Byrne. The mother and sister, Ann, of Sister M. Paschal O'Callaghan presented a beautiful statue of Our Lady of the Miraculous Medal to the kindergarten. Father Michael Fullen, P.P., celebrated an opening Mass there on 8 September 1946; the little school was blessed and 16 children enrolled.

Each day Sister M. Mercy Cummins and Sister Colette Fitzsimmons (and later Sister M. Finbarr Maloney) travelled to Ballyholme from the convent in Bangor. As time moved on the number of children attending the kindergarten dropped, so it was closed and the house later used as the residence for the curate.

For the first 16 years the convent school in Bangor educated the girls until school-leaving age. The year 1948 saw the introduction of the 'qualifying examination'. Girls who qualified for grammar schools went daily to Belfast, to St Dominic's High School or the Dominican College, Fortwilliam. Some went as boarders to Kilkeel, Ballynahinch or Ballycastle. A few who did not wish to travel or board went to the local non-denominational grammar schools – there was no Catholic grammar school in Bangor.

Over the ensuing years, many Sisters came to serve in Bangor for longer or shorter periods. Besides the school, they were involved in many of the activities of the parish. They cared for the church, keeping the altar linens and vessels in perfect order; they participated in the parish choir and, when necessary, trained it. Instructing converts for baptism was a very important apostolate, especially since Bangor was a place of many mixed marriages. The Sisters were also the directors of the Junior Legion of Mary and active members of St Joseph's Young Priests' Society. They encouraged vocations to the priesthood and religious life by word and example and the convent was a place of encouragement and advice for married couples. No work of mercy was outside their scope and their presence was much appreciated by the people.

During the early 1950s, the school had large numbers of pupils for whom there was insufficient accommodation. Relief came when, in 1956, the school committee decided to build a new extension at a cost of £12,000. In 1958 the extension was ready for occupation, giving three additional classrooms. This building was a great asset to the school, as the rooms were large, well heated and ventilated and bright, owing to the many windows. The principal at this time was Sister M. Paschal O'Callaghan; she was assisted by Sister M. Patrick Kelly, Miss McDevitt and Mrs Caughey.

In addition to the important purposes being served by the presence of the Sisters in Bangor parish, it was of no small importance that occasionally Sisters from Belfast could spend a few days' holiday there, especially during the summer when the Sisters teaching in Bangor during the year went elsewhere for a change. The convent was beautifully situated, comfortable, commodious and convenient for refreshing walks by the sea or in the country. Over the years many Sisters from the city availed of this opportunity and always found a most hospitable welcome from the resident community.

[1]   St Bernard of Clairvaux, *Life of Malachy* (London: Society for Promoting Christian Knowledge, 1920).

[2]   C.F., Comte de Montalembert, *The monks of the west, from St Benedict to St Bernard* (Edinburgh and London: Blackwood, 1860), vol. ii, Book 7.

[3]   O'Laverty, *op. cit.*, vol. ii, p. 40.

[4]   P. Winder, minister of Bangor, to clerk of parliament (Archives, SPCMB, 12 April 1766).

[5]   Archives, SPCMB, 1930s.

[6]   Ibid.

[7]   Sister M. Clare (Josephine) McAteer, college project on Belfast Mercy Sisters (unpublished, 1965).

[8]   The exact details about this matter could be questioned. They came from Father McGowan, P.P., years after the event and even after the death of Canon Scally. However, the controversy did reflect the distrust the Catholic hierarchy had of the new government of Northern Ireland.

[9]   In the convent the first Sunday of each month was a day of recollection. Strict silence was kept until recreation time at 4.30 p.m.

[10] Sisters of Mercy, Convent of Mercy, Bangor: annals (MCA).

[11] Ibid.

[12] M.M. Feeny, personal memoirs, Bangor (Archives, SCPMB, 1980s *et seq.*). See also J. O'Hanlon (ed.), *St Comgall's Primary School centenary, 1890–1990* (Bangor, 1990).

[13] Ibid.

[14] Ibid.

20

CENTENARY OF FOUNDATION

The big event of 1954 was the centenary of the arrival of the Sisters of Mercy in Belfast. It was an event for which preparations had been made all through the preceding year.

First of all, in the spring of 1953, a full-scale redecoration of the convent commenced, beginning with the chapel. At the same time, during the weeks of Lent, another kind of activity was going on: a modification of the Sisters' religious dress. This was to be a simplification of the traditional, more cumbersome, religious habit which had been distinctive of the Sisters of Mercy over the preceding 90 years or so. The results were to be seen for the first time at Mass on Easter Sunday and were met with general approval.

In the course of the year other intensive preparations for the coming centenary were made, and each Sister undertook her share in these. A centenary magazine was prepared, recounting the history of the community over the previous hundred years.[1] The Sisters in each school set to work to prepare the entertainments. The first production was an operetta, *Pearl the fishermaid*, performed by the pupils of St Malachy's Convent Primary School, Sussex Place, on 8 December 1953 (in the 'red room', the school's performance hall). The pupils of St Paul's Convent School were preparing a play, *Our Lady of Guadalupe*, for the centenary day, and the children of the Star of the Sea Convent School were working on a variety concert.

At last the great day dawned – Monday, 25 January, the feast of St Paul. The previous Saturday and Sunday had been busy days, spent decorating the convent and making ready the dining rooms. The chapel was prepared for the thanksgiving Mass, with a throne erected in the sanctuary for Bishop Mageean, who was to preside. The celebrations commenced in the morning with solemn High Mass, at which the bishop presided in *cappa magna*. The celebrant was the Right Reverend Monsignor James Hendley of St Paul's Parish, Belfast, assisted by Very Reverend J. McMullan of Duneane as deacon and Reverend J. Maguire of St Malachy's College as sub-deacon. The Very Reverend F. McCorry of St Malachy's College (chaplain to the convent) was master of ceremonies. The Mass was sung by the community choir under the direction of Reverend P. O'Kelly of St Mary's Teacher-Training College. The Very Reverend G. McDonnell, C.Ss.R., rector of the Redemptorist Monastery, Marianella, Dublin, preached the sermon.

An especially valued tribute for the occasion was a telegram from the Vatican:

HAPPY OCCASION CENTENARY SISTERS OF MERCY CRUMLIN ROAD HOLY FATHER SENDS CORDIAL FELICITATIONS INVOKES CONTINUED DIVINE BLESSINGS PRAISEWORTHY WORK IMPARTS COMMUNITY APOSTOLIC BENEDICTION. MONTINI PROSECRETARY.[2]

After the religious ceremonies lunch was served to all who had attended. Outside the rain poured unceasingly but this did not mar the festivities within. In fact, it highlighted the bright and joyous atmosphere.

When lunch was over the bishop and clergy (over a hundred had attended the celebratory Mass) repaired to Fatima Hall (the school performance hall) for the drama. The medical and surgical staff of the Mater Hospital, with their spouses, were also invited. Afterwards there was Benediction of the Blessed Sacrament and a solemn 'Te Deum' was sung alternately by the clergy and the community choir. The hospital guests were then entertained to high tea in the refectory and the clergy had light refreshments in the noviceship. Thus ended the actual centenary day – a memorable and happy one for all. The next day, the seminarians from St Malachy's College were entertained to lunch, after which they gave a most enjoyable entertainment for the community.

On the following Sunday members of religious communities of women from convents throughout the six counties were invited. The drama (*Our Lady of Guadalupe*) was staged for them and this was followed by Benediction and the 'Te Deum'. High tea was served in the refectory. In the evenings of the following week, staff of the schools and hospitals, as well as friends and associates of the community, were invited. On Sunday, 7 February the pupils of the Star of the Sea School staged their variety concert for the community and the student nursing Sisters. On Sunday, 14 February the community was invited to the hospital to view a film, followed by tea. During the course of the weeks of celebration the children in the schools had their own parties.

After a very full and exciting couple of weeks the festivities came to a happy conclusion. Many greetings telegrams were received from all over Ireland for the occasion and many holy Masses offered in thanksgiving and for the community's intentions. Fine commemorative gifts were also received, which were much appreciated and admired. A fitting conclusion to the year of celebration came with the blessing, on 8 December, of the new grotto of Our Lady of Lourdes in the front garden of the convent, in special commemoration of the Marian Year (1954). The grotto was presented to the community by the past and present clergy of St Malachy's College. The blessing was followed by solemn Benediction of the Blessed Sacrament in the convent chapel.

The centenary celebrations had been a great success, but no doubt the Sisters were glad to settle down again to the common life. There was a lot to be grateful for and the community gave heartfelt thanks to God for the many blessings of the previous hundred years and the present.[3]

Convent life resumed its normal flow, but the year 1956 saw a far-reaching innovation. The community purchased a green minibus. Joseph Quinn (of the lodge) learned to drive; so did Mother M. Bernard McKillop and Sister M. Benignus Morgan. At one period, during a summer course which was held in St Teresa's Hall, Glen Road, when many visiting Sisters were staying in the convent and needed transport, two minibuses were running simultaneously and cars were constantly on the road. They saved invaluable time and travel expense.

The first minibus travelled over half of Ireland when community outings were organised: to Dublin and the midlands; to the Glens of Antrim; to Glenties and Bundoran in south Donegal and to Fanad and Malin Head, north Donegal. Many films of the journeys were made by Mother M. Bernadette Agnew, then bursar. The prime movers behind the purchase of the minibus and cars – and the newly enlivened lifestyle – were Mother Marie Thérèse Laverty, superior, and Mother M. Bernadette Agnew. Both were far seeing and progressive for their day, while at the same time retaining a great regard for the traditional values and regularity of community life. Several other Sisters learned to drive in the ensuing years and in time that first car gave place to a fleet. If they could talk, the community cars would have many tales to tell.

Immaculata Special School

One reason why the new style of vacation was introduced was that the home in Abbeyville was no longer available for community holidays. As has been mentioned elsewhere, the building had suffered considerable in a fire. The top floor – the dormitory, which accommodated the Sisters on holiday – had been completely destroyed. Sisters M. Aidan Mullarkey and M. Ailbe (Elizabeth) Gray were there at the time and actually in the dormitory when the fire started, but no one was injured. St Brigid's Home and School for the Blind in Abbeyville finally closed in 1956.

Before the blind children left Abbeyville plans were already under way for the school to be used for a new educational apostolate. After the fire, when the home's future was in question, the bishop had put to the superior of Crumlin Road the urgent need for a school for children of slower learning abilities, as no such Catholic school existed in Northern Ireland. As the intake would be from all over the north boarding facilities would be needed. For this Abbeyville seemed ideal. The proposal was agreed to by the community and, when the blind children had left, the necessary refurbishment got under way. Sister M. Carmel Laverty had already gone to London (on a grant from the Ministry of Education) to take her diploma in the teaching of children with special educational needs and she supervised the preparations for the new school. Abbeyville was about to enter into a new phase of its interesting history.

On 12 September 1957 Bishop Mageean blessed and formally opened Immaculata Special School for Educationally Sub-normal Children (ESN), Abbeyville. Reverend Christopher Dallat, C.C. of Whitehouse, was appointed manager and Sister M. Carmel Laverty principal. She was assisted by Sister M. Alphonsus McKernan as vice-principal, along with Sisters M. Clement (Ann) McKeever, M. Annunciata Caffrey and two lay teachers, Marie McKenna and Beth Gormley.

Sister M. Carmel recalls that the names of the pupils who were to attend the school were received in June, three months before the opening, and she and Sister M. Alphonsus visited the homes of as many of these as possible during the summer months. As can be understood, some Belfast parents were a little apprehensive about their children leaving the local primary school and travelling to this new, unknown establishment on the outskirts of the city. An amusing anecdote was recounted at the time by Sister M. Mercy Cummins, who was then teaching in Sussex Place Convent School in the Markets, from which several of the new school's pupils were to be drawn. This was a conversation between two mothers which she had overheard. One remarked rather scornfully that her neighbour's daughter had to go to 'the backward school', to which her neighbour, with typical ready Belfast wit, replied, 'It's not a backward school. It's a pushing on school!'

The first pupils arrived on 25 September. It was to be for girls only: boys attended St Aloysius Special School, Somerton Road, Belfast. The school at first had an enrolment of 60 girls from Belfast and district, all day pupils. On 11 February 1958 11 boarders were taken from various parts of Northern Ireland, and by September 1958 the full number on roll had risen to 102, 19 of whom were boarders. (The number of pupils was later to rise to 120, 25 of whom were boarders.) Sister M. Xavier Larkin was house mother, assisted by Sister M. Celsus Daly. Sister M. Kevin Drain very ably fulfilled the role of catering supervisor. Lily Campbell, formerly a resident of Abbeyville, remained on to manage the laundry, a job which she accomplished with great skill and efficiency, while James (Jimmy) Joyce of the lodge continued as caretaker.

Immaculata Special School was a happy place, especially as the children, many from problematic backgrounds, got individual tuition and attention. Though every care was taken to improve intellectual skills, much attention was also given to developing their natural talents for music, art, drama, cookery, craftwork and athletics. All members of the staff had special qualifications for teaching children who were, in the parlance of the day, 'slow learners'.

The community in Abbeyville Convent at this time (the late 1950s), besides those engaged in the school, were: Sister M. Patricia Doran, local superior, Sister M. Antonia Downey (the oldest member), Sisters M. Ercnat Kelly, M. Philomena McMullan, Colette Fitzsimmons and M. Colman McGurk.

Craigdarragh

In 1957 also another work was entrusted to the Belfast community – a second home for the elderly infirm. Our Lady's Home, Beechmount, was overcrowded and could not accommodate all those who sought admission. In 1955, in response to the need for more places, Bishop Mageean bought an extensive property (27 acres) including a large mansion, known as Craigdarragh, at Helen's Bay, County Down, with the intention of having the house modernised and extended as a home for elderly men who could be moved from Beechmount. The mansion was a beautiful Regency-style building surrounded by acres of terraced lawns overlooking Belfast Lough and opposite Carrickfergus. With the house came fields where cattle grazed, woods, a glen and little beach on the lough shore. The house had been built around 1850 for the Workman family, shipping merchants. John and Robert Workman, brothers, had come to Belfast from Scotland in the early nineteenth century to set up a muslin business in Upper Arthur Street (R. and J. Workman). The family later joined with the Clark firm to form a shipbuilding company in Belfast. The last Workman descendant who lived there sold the property to the diocese of Down and Connor. Renovations to the house and a three-storey extension commenced in May 1955 and were completed in 1957. The extension included some accommodation for the staff of the new home.

St Columbanus's Home, as it was named, was entrusted to the care of the Sisters of Mercy. The bishop officially opened it on 26 November 1959. Sister M. Patricia Doran was the first superior. The Sisters on the nursing staff were Sister M. de Lourdes Keaveney and Sister Marie Goretti McDevitt; Sister Laurence McCann supervised the catering. The nursing Sisters travelled from Belfast each day until the convent section was ready. Part of the basement of the house was converted into a beautiful chapel, one of the first to possess a modern 'rubrical'-style altar and Gothic vestments. Father Oliver Breslin (on loan from the diocese of Dromore) was appointed chaplain. On the opening day the first Mass was celebrated by Reverend Dan Murphy, P.P. of Holywood, with the bishop presiding. On 8 December the first residents, nine male patients, were transferred from Beechmount; the remainder arrived a fortnight later.

On 28 January 1976 St Columbanus's was registered with the Eastern Health and Social Services Board as a voluntary residential home for aged, infirm and physically disabled persons with a maximum of 40 residents. As with Beechmount, control of St Columbanus's was exercised by the Down and Connor Management Committee, which was responsible for major policy decisions and the provision of funding. The day-to-day management of the home was the responsibility of the Sisters of Mercy.

The 1950s, then, were eventful years for the Sisters of Mercy in Down and Connor. The community was large and youthful, with an average of two postulants entering each year. The works were expanding and the centenary gave an opportunity for stocktaking and expressing gratitude for what had been achieved.[4] Sixteen Sisters had died, most of them in old age after many fruitful years. Plans were being made for the future, especially in the areas of education and nursing. Sisters who would work in these apostolates were receiving third-level education and the new government health and education reforms were imposing many challenges, which the community hoped, with God's help, they would be well able to meet. The 1960s were to bring a widening of horizons as the community entered into the new enterprise of secondary education.

---

[1] Sisters of Mercy, 'Convent of Our Lady of Mercy, St Paul's, Belfast: centenary souvenir, 1854–1954' (MCA).

[2] Archives, SPCMB, 1950.

[3] I am indebted to the late Sister M. Brendan Blanche for this account of the actual centenary event and the days following it. The drama *Our Lady of Guadalupe* was later staged for the public in St Mary's Hall, Berry Street, Belfast.

[4] Sisters of Mercy, 'Convent of Our Lady of Mercy, St Paul's, Belfast: centenary souvenir, 1854–1954' (MCA).

21

THE 1960s: A DECADE OF EXPANSION

Involvement in modern secondary education became a new undertaking for the Mercy community. In 1957 the school-leaving age had been raised to 15. Pupils who had not qualified for places in grammar schools went to the secondary intermediate schools to complete their final years of mandatory schooling. However, as yet Mercy Secondary Intermediate School was not ready, so interim arrangements had to be made for extra classes for the 14–15-year-olds who were to remain on in both the Crumlin Road and the Star of the Sea Convent Schools for another year. The Crumlin Road School was able, after the departure of the 'qualifiers', to provide senior classes for those pupils who would be staying on. The Star of the Sea School, however, already quite overcrowded, did not have sufficient space, so the senior pupils from there had to move to St Patrick's Girls' School on Donegall Street. The girls from this school had moved elsewhere – the primary-age children to a new school nearby, and those over 11 years old to the new parish secondary intermediate school, the Little Flower, Somerton Road. Here they would remain for one year until the opening of the new secondary school at Ballysillan.

The old St Patrick's School had been left in a state of disrepair since it had been vacated, so it was in very poor condition. However, all that could be done was to knuckle down to the situation and make the most of it. Three teachers were appointed, Sister M. Emilian Moloney from the Star of the Sea School, Mrs Carville, formerly a teacher in St Patrick's, and Sister M. Assumpta Duddy, who had just finished college. There were three classrooms in all and an extra cookery and needlework class was taken by Sister M. Emilian. The oldest girls were hard to manage because they were aggrieved at having to stay on at school an extra year and because they found themselves in class with girls a year younger than themselves. However, despite their sometimes boisterous behaviour, the youngsters were good and always loyal to their old *alma mater*, the 'Star'. The 11–14-year-olds, for their part, were looking forward to the novelty of the new secondary school, which they hoped to attend the following autumn. Sister M. Emilian and Sister M. Assumpta walked to and from the school each day, returning to the convent for lunch at midday and usually with a sigh of relief in the evening.

In 1960 Sister M. Carmel Laverty left Immaculata Special School in the capable hands of Sister M. Alphonsus McKernan, to become the first principal of Our Lady of Mercy Secondary Intermediate School. At last the school, the building of which had seen so many vicissitudes between the cutting of its first sod in August 1954 and its completion in 1960, opened in September of that year with 352 pupils and 14 staff. The staff comprised six Sisters (besides Sister M. Carmel) – Sister M. Paschal (Briege) O'Callaghan, vice-principal, Sister M. Berchmans (Deirdre) O'Leary, Sister M. Gabriel Deignan, Sister M. Assumpta (Marie) Duddy, Sister M. Pius (Eileen) McNicholl and Sister M. Concilio (Thérèse) Larkin – and seven lay teachers – Ethna Kearney, Brea McCabe, Philomena Bradley, Margaret Higgins, Ann McAlinden, Pat Hamill and Geraldine McErlean. Although the building was not yet quite ready for use, Sister M. Carmel's wishes prevailed. As she felt that the completion of the school had been long enough delayed she was determined to make a start with a blessing and opening ceremony on 15 September, the feast of Our Lady of Dolours.

On this day the pupils and staff gathered in the gym hall as the floor of the assembly hall was not yet finished (and would not be for several weeks). After the formalities the pupils went home and the staff set about the task of sorting out desks, chairs and parcels of books and sweeping back sawdust and debris in the wake of the workmen, who were still at their jobs.

Under the able supervision of Sister M. Carmel things were gradually becoming shipshape. Equipment was installed in science labs, cookery rooms, art rooms, the gym, the canteen and the kitchen and classrooms were in order when the formal blessing and opening took place on 27 October. Besides the girls from the Crumlin Road and Star of the Sea some others were admitted from St Vincent de Paul Girls' Primary School, Ligoniel, in which parish the school was situated. There were 11 classes to start with and, with form teachers duly assigned, things began to take shape. Some of the Sisters and teachers were familiar to the girls, having come up from the primary schools with them, and that made things easier. Still, however, the environment was new and took some getting used to. An interesting fact was that, at lunchtime, the girls did not know what to do with themselves in the spacious play area (later laid out as playing fields and tennis courts) around the school, having come from such confined playgrounds in their inner-city schools. Needless to say, this strangeness was soon overcome. Changing classes at the sound of the bell, and the variety of subjects to be studied, were other big novelties for them – as was bus travel to and from school, which was soon efficiently organised. (One day some years later one bright young lady arrived on her pony.)

The school uniform was navy and white, with a royal-blue and gold tie. The motto on the school badge, in Irish and in English, read 'Truth in our hearts'. The challenge of this motto was brought home to the girls (and the teachers) in the words of Bishop Mageean, on the opening day:

> The purpose of this school is to make you women of character, and by that I mean the supernatural person who thinks, judges, acts constantly and consistently in accordance with the principles of right reason as elevated and illuminated by the teaching and example of our Divine Lord.[1]

Our Lady of Mercy School was off to a good start![2]

Also in 1960, a Catholic parish coeducational secondary intermediate school for 600 pupils was opened in Bangor, County Down – St Columbanus's, Ballymaconnell Road – and the Sisters of Mercy were asked to join the staff there. Those appointed were Sister M. Alacoque McDonagh (as vice-principal), Sister M. Louis Donaghy and Sister M. Emilian Moloney. (Later, Sister M. Pius McNicholl moved from Our Lady of Mercy to join the staff in Ballymaconnell.) As a corollary to the appointment of the Sisters to the staff a contract was drawn up between the diocesan trustees of the school and the Belfast Mercy community. According to this agreement, the community undertook to pay one quarter of the cost of the internal maintenance of the school and of the heating, lighting and cleaning costs, one quarter of the insurance premiums and one quarter of the cost of national insurance for the teaching and non-teaching staff during such time as the Sisters should be staff members of the school.[3] The Sisters resided in Bangor Convent and travelled to school daily. However, after some years the Sisters were required for the Belfast schools so had to be withdrawn from St Columbanus's. Because of a lack of available personnel in the community they could not be replaced.

One of the reasons for the removal of the Sisters from the secondary school in Bangor was that a new secondary intermediate school was opening nearer to Crumlin Road Convent. St Gemma's, on the Oldpark Road, would serve the Ardoyne and Sacred Heart Parishes (from which some children went to the convent primary school on the Crumlin Road). An urgent request was made to the Mercy community for Sisters to staff it – in particular, for a principal. Sister M. Emilian was appointed to the post and Sisters M. Pius McNicholl and M. Annunciata Caffrey joined her on the staff.

Sister M. Emilian Moloney was principal from 1967 to 1979. When she became superior of the community in 1979 she was replaced by Sister M. Gabriel Deignan (principal until 1988). Sister M. Emilian was later appointed principal of Mercy Primary School. Sister M. Pius took early retirement in 1984 (to go to Africa) and Sister M. Annunciata retired in 1992. There had also been a request to the community, in 1960, to adopt, finance the building of and staff a girls' secondary school in St John's Parish (upper Falls Road, Belfast). This was a large Catholic area, which had originally been middle class but now included new, densely populated, poorer housing estates. In the event, this undertaking did not prove feasible as the request came at the same time as that to staff St Gemma's. The school was then built by the parish and became, in time, the highly successful St Louise's Comprehensive School under the principalship of Sister Genevieve, Daughter of Charity.

The convent primary school

At the end of the 1950s the Northern Ireland Ministry of Education gave planning permission for the building of a new, modern primary school on the site of the existing convent school on the Crumlin Road, now almost a hundred years old. The community decided, in 1962, that the school, the girls' club and the lodge on Convent Avenue be demolished with a view to rebuilding on the site. In preparation for this the school had to find temporary accommodation and it was not easy to find a suitable place in the district. However, at last, a lease for three years of the old Belfast High School (which had moved to new premises in Jordanstown) in Glenravel Street and a row of adjacent terrace houses was acquired. Since Glenravel Street (which was later demolished to make way for the Westlink) was not far distant from the convent, this was as satisfactory as could be hoped for.

In June 1964 the move was made. One of the younger Sisters on the staff at that time, Sister M. St John (Frances) Forde has left us an account of the circumstances and event:

> The building in Glenravel Street had been the former premises of the Belfast High School. It had been derelict for more than a year when we moved there in June 1964. It was inevitable that a lot of work needed to be done to prepare for the transfer of the school. However, with the use of mops, buckets, soap, water, dusters and polish and most of all willing hands, it became quite a pleasant place for the children. Perhaps the fact that we had to improvise and make do helped to create the warm atmosphere, which was experienced by the staff and pupils alike.[4]

There were six Sisters on the convent-school staff at the time of the transfer: Mother Marie Thérèse Laverty (principal), Mother M. Bernadette Agnew, Sister M. Mercy Cummins, Sister M. Benignus Morgan, Sister M. Angela Deignan and Sister M. St John (Frances) Forde. Sister M. Aquinas (Grace)

Quinn and Sister M. Gertrude Monaghan joined the staff in Glenravel Street. Most of the lay staff of the school also generously participated in the move. With 850 children on roll the transfer was, no doubt, a big undertaking, but with the cooperative spirit of staff and pupils things were soon put in order and a regular school routine resumed after the summer holiday.

Meanwhile, as temporary accommodation pending the intended rebuilding of the convent lodge, Joseph Quinn and his sister got a house in Thorndale Avenue. The girls' club, or hostel, also moved to two adjoining houses on the same road. Sister M. Mercy Cummins was appointed in charge of the hostel and undertook extensive renovations to the houses, which resulted in a most comfortable, homely and convenient residence.

Then began the grand work of funding the building of the new school. A monster bazaar was held before Christmas, which proved very rewarding. There was a great response from pupils, their families and all the friends of the community.

At this point, unexpectedly, matters took a new twist. When demolition was under way Bishop William Philbin requested that the school site be used for an extension of the Mater Hospital which, he said, was necessary if the hospital was to be recognised as a medical training school. This request caused great consternation in the community, especially as plans for the construction of the new school on the original site had been drawn up and approved by the Ministry of Education. However, the superior of the time, Mother M. Ercnat Kelly, felt obliged to accede to the bishop's request. This request was the beginning of a long-drawn-out controversy between the bishop and the community in the years following with regard to releasing convent property for the expansion of the Mater Hospital.

The change of plan opened a totally new aspect of the rebuilding scheme. A new site was now needed and a search began. The community felt it desirable, if at all possible, to keep the school within St Patrick's Parish, for which the first school had originally opened and from which most of the intake still came. An additional complication was that Hamill Park, which had been earmarked for the new gate-lodge, could not be used either, in view of the hospital plans.

At last, in December 1966, a site for the primary school was found and purchased. It comprised a house and six acres of land and cost £30,000. The community bought the site against competition from the Belfast Corporation, who wanted it for a fire station for trainee firemen. It had, unfortunately, not been possible to find property in St Patrick's Parish, but the community considered themselves very lucky that, after a long and seemingly almost futile search, which had ranged from Carlisle Circus to

Glengormley, a suitable, spacious property about two miles up the Crumlin Road from the convent – in fact, en route to the secondary school – had at last been found. This was Ballysillan House, at 614 Crumlin Road (in Holy Cross Parish, Ardoyne). It was in a residential part of the Crumlin Road and beautifully located on a rise of the hill in the (then) northern outskirts of the city.

This property had originally been owned by J. Salters of Salters and Anderson, linen merchants, who had built it just after World War I. The architect, Tom Henry (brother of the Irish painter Paul Henry), had designed it in 1919.[5] It had been acquired by the Ewart family in 1927 and was the home of one of the managers of Ewart Mills, one of the two great linen mill companies on the Crumlin Road which had been so productive from the mid-nineteenth to the mid-twentieth centuries and which had given rise to the growth of population in the Ardoyne and Woodvale areas of north Belfast. (The other mill was the Edenderry Mill on the opposite side of the Crumlin Road.) The Ewart family itself, of Glenbank House, Ligoniel, was one of the most active in philanthropy in Belfast. Their commitment began with William Ewart Junior, chairman of the firm, a town councillor, twice mayor, and MP for north Belfast. He served on the town relief committees in 1858 and 1879 and on the committees of the Workshop for the Blind, and the Prison Gate Mission for Women. In recognition of his services to the town he was made a baronet. Perhaps, then, it is no little coincidence that the Ballysillan property should have come into the possession of the Sisters of Mercy, dedicated to the service of the poor and the cause of education. However that may be, it was a very suitable site, both in extent and in situation.

Building began on the site in early 1968; the architects were McCusker, Power and Leeson. In August 1968 a proposal came from the bishop suggesting that, in view of the cost of the building and setting up of the new school, application should be made for maintained status. The new education legislation, an amendment act passed in 1968, came to the aid of voluntary schools by providing that church authorities could receive an 80-per-cent grant towards capital expenditure, and a 100-per-cent grant for maintenance. This depended on their agreement to be managed by a 'four-and-two' committee and was known as maintained status. If the trustees followed the bishop's proposal, Mercy Primary School would be a pioneer beneficiary of this new legislation as the bishop had advised that other Catholic voluntary schools not go into the system at that time.

In October of the same year, Our Lady of Mercy Secondary School made plans to enter the maintained scheme. When the school formed its first 'four-and-two' committee, Matthew G. Salters was invited to join the new board of governors and served on it for 30 years.

The Ballysillan House property had been purchased primarily for the six acres of land on which the new primary school would be built, but there were also plans to use the house itself as a voluntary nursery school. This proposal was put to the Ministry of Education in May 1967 but was then put on hold pending the opening of the primary school. In the end it was never followed up and the house was reserved for other purposes.

The house itself is a handsome building – two storeys high, pebble-dashed, with a noble portico at the entrance and bays on either side. A pretty glass sun-porch fronted the morning room, facing east, and a large conservatory extended from the west gable facing Divis Mountain and, in the days of the house's use as a family dwelling, looked down on terraced rose gardens to the small stream of the Forth River. Here the westering sun is caught in the evening and the view extends to the majestic Mourne Mountains in the south. Unfortunately the rose gardens and extensive front lawns had to be sacrificed for the building of the new school and playgrounds, but some of the lawns and gardens in the immediate vicinity of the house were retained. Trees and shrubs were planted which, over the years, have grown to maturity and provide a pleasant oasis of calm alongside a very busy thoroughfare.

In September 1970 the new Mercy Primary School was ready for occupation. We take up the story from Sister M. St John Forde:

> The change from Glenravel Street to the present surroundings in 1970 was a real culture shock. We moved from very cramped conditions to spacious grounds, from concrete to grass. In our first year here, because of the more extensive school premises, the members of staff felt cut off from one another, but we soon learned to adapt to these new conditions.[6]

For the convent school it was simply a matter of a change of site. Mother Marie Thérèse Laverty continued as principal; the other Sisters on the staff were Mother M. Bernadette Agnew, Sisters M. Paschal O'Callaghan, M. Benignus Morgan, M. Angela Deignan, M. St John Forde, M. Aquinas Quinn and M. Gertrude Monaghan. Sister M. Mercy Cummins retired at this time. The school was designed to take up to 700 pupils, with 22 classrooms, an assembly/gym hall, offices, a dining room and a meals kitchen. It would see various additions and extensions in the ensuing years.

Changes in the deployment of the teaching Sisters, necessitated by the undertaking of secondary education in three new schools, inevitably affected the staffing of the primary schools in which these Sisters had been engaged.

In June 1969 a community decision was made that the convent in Sussex Place should be closed for a trial period of some weeks or months after the summer, as there were only two Sisters now engaged in the school – Sister M. Vincent Donnelly, principal, and Sister M. Clement (Ann) McKeever, assistant teacher. It was arranged that these two Sisters should travel daily from Crumlin Road. The experiment proved satisfactory. Sussex Place Convent no longer had a resident Mercy community, but new developments were to take place there in the course of the next two decades, as the later story will tell.

The Sisters continued to teach in the Star of the Sea Girls' Primary School, but in the course of the 1970s their number was reduced to two. The same course of events took place in Bangor. Priority was given to the staffing of the secondary schools and Immaculata Special School, as the greatest need was considered to exist in these sectors at that time.

Community life in the sixties: winds of change

The 1960s ushered in a whole new era in the western world. These were the opening years of a period of rapid change such as had never been experienced before, which would continue for the decades to follow. It was also a decade of great wars and violence – in Africa, Vietnam, China and elsewhere and with the assassination of such figures as President John Kennedy and Dr Martin Luther King Junior. Before the end of the decade, violence was to erupt in Northern Ireland itself. Unquestionably, though, the most historic event for the Catholic Church (one which was also to have a considerable impact on the wider world) was the Second Vatican Council, convened by Pope John XXIII and held in Rome between 1962 and 1965. However, before this momentous event, gradual changes continued to take place in the Mercy community's lifestyle in Belfast. A cautious modernisation happily prepared the way for greater and more rapid and far-reaching changes in the 1970s, 1980s and 1990s.

Changes took place on various levels: in the structures of the community, the prayer life and liturgy, the convent building itself and, yes, even more modification of the religious habit. For the sake of clarity and consistency it might be best, from this point on, to follow in broadly chronological order the notable stages of this evolution in community life as it occurred.[7]

In September 1963 a very important event took place. By an indult[8] from the Holy See, and in accordance with the decisions of the chapter of the community, the lay Sisters were accorded all the rights and privileges of choir Sisters, including full voting rights, so that the distinction between choir and lay Sisters no longer existed. This indult was warmly welcomed by the community. The former lay Sisters were given their places in the community according to the date of their profession and the rank of lay Sister was abolished.

Various changes were made in the customs for community prayers. Some years previously (in 1958) a change in the recitation of the Office of the Blessed Virgin Mary (the 'Little Office', in Latin) had been introduced. It was now to be recited in monotone and many of the additional prayers that had usually followed were to be omitted.[9] This innovation, like all the others, brought many amusing anecdotes in its train as the Sisters made valiant, though sadly not always successful, efforts to reach the pitch and maintain it throughout.

About this time it was also decided that Sisters who had to go on educational visits with children, nurses, etc., and those attending courses or classes, might go out unaccompanied by another Sister if it would be inconvenient to find a companion. Express permission was always required for these occasions – as, in fact, for any occasion to leave the convent.

Welcome renovations were made to the convent building itself for the convenience of the community. A three-storey extension was added to the convent's south wing by the erection of an infirmary block on the ground floor along Our Lady's Cloister. Above this were additional rooms on the first and second floors; a lift was also installed. A new community library was comfortably furnished with carpet, curtains, easy chairs, a heater and built-in bookcases of beautiful oak with sliding glass fronts. These bookcases were a gift from the family of Sisters M. Gabriel and Angela Deignan. They were later transferred to the library of Ballysillan House when the convent was closing. Great pleasure was taken in stocking the library with the best books on contemporary spirituality, theology, scripture, etc. available, and no expense was spared to purchase these.

Also in the 1960s the teaching Sisters began to become very much involved in wider educational circles, both with the Ministry of Education and with other schools. This involvement was necessary for the progress of Catholic education in Belfast, especially as the secondary schools were in a state of evolution. The Sisters were invited to give ideas, suggestions and opinions and gradually found themselves accepted on an equal footing with the 'controlled' schools (which were managed by the government). Times were changing. The Sisters also undertook night classes (though this was no great innovation in the history of the Sisters of Mercy in Belfast) in Our Lady of Mercy Secondary School. The enrolment was 30 to 40 young (and not so young) women and the subjects were cookery, needlework, physical education, commercial subjects and English. This undertaking required the

Sisters involved to travel back to the school at Ballysillan on Tuesday and Thursday evenings for classes at 7–9 p.m., which was demanding. Also, the school was quite out of the way for those who wished to attend the classes, many of them from the New Lodge and Antrim Road area. When the winter months came attendance dropped and the scheme was abandoned.

In the course of these years many requests were made to the community for Sisters for the missions – in particular for the USA (Florida and Alabama), Canada (British Columbia), South America and Africa. Several Sisters were eager to volunteer but the bishop would never give permission as he claimed that there was more than enough work to be done at home.

During the 1960s a fine spirit prevailed in the community. Much credit for this was due to Mother Marie Thérèse Laverty, supported by her council, for her open-mindedness, her willingness to enter fully into the mind and spirit of the church and her desire to prepare the community for the renewal intended by the Vatican Council. Being someone who kept up to date with current trends in religious life, she respected the new emphasis on the uniqueness of the individual and the need to foster personal responsibility and initiative, being careful at the same time to safeguard the religious spirit and always to call for a response of loyalty, obedience and respect towards the community and the institute as a whole. It was not an easy task to try to establish such a balance. Mother Thérèse believed that trust in the Holy Spirit and confidence in people were key elements of renewal. She was a woman of faith, courage and inspiration, a visionary for her time.

[1] Opening of Our Lady's Mercy School (Archives, SPCMB, 1960s).

[2] For the history of the school in its first 25 years see school publication, Our Lady of Mercy Secondary Intermediate School, *Our Lady of Mercy, Belfast: silver jubilee, 1960–1985* (Belfast: Our Lady of Mercy Secondary Intermediate School, 1985), p. 8.

[3] See legal agreement per T.H. Cairns and Co., Solicitors, Belfast (Archives, SPCMB, 17 August 1960).

[4] Sister M. Frances Forde, 'Personal memoirs of Mercy Primary School, Belfast' (Archives, SPCMB, 1960s).

[5] See P. Larmour, *Belfast: an illustrated architectural guide* (Belfast: Friar's Bush Press, 1987), p. 81, no. 186.

[6] Sister M. Frances Forde, 'Personal memoirs of Mercy Primary School, Belfast' (Archives, SPCMB, 1960s).

[7] Annals, SPCMB.

[8] A licence granted by the pope authorising a specific change to some rule for an important purpose. Since the Mercy Congregation was of pontifical rite, permission from the pope was needed at that time to make changes to the rule and constitutions.

[9] Reverend Dom Winnoc, O.S.B., of Glenstal Abbey, introduced the 'new' office and taught the Sisters to recite it.

22

THE 1970S: FERMENT AND CHANGE

The year 1969 saw the beginning of an era of serious disruption in the society of Northern Ireland which – though no one could have foreseen it – was to continue through the next 30 years, a saga of sectarian violence.

As is well recorded, Northern Ireland society suffered from sectarian unrest, which was aggravated by inequitable politics in the state and consequent inequality and injustice for some people. By the 1960s the nationalist youth of Northern Ireland had, it might be said, come of age, a long-term consequence of the 1947 Education Act. This had provided opportunities for secondary and third-level education for the minority section of the population who could not otherwise have aspired to continue their education after primary school. Education brought awareness; the nationalist youth saw that, though academically they could have matched their peers on the unionist side of society, opportunities in the professions and in business, as well as for housing and jobs, were far from equally shared between the two communities.

Such awareness brought the idea of a civil-rights movement, inspired by the civil-rights movements in the USA and intended to promote peaceful protest and a demand for fair treatment and equal opportunity for all. The Northern Ireland Civil Rights Association was founded in Belfast on 1 February 1967.[1] Predominantly (but not entirely) nationalist, socialist, Catholic and, to a certain extent, republican, the movement posed a threat to the non-sympathetic section of the population. Unrest had been simmering through the early years of the decade, welling to the surface in June 1966 when Dr Ian Paisley had led a demonstration in Belfast protesting against 'liberal' attitudes which he believed were destroying the sacrosanct structures of the state and exposing it to the encroachments of Romanism, nationalism and republicanism. The demonstration in the city centre had spilled over into a neighbouring nationalist area, the Markets, no stranger to sectarian antagonism, and rioting had ensued. The spark had been ignited and by the close of the decade sectarian conflict had flared up once more – this time more sophisticated, more deadly and more destructive than ever before.

It is not my intention to give here a history, even the briefest, of the Troubles. Many others have done this in a very expert way. Suffice it to say that scarcely anyone in Northern Ireland escaped the consequences of the terrorist conflict, least of all the poorer sectors of the Catholic nationalist population in Belfast, especially in the north, west and east of the city – the communities within or near which the Sisters of Mercy lived and with which they were pastorally involved. The convents, the hospitals and especially the schools came under frequent attack and the Sisters themselves felt threatened as targets of hatred from some quarters. Many stories could be told about these troubled years when bombings, shootings and assassinations were everyday fare and Northern Ireland was ravaged with great suffering and many terrible tragedies.[2]

The convent schools, especially those in north Belfast – Mercy Primary and Our Lady of Mercy Secondary – suffered many bombings and arson attacks. Scarcely a pupil came from a family that did not suffer bereavement of one sort or another. Some pupils died from terrorist attacks. In one of the first of these two Sisters, recent past pupils of Mercy Secondary School, Rosaleen and Jennifer McNairn, were both terribly maimed when they were caught by a bomb ruthlessly planted in a city-centre café. Immediate-family members and other close relatives of some of the Sisters were also killed or gravely injured in assassinations, crossfire shootings and bomb attacks; other endured loss of homes and property.

As has been recorded, in September 1970 the new Mercy Primary School opened at the Ballysillan House site (the Sisters travelled each day from the convent) and all went well there for the next couple of years. At first there were some minor sectarian attempts to cause damage to the school; then, in September 1973, both the primary and the secondary school, Our Lady of Mercy, suffered severe bombing on the same night. Much damage was done to both schools. Part of the primary school was out of use for the remainder of the school year while rebuilding work was being done. The classes affected moved into Ballysillan House for the duration. The secondary school had, in the earlier 1970s, suffered several vicious attacks resulting in three major fires, but had survived. This latest attack caused, once more, serious destruction, disruption of classes and an abiding sense of threat for teachers and pupils alike. By September 1974, however, the schools were completely repaired and ready to reopen.

That year was a difficult one for the schools. In the case of both schools the staff, both religious and lay, rose generously and uncomplainingly to the occasion, in spite of the loss of classrooms, furniture, books and equipment and the great inconvenience entailed. They had determined that school life should go on and that the children and young people should not be deprived of their rightful education because of the antagonism, and even hatred, around them. In most cases the Catholic schools in Belfast provided a haven of relative peace and stability for the children in a seriously disrupted society.

The attacks continued throughout the next 20 years. They varied in severity but always caused unwelcome disruption and untold expense. The most serious attacks of all on Our Lady of Mercy Secondary School took place in July and August 1996, after the controversy surrounding the Orange parade at Drumcree, Portadown. But this is outside the scope of our story. It is enough to say that the long-suffering principal, Sister M. Regina Caffrey, showed unparalleled resilience and courage in facing the heart-breaking devastation of that time. She fortunately had the whole-hearted support of the Board of Governors and staff. Two pupils of the secondary school were shot during the 1970s, one of them in crossfire on her way home from school, but fortunately no lives were lost nor injuries sustained in any of the Mercy convent schools.

Recounting the conflicts and strife of those years could take a long time, but it is not the only immediate purpose of the present narrative. The suffering was profound, intense and at times very tragic for all the people who were part of Northern Ireland society. On the other hand, these were years which also saw heroic generosity and self-sacrifice from people who made every effort to promote peace and to counter hatred with tolerance, injury with forgiveness and alienation with acceptance.

The Cave House

The 1970s saw a dramatic rise in the level of sectarian conflict in Belfast, and all over Northern Ireland, with many riots, shootings and bombings. Much of it took place near the convent and the convent schools on the Crumlin Road and the New Lodge, as well as in the Markets area of the city, which was served by Sussex Place Convent School. The tension was great and the stress of life in Belfast took its toll on everyone. During these years the Sisters were blessed in having a 'bolthole', a holiday house miles away, to which they could escape for a summer vacation, for the Christmas or Easter break or for an occasional weekend when commitments allowed. This was the Cave House in the Glens of Antrim, a place of blessed peace and tranquillity.

Cave House had been acquired in the summer of 1966. Since the fire in Abbeyville in 1953 there had been a lack of holiday accommodation there for the community. A disused premises at the rear of Abbeyville Convent, known as Lourdes, had been restored, mostly for the holiday use of the novices and junior professed (the professed Sisters could go for their holiday to other convents if they wished). For some years this fulfilled the need for holiday accommodation but it could not be considered suitable in the long term. So there was a search for an alternative, preferably by the sea. Eventually, by great good fortune, an ideal place was found, the Cave House in Cushendun, County Antrim.

The house has a panoramic setting in a secluded cove on the Antrim coast close to the picturesque village of Cushendun. With its own little private bay, it is surrounded on three sides by a semi-circle of headlands and cliffs and faces the open sea, with clear views across to the Mull of Kintyre in Scotland. John Masefield, the one-time poet laureate, who was married into the Crommelin family, former owners of the property, sometimes visited the house and remembered it as 'a lovely old place in an odd position on the Ulster Coast'.[3] It has been said, indeed, that Masefield's popular poem, 'I must go down to the sea again' was inspired by visits to the Cave House.

Cushendun is a charming place to visit, especially in spring and summer. It is a quaint Ulster village, situated on the coast of County Antrim some 50 miles from Belfast. The Cave House itself is a historic eighteenth-century residence, though partially rebuilt and modernised, and the immediate locality has an extremely rich history. Apart from past history, in recent times many famous names have been associated with the little coastal village, which has always attracted famous artists and poets. It was the home of the poetess Maire O'Neill, descendant of an historic glens clan.

For the visiting Sisters, the Cave House provided an ideal holiday environment. The day usually started with a refreshing walk to the parish oratory for Mass; the car was available for the use of the less able. Normal convent routine was set aside and the whole day was completely at each Sister's disposal. Any Sisters who wished could have use of the car to go for drives to Ballycastle, the Giant's Causeway, the glens or any accessible part of the beautiful surrounding countryside. It can be understood that the amenities of the Cave House were appreciated more than can be described by the Sisters, especially during those stressful times.

Anniversaries and celebrations

In spite of the Troubles, the vicissitudes of which so preoccupied the minds of everyone in the community, there were also occasions in the seventies for celebrating and rejoicing: golden jubilees, silver jubilees, receptions and professions – though these latter, as the years passed, became fewer in number. True, several young women came to sample community life and the Mercy apostolate, but most passed on, either immediately or at some stage of novitiate or juniorate formation. In this decade – and later, in the 1980s – the trend seemed to be universal for most religious congregations in the western world. Older Sisters retired and there was no one to replace them.

One great event of the 1970s was the celebration of the centenary of St Patrick's, the parish church of the Crumlin Road community and a pro-cathedral of the diocese of Down and Connor. This was held on Sunday, 20 November 1977. The Crumlin Road Sisters had been asked to do the catering for a banquet to be held in St Kevin's Hall following concelebrated Mass in the church at 3 p.m. This had created a flurry of activity during the week preceding the event, as 300 guests were expected. Apart from the preparation of an abundance of food, ably done by Sister Colette Fitzsimmons and Sister Margaret Mary Daly with a few willing helpers, table linen, crockery, cutlery and other requisites borrowed from convent and schools had to be transported to the hall, which also had to be decorated appropriately. The whole celebration passed very successfully, fortunately undisturbed by bomb scares or any other unpleasant happenings in an area where terrorist attacks were not uncommon.

When the activities had finished the Sisters were back in the convent before 8 p.m., weary but pleased that everything had gone well and happy to relax and discuss the events of the day. On the following Tuesday there was a centenary Mass for the schoolchildren of the parish. On 30 November the priests of St Patrick's Parish, Reverend M. Blaney, Adm., and Fathers Magee, McMullan, Maguire, Downey and Gallinagh, concelebrated Mass in the convent chapel at 5.30 p.m. as a token of gratitude to the Sisters for their help with the centenary celebration. Afterwards they were entertained to tea in the refectory, where they presented a beautiful inscribed silver platter to the community.

The year 1978 marked the centenary of St Malachy's, Sussex Place. In those hundred years, 100 Sisters had served in the school, along with 50 lay teachers, and the 'Mercy nuns' were inextricably linked with the Markets area in the heart of Belfast. With the redevelopment of the inner city and the insecurity of the city centre, where businesses were constantly being bombed throughout the 1970s, many families had gone to live elsewhere. Consequently, school enrolment had decreased from a healthy 450 in 1970 to only 190 in the centenary year. The Sisters of Mercy had moved out of Sussex Place Convent and been replaced by the Good Shepherd Sisters, who were involved in social apostolates in the district. However, with two Sisters still teaching there (Sister M. Vincent Donnelly, principal, and Sister Ann McKeever), the Mercy presence in the school continued and many past pupils were happy to join, on Pentecost Sunday, in the centenary celebrations.[4]

The bicentenary of Catherine McAuley's birth was 29 September 1978. By coincidence, 24 September of the same month marked the 150th anniversary of the opening of the first House of Mercy, by Catherine, in

Baggot Street, Dublin. The bicentenary was commemorated by many celebrations organised by the Mercy Association of Ireland: a special Mass in Westland Row Church in Dublin, Catherine's parish church; an exhibition in the Bank of Ireland, next door to the Mercy Convent, Baggot Street; a pilgrimage to Knock shrine, County Mayo; the publication of a centenary souvenir booklet. In addition, the Mercy Mission Bourse was set up and contributed to by all the member communities of the association to aid students in Mercy missions in the developing world.

An interesting historical note can be added. In the 200 years between the birth of the foundress and the bicentenary, and the 150 years since the founding of her institute, the Mercy Congregation had spread into all five continents and into more than 20 different countries in these. This was an outstanding achievement, well worthy of the grandest of celebrations. A key dictum of this woman of great faith and confidence was, 'Put your whole trust in God; He will never let you want.'

Bangor and Downpatrick Convents held their own celebrations, and in Belfast the bicentenary event was celebrated with a Mass in St Patrick's Church, Donegall Street, at 10.45 a.m. on 3 October, which was attended by up to 2,000 Mercy pupils. Bishop Philbin presided and the concelebrants were the priests from all the city parishes in which there were Mercy schools or a Mercy presence: Mercy Primary School (Ardoyne), Our Lady of Mercy Secondary School (Ligoniel), Star of the Sea (St Patrick's), St Malachy's (Sussex Place), Immaculata Special School (Whiteabbey) and St Gemma's Secondary School (Sacred Heart). A massed choir of pupils from all the schools was conducted by Sister M. Anthony Cairns. For this great occasion Sister M. Brendan Blanche composed a 'Tribute in verse':

Mother Mary Catherine McAuley, 1778–1841

'Whatever you do,' said Jesus, 'to the least of my brethren here,
the poor, the sick, the orphan, you do unto me' – you care.

'Stretch out your hands, my daughter, in mercy and in love,
to the outcast and forsaken – your reward is heaven above.

'See, they are cold and hungry. See, they are homeless and lone.
Stretch out your hand and feed them, and lead them safely home.'

She heard the saviour's pleading. She heard his promise too:
'What you do unto these, my little ones, to me you also do.

'Stretch out your hands and save them, the souls for whom I died.'
In the lanes of the city she sought them for love of the crucified.

'One pair of hands,' she pondered, 'and the harvest fields so great!'
Yet the great heart of Catherine McAuley did not fear or hesitate.

She saw, with wondrous vision, helpers ready to share,
Willing to gather the harvest by sacrifice and prayer.

Brave souls she gathered round her, Sisters of Mercy were they,
To help the poor and the outcast and lighten their misery.

The spirit of Catherine McAuley lives on in her daughters today;
May the Sisters of Mercy ever be true to her loving precepts, we pray.[5]

As what seemed to be an appropriate sequel to the bicentenary commemoration, in May 1979 a unique event took place for the Belfast Sisters of Mercy: an Ulster Television crew came to film convent life. They filmed the community at evening prayer, at Mass and later at evening recreation. Over the next few days they visited several Sisters engaged in various occupations and apostolates. On hindsight the recording seemed to be providential, as this style of convent life was not to last much longer. It could be said that the late 1970s marked the end of an era, as the history of the 1980s and 1990s will show.

Mercy Federation and Mercy Association
Despite the conflicts, the life of the Mercy community, as part of a larger congregation, had to move forward, and the decades of the 1970s and 1980s were ones of rapid change and development.

In the summer of 1969 the Mercy communities of Belfast and Downpatrick became members of the newly formed Federation of the Sisters of Mercy of the Armagh Ecclesiastical Province. The genesis of the federation could be said to have been the meeting of the superiors and mistresses of novices from around the northern dioceses that had taken place in Crumlin Road Convent, Belfast, in March 1968 with the purpose of investigating the possibility of creating a common novitiate for the northern communities. It came into being as a response to the movement for the renewal of religious life after the Second Vatican Council. From collaboration on the matter of formation – that is, induction of new members into the religious life as lived in the Mercy Congregation – it was suggested that there could also be collaboration on the revision of the Mercy constitutions as recommended by *Perfectae caritatis*, the Second Vatican Council's decree on the adaptation and renewal of religious life, and other issues such as dress and overseas missions.

The federation came into being in March 1969 as a 'friendly alliance' of the 28 autonomous communities of the nine dioceses of the Armagh Ecclesiastical Province: Armagh, Ardagh and Clonmacnoise, Clogher, Derry, Down and Connor, Dromore, Kilmore, Meath and Raphoe (with approximately 1,450 Sisters in all). Mother M. Gertrude Gallagley, superior of the Derry community, was elected president, Mother M. Cecilia Flynn, superior of Tullamore, vice-president and Mother Marie Thérèse Laverty, superior of Belfast, secretary.

The primary undertaking was the revision of the Mercy rule and constitutions. The different communities were already engaged in this task but it was understood that a revised version of the constitutions, if coming from a group of communities, was more likely to be approved by Rome than one from individual communities. A working party was formed with members from each of the dioceses and Father Frederick Jones, C.Ss.R. was requested to direct and facilitate this work of revision. This he generously agreed to do and there began a series of meetings, work-days and weekends, mostly in the retreat house of the Handmaids of the Sacred Heart in Finglas, Dublin. Such a venue proved, according to general consensus, the most accessible one for the Sisters travelling from many locations in the archdiocese.

The formation of the federation proved to be of benefit to all the communities concerned. By the end of the first year Mother M. Gertrude Gallagley was able to write:

> During the past year we have come to know our Sisters in the Province and have been helped and encouraged by their example. We have worked hard in the drafting of our proposed constitutions. We have considered the possibility of a South American Mission. We have discussed our problems concerning the Formation of our young Sisters and planned one Course and Retreat for a group from various communities.[6]

A year later, on 1 May 1971, the federation hosted the visit of a group of Sisters of Mercy from the USA. The venue for this was St Malachy's Convent of Mercy in Seatown Place, Dundalk – chosen as the first Mercy convent to be founded in the northern half of the country – that is, north of Dublin. It was founded in 1847. (Tullamore Convent, which was also in the northern federation, was the first Mercy convent founded outside County Dublin. It is south of Dublin city.) The welcome address was presented by Mother M. Gertrude Gallagley. She paid tribute to the American Sisters of Mercy, in particular those in Burlingame, California, for the help given to date to their sister communities in the federation with work on the renewal of the constitutions, which was their primary project. A response was given by Mother M. Silverius Shields of Dallas, Pennsylvania, president of the American Mercy Federation, who offered a survey of the 'developmental stages' in the life of a Sister of Mercy, as experienced in the United States, in the context of their understanding of the vision and charism of the foundress, Catherine McAuley.[7]

The collaborative work in the federation, acknowledged by Mother M. Gertrude, continued for the next three years. However, as horizons were broadening on the part of many of the autonomous Mercy communities, and the work of revision of the constitutions was going on in most of these, wider collaboration, firmly encouraged by Father Jones, who acted as advisor to many of the working parties, was taking place. The result of this was the formation of the Mercy Association of Ireland. (At this time there were Mercy communities in every diocese in Ireland, with a total of approximately 5,000 Sisters.)

When the idea of forming an all-Ireland association was broached, Sister M. Cabrini Moloney of Limerick arranged for a plenary meeting to be held in the Redemptorist retreat house, Cluain Mhuire, Galway, on the weekend of 30 March–1 April 1973, to which delegates from all the Mercy communities in the country, one superior and two Sisters from each, were invited (84 Sisters in all). At the close of the meeting it was decided unanimously to form an association with flexible structures and loose constitutions. A steering committee was formed of 12 elected Sisters, three from each ecclesiastical province, one of whom was a diocesan superior. Each Sister of Mercy, through her community, was a member of the association. Its first meeting was held, significantly, in the Convent of Mercy, Baggot Street, Dublin, the foundation house of the congregation. Sister M. Cabrini Maloney was elected president with Mother M. Josephine of Carysfort as vice-president. The aim of the association was to foster closer bonds among the individual Sisters of Mercy and closer bonds between communities and diocesan unions throughout the country. One of the first collaborative tasks embarked upon was to draw up national Mercy constitutions. A working party was formed for this purpose in 1974.

With the formation of the all-Ireland Mercy Association the federation was no longer considered necessary. It was dissolved by almost unanimous consent in October 1975. By this date five of the member dioceses of the federation were initiating, or had completed, a process for union within their own diocese. The others – Armagh, Derry, Down and Connor and Dromore – began to investigate the possibility of forming an inter-diocesan union among themselves. In the event this did not take place; instead union was created within each diocese at different times over the next six to seven years. The Belfast and Downpatrick communities united in 1981.

Iceland

The proposed project of a South American mission did not materialise, but the federation did undertake a mission to Iceland. This was in response to a request to the federation in 1974 from Bishop Frehan, the Roman Catholic bishop of Iceland, who represented the great need for Sisters in that very secularised island, where the Catholic population was minimal (about 0.5 per cent; the main church was Lutheran). His need was for Sisters who would take over the running of a hospital in Reykjavik, from which the Sisters of St Joseph of Chambery were to withdraw because of increasing age and lack of personnel to continue the work. The federation took up the challenge and a small party consisting of Sister M. Peter of Navan, Sister M. Enda of Loughrea, Dr James McKenna, a medical doctor and Pat Kinder, senior finance officer of the Department of Health and Social Services, Northern Ireland, undertook to visit the hospital and explore the proposal. They spent four days in Iceland for that purpose. The report produced by the visitors gave the impression that the Reykjavik hospital was too big for the federation to take on. However, a smaller hospital in Hafnarfjordur, with a resident community of Sisters, was offered. When this offer was examined the federation judged it acceptable. On 15 September 1975 three Sisters of Mercy went to Iceland, and so the Iceland mission began. Mother M. Gertrude Gallagley, as president of the federation, gallantly took up the cause and spared herself no trouble to encourage the mission and support it with personnel for as long as that was possible and feasible. When the federation became part of the Mercy Association, Sisters from various dioceses in Ireland volunteered for the mission. They spent periods of time in Iceland, from weeks to years, in the hospital and in a small primary school and engaged in the usual Mercy apostolate of visitation.

The story of the Iceland mission is a most interesting one, well documented in the provincial archives. The Sisters of Mercy withdrew from the country in 1984. Factors influencing the decision were: that no one Mercy diocesan group or canonically established body was responsible for the mission, and therefore it was difficult to ensure continuity; that the Icelandic language was difficult and casual communication with the people was curtailed for lack of fluency; that surgery carried out in the hospital tended to be cosmetic rather than urgent or even necessary and this called into question the role the Sisters were playing there. In spite of these limiting factors it was agreed that Iceland remains a challenging mission for the Sisters of Mercy.

In this whole movement towards collaboration through the federation and the association, as well as the great and successful work done on the revision of the constitutions, inestimable credit is due to Father Frederick Jones, C.Ss.R., who was an unfailing and indefatigable mentor, guide and inspiration to the Sisters of Mercy during the 1970s. [8]

Renewal at local level

Meanwhile, encouraged by these innovations at wider congregational level, daily life in the Belfast community went on. The renewal initiated by the Second Vatican Council was effecting changes in many dimensions of the church and religious life. In the chapel of the Crumlin Road Convent quite radical renovations were carried out to meet the new liturgical recommendations. The beautiful traditional marble altar and reredos were removed and replaced with a free-standing plain white marble altar, brought forward to the front of the sanctuary, with a matching pedestal for the tabernacle situated at the rear wall. The rich mosaic back wall of the sanctuary, with its golden cherubs, was covered with a dark hessian screen. The mosaic sanctuary floor was redesigned to suit the new layout of the sanctuary and a white marble ambo was set up on either side. The side altars underwent the same transformation. The large pipe organ on the organ gallery was dismantled and replaced by a small electric organ in the nave of the chapel. The choir stalls were all removed and rows of *prie-dieux* facing the altar took their place. The beautiful carved oak screens separating the transepts on either side of the nave were also removed and the life-sized statues of the Blessed Virgin Mary and St Joseph were replaced by smaller and more modern carved ones, fixed to the pillars of the sanctuary. Similar forms of adaptation were carried out in the chapels of the branch houses. The changes in the chapel took some getting used to and were not pleasing to all. However, they were carried out with the best of intentions and in a spirit of conformity to the requirements of a new era of liturgical practice in the church.

On a more personal level, the Sisters were told that if they wished they could drop the religious names assumed at their reception into the congregation and resume their baptismal names (effected in January 1971), since baptism, effecting integration into the Christian community, is considered of primary importance. Regarding community government, the new interim Mercy statutes now stipulated that the superior's council would consist of the assistant, the bursar and three elected councillors. The mistress of novices would no longer be, *ex officio*, a member of the council.

Gradually these changes, and others touching various aspects of lifestyle and the daily horarium, were assimilated by the community, all effecting a progressive transformation of religious life as it had been known and lived over many decades. In effect, it was a transition from a monastic lifestyle, which the Mercy Institute had assumed, inadvertently or not, over the previous 130 years, towards a rediscovery of what did in fact constitute active apostolic religious life – the genesis of the Mercy charism. Active apostolic life, without enclosure and formal monastic dress, was a new phenomenon in the nineteenth century. The Mercy Congregation was the first such institute to be canonically recognised. However, the transition in lifestyle and dress only took place gradually.

[1] *Sunday Times* Insight Team, *Ulster* (London: Penguin Books, 1972).
[2] See, for example, *Irish News*, 5 August 1969. See also records kept in Our Lady of Mercy Girls' School ('Ballysillan'), Bilston Road, Belfast.
[3] J. Llewellan, *A guide to Cushendall* (privately published, 1996).
[4] *St Malachy's Convent Primary School Centenary Brochure, 1878–1978* (Belfast: St Malachy's Convent Primary School, 1978).
[5] For this and other events of the bicentenary celebration see Archives, SPCMB, 1978.
[6] Mother M.G. Gallagley to superiors (MCA, 18 May 1970).
[7] See Mercy Northern Province Archives (MCA).
[8] Father Frederick Jones passed away, very suddenly, in 1996. The Irish Sisters of Mercy are much indebted to him. May he rest in peace.

23

THE MATER INFIRMORUM HOSPITAL – A NEW ERA: 1960s–90s

The story of the Sisters of Mercy in Belfast is inextricably linked with that of the Mater Infirmorum Hospital, which they founded. In the century and more of its existence it flourished steadily and extended its services in spite of the inevitable financial limitations which are the lot of all voluntary institutions. The Mercy connection with the hospital was eventually to come to an end but the great work the Sisters started continues to expand even more rapidly.

When the National Health Service was introduced in 1948, the Mater Infirmorum Hospital opted to retain its voluntary status under Catholic trusteeship, and so it remained for the next 24 years. In 1972 it became fully integrated into the National Health Service under the Northern Ireland Hospitals Authority, subject to special conditions, principally that of safeguarding the hospital's 'character and association'. Within two years, with the introduction of the health and social services boards, it became part of the North and West District of the Eastern Health Board.[1]

To put these developments in context we refer back to the early history of the hospital. Since its foundation the Mater Infirmorum Hospital had been supported primarily by the Sisters of Mercy and by voluntary contributions from the Catholics of Belfast and further afield. After the earliest years a weekly collection (one penny) was introduced, which brought a small but regular income; later yearly church, house and street collections were carried out in which the Mater nurses played a very active part. The hospital depended totally on these and other voluntary contributions. The Sisters who worked in the hospital, as well as many of the consultants and surgeons, gave their services free. The upkeep of the hospital, and the fact that they were responsible for such a big undertaking with no assured source of income was, naturally a constant cause of anxiety for the Crumlin Road community. As Mother M. Magdalen Toner, superior in the 1940s, put it:

> The expense of such a big hospital, with no means of support, is a great worry and anxiety to the Sisters of Mercy responsible. It is only God, who blesses the work miraculously undertaken for his poor and his

glory, who can provide what is needed. Numberless souls have been saved and brought back to God there which will only be revealed on the Great Recording Day.[2]

Prior to the integration of the hospital into the National Health Service, it had been managed by a board appointed by the Roman Catholic bishop of Down and Connor and was under the care and control of the Sisters of Mercy and under the general guidance, direction and supervision of the said bishop.[3] There were serious reasons why the hospital did not join in with the National Health Service in the late 1940s. When the Comprehensive Health Act was passed in 1948 the minister of health presented the management committee of the Mater Hospital with a stark ultimatum: they must choose to be fully in or fully out of the state service; there could be no halfway arrangement. As the government of the time could give no guarantee that, in the event of the hospital's coming under the state, the Catholic character of the hospital would be maintained, the board, under the chairmanship of Bishop Mageean, opted for the hospital to remain a voluntary institution. Consequently it did not qualify for the benefits of the Health Act. The patients attending the hospital could not claim the free medical treatment and medicines available in the state hospitals and the salaries of the hospital employees were lower than under the NHS. The board paid the doctors and nurses, but the Sisters of Mercy working in the hospital – the matron, tutors, nurses and those in catering and ancillary work – gave their services free until the hospital was integrated into the NHS in 1972.

Given these circumstances it is not surprising that the Board of Management of the Mater Hospital, out of economic necessity, began in the mid-1960s to consider coming to some arrangement with the NHS. They were supported by the then prime minister of Northern Ireland, Captain Terence O'Neill, who pledged that his government would seek an equitable solution. In 1967 the minister for health and social services, W.J. Morgan, was invited to pay a courtesy visit to the hospital with a view to its obtaining some benefit from the welfare schemes. The bishop was present to welcome the minister, who visited the whole hospital, the Maternity Unit and St John's Private Nursing Home. He expressed approval of what he had seen. The hope was that by some arrangement the hospital could become integrated into the NHS and still retain its Catholic character.

The negotiations proved fruitful and in 1971 an agreement between the government and the board of management of the hospital led to the leasing of the institution to the state for a period of 999 years at the nominal rent of five pence per year. In consequence all hospital property – that is, the main hospital including the chapel and the 'convent portion', along with

MATER HOSPITAL ANNUAL COLLECTION
★ TO-DAY ★

THIS BED

could be
waiting
for

YOU

so

give generously to

MATER
HOSPITAL ANNUAL
COLLECTION
FRI. & SAT., JUNE 25 & 26

On This Day/December 27, 1924

Christmas cheer on the Mater Hospital's wards

THE PATIENTS compelled by circumstances over which they have no control to spend Christmas in hospital are subject to special commemoration.

Those, however, who found themselves within the neat wards of the Mater Infirmorum Hospital during the festive season have nothing but grateful memories of the occasion. The Sisters of Mercy, to whose self-sacrifice in the interests of the poor and needy whom God entrust to their care, and the highly efficient medical, surgical and nursing staffs, are ladies and gentlemen to whom those who have benefited in the institution can never be too grateful.

The Holy Season was ushered in the most solemn way by the celebration of Midnight Mass by the Rev Fr Gogarty, CC, St Patrick's. The sacred music was rendered in a highly impressive manner by the choir.

A sumptuous dinner was set before the patients on Christmas Day, the menu consisting of turkey, chickens, dessert, etc, the meal being keenly relished by all. All previous records were excelled in the scheme of decoration which was on an artistic and lavish scale. Lights, coloured in various hues, fairly lanterns and candelabra, cast a warm glow in the wards, Members of the Rotary Club, one of whom was dressed as Father Christmas, distributed toys and games to the children.

the nurses' home, St John's Nursing Home, the Maternity Unit, the School of Nursing and the doctors' residence – was transferred to the state. The transfer also included all endowments and other incomes. The state did not clear past debts; the board of management had to clear all outstanding debts and overdrafts up until the beginning of 1971 and to pay for the running costs up until 1972 insofar as they could be met by the hospital's income.[4] In spite of these stringent conditions the arrangement was found acceptable to both parties, in particular since the deed of arrangement safeguarded the religious interests of the hospital and Catholic ethical practices, specifically in obstetrics, gynaecology, geriatrics and psychiatry. At a later date (the celebration of the centenary of the hospital in October 1983) Bishop Cahal B. Daly described the agreement that had been arrived at as a model for the type of structure that must be worked out in every aspect of public life if Northern Ireland is to have a future.

By the time of its integration into the NHS the Mater was being served by 18 consultants in a variety of specialties and had 252 beds, which included 66 in general medicine, 65 in general surgery, 30 in gynaecology and 24 in obstetrics. Also the Mater Nurse Education Centre became part of Belfast Northern Group School of Nursing, in which Sister M. Jarlath Mannion became a senior nursing tutor.

Preparations for this transition had been going on since the 1960s. In the intervening years the services of the hospital had been steadily expanding. In the years between 1960 and 1970 the hospital had treated approximately 550,000 outpatients and 50,000 inpatients. The facilities provided, besides general medical and surgery, were maternity, psychiatric, geriatric and paediatric. These services put great strain on the meagre financial resources, strongly dependent at this time on voluntary contributions and the money collected by the Young Philanthropists' Society and the Y.P. Football Pools.

There was a particular need for better maternity services (there was no Catholic maternity hospital in Belfast), the existing unit coping with constant demands in conditions which, though exploited to the full by a very professional, competent and caring staff, were barely adequate. In 1959 the unit had been extended with a view to setting up a midwifery training school, and Sisters M. Dolores Morton and M. Jarlath Mannion were sent to Drogheda and London to train as tutors. The extension had necessitated the demolition of houses which formed the end of the terrace of which the Maternity Unit was part. These houses (known as Fatima House) had provided accommodation for the student nuns of the hospital. They lived temporarily in the convent and later moved to the nurses' home, to which an extension had been added.

However, conditions were far from ready for the midwifery school to be set up. The unit had 24 beds and consisted of three converted terrace houses on the block between Lonsdale and Fairview Streets on the Crumlin Road. One can imagine the limitations this arrangement imposed (as is the case with many converted buildings). However, despite the difficulties, the Mater Maternity Unit was always a homely and caring haven for the hundreds of expectant mothers who came time and again to have their babies delivered. The unit could have, on average at that time, about 400 admissions annually. There were dreams of a new maternity hospital, modern, purpose built and fully equipped, with more than three times the current bed complement, as well as antenatal clinics and ancillary services. With that in operation it was hoped that the new hospital would be recognised as a training school for midwives and, in time, provide practical training for medical students.

On the subject of training, in 1965 new premises were found for the Mater School of Nursing. These, too, were badly needed. In previous years the Christian Brothers Old Boys' Club, opposite the nurses' home on the Crumlin Road, had been used by the School of Nursing, but it was inadequate. Subsequently the hospital management board purchased the recently vacated synagogue on Annesley and Fleetwood Streets, hoping to convert it into a modern nurse-training centre. The first Mater Infirmorum Hospital nurses' prizegiving ceremony was held there on 23 November 1965.

In the main hospital 1963 saw the remodelling of the theatre block, 1970 the opening of an intensive-care unit and 1971 a new midwifery and gynaecological clinic.

During the 1960s Mother M. Eugene Murphy was matron of the hospital, but she was due to retire at the end of the decade. In 1969 the convent's community council nominated Sister M. Ignatius McAvoy, a member of the staff, to the Mater board of management for the post of matron 'in order to have this post officially established'.[5] Sister M. Ignatius had first started work in the Mater as a radiographer and then trained for nursing and later administration. On Mother M. Eugene's retirement she was appointed matron (later designated senior nursing officer), a post she held until her retirement in 1987, when she was succeeded by Mary Waddell.

The 1970s and 1980s, because of the Troubles, were very difficult years for Northern Ireland and especially for the hospitals in Belfast because of the many casualties of the bombings, shootings and other acts of terrorism that arrived at their doors for treatment. The Mater was to the forefront in the care and treatment of victims of explosions and terrorist attacks. It was the first hospital in Northern Ireland to care for injured British soldiers when violence erupted on the Shankill Road in October 1969. Despite its well-known Catholic ethos, the hospital had always had a high proportion of non-Catholic patients, who were treated without the slightest discrimination and happily shared the wards and the outpatients' clinic with their Catholic counterparts. The Mater Hospital played its role in full, as it had done during the years of World Wars I and II, and coordinating services and confronting crises during those years was no mean task for the person in charge. In June 1977 Sister M. Ignatius was awarded the OBE for her services as matron and in recognition of the hospital's 'continuing ability to play its full part in treating casualties of all denominations arising out of the current disturbances'.[6]

Another part of the award citation referred to Sister M. Ignatius's services in assisting, as matron, the smooth transition of the Mater Hospital from voluntary to statutory status within the NHS.

Further expansion

We have seen how, after years of protracted negotiations, the Mater Infirmorum Hospital was finally integrated into the National Health Service in 1972. Now the pressure was on to expand and specialise; this necessitated a building programme. Because of the limited confines of the hospital, the only possible direction for expansion was towards the convent and grounds – the only property between the hospital and St Malachy's College. Plans for an extension were already in mind when, in 1964, Bishop William Philbin asked for the sites of the convent primary school and the lodge for this purpose. These he acquired. Eight years later he approached the community for Hamill Park, Convent Avenue and the site of the girls' club. This request was not so easily acceded to as the community suspected that it heralded even further incursions into convent property. They requested to see the proposed plans for the extension before they would give a definite response.

Their suspicions were not unfounded. The next request was for the site of the convent chapel (which would be demolished) and the adjoining porch wing. At this point the community's reaction was strong: it was thought that this was going too far. The future of the convent itself was threatened – if surrounded with hospital buildings and traffic it would be virtually inaccessible and impossible to live in, without any privacy or quiet. Thus was set in train a long-drawn-out controversy between the bishop and the community that would continue over the next ten years.[7] During this time there was an additional request from the hospital trustees (in October 1978) that the convent itself be made available for inclusion in the building programme. Since all convent property next to the hospital was entirely owned by the community (though, according to canon law, all property held by religious communities ultimately belongs to the church as a whole) there was no legal obligation to sell or dispose of any of it. In the end, after much community discussion, and advice sought from all the right quarters, it was a sense of moral obligation that led to the decision (in February 1983) to let go, first of all, of the convent chapel, Convent Avenue and Hamill Park. The final reasoning that swayed the community was that, since the Sisters of Mercy had come to Belfast to help the poor, the sick and all others in need, they should not hold on to convent property simply for sentimental reasons if the hospital needed more accommodation in order to dispense its services more efficiently.

June 1983 saw the conveyance of that part of the convent property adjoining the Crumlin Road – that is, the sites of the (demolished) school, lodge and hostel and St Anthony's Chapel, Hamill Park and Convent Avenue. On 20 June 1984 the demolition of St Anthony's Chapel commenced. Witnessing this sad operation was very traumatic for the community, as one can well imagine. In March 1986 the construction of the new hospital tower block began.

Having made the painful decision to let the chapel go, in December 1985 the community reaffirmed its intention to survive by undertaking a full redecoration programme in the convent itself. However, as the next few years went by, other important elements entered into the equation regarding the future prospects for the convent. In the first place, access was becoming more and more difficult as the hospital building programme advanced. Though such access had been guaranteed by the contract, in actual fact, with heavy building plant holding ground in every available spot, keeping an open right of way to the convent was not always practicable.

Another consideration was that, as the years went by, fewer Sisters remained in the convent. The schools were at a distance and there were fewer Sisters on the hospital nursing staff. Besides this, new trends in community living and apostolates saw Sisters requesting to live in smaller communities, in houses closer to parish facilities and housing estates. Permission was gradually given for experimentation in this new lifestyle, leaving mostly only the older Sisters in the larger community. This situation was far from ideal for them, though they accepted the changes with great open-mindedness and tolerance, trying to understand the motivations of the younger generation. Finally, in July 1989, at an assembly of the Down and Connor Mercy Congregation (the St Paul's and Downpatrick communities, which had united to form one diocesan unit in 1981),[8] a definitive decision was taken to be prepared to move out of St Paul's Convent and offer it to the hospital trustees. Negotiations ensued and an agreement was reached. In December 1992 the front-door keys were handed over.

Mater Infirmorum Hospital centenary

The year 1983 saw the centenary of the founding of the first Mater Infirmorum Hospital in Bedeque House, Crumlin Road. The first centenary event, held on 1 January 1983, was the unveiling of a commemorative plaque at the entrance to the hospital by Bishop Cahal B. Daly. He was joined by the lord mayor of Belfast, Councillor Tom Patton, the chairman of the Eastern Health and Social Services Board, Sir Thomas Brown, and many other distinguished guests. On this occasion Bishop Daly spoke of plans for the future development of the hospital:

> The Mater is about to launch into a new phase of building because the medicine of the nineties will be radically different from today's. The same dedication and skill will be found in the new computer age as has been present throughout the first hundred years.[9]

He expressed thanks, on behalf of the trustees and staff of the hospital, to the Department of Health and Social Services for the 'generous infusion of public money … needed to update the building, the equipment and the services of the hospital and bring it up to the best standards of contemporary health care for the benefit of the public'.[10] The hospital was facing the challenge of expansion with the planned building of a £10.6 million tower block. The bishop also underlined the Mater's 'distinctive ethos', and paid tribute to the Sisters of Mercy 'by whose holiness, whose prayers and whose selfless services the walls and wards of the hospital have been hallowed for a century'. He added that most important for this Catholic ethos was the chapel, 'where the Eucharistic Lord has been lovingly encountered for the inspiration of the staff and the consolation of the patients down the decades'.[11]

On this occasion the lord mayor presented to the hospital a commemorative plaque of the city's coat of arms, 'maintaining a link established when Sir Robert McConnell, the then Lord Mayor, performed the opening ceremony of the main hospital on 23 April 1900'.[12] He congratulated the hospital for its services to the citizens of Belfast 'of all creeds and classes' and said that he hoped the plaque of the city's coat of arms might remind everyone of 'the very important part which the hospital plays in the life of the great city of Belfast and of our city's gratitude for the unfailing skill and devotion of all who serve here'.[13]

Other civil events that marked the centenary included a St Patrick's Day dinner held by the Mater Students' Society, centenary lectures in September and a medical-staff dinner in December. A special centenary commemorative booklet was published.

The biggest event was the centenary Mass in St Patrick's Church, Donegall Street, on 30 October. The celebrant was Bishop Daly; he was aided by five other bishops including the retired bishop of Down and Connor, Dr William Philbin. Cardinal Tomás Ó Fiaich presided. The singing was led by the nurses' choir and the choir of St Malachy's College, accompanied by Robert Leonard, organist. The lord mayor of Belfast, along with the chairman and other members of the Eastern Health and Social Services Board, were among the special guests, as were Rita Kavanagh and Teresa Robinson – two great-grandnieces of the Sister who inspired the founding of the hospital, Mother M. Magdalene Malone. Their presence added a special dimension to the occasion.

The bishop presented a papal blessing for the Mater staff to the senior nursing officer, Sister M. Ignatius. In his sermon the bishop spoke again about the bright prospects for the future of the hospital:

> Plans are now well afoot towards the building of a tower block within the hospital site to contain departments in Accident and Emergency, in Out-Patients and in Radiology, an Operating Theatre Suite, a thirty-five bed Maternity Unit and various other ancillary facilities.[14]

Thus the centenary marked what could be called the end of an era for the 'old' Mater, though all agreed that it was important that its special character and ethos as a Catholic hospital should be carried on into the 'new'. By 1984 it was a 300-bed hospital of diocesan ownership integrated with the NHS. The administration was now tripartite: a lay administrator along with the chairman of medical staff and the director of nursing service. For nurse training the hospital became part of the Belfast Northern Group School of Nursing and also continued its long association with Queen's University, Belfast, for the training of doctors.[15]

In 1984 there were still 12 Sisters of Mercy working in the hospital and now receiving salaries from the state. Mass continued to be celebrated daily in the hospital chapel and, in order to preserve a Catholic code of practice, an ethics committee was established early in that year.

Attached to the Mater trusteeship were Our Lady's Home, Beechmount, Belfast, and St Columbanus's Home, Helen's Bay, County Down. Both establishments were diocesan property, subsidised by the state and run by the

Sisters of Mercy. Beechmount had 80 female patients. Sister M. Emmanuel O'Rawe was matron and there were five Sisters of Mercy in the community. St Columbanus's had 45 male patients. Sister M. Benedict Monan was matron and there were six Sisters in the community.

Papal awards

Another special day for the Mater Hospital was 4 June 1984, when Bishop Daly presented eight papal awards to current and former staff of the hospital for services over the years. One of the highest papal awards, Pro Ecclesia et Pontifice, was given to Sister M. Ignatius McAvoy, director of nursing services, and Sister M. Genevieve Martin, former principal nurse tutor. Five Benemerenti Medals were also presented – to Mary Ann Gibbons, Maire O'Donnell, Norah Moore, M.K. Fegan and Dr Raymond Magill. Vincent McCaughan was granted a posthumous award.

It was an historic occasion for the Mater because it was the first time the Pro Ecclesia et Pontifice award had been made in the diocese of Down and Connor. The medal is conferred for outstanding services to the church and pontiff. The presentations were made at a special Mass concelebrated by the bishop and former chaplains in the hospital chapel. The Sisters honoured certainly had given outstanding service over the years to the Mater Hospital and to the nursing profession. Sister M. Ignatius had been associated with the Mater for 30 years – first as a radiographer, a post she held until 1960, when she undertook training for general nursing and then worked in the wards. She later trained for administration and was appointed matron in 1969. Sister M. Genevieve's association with the hospital dates from 1941. She completed her nurse training at the Mater during the war years, took a tutor's course in Birmingham and was appointed tutor at the hospital in 1949. She acceded to the post of principal tutor six years later. She took up the position of principal nursing officer for education in the Belfast Northern Group School in 1974 and between 1950 and 1980 was active in nurse education for post-basic courses in the Northern Ireland Royal College of Nursing. She was later awarded an honorary degree in nursing from the Royal College of Surgeons, Dublin, for her services to nurse education. She retired from nurse education to take up the post of first superior general of the Congregation of the Sisters of Mercy of Down and Connor in 1981.

As we have seen, the community and the hospital had much to celebrate in the early 1980s, but in March 1985 a great personal tragedy struck the Down and Connor Sisters of Mercy and the Mater Hospital. Two former nurses, Sister M. Immaculata McClory and Sister Ethna O'Boyle, were killed in a car accident on the Belfast to Dublin road. Sister M. Immaculata

Beechmount Convent, Falls Road, Belfast

Our Lady's Home, Beechmount

St Brigid's Home for the Blind, Abbeyville

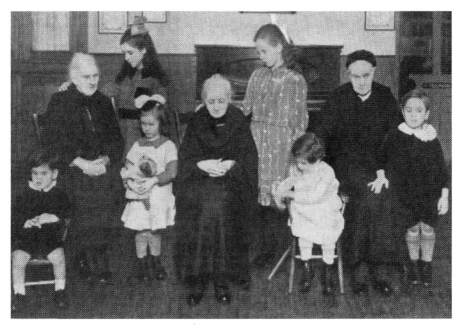

Home for the Blind: children and adults

Mother M. Magdalen Toner with her sister, Sister M. Clare Toner, *c.* 1918

Community group, St Paul's, Belfast, *c.* 1940s

Convent of Mercy, Brunswick Road, Bangor

St Columbanus' Home, Craigdarragh House, Helen's Bay, County Down

Annadale Street, 22 June 1941 (GAR 055)
© National Museums Northern Ireland 2010
Garland Collection, Ulster Museum
Photograph reproduced courtesy the Trustees of National Museums Northern Ireland

Annadale Street, off the Antrim Road
CAB/3/A/68. Courtesy of the Public Record Office of Northern Ireland

St Anthony's Chapel, St Paul's Convent

Statue of Our Lady of Mercy, St Anthony's Chapel

Reception ceremony: a postulant is received into the community

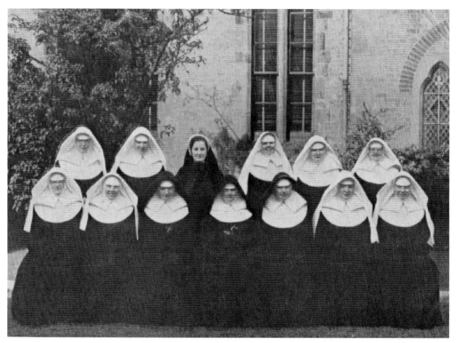

Members of the novitiate, St Paul's Convent, 1954

Novitiate group, St Paul's, 1970s

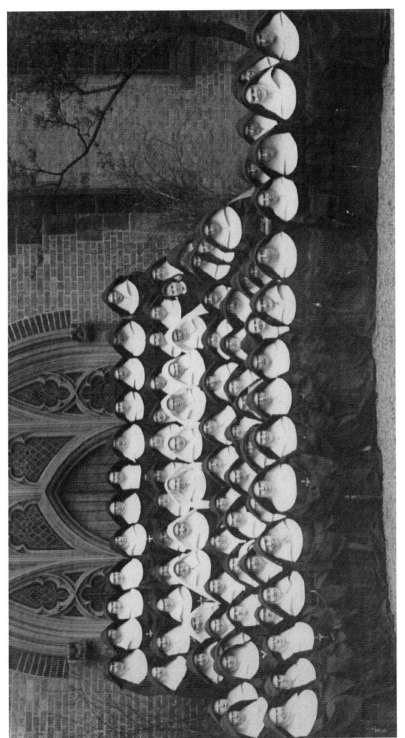

Community, St Paul's, centenary photograph, 1954

Our Lady of Mercy Girls' School, 'Ballysillan', Belfast

St Mary's High School, Downpatrick

Mater Infirmorum Hospital, old and new (on right, the tower block)

The McAuley Building, Mater Infirmorum Hospital

Sisters of Mercy, Down and Connor Mercy Diocesan Union, at Trench House, Belfast, July 1981

had worked in various wards and departments in the general hospital and had been matron in the Maternity Unit for 12 years. She had also served in St John's Private Nursing Home and in St Columbanus's Home and as matron in St Malachy's College. She had retired from nursing the previous February and was undertaking a course in pastoral care in the Mater Hospital, Dublin at the time of the fatal accident. Sister Ethna had spent most of her working life in St Columbanus's Home and in the nursery of the Mater Maternity Unit. She had also worked in the Mercy mission in Iceland for a short period and had returned to Ireland to do a course in pastoral care at the Dublin Institute for Adult Education. The Sisters were returning to Belfast for a congregation assembly when the accident occurred. Both Sisters were beloved by their community, friends, colleagues and former patients for their gentle and caring manner and admired for their deep spirituality. Their deaths were a great shock and loss to all who knew them. A memorial Mass was celebrated in the hospital chapel in their honour, and a new 'Way of the Cross' erected there in their memory.

The tower block

The construction of the new tower block for the Mater Hospital began on 19 March 1986. This was a massive undertaking: the new building was to take all the space between the original Mater and the nurses' home, except for a limited driveway on either side for service-vehicle access. The new structure fronts the Crumlin Road and its design is in striking contrast to the adjacent buildings. It has a sheer façade, with an outer skin of glass curtain-walling which seems to reflect a reddish hue – the only concession to the mellow red brick of the older buildings. The completed building, said to be equipped with the best of contemporary technology for medical and nursing care, was handed over to the Eastern Health and Social Services Board on 6 April 1990 and officially opened on 11 September 1991. By this time the trustees were already planning for further extensions on the site of the convent, which the Sisters by now had agreed to make available. Soon the former convent was demolished and construction began on the site in 1999.

St John's Private Nursing Home had long since gone. The buildings were being used for various administrative and other purposes and the block that had housed the Maternity Unit had been demolished. The former nurses' home had been reconditioned to provide an inpatient psychiatric unit on the two lower floors and a day hospital on the upper levels. Accommodation for nurses and other staff was provided in a new block of 84 flats on Fleetwood and Annesley Streets. The configuration of the original hospital and its dependent establishments was undergoing a radical sea change as the services continued to expand. A 'Factfile' for the hospital was published in 1992, which gives interesting statistics:

- The Mater employs 810 staff: 635 female and 175 male.
- The Mater will spend in excess of £13.5m this year in treating patients.
- The Mater's land and buildings are valued in excess of £14m. The building houses in excess of £6m of plant and equipment.
- The Mater currently treats 9,044 inpatients and 45,501 outpatients per annum.
- 43,058 people visit our Accident and Emergency Unit every year.[16]

[1] See *Centenary year, 1883–1983* (Belfast: Mater Infirmorum Hospital, 1983).
[2] Annals, SPCMB.
[3] See deed of arrangement regarding transfer of the Mater Infirmorum Hospital to the Department of Health and Social Services (MIHA and Archives, SPCMB, *c.* 1950s), Schedule, Part 2, Section 3.
[4] See deed of arrangement, state rules and orders of Northern Ireland, regarding transfer of the Mater Infirmorum Hospital into the National Health Service (MCA, 30 November 1971).
[5] Acts of chapter, SPCMB, 1969.
[6] Roy Mason, secretary of state for Northern Ireland to Sr M. Ignatius: letter of notification of award of OBE (MCA, 10 June 1977).
[7] See documentation on this matter (MCA).
[8] See Chapter 25.
[9] Address by Bishop C.B. Daly (MIHA, 1 January 1983).
[10] Ibid.
[11] Ibid.
[12] *Irish News*, 3 January 1983.
[13] *Belfast Telegraph*, 3 January 1983.
[14] *Irish News*, 31 October 1983.
[15] Deed of arrangement, state rules and orders of Northern Ireland, regarding transfer of the Mater Infirmorum Hospital into the National Health Service (MCA, 30 November 1971).
[16] *Belfast Telegraph*, 23 April 1992. See also Appendix to Chapter 23.

24

THE DOWNPATRICK
MERCY COMMUNITY IN
THE TWENTIETH CENTURY

The early history of the Downpatrick Mercy community has been recounted, and it is appropriate at this point to trace the story of the community over the six decades (between 1923 and 1981) during which it had autonomous status.

When, after 12 years of union with the Belfast community (1911–23), the Downpatrick community again became autonomous, Mother M. Ethna Grene, who had been superior of the amalgamated communities and had resided in Crumlin Road Convent, returned to Downpatrick to be superior there. She was joined by Sister M. Anthony Crangle, who had been mistress of novices in Crumlin Road. She returned to Downpatrick to take up the same office there, accompanied by a novice, Sister M. Kieran O'Carroll, who had volunteered to go to Downpatrick. On 14 August 1923 the novitiate in Downpatrick was reopened. Sister M. Kieran made profession there on 24 July 1925. From then on the Downpatrick community continued to flourish and expand.

The Donaghadee foundation

The early 1930s saw the setting up of a new branch house in the small seaside town of Donaghadee on the north-east coast of County Down. This town was, at that time, badly in need of support for the small Catholic community that formed part of the parish of Newtownards. The town, traditionally a port for the shipment of cargo and people to Scotland and England, was predominantly a Presbyterian settlement dating from the post-Reformation years in the seventeenth century. From that time up until the mid-1800s there was no record of Mass being celebrated there. Gradually, however, as the import/export trade developed in the early nineteenth century, a number of Catholics came to find work and live in the town. When this became known, the parish priest of Newtownards organised the celebration of Mass occasionally in a private house, the home of a man named Kelly, of the Ford on the Newtownards Road, and afterwards in an old house in Scorr's Lane in Donaghadee. Eventually, in the 1840s, a small church was built, St Patrick's. (It was later rededicated to St Comgall, the patron saint of the area.) But as the number of Catholic children was small, there was as yet no school.

In the 1920s, with the growing number of Catholic families, the parish priest of Newtownards, Reverend A. Kennedy, saw the necessity of having a small Catholic school in Donaghadee. He tried, unsuccessfully, to find a religious teaching congregation to take on this work; eventually his curate, Reverend Seamus McKeown, suggested he approach the Sisters of Mercy in Downpatrick. With the support of the bishop he did so and here he was successful. The Downpatrick annals record:

> [Reverend] Mother M. Benignus [Markey] and Mother M. Ethna [Grene], after mature deliberations, agreed to send Sisters to Donaghadee if suitable accommodation could be provided.[1]

Such accommodation did come on the market in July 1931 – a shop with an attached dwelling on High Street. The property was up for sale in an auction held in the Orange Hall on 21 July and, through intermediaries (for Bishop Mageean, 'was most particular that the nuns not be seen in Donaghadee until after the sale'),[2] the Sisters bought the premises. On 22 July Reverend Mother M. Benignus and Mother M. Ethna went to Donaghadee for the first time, Father Kennedy joining them at Newtownards. They met the surprised (and perhaps dismayed) former owner, Mrs Atkinson, who had never suspected that the purchasers were nuns. They were shown through the house, which had five storeys, was in perfect repair and had every convenience as far as the nuns could see. At the request of Mrs Atkinson a month was set aside so that she might settle her affairs. The time was further extended until 25 September and on Sunday, 27 September the Sisters took up residence in the house. These were Mother M. Ethna Grene, Sister Margaret Mary Hogan and Sister M. Dympna Greene. The parish church of St Comgall was just three minutes' walk away from the new convent and on that first Sunday Father Kennedy told the people that at last he had secured the services of the Sisters of Mercy to teach their children. On 7 October 1931 the new convent, St Anne's, formally opened.

The property on High Street was large, consisting of the ground-floor shop premises, four upper storeys and attics. The first floor had an office and bathroom. The second had three large rooms which served as an oratory, a community room and a parlour. The bedrooms were on the third and fourth floors and in the attic rooms. The refectory, kitchen and scullery were on the ground floor, to the rear. For the renovations, the Sisters had the help of a generous benefactor, Thomas Maguire, solicitor, of Holywood. Maguire also had electric light installed and the oratory painted and suitably furnished.[3] Various adaptations were necessary to provide suitable living accommodation for the Sisters and to turn the ground-floor shop into a school – which consisted of one large classroom, divided by a lace curtain, where the classes would be conducted by two teachers. To the rear of the school were the playground and garden.

Because of the necessary refurbishing it was decided to postpone the date for the opening of the school until the new year of 1932, and at the Christmas Masses in the town it was announced that the school would open on 4 January. This meant that the Catholic boys and girls who had attended the non-Catholic schools in Donaghadee could transfer to St Anne's. On that auspicious day Mother M. Ethna (now superior of the little community) received the children and their parents. Sister M. Dympna was appointed principal and teacher of the juniors, while Sister M. Columba Kirkwood (who had joined the community) was to have the seniors. On his first visit, the inspector of schools, Mr Scott, was impressed by the excellence of the education being provided. These high standards were upheld through all the years that followed.

The activities of the Sisters were not restricted to the classroom. Mother M. Ethna soon opened a club for girls at the convent. This was for the benefit of Catholic girls who were working or in service in non-Catholic situations. The club was open from 7 p.m. to 9 p.m. and the girls occupied their time in sewing, knitting and at games. By their contact with the Sisters the girls were given personal and moral support and encouraged to keep faithful to their religious duties.

Life was not all plain sailing for the Sisters when they came to Donaghadee. There were at that time many superstitions in non-Catholic circles about religious Sisters. History has recorded that when the Sisters of Mercy took up residence in High Street on 27 September, on their first evening a public meeting of protest against their presence was organised by the Freemasons. They were determined to take action to prevent the Sisters remaining in their midst. So vehement was their opposition that Father Kennedy had to get the police to put a guard on the convent. Fortunately they had one defender in the person of a member of the local ascendancy, the De Lacherois family, who stood up at the meeting and, with considerable courage, declared to the protesters: 'These nuns who have come into the town are ladies and should be treated as such!'[4]

The Sisters did much to demolish such prejudice during the 57 years of their presence in Donaghadee and developed strong friendships with their neighbours and the people of the town and its surrounding area.

In 1936, sadly, Mother M. Ethna Grene's health began to fail but she still continued her labours in St Anne's. Mother M. Ethna Gonzaga Joseph, born Anna Maria Grene in County Tipperary on 23 March 1855, had entered the Convent of Mercy, Mount St Patrick, Downpatrick, on the feast of the Immaculate Conception, 8 December 1874. She had made her first profession there on 10 July 1877. In July 1938, having returned to the convent in Downpatrick for the annual retreat, she became ill. At her own wish she went back to Donaghadee on the feast of St Anne, 26 July. On 17 August she died peacefully in the convent which she had founded and in which she had spent the last seven years of her life. Her remains were brought back to Downpatrick. She was laid to rest in the little community cemetery with those of her younger sister, Sister M. Philomene Grene, who had died in October 1882, just two years after making her religious profession. Mother M. Ethna had surely completed her life's work. Besides her years of leadership of the communities of St Paul's, Belfast, and Mount St Patrick, Downpatrick, in Donaghadee she left behind her the legacy of her great generosity to the poor and her dedication to the children and people her of adopted home.

When Sister M. Dympna Greene (no relation of Mother M. Ethna and Sister M. Philomena Grene) was elected superior in Downpatrick, Sister M. Columba Kirkwood succeeded her as principal in St Anne's. Over the years various Sisters from Downpatrick interchanged as assistant teachers. One of these was Sister M. Comgall McCourt, who spent 13 years in Donaghadee until she, too, was appointed superior in Downpatrick in 1959. Sister M. Philomena McDonagh replaced Sister M. Comgall as principal. She quickly set about raising money for the school through raffles and the funds she collected provided for the repainting of the schoolroom. The old lace curtain was discarded and a partition, obtained from a classroom in Downpatrick Convent School, set in place.

About this time other changes were taking place for the parish of Donaghadee. Back in 1934, while the convent and school were being established in the town, the diocese had purchased, at great expense (£3,376) and amid some local controversy, a large site on the southern outskirts between the Millisle and Killaughey Roads, with a view to building a church there later. The house on the property, Shandon, was used as the parochial house, the first home of the resident priest, Father Gerard Haughey, who since his appointment to Donaghadee in 1931 had lived in rented accommodation in the town. Father Haughey was tragically killed in a motorcycle accident not long afterwards. He had a great relationship with the first Sisters in Donaghadee, as their first curate, and they recorded that he had a marvellous sense of humour and 'helped immensely to keep their spirits up when times were bad'. His twin brother was Father Arthur Haughey, who survived him by about 50 years. Their only niece, Sister M. Dolores Morton, is a member of the Belfast Mercy community.

In 1958 two fields adjacent to Shandon were purchased from a Mr Weathercup, a move which was to prove important for the future of the Mercy school in Donaghadee. With this background, let us take up the story as Sister M. Philomena told it:

> There [were] many ups and downs, with the numbers of pupils fluctuating, sometimes down so low we feared a teacher might become redundant. A Miraculous Medal was placed over the school entrance door, and within three months the rooms were too small to hold the pupils and we were forced to send the three top classes to the clubroom behind 'Shandon', then the curate's house.
>
> Sr. M. [*sic*] Elizabeth McKeown was teaching [t]here at this time, getting her teacher's diploma. The clubroom was in a very bad state. It was so dark that the electric light was on all day, and in winter it was very cold because there was only one thin heating pipe along one wall. The children were forced to wear heavy coats all day.[5]

It was during this time that two more teachers joined the staff, Esther Ward and B. McParland. Sister M. Philomena added to her account some unsavoury details:

> I cannot leave out of this account what we suffered from rats in the clubroom. One morning I went in and found a piece of candle stuck in a hole at the side of the door. This had been dragged from the room above which was used on Sundays by the Vincent de Paul and the Legion of Mary. Rats were seen at night and described to me as being 'as big as a pup, Sister'. We laid two large boxes full of rat poison. This must have killed many families of these pests because each morning we entered the 'schoolroom' we almost smothered with the odour. We were forced to call the roll outside.[6]

During all these years the people of Donaghadee were collecting money for a new school but still there was no financial contribution from the diocese. On 2 January 1962 Sister M. Philomena telephoned Bishop Mageean and put him in the picture, telling him also that she herself had contracted bronchitis as a result of the impossible conditions in the Shandon clubroom. She also stated that her absences from school through illness were a cause of great neglect of the pupils and inconvenience to the assistant teachers. The bishop told her that he had been unaware of the circumstances and promised to have a new school built by the end of the year.

True to his word, the new building, to replace the first school on High Street and the clubroom annex, was erected on the Shandon grounds (at a cost of £14,500) and blessed on 23 May 1963. Sadly Bishop Mageean did not live to see the opening of the new St Anne's Primary School. The opening ceremony was carried out by his successor, Bishop William Philbin. Prior to the opening ceremony High Mass was celebrated in the open air on an altar erected on the outside porch of the new school. The celebrant was Reverend J. Magee, C.C. of Downpatrick, with Reverend Charles Denvir, C.C. of Ballycastle, as deacon, and Reverend E. O'Brien, C.C. of Newtownards, as subdeacon. Reverend Felix McLaughlin, C.C. of Donaghadee, was master of ceremonies and Reverend Leo McKeown was assistant to the bishop. The cantors were Reverend Noel Watson of St Joseph's Training College, Belfast, and Reverend F. Kennedy, chaplain of Nazareth Lodge, Belfast. The choir was composed of clergy from the neighbouring parishes.

The new school building uplifted the morale of both children and teachers. High standards of good behaviour and refinement, as well as of academic work, were encouraged and pupil enrolment increased yearly. In 1964 Sister M. Agnes Woods joined the staff and Sister M. Oliver (Brigid) Quinn and Mother M. Comgall McCourt, who were now teaching in the parish primary school in Newtownards, came to live with the community in High Street in Donaghadee.

In 1968 Sister M. Philomena McDonagh was appointed to the new Downpatrick foundation in Hannahstown, west Belfast. There she became principal of the new Blessed Oliver Plunkett Primary School and Sister M. Agnes Woods replaced her as principal of St Anne's.

The former classroom at the convent in High Street did not fall into disuse. In fact it was destined for an even more elevated purpose. As a consequence of the Troubles that then afflicted Northern Ireland, Donaghadee's little parish church, St Comgall's, in which the Catholic community had worshipped for almost 130 years, suffered. On the night of Friday, 25 August 1972 it was destroyed by a bomb, leaving the townsfolk without a place of worship. It was then that the Sisters of Mercy donated the old school to be used as a chapel. The Sisters continued to live in St Anne's Convent, High Street, until after the Down and Connor Mercy Congregation united – that is, until June 1982. The last Sisters to live there were Sisters M. Angela Deignan and M. Kieran Morrison. St Anne's was sold on 14 July of that year to a Mr Shortland. Sister M. Angela and Sister

M. Kieran lived in Bangor and travelled each day to Donaghadee for the next seven years.

The chapel served the small Donaghadee Catholic community for five years until, by a marvellous effort on the part of the people and the generous help of friends and benefactors, work began in May 1977 to build a new St Comgall's Church on the Millisle Road, beside the primary school. The building progressed rapidly and Bishop Philbin blessed and opened the church on Sunday, 13 November 1977. It must be mentioned here that Sister M. Catherine Molloy, who had since joined the Donaghadee Mercy community, did wonderful work towards the building of the new church. Through sales of work and other fundraising events in Donaghadee and Newtownards she, with organised parish groups, soon left the new church free of debt. Sister M. Catherine was also a well-known visitor of the sick and the needy in Donaghadee. For that she is fondly and gratefully remembered by the many people who knew her.

The schools

In Downpatrick itself the end of the 1930s saw another very important venture, the opening of a commercial school in St Michael's Home, beside the convent. This was pioneering work which was started by Mother M. Aloysius McCusker and Canon (later Venerable Archdeacon) D.J. McWilliams, then parish priest of Downpatrick. Long before the Education Act of 1947 introduced mandatory secondary education for all children, this school was providing free post-primary education for the girls of Downpatrick.

The commercial school opened on 25 September 1939. The moving spirit was Canon McWilliams, who was involved in education circles both north and south of the border and was influenced by his knowledge of the commercial schools ('secondary tops') already in existence in Mercy convent schools in the south of Ireland. These provided for girls who wished to continue their education after primary school with a view to getting employment mainly in secretarial work. The commercial school in Downpatrick was formed from Standard 7 of the primary school in order to meet the needs of the many young girls of the parish and surrounding districts who desired further education. The main focus was on commercial subjects – typing, shorthand, book-keeping – skills that would help them to secure jobs in the civil service, secretarial posts and other suitable positions. But the curriculum was much wider, including general subjects, domestic science and the arts. The school attracted a large number of pupils, the average enrolment being between 70 and 80. Some of the girls who attended the commercial school were boarders in St Michael's. They came from Portaferry, Kilkeel, other parts of County Down and even Belfast. Some of these girls later joined the Downpatrick community. Almost all the others got good situations, often with the help of Mother M. Aloysius and Canon McWilliams, who were always ready to seek out employment and give the girls good recommendations.

Commercial-school life was not all academic and job orientated. The pupils staged musicals and operettas for special occasions, which were highly acclaimed. The senior girls joined the Sodality of Our Lady – the Children of Mary – and each year, dressed in their striking blue cloaks and white veils, led the May procession. This was a tradition that had begun in 1940 and one in which the parish liked to participate. The girls, some carrying banners, processed from the commercial school at St Michael's down the Folly, thence along St Patrick's Avenue, up the hill to the parish church and into the cloister garden of the convent. Each girl carried a bouquet of flowers. The May queen was always one of the senior girls and was dressed all in white. She crowned the statue of Our Lady and each girl in the procession followed her, placing their bouquets of flowers at the statue's feet. An outdoor altar had been set up in the cloister garden and the procession ended with solemn Benediction of the Blessed Sacrament. At this time also, extra-curricular night classes were conducted at the convent for girls requiring instruction in domestic economy. Others came to attend classes for music, drawing, painting, French and Irish. Quite a number of non-Catholics from the town were among those who attended and non-Catholic lay teachers were among the instructors.

After the legislation stipulating free secondary education for all young people, the provision of secondary intermediate schools for the boys and girls of Downpatrick and the neighbouring parishes of Strangford, Saul, Killough and Dundrum became a priority. De La Salle Secondary Intermediate School for Boys was opened in Edward Street in 1953. Shortly after this, Archdeacon McWilliams encouraged the Sisters of Mercy to consider setting up a secondary intermediate school for girls. Mother M. Aloysius, headmistress of the commercial school, responded wholeheartedly to the suggestion. A suitable site for the school, on the Ardglass Road, was purchased from Lord Dunleath. Archdeacon McWilliams cut the first sod on 19 February 1956. The building was completed a year and a half later and Bishop Mageean officially blessed it on the feast of the Nativity of Our Lady, 8 September 1957. The architects were McLean and Forte; the building contractor was H.J. O'Boyle. The commercial-school pupils formed the nucleus of the new school, which opened with 286 pupils and

12 teaching staff. Seven of the staff were Sisters of Mercy. They were: Mother M. Aloysius McCusker, Sister M. Teresa Kielty, Sisters M. Mercy McKeown, M. Augustine (Elizabeth) McKeown, M. Baptist (Mairead) McKiernan, Marie Therese (Margaret) Heffron and M. Joseph Deeny. The lay members of staff were: Mary McCavana, Bernadette Mulholland, Irene Crumlish, Felicity Rogers and Una Crawley.

Mother M. Aloysius McCusker was appointed principal of the new school with Sister M. Teresa Kielty as vice-principal. It has been said that while Archdeacon McWilliams was the moving spirit behind the schools, Mother M. Aloysius was the driving force. Very experienced in the field of education and administration, she was well suited to lead the new secondary school into the future. As one former colleague recalled:

> The administration of St Mary's, as moulded by her [Mother M. Aloysius], demanded personal knowledge of each pupil and frequent contact with them. During school hours she gave her time and attention generously to the pupils, and this service did not cease when the school gates were closed. Many evenings, week-ends and holidays had to be devoted to the work of administration, but all was done in a spirit of cheerful service, giving without counting the cost.[7]

Mother M. Aloysius died in Downpatrick in May 1978. She had also served as superior in the community for several years.

Memories of the opening of the new school are recorded. A former pupil, Ita Cunningham (*née* Braniff), whose name was the first to appear on the new school register, wrote:

> I remember well the transfer from the homely surroundings of Irish Street, known as the Sisters of Mercy Commercial School. We were one big happy family there, so it is true to say I had mixed feelings about going to St Mary's on the hill.
>
> On that first school day ... I walked through the gates of this significant looking building for the first time. The sun shone and the air was scented with flowers. There was a constant flow of girls in blue making their way to the main door where Mother Aloysius awaited their arrival. Sister M. Mercy and Sister M. Teresa directed us to the new cloakrooms and then to the assembly hall. There was a buzz of excitement as we made our way to the main hall, glancing into each new classroom as we passed by. The highly polished desks, gleaming floors, roller blackboards and rows of brand new typewriters all added to the mystery and glamour of this serene building.
>
> With Mother Aloysius at the helm very little time was wasted. Morning prayers were said, a few welcoming words and a short stern

talk on behaviour inside and outside the school. It did not take long for those who did not know her to realize she meant what she said.[8]

The same former pupil also paid a special tribute to another Sister, who was always there as a supporting hand and guiding light in her own quiet, unobtrusive way:

> I would like to take this opportunity to refer to a gifted teacher, a lady in every sense, Sister Mary Mercy [McKeown] who enriched our school lives simply by being there. She was a constant figure, and eased the transition between old and new at a time of great change.[9]

And so life in the new school got under way. Soon the curriculum expanded to take in a wide variety of subjects and in the 1960s the school was given permission from the Ministry of Education to provide a 'grammar stream'. It was one of the first secondary schools to achieve this status. This enabled pupils to take junior, senior and advanced certificates in general subjects as well as qualifications in commercial subjects. Time was made in the curriculum also for music, drama and sport, and musicals were staged each year with great success. The school steadily increased in numbers, even over the first decade of its existence, and it was soon foreseen that in the not-too-distant future it would need to expand.

In 1976 the Convent Primary School in Downpatrick celebrated its centenary. This was commemorated in various ways, including the publication of a booklet, which gave something of the history of the community and the schools since the arrival of the Sisters in the parish in 1855. In a foreword to the booklet Bishop Philbin wrote a worthy tribute:

> It is hardly possible to exaggerate the contribution of the Sisters to family and community life. Generations of girls from the town and a wide adjacent countryside have passed through the Convent School whose centenary is being celebrated this year. This booklet marks 100 years of achievement in education. The people of Downpatrick rejoice with the Sisters of Mercy in reaching a notable milestone in their history … I join in the joy of the Sisters and in the well-merited words of congratulations and gratitude that are being offered them by past pupils and parents. May they continue to be blessed in their apostolic work in this parish of the National Apostle for many years to come.[10]

The centenary coincided with another milestone – the transfer, then in process, of the convent school to a new site. The course of the 1970s had brought some educational changes to Downpatrick. After the outbreak of the Troubles there was a migration of many families from Belfast to Downpatrick for safety. This meant that there was a large influx of children into the primary schools, both boys and girls. When the new pupils came seeking places in the convent primary school, there was not enough room for them. Some classes moved into St Michael's but even more classroom space was needed. A solution was to purchase a house on Irish Street, two doors from St Michael's, the property of a Dr Kelly. The attraction of this house was that it had a large garden at the rear, next to that of St Michael's, and the long-term plan was to build a new primary school on the site of the two adjoining gardens, which together formed quite a spacious plot of land. However, when the plans were submitted to the Department of Education they were turned down as the site was considered too small. As an alternative, the department suggested that the convent primary school move into the school premises in Edward Street, which had been vacated when the De La Salle Brothers built their new secondary school on Saul Street.

This had also been necessitated by the influx of new pupils from Belfast. In 1937 St Patrick's High School, a grammar school for boys, financed by the De La Salle order, had been completed and officially opened. After the 1947 Education Act, when new secondary intermediate schools were needed, the boys' primary school had been transferred to a new school built in Dillon's Avenue (opened in 1951) and the school in Edward Street had been altered and extended to become De La Salle Secondary Intermediate School for Boys. This had served four parishes: Strangford, Saul, Killough and Dundrum, each parish contributing its share financially.

The Sisters accepted this solution and the community purchased the vacated school property in June 1975. In a temporary arrangement, Sister Brigid Quinn, principal of the girls' school, moved there with the top two classes. Sister M. Vianney remained with the pupils in Irish Street and the convent school operated on two sites for two years. Eventually the school on Edward Street was refurbished to make it suitable for girls. An extension was added, consisting of four classrooms, two offices, a medical room, cloakrooms, toilets and other facilities. When everything was in readiness all the children moved in. The official opening was held in September 1976.

When the plans for a new primary school in the garden of St Michael's and Dr Kelly's house had been turned down, a convent nursery school was built on the site instead. Both it and the primary school on Edward Street were blessed and opened by Bishop Philbin on the same day in June 1977 – in quite an unseasonable snow shower.

With the relocated primary school in Edward Street, the former school premises beside the convent became vacant and the community decided to demolish them to make way for a new convent extension. Plans for this were made in 1979 and work got under way. The new building was modern in design and incorporated many features that added to the comfort and convenience of the community. The new wing was planned for a novitiate on the two upper floors with, on the ground floor, bedrooms, bathrooms, an oratory, a kitchenette and stores for the convenience of the invalided and infirm Sisters. A lift was also installed. A spacious new dining room was built, with an adjacent large kitchen and stores. A new rear entrance with parking opened from Folly Lane. Again, the architects were McLean and Forte and the builders were H.J. O'Boyle. The new building was blessed and opened on 21 June 1980. Necessary renovations to the original building were also made at this time, but the character of the original convent remained intact – its wide entrance hall, the light-filled St Joseph's Cloister with its Gothic-style windows giving a view of the front garden and the parish church, and the bell-tower with its elegant spire surmounting all.

Community life, 1920s–1980

The community in Downpatrick, during these decades of expansion, followed the same 'Common Life' – a round of prayer, work, recreation and special events – as could be found in any Mercy convent at home or abroad. In Downpatrick, however, it was Canon McWilliams, the parish priest, and not the bishop who presided, with great dignity, at receptions and professions. He had a fatherly care and concern for the community, which was recognised and appreciated. Besides the regular apostolates of teaching, visitation and work with parish groups, another service the community provided at this time was the making of altar breads for all the local churches. This work was in the hands of two skilled local women, Annie Troy and Maura Blaney. They worked in a room in the convent that later became St Catherine's Parlour. The novices helped out at times, counting and packing. This service ended around the time of the convent centenary, 1957.

By the summer of 1939, western Europe was caught up in war. Downpatrick was not affected by the bombing raids which swept over the cities, but the sound of the siren was not unknown. When it was heard the Sisters went for shelter down to the furnace room in the basement below the chapel. They also, of course, experienced the rationing and blackout precautions. But, as Downpatrick was considered to be a safe place, many families went there from Belfast to escape the dangers of the city. After one particular raid, evacuated children arrived in the town and, as a temporary measure, slept in a school classroom until better accommodation was found.

The influx of families and children considerably increased the enrolment in all the schools. The Sisters of Mercy worked over the years in agreeable collaboration with the De La Salle Brothers, who ran the schools for boys. The convent school took the boys in the infant and junior classes, up to the age for First Communion, after which they passed on to the De La Salle Brothers' primary school in John Street. This arrangement continued until 1968.

But convent life was not 'all work and no play'. For all communities, at this time living a semi-enclosed life, holidays were a special event. The Downpatrick community in the 1930s and 1940s took their holidays in Killough, a pretty, quiet, seaside village on the coast of County Down, about six miles from Downpatrick. A kind benefactor had given the Sisters a cottage on the seafront for their holidays and they took turns to spend time there. Living conditions were basic, but they were surrounded by the beauty of the open countryside and the wide sweep of shoreline and sea. Promenades were made to nearby beauty spots, in particular St John's Point and the beach at Rossglass, with its stupendous view of the majestic Mourne Mountains directly across the bay.

The 1950s and 1960s brought a whole series of memorable events for the people and the Mercy community of Downpatrick. The first of these was Father Peyton's Rosary Rally, which took place in the summer of 1954 and was a great occasion for the whole parish and hinterland. The Sisters of Mercy and their pupils played an active part in its organisation.[11]

The Rosary Rally was followed the next year by two very special anniversaries, separated by only two days. The first of these was the centenary of the Sisters of Mercy foundation in Downpatrick, a milestone in the history of the parish and of County Down. A worthy commemoration was in order. On the centenary day itself, the special event was the Eucharistic celebration of thanksgiving in the parish church. The celebrant was Archdeacon McWilliams. Bishop Philbin presided and many other clergy were in attendance. Following this, the community invited parishioners, hierarchy and clergy, friends, benefactors, associates and past and present pupils to join them for many social, musical and cultural entertainments organised by the schools. Also, Sisters of Mercy from many counties of Ireland and from abroad, some of them past pupils, joined the Downpatrick community for the centenary celebrations, which extended over a full week.

Within two days of the convent centenary celebrations, all roads again led to the 'city of Down' for the celebration of the diamond jubilee of Archdeacon McWilliams's ordination to the priesthood. Archdeacon McWilliams was the parish priest of many years standing and a great friend of the Downpatrick Mercy community. He had been ordained a priest in June 1895. He came to Downpatrick as parish priest in 1933 and from his earliest days there engaged himself fully in the work of the parish, with a special interest in the schools. As we have seen, he was the moving spirit behind the setting up of the convent commercial school in 1939 and, when the new secondary intermediate system came into being, he saw that secondary schools for both boys and girls were constructed and opened in the parish at the earliest possible opportunity.

The biggest event of the 1960s in which the Downpatrick Mercy community was fully involved was the Patrician year. This was to commemorate the fifteenth centenary of the death of St Patrick, patron saint of Ireland, who reputedly died in the year 461 CE. This centenary had special significance for the town and parish of Downpatrick because of the particular associations with the patron saint. Many celebrations were held and Downpatrick Mercy convent and schools ranked high among the venues associated with the commemorative events.

A new foundation

The mid-1960s saw an important new venture undertaken by the Downpatrick community, a foundation in west Belfast. The involvement of the Sisters of Mercy in the parish of Hannahstown, on the outskirts of Belfast, began in 1965, when the parish priest of Hannahstown, Reverend Charles Donnelly, approached Bishop Philbin to request Sisters for the new primary school which was required for the expanding parish.

A few years earlier the Sisters of Mercy in Downpatrick had spoken to Bishop Philbin of their desire to open a mission in Tampa, Florida. He had responded by saying that there was a greater need for their services in their own diocese, where new Catholic housing estates were rapidly developing in which new primary schools would need to be built and staffed. So, when Father Donnelly's request came, the bishop asked Mother M. Comgall McCourt, superior of the Mercy Convent, Downpatrick, if the community would contribute to the building and staffing of a new girls' primary school in Hannahstown. Mother M. Comgall agreed, and the school, dedicated to Blessed (later Saint) Oliver Plunkett, opened in 1968, with Sister M. Philomena McDonagh as principal. She was assisted by Sister M. Leontia Crilly as vice-principal. The following year Sister M. Vianney McVeigh joined the staff.

The Sisters first lived in a bungalow in Glengolan Avenue, Stewartstown Road, but early in 1969 they purchased a house, McAteer's, at the top of the Glen Road. In 1970 Sister M. Joseph Deeny joined the school staff and

Sister M. Vianney returned to Downpatrick. In July 1972 Sister M. Philomena retired (but remained in the Glen Road community) and Sister M. Joseph became school principal. The number of Sisters teaching in the school increased to four when Sisters Irene Sheridan and Mary De Largy joined the staff in 1974 and 1976 respectively. In 1977 the community moved to a larger house on the corner of Fruithill Park and the Andersonstown Road, in St Agnes's Parish. By the beginning of the 1979–80 school year, however, the number of Sisters in the school was again reduced to two. At Christmas 1977 Sister Irene had moved back to Downpatrick to open a new nursery school built by the community; in the summer of 1978 Sister M. Leontia had retired (Sister M. Francis McCashin became vice-principal); and early in 1979 Sister Mary De Largy had taken sabbatical leave. By then, however, the school was well established with, in addition to the Sisters, a dedicated lay staff.

With 125 years of successful apostolic work to look back on, the Downpatrick Mercy community was now prepared for a new phase of its history which would be heralded by events at the opening of the next decade, the 1980s.

---

1   Annals (SMD, 1920s).
2   Ibid. The bishop's caution was not without reason since at that time Catholics were barely tolerated in the town.
3   Personal memoirs of Sister M. Agnes Woods (Archives, SMD, 1930s).
4   Father Leo McKeown, an eyewitness to the scene, quoted by Reverend H. Armstrong, P.P., in an address in the Convent of Mercy, Bangor, 20 June 1989, Bangor (Archives, SPCMB, 1980s).
5   Sister M. Philomena McDonagh (Archives, SMD).
6   Ibid.
7   'A tribute to deceased members of staff' in St Mary's High School, Downpatrick, *St Mary's High School, Downpatrick, commemorative booklet* (Downpatrick: St Mary's High School, 1993), p. 8.
8   Ibid. p. 23.
9   Ibid.
10   Dr W. Philbin, 'Foreword', Downpatrick Convent of Our Lady of Mercy Primary School, *Centenary souvenir* (Downpatrick: Downpatrick Convent of Our Lady of Mercy Primary School, 1976).
11   Father Patrick Peyton, an American priest, followed a special worldwide mission in the middle decades of the twentieth century, spreading Catholic devotion to the rosary of the Blessed Virgin Mary.

25

DOWN AND CONNOR MERCY DIOCESAN UNION

An important new phase in the present history came when the two autonomous Mercy communities, Belfast and Downpatrick, with their respective branch houses, came together in July 1981 to form the Congregation of the Sisters of Mercy of Down and Connor Diocese. This was part of a process of changing structures in the Mercy Institute – that is, all the Catherine McAuley Mercy congregations in the world – throughout the country.

The later 1970s saw a steady movement towards a closer integration of Mercy communities in Ireland, on a diocesan basis to start with. This was a development responding to societal changes at the time. From the earliest days a strong and valuable characteristic of the Mercy Institute had been local autonomy: as soon as a newly founded community had become reasonably self-supporting it had become self-governing and independent, creating its links with and establishing its identity within the parish community to which it had been called. It had its own governing structures and its own novitiate. Though Mercy communities were not diocesan but of pontifical rite, they worked closely under the direction of the bishop of each diocese, as their whole focus was on pastoral work and service to the church in the parishes. There was no central governing body, or generalate, to which they were answerable.[1] Decisions about life and apostolate were made in the light of local needs and conditions. This proved to be a great strength and was most probably a key to the notable growth of the institute, worldwide, over the decades since its foundation. However, in spite of this local autonomy and identity there were strong bonds of kinship between the various Mercy communities, sustained by a 'Common Life' lived in accordance with the Mercy rule and constitutions, which were observed in each community, and a common sense of dedication to the service of the poor, sick and ignorant, as the fourth vow stated.

In parts of the world other than Ireland, where Mercy communities were more widespread and perhaps, because of circumstances, more fragile, amalgamations and unions between communities had been formed early on – for example, in the USA and Australia. In Ireland the Sisters were more numerous and the communities easily self-sufficient and firmly rooted in their local soil.

As has been indicated in the story of the Federation of the Sisters of Mercy of the Armagh Ecclesiastical Province and the all-Ireland Mercy Association, the communities in Ireland were gradually forming closer bonds. The movement was first towards diocesan amalgamation, in many cases instigated by the wishes of the local bishop. In the 1970s the impetus came from the Second Vatican Council's *Perfectae caritatis* decree.

By the time the federation had come to an end, five of the communities in the archdiocese of Armagh were already amalgamated within each of their own dioceses and the issue of possible interdiocesan union for the other four diocesan groups – Armagh, Derry, Down and Connor and Dromore – arose. The Belfast community did not favour this option. However, the process of discussions and discernment did not cease, and, on 6 September 1980, the Belfast Sisters met with the Downpatrick community to discuss the possibility of forming a Down and Connor diocesan union. Some progress was made and the Sisters agreed to continue the discernment process over the following three months. For this, joint commissions under various headings were set up to examine the implications of such a union with regard to personnel, apostolates, properties, finance, etc. Inter-community meetings were facilitated by Reverend Frederick Jones, C.Ss.R. A definitive vote on diocesan union was taken in December 1980 and the response was in favour. Permission to form the union was sought from the Sacred Congregation for Religious and for Secular Institutes in Rome. This was granted in a decree issued on 16 February 1981:

> The Superiors of the autonomous communities of Sisters of Mercy of Belfast and Downpatrick, located in the diocese of Down and Connor in Ireland, having consulted all the members of the communities, and having received a majority of affirmative votes, have petitioned the Holy See that their communities be permitted to form a Union.
>
> This Sacred Congregation for Religious and for Secular Institutes, having carefully considered the matter and obtained the opinion of the Local Ordinary of Down and Connor, by this decree grants permission for the above-mentioned fusion and entrusts the execution of it to the Local Ordinary of Down and Connor who will promulgate it in the presence of the Superiors and the Assistants of the communities of the Sisters of Mercy of Belfast and Downpatrick.[2]

In July of that year the communities of Belfast and Downpatrick, motherhouses and branch houses, united to become the Congregation of the Sisters of Mercy of Down and Connor.

The first general chapter of the new congregation was held in July–August 1981 and a leadership team was elected: Sister M. Genevieve Martin, superior general, Sister M. Joseph Deeny, first councillor, and Sisters M. Carmel Laverty, M. Vianney McVeigh and M. Bernadette Park, additional councillors. Their term of office was six years.[3]

Inauguration of the Union and of the new leadership team was held on 15 August, feast of the Assumption of the Blessed Virgin Mary. Central to the ceremony was the celebration of the eucharist, which focused on the theme 'peace and joy'. Later, at the communal celebration of evening prayer, Sister M. Genevieve, the new superior general, gave her inaugural address. She took for her text the beautiful verses of St Paul's letter to the Ephesians:

> I bow my knees before the Father from whom every family in heaven and on earth is named, that according to the riches of his glory he may grant you to be strengthened with might through his Spirit in the inner man, and that Christ may dwell in your hearts through faith; that you, being rooted and grounded in love, may have power to comprehend with all the saints what is the breadth and length and height and depth, and to know the love of Christ which surpasses knowledge, that you may be filled with all the fullness of God.
>
> Now to him who, by the power at work within us, is able to do far more abundantly than all that we ask or think, to him be glory in the church and in Christ Jesus to all generations. Amen.[4]

A business chapter followed and Sister M. Dolores Morton was appointed congregation treasurer and secretary general. The convent in Abbeyville was chosen for the new generalate and Sisters M. Genevieve and Joseph resided there. (Other Sisters in the Abbeyville community were Sisters M. de Lourdes Keaveney and M. Immaculata (Margaret) Campbell.) Thus began a new era for the Sisters of Mercy of Down and Connor.

The total number of Sisters in the new congregation was 93. Of these 24 were in the Downpatrick community. Each of the former autonomous communities brought to the union its own rich history and legacy, such as has been recounted in this story. At the time of union the Belfast Sisters were dispersed over five communities, taught in eight schools and were engaged in nursing in the Mater Hospital and the various nursing homes. The Downpatrick Sisters resided in three communities and were engaged in five schools. Both community groups also had Sisters engaged in visitation and pastoral work in the parishes as well as other forms of educational ministry.[5] From the summer of 1981 onwards the story of the Downpatrick community coincides with that of Belfast and its branch houses.

At this time postulancy was located in St Paul's Convent, Crumlin Road, and in the succeeding years the novices were sent to do their novitiate formation in various centres in Ireland. Numbers were small in all the communities and it was believed that the best novitiate programme could be presented in collaboration.

The new diocesan union, with its new form of government, opened up new perspectives in the lives of the Sisters in the respective communities. There was a certain movement of personnel to different apostolates as the need arose or where particular Sisters wished for a change. New appointments were made and collaboration among communities was encouraged. Naturally, the new regime required some getting used to, but on the whole it did not cause any significant difficulties, and in the end proved to have many more advantages than inconveniences. The Congregation of the Sisters of Mercy of Down and Connor could now move ahead along with the other Mercy congregations in the country with the work of renewal – in particular, seeking approval from the Holy See of their renewed national constitutions. (This would be granted in 1986.)

Missions

While the process towards the union of the Down and Connor communities was in train, life was moving on, meeting the needs of every day at home and abroad. The call of the missions had been heard and in 1976 Sister M. Bernadette Kielty of Downpatrick had gone to teach for one year with the Carysfort Sisters of Mercy in Nairobi, Kenya. The Belfast and Downpatrick Sisters of Mercy had also been involved, during the years of the federation, with the mission in Iceland, mainly in a supportive role. In 1977 Sister M. Perpetua Murphy of Downpatrick had gone to join the Sisters in Hafnarfjordur, Iceland, where she served for five years. Sister M. Joseph Deeny and Sister M. Pius McNicholl went to Iceland on a working holiday in 1982. When Sister M. Perpetua came home for good from Iceland in 1982, Sister Ethna O'Boyle took her place for one year.

The Sisters of Mercy from Dungarvan, County Waterford, had opened the first Nigerian mission in Yola, in the north-east of the country, in 1969. The summer of 1980 saw the beginnings of involvement in the Mercy mission in the town of Minna, in Niger state. In June 1980 a request had been made to the Belfast community for a Sister or Sisters to teach in northern Nigeria. The Strabane Sisters of Mercy were already in Minna. Mother M. Emilian Moloney, superior of the Belfast community, asked for volunteers. The lot fell to Sister Marie Duddy, who gave up her lectureship in religious studies in St Joseph's College of Education, Belfast, to take up a similar post in Minna, where the need was immensely greater. She set off for Nigeria on 26 January 1981. In October 1984 Sister M. Pius (Eileen) McNicholl, having taken early retirement from St Gemma's Secondary School, Belfast, joined Sister Marie in Minna, where she took up a wide-ranging pastoral apostolate. Sister Marie returned from Nigeria in the summer of 1986. Sister M. Pius (Eileen) McNicholl remained in Nigeria for 23 years.

In the autumn of 1981 Sister M. Alacoque McDonagh, recently retired from St Columbanus's Secondary School, Bangor, went to join the Ardee Mercy mission in Melbourne, Florida. She gave generous service there for several years. In 1988 Sister Rosemary McCloskey joined two other Sisters of Mercy on a mission to Chivu, Zimbabwe, to work with the Irish Franciscans there.[6]

Congregational events, 1980s

The 1980s was marked by special events, which were milestones in the history of the Mercy Congregation in Ireland. These were Trócaire '81, the formation of Mercy Ireland and Knock '86, the promulgation of the revised Mercy constitutions.

The first of these – Trócaire '81 – which took place on 23 July–1 August, was an historical event for the whole worldwide Mercy Institute. It was the first international gathering of Sisters of Mercy. After 150 years of growth and expansion, and after several years of planning, Sisters of Mercy from across the world met in Dublin, birthplace of the institute. Held in St Patrick's College, Drumcondra, the gathering was attended by 130 delegates. The purpose of the meeting was to forge closer bonds between the more than 22,000 Sisters in communities throughout the five continents. They formed the largest congregation of women religious in the Catholic Church at that time – a miraculous flourishing since, over the century and a half of its history, the Mercy Institute had had no central organisation nor dominant charismatic leadership since the death of its foundress, Catherine McAuley, a mere ten years after its inauguration.

Trócaire '81 had a fruitful outcome. An international planning committee was formed to strengthen relationships by various means of communication and ideas for the setting up of the Mercy International Centre in Baggot Street Convent, Dublin, were put forward. This important project materialised in 1994.

The success of the Mercy Association of Ireland paved the way for its evolution, in 1985, into a full policy-making body under the new title of Mercy Ireland. A full-time team of three Sisters was elected. They were backed by a committee made up of two Sisters from each of the four archdiocesan groups of communities. The task of the Mercy Ireland team was to explore possibilities of even closer bonding and, on behalf of all the communities of Ireland, to look into possible collaborative initiatives with regard to the needs of the homeless, youth and women, to promoting the role of the laity in the church and to other issues, particularly concerning the poor and the 'voiceless', that needed attention. So that cooperative action could be taken in the years ahead they set up commissions to implement the decisions taken. In the event the greatest work carried out by the Mercy Ireland team was to pave the way for the eventual realisation of the Mercy Ireland Union.

The big event for the Sisters of Mercy in Ireland, Knock '86, was the promulgation of the revised Mercy constitutions, which had been accepted by all the communities in Ireland. As we know, work on this revision had been going on for over 15 years, firstly at local and then at inter-diocesan level. It was one of the tasks that newly-formed Mercy Ireland executive took in hand, with the aim of finalising a version acceptable to all the Sisters in the country and, of course, to the Sacred Congregation for Religious and Secular Institutes in Rome, the final arbiter. Eventually, in 1985, this work was completed and the new constitutions approved. The constitutions had been revised, taking into account developments in the work and mission of the Mercy Institute in recent times, and would now become the guideline for each Sister's life and apostolate. They applied to 4,500 members of the congregation then in Ireland who, over the previous 14 years, had successfully amalgamated their multiple autonomous communities into 26 diocesan unions.

To mark the promulgation of the new national constitutions a special event was organised for 5 April 1986, a liturgy of thanksgiving at the national shrine of Our Lady, patroness of the congregation, at Knock, County Mayo, during which a copy of the constitutions was formally presented to each of the 26 superiors general. Cardinal Tomás Ó Fiaich was chief celebrant, assisted by bishops and priests from many dioceses, and thousands of Mercy Sisters from home and abroad attended the Mass. The cardinal congratulated the Sisters on what they had achieved and added, 'The new constitutions, based on the gospels and preserving all the essentials of Catherine McAuley's legacy, will provide the Sisters with a sure guide for living out their vocation.'[7] Later, in summing up the occasion, Sister M. Regina Kelly, president of Mercy Ireland, echoing the words of the cardinal, said:

> I believe that this is a moment full of hope and promise for the order and for the church. The shared work of re-examining and re-expressing the mercy vocation in the light of today's needs has resulted in a sharpening of focus regarding this vocation and its call to be with the poor and deprived.[8]

The Knock event was not just the completion of a task undertaken but the opening of a new phase in the life of the congregation in Ireland with a new outreach to all the Mercy communities throughout the world.

Movement and change

Subsequent to the formation of the Congregation of the Sisters of Mercy of Down and Connor it was necessary to study the congregation's assets – works and properties – and, in order to make the best of these, some rationalisation was necessary along with some reallocation of personnel. As part of the process, decisions had to be made about the branch houses of the now-combined Belfast and Downpatrick communities, especially as some school Sisters were retiring and not being replaced.

In 1982 a decision was made to sell the convent, St Anne's, in Donaghadee, County Down. In September 1981 Sister M. Angela Deignan had become principal of St Anne's Primary School, succeeding Sister M. Agnes Woods, who had retired (there were then just 39 pupils in the school). With changes in personnel over the next year, the community of St Anne's Convent was reduced to two. These, Sister M. Angela and Sister M. Catherine Molloy, continued to live in the convent in High Street until it was put on the market. After this Sister M. Angela and Sister M. Bernadette Kielty, who was engaged in pastoral work in Donaghadee, travelled there each day from Bangor. When the Sisters of Mercy left Donaghadee the Sisters of the Adoration came to the town and took up residence in the presbytery in the absence of a resident parish priest.

In 1982 the Sisters celebrated 50 years of their presence in Bangor. They continued their active service in the parish but in the late 1980s it had become evident that, because of the lack of Sisters available, a community presence in Bangor could no longer be sustained. By 1988 the community numbered just four Sisters, with only two teaching in the schools – Sister M. Angela Deignan in Donaghadee and Sister Grace Quinn in St Comgall's. Sister M. Benignus Morgan had been transferred to Belfast and Sister M. Mercy McKeown, from Downpatrick, succeeded her as superior of the Bangor community. Sister M. Bernadette Kielty had returned to Downpatrick and Sister M. Kieran Morrison came back to Bangor to replace her.

In June 1989 Sister M. Angela retired from the principalship of St Anne's and a lay principal, Mr M. Conway, took over. Sister Grace also resigned from her teaching post in St Comgall's Primary School. By the summer of 1989, therefore, both Sisters had left Bangor. The last Sisters to remain in the convent were Sisters M. Mercy McKeown and M. Kieran Morrison. To them fell the painful task of closing down the convent, home to the Sisters for over 50 years. On 22 April 1990 a Mass of thanksgiving was celebrated in the parish church at which Bishop Cahal Daly presided. The parish priest, Reverend Hilary Armstrong, was celebrant and he conveyed the gratitude of the parish to the Sisters for their 58 years' service there. Sister M. Emilian Moloney, superior general, expressed in response the Sisters' appreciation for the welcome and support they had always received from the priests and parishioners and the regret with which they felt obliged to withdraw. The Mass was attended by a large congregation and was followed by refreshments provided by the ladies of the parish.

On 2 May the last Mass was celebrated in the little convent chapel and the Sisters vacated the convent shortly afterwards. The house was purchased by the parish and became the residence of the parish priest. Another mission had been accomplished.[9]

In October 1982 the convent, school and grounds at Sussex Place were put on the market, along with convent properties in Joy Street and Little Joy Street. At first the convent was rented by the parish priest at a nominal rent (£5 per year) and it was used as a playschool, a dinner centre for elderly people and a nightclub for men. The school itself could not be vacated for five years until the new parish school was ready. In August 1983 the Sisters of the Good Shepherd, who were engaged in pastoral work in the area, purchased the convent.

October 1982 also saw the beginning of the demolition of the original convent, Abbeyville, Whiteabbey. The Down and Connor Mercy Generalate had been established there but the house was in need of considerable repair. It was old and extensive restoration would have entailed considerable expense, so it was decided to demolish it and build a new convent on the site. The site was purchased from the diocese in exchange for the chapel, which was community property and had been used as the parish church since the early 1970s. In the interim, the generalate and the Abbeyville community rented temporary accommodation next door in houses belonging to their neighbours, the Sherlocks. This arrangement proved satisfactory.

Father Hugh Crossin, the parish priest, completely modernised the former convent chapel, now the new parish church of St James's Parish, to create what was considered the ideal liturgical setting. The former gate lodge was demolished to give place to a new residence for the priest.

In St Paul's Convent, Crumlin Road, the Sisters braced themselves for the loss of their convent chapel, St Anthony's Oratory, which would have to be vacated after Easter 1983. To replace it the common room was adapted as a *pro-tem* chapel. This was a case of history repeating itself – the common room, formerly the noviceship, had been the community chapel until St Anthony's Oratory was opened in 1910. The last Mass was celebrated in the oratory on 10 June at 6.15 p.m. A week later demolition started and one Sister, witnessing the scene, saw the beautiful figure representing St Luke, in mosaic, crumble under the force of the bulldozer. It was a sad day. With the chapel went memories of many ceremonies – receptions, professions, requiems, solemn high Masses and Quarant' Ore, holy days and great feasts, vigils of Christmas and Easter celebrated in all their liturgical splendour. Life would never be the same again. In the subsequent years the Sisters attended the vigil Masses in the hospital chapel; other ceremonies and funerals were held in the parish churches according to where the Sisters were engaged.

The 'Common Life' had gone and religious life was undergoing a radical change. While some property had, perforce, to be disposed of, other property had been acquired. Ballysillan House, 614 Crumlin Road, Belfast, with its grounds, had been purchased by the community in 1966 as the site for the new convent primary school. Originally there had been plans to use the house for a nursery school, but the idea had been dropped. At the end of the 1960s a decision was made to use it as a formation house for the Mercy communities of the northern federation and it was used for this purpose from 1970 until 1971, when Sister M. Gabriel Deignan brought the novices to live there. The school Sisters also used a room on the ground floor of the house for their staffroom and, when the novices moved out in 1971, the school used more of the house during the day.

In September 1973, after a bombing of the primary school in consequence of which the front of the house also suffered severe damage, the whole house was given over to the school for classrooms until the school building was restored. Afterwards the school retained the ground floor for use as music rooms, an interview room, a staff and Sisters' dining room and a kitchen. The flat and annex at the rear were used as storage space. In the summer of 1987 Sister Marie Duddy got permission to use a room on the upper floor of the house as an office for the Northern Ireland Council of the Conference of Major Religious Superiors (Ireland), of which she had been appointed secretary coordinator. Some of the rooms on this floor, which were used for storage, were cleared and redecorated. Eventually two additional rooms were used for meetings. The school continued to use the ground floor.

In the grounds of Ballysillan House were two other houses. One used by the school caretaker, Peter O'Reilly and his family. Peter O'Reilly worked for many years as an excellent caretaker until his sudden death on 6 June 1997. The other adjoining house was leased to a tenant. There was also an extensive stable area which, when the stabling was demolished, provided an ideal building site for a new community house.

The schools

Our Lady of Mercy Secondary School celebrated its silver jubilee in 1985. Since its foundation it had expanded in numbers and size. In 1977 Sister M. Carmel Laverty retired and Sister M. Regina Caffrey succeeded her as principal. The school suffered considerably during the 1970s and 1980s from bombings, arson attacks and serious vandalism but continued to maintain its high standards of education, both academic and vocational. In spite of all the problems, morale was high among staff and pupils.

As the 1980s progressed, further extensions were built for the teaching of new specialised subjects of the curriculum. A highly equipped technology suite was added for the introduction of courses in design and technology. This was a breakthrough as up until this time there had been no provision for design and technology in girls' schools. Following this came an extension of the science facilities, a refurbishment of the computer-studies suites for the teaching of information and communication technologies (ICT) and an extension of the computer network for which the most up-to-date equipment was installed. B-Tech National and GNVQ courses were introduced. Later the facilities were to be expanded with the addition of new music, drama and fitness suites (in the 1990s). Every opportunity was given to the pupils for a wide choice of careers. They were prepared for usual GCSE and other academic examinations up to A level and artistic and musical talents were also actively nurtured.

By the mid-1980s Mercy Primary School was well established in the grounds of Ballysillan House. It also suffered from sectarian attacks, the worst being in 1973 but, like the secondary school, it continued, undaunted, to provide an excellent curriculum for the young pupils. The principal of Mercy Primary School was Mother M. Emilian Moloney, who succeeded Sister M. Bernadette Agnew in 1979. She in turn was succeeded by Sister M. Gertrude Monaghan in 1986 and Sister Frances Forde in June 1989.

As has been recorded, Sussex Place Convent closed in June 1969, but there was still a flourishing convent primary school, St Malachy's, which celebrated its centenary in 1978.[10] However, with the movement of the population away from the city centre to the outskirts following both political disturbances and new urban development planning, the number of pupils decreased (from 450 to 190 between 1970 and 1978) and eventually plans were made to amalgamate the girls' and boys' schools in a new school in the parish.

St Malachy's Convent School, Sussex Place, closed its doors to the children on Tuesday, 23 June 1987 after 110 years of service to the parish. The convent school joined with the boys' school to form the new St Malachy's Primary School, Cromac Street. Sister Ann McKeever was the last principal of the convent school. She was appointed principal of the new school and remained there until her retirement in 1989. She had spent 24 years as a teacher in the Markets area.

The Star of the Sea Girls' School in the New Lodge area also had its share of harassment during the Troubles. Situated at the upper end of the New Lodge and in proximity to Tiger's Bay, throughout the 1970s the pupils and their families endured street riots, burnings, bombings, shootings, midnight searches and the internment and imprisonment of their fathers, brothers, uncles and cousins. It took great courage and determination on the part of everyone to keep the school going and through it all the children struggled bravely to attend school, where they felt comparatively safe from the ever-present dangers of the streets. The last Sister to be principal of the school, Sister M. Louis Donaghy, retired in 1980 and was succeeded by a lay principal, Miss Agnes Devlin, a very dedicated teacher who had served many years in the school as a member of staff. One Sister, Sister Josephine McAteer, remained until she was appointed principal of Immaculata Special School in 1986. Thus ended another chapter in the history of St Paul's community, with the withdrawal of Sisters from the 'Star' after 99 years' service there. In 1989 the 'Star' celebrated its centenary and the occasion evoked many nostalgic memories from past pupils and teachers alike.[11]

In Bangor Parish, the old primary school – the former convent school – was considered unfit for further use and in 1974 a new building was constructed for an amalgamated girls' and boys' primary school. This was handed over to lay administration. The next five years saw a steady decline in enrolment, when a second Catholic primary school, St Malachy's, was opened in the parish to serve the new Kilcooley estate. By this time the number of Sisters teaching in St Comgall's was reduced to two – Sisters M. Angela Deignan (who, in the summer of 1981, left the school to take up the principalship of the school in Donaghadee) and Sister Grace Quinn. Sister Grace remained on for some more years (until 1989), being the last Sister of Mercy to participate in the primary education of girls in Bangor. The year 1990 marked the centenary of St Comgall's Primary School and the Sisters' contribution over more than 50 years was graciously acknowledged.[12]

Immaculata School in Whiteabbey continued to provide for girls with special educational needs. However, towards the end of the 1970s enrolment went into steady decline until a decision was reached in 1989. The school authorities decided, in conjunction with the Department of Education, that it was in the best interest of the pupils' further education that Immaculata School amalgamate with St Aloysius's Boys' School, Belfast, and move to the vacated premises of Gort na Móna Boys' School in Holy Trinity Parish, to form St Gerard's Educational Resource Centre. The new school duly opened in September 1989 and Sister Josephine McAteer served there for a short time. She later moved into a new ministry.

In 1976 Sister Bernadette Park had gone to work in the New Lodge Nursery School, an important apostolate in a very troubled area. The school had opened in 1968, a two-teacher school with two assistants. Sister Bernadette was appointed principal of the nursery school in 1984 and remained there until she was seconded for further studies.

With the union of the Belfast and Downpatrick communities, the new congregation also included the convent schools in Downpatrick and Donaghadee. In Downpatrick were the convent primary school and the parish girls' secondary, St Mary's High School. In 1976 the convent primary school moved from Stream Street, where it had been founded, to Edward Street. Sister Irene Sheridan was appointed principal of the convent nursery school when it opened in 1977 and the new school soon attracted many small pupils.

The first principal of the high school when it opened in 1957 was Mother M. Aloysius McCusker. On her retirement in 1974 she was succeeded by Sister M. Teresa Kielty, who in turn retired in 1982 to be succeeded by Sister Anne Kerr. Sister Anne remained in the principalship for only a couple of years, with Sister Margaret Heffron as an assistant teacher. With the retirement of Sisters Anne Kerr and Margaret Heffron, there were no Sisters left on the teaching staff of the school. However, their leaving did not end the Sisters' involvement with St Mary's. Sister Elizabeth McKeown, who had formerly taught in the school, remained on as a chaplain. She took responsibility for organising the school retreats, some of which were conducted in the convent, where two large rooms were made available. Along with the clerical chaplain, she also organised the liturgical celebrations and encouraged the formation of prayer groups and groups of social concern in the parish. She continued this work until she moved to west Belfast in 1993.

The early history of St Anne's Girls' Primary School, Donaghadee, has been told in Chapter 24. Sister M. Angela's retirement in 1989 marked the end of an era for the school, which had been run by the Sisters of Mercy ever since its opening in the shop in High Street in 1932. At the thanksgiving Mass on 21 June marking the years of service the Sisters had given, the parish priest, Reverend Hilary Armstrong, paid tribute to the role the Sisters had played not only in the school but also in the town of Donaghadee. In addressing the congregation he said:

> [They] had a widespread pastoral role in this area. The friendship, comfort, counsel and support they gave over the years to parishioners and especially to the families of pupils is one you can attest to and I am sure you have many anecdotes about this ... How many of you still remember the club for girls which the Sisters set up in the old school and later in what is now called the retreat house? How many priests also thank the Sisters for the care they lavished on the old St Comgall's Church and their musical direction of its choirs?[13]

The girls' primary school in St Oliver Plunkett Parish, Lenadoon, west Belfast, which had been opened by the Downpatrick community, now also came under the umbrella of the Congregation of the Sisters of Mercy of Down and Connor, as did the community house in Fruithill Park. Sister M. Joseph Deeny was principal of the school and the former Fruithill Park community expanded and diversified. The members were: Sister M. Emilian Moloney (principal of the Mercy Primary School), Sister M. de Lourdes Keaveney (retired), Sister M. Colmcille Kennedy (pastoral work), Sister M. Jarlath Mannion (senior tutor, Royal Victoria Hospital), Sister Frances Forde (Mercy Primary School) and Sister M. Francis McCashin (Oliver Plunkett Primary School). Sister Frances Forde was appointed local superior.

As can be seen, the engagement of the Sisters of Mercy in the schools of the diocese was gradually declining. Throughout the 1990s the numbers further decreased both by natural attrition (through retirement) and change of apostolates. In 1994 the profile was as follows: Our Lady of Mercy Secondary School had two Sisters; Mercy Primary School, Belfast had one Sister; Downpatrick Convent Primary School had one Sister; Oliver Plunkett Primary School had one Sister and Downpatrick Convent Nursery School had one Sister.

Visitation and pastoral care

In spite of many changes, the traditional Mercy apostolate of visitation still held a prominent place in the Sisters' mission, though with a broader interpretation of this work of mercy in keeping with the needs of the times. According to the revised Mercy constitutions:

> Visitation is a particular expression of our Mercy apostolate
> bringing us close to those in need.
> The Laity are our associates and co-workers
> in the spiritual mission of the Church,
> and we collaborate with all
> who make the Gospel of Mercy live in today's world.[14]

As long as there were still Sisters in Crumlin Road (St Paul's) Convent the apostolate of visitation was continued, though to a reduced degree. The surrounding area had changed demographically and many Sisters had changed their work locations and patterns and their manner of serving the poor and needy. However, visitation of the sick and aged in hospitals and in their homes continued to be very important for all the communities of the diocese. Also, the time-honoured works of mercy, feeding the hungry and giving drink to the thirsty who arrived on their doorstep – in particular men and women 'of the road' – had been established practice for as far back as the Sisters of Mercy could remember. This continued at St Paul's as long as the porch (a small entrance hallway to the side of the convent, where those who came for food or other needs were served daily) existed and there were Sisters in the convent to attend to those who came. The same hospitality was, of course, practised in the other convents insofar as this was feasible.

Visitation in Crumlin Road Jail had been an important duty for the Sisters in the early days. This also, by necessity, had had to be abandoned because prison regulations had changed. However, for as long as the Sisters remained in St Paul's Convent a Sister (Ann McKeever) went each Sunday to provide music for Mass in the prison, and usually at Christmas time security was relaxed in order to allow other Sisters to join in for the Christmas carols. These visits to the prison next door were salutary experiences for the Sisters and hopefully brought some Christmas cheer to the unfortunate prisoners who were detained there.

In the late 1980s and the 1990s the apostolate of visitation took on a much wider connotation in all the Mercy communities in the diocese. It took the form of fuller involvement in parish activities along with, and supporting, the laity, and in specific fields of pastoral work for which several Sisters were specially trained. With greater flexibility and availability than in former years, Sisters could now participate in the work of the many pastoral organisations and societies in their own parishes. These included the Society of St Vincent de Paul, the Legion of Mary, the Pioneers, Apostolic Work, prayer, Bible-study and meditation groups; Special Religious Education for the Disadvantaged (SPRED), youth-work, adult-education and family support groups. The general comment was that there was too much work to be done and too few Sisters to do it.

At this time also several Sisters undertook clinical and pastoral education (CPE) courses to prepare them for chaplaincy work in hospitals and hospices, others training for counselling and therapy in preparation for work in family and youth ministry and with the bereaved and those traumatised by violence in Northern Ireland society. Visitation of the sick, the elderly and the needy, of course, also continued to be important; associated with this was the role of eucharistic minister (a person delegated to bring holy communion regularly to the housebound).

In these decades a special ministry was to those smitten by the dreaded and ubiquitous disease of cancer. In 1980 Sister M. Genevieve Martin became a founding member of the Northern Ireland Hospice on the Somerton Road, Belfast, and served there for 16 years (until 1996) as a chaplain and member of the council of management. In the 1990s Sister M. Ignatius McAvoy became engaged as a chaplain in the Northern Ireland cancer-treatment hospital at Belvoir Park, Belfast.

The political climate
The need for pastoral care was hardly ever more urgent. Political and social insecurity created many problems. In the 1980s the social disruption in Northern Ireland had by no means diminished; at times it exploded into full-scale violence with the loss of many lives through bombings, shootings and the wholesale destruction of property, especially in the main towns. The province was flooded with thousands of British troops whose task it was to try to contain the sectarian violence and to protect lives and property. Not an easy task in conditions of guerrilla warfare. No one was spared, though the conflict was localised to some areas more than others. Except for targeted bombings of businesses in the cities and towns, the working-class religiously divided ghetto areas bore the brunt of the attacks and reprisals. By now the province was under direct rule from Westminster and there seemed to be no political solution in view.

In 1986 elections took place in Northern Ireland and, as usually happened on such occasions, sectarian allegiances were reinforced and the aftermath of the elections brought renewed rioting. The lower Crumlin Road, an interface of the two communities, was always a flashpoint and the convent and hospital did not escape the consequences. On more than one occasion the front hospital wards had to be vacated. When the Maternity Unit was attacked late one evening, the mothers were moved to the rear of the building and the infants were brought across the road to the convent community room. Despite the fear and disruption involved, the roaring fire surrounded by cosy cots and peacefully sleeping babies must have been a delightful sight the following morning. One evening rioters broke into the convent grounds and vandalised the statues in the front garden; on another evening they burned the cars. They broke into the hospital chapel during the quiet hours of the night and perpetrated a considerable amount of damage. A particularly horrifying incident for the Mater Hospital was when sectarian assassins broke through the security and murdered Máire Drumm, a leading member of the IRA, in the hospital ward where she was a patient. This ruthless murder shocked everyone.

These are only some examples of what became regular occurrences during those terrible years. Fortunately, though, and through God's mercy, no Sister suffered any serious physical harm, though personal harassment on the public thoroughfares was not unknown. The Sisters who had to be out frequently resorted to wearing mufti, since the very appearance of religious dress could be offensive to some people of strongly anti-Catholic persuasion. At times the future looked very dark, but ordinary people continued to live in hope and counter the violence and destruction by participating in peace initiatives and movements for inter-faith and inter-community understanding and reconciliation. Forgiveness and prayer were their response to hatred and violence and sometimes this forgiveness reached a heroic level.

Overview

As we have seen, the 1980s was a decade of many changes, not only on the wider perspective of the congregation's corporate life but also affecting the day-to-day lives of the Sisters at local level. One significant and noticeable change was a certain secularisation of religious dress. This change had been taking place gradually and informally – and the fact of living in Belfast during these years of sectarian conflict played no small part in it. It was, besides, a trend that was making itself obvious among most active apostolic religious, especially in the western world, for various reasons. Following a Down and Connor congregational assembly in the summer of 1986, at which this controversial matter had been discussed at length, Sister M. Genevieve Martin, superior general, issued the following circular to the congregation:

> The religious dress of the Congregation is simple attire suited to the local circumstances and modern conditions, and worn with a Mercy symbol [usually the Mercy cross]. It is an external sign of our consecration and must be in keeping with our profession of religious poverty and with our apostolic mission.[15]

While a modest form of secular attire was permitted in appropriate circumstances, at the same time Sisters who wished to retain the traditional religious habit (in a modified form) were quite at liberty to do so. With secular dress the veil was optional. In the late 1980s the Sisters were given personal budgets (monthly allowances) to cover clothes, shoes, stationery and stamps, gifts, recreation and entertainments, and incidental travelling expenses. All these changes implied and promoted individual responsibility in the use of material goods and a new understanding of the practice of religious poverty and of obedience, as they left a high degree of choice to each Sister.

The changes also extended to the daily horarium, community prayer and various other aspects of everyday life. A modern understanding of religious life was evolving and needed to be learned and appropriated by the religious Sisters of the late twentieth century. The structures of the previous decades and centuries were being gradually dismantled. There were new perspectives and challenges for all.

The 1980s, then, was a decade of vitality, which saw a widening of visions and horizons, new perspectives on the charism of Mercy and a new understanding of it. However, visions of the future rest on the shoulders of the past and the communities of the 1980s owed their existence to those who had gone before them and the legacies they had bequeathed. Though the individual stories of all these valiant women cannot now be recounted, we can remember their passing. The 1980s had seen 17 Sisters of the Congregation of the Sisters of Mercy of Down and Connor pass away, most in the fullness of their years.

---

[1] The generalate of a religious congregation is the central administration. Besides an international generalate, where this applies, each autonomous Mercy congregation had its own generalate for its local administration. Over recent years, this title has modified to central leadership team for the administration of a number of provinces and provincial leadership team for the administration of each individual province.

[2] See Down and Connor Mercy Archives (MCA).

[3] Details of the procedures of this general chapter are to be found in the Down and Connor Mercy Archives (MCA).

4   Ephesians 3:14–21.
5   The particulars of these communities and apostolates are given in following chapters of this story.
6   The stories of all these missions are documented in the reports of Mercy Missions in Iceland and Nigeria in the Mercy Northern Province Archives (MCA).
7   Cardinal T. Ó Fiaich, address to Knock '86 (5 April 1986).
8   Sister M. Regina Kelly, address to Knock '86 (5 April 1986).
9   For this and earlier information about the Bangor convent I am indebted to the annals of the Bangor community (written up in the 1980s), the memoirs of M.M. Feeny (written 1982), the research done by Sisters M. Brendan Blanche and M. Mercy Cummins, St Comgall's Primary School centenary publication, 1983, Sister M. Clare (Josephine) McAteer's minor thesis (1965) and Ann McCann, unpublished thesis (NUU, 1994) (Archives, SPCMB).
10   Cummins, *op. cit.*
11   See Sisters of Mercy, *Star of the Sea Girls' Primary: centenary magazine* (Belfast: Star of the Sea Girls' Primary School, 1989).
12   See the centenary publication, J. O'Hanlon (ed.) *St Comgall's Primary School centenary, 1890–1990* (1990), for a very comprehensive history of the school.
13   Reverend H. Armstrong, address at thanksgiving Mass, St Comgall's Church, Donaghadee, County Down (21 June 1989).
14   Revised Mercy constitutions, Sections 43 and 44.
15   Sister M. Genevieve Martin to Mercy Congregation (Annals, SPCMB, 1986).

26

New horizons – the diaspora

While the decades of the 1970s and 1980s had been periods of integration and closer cooperation between communities, the latter years of the 1980s saw what appeared to be a movement in the reverse direction – a trend away from large community living and the 'Common Life' and from concentrated community apostolates as such. 'Freedom for mission' became a slogan and an assertion of individual personal discernment with regard to each Sister's role in the corporate mission of the congregation.

This new face of apostolic religious life had been emerging throughout the Catholic Church as a whole. It was attributed to the action of the Holy Spirit in a new social era which was strongly characterised by rapid change and by trends that threw up diverse social problems in a world struggling with the dichotomy of great wealth on one hand and extreme poverty and deprivation on the other. These changes, which seemed to require radical responses, found echoes in new concepts of apostolic religious life and community. These were not slow in affecting most apostolic religious communities, not least those of Down and Connor.

By the late 1980s the idea of moving out of the larger communities to form smaller communities was already in fashion. Back in February 1983, in a circular letter to the communities, Sister M. Genevieve Martin, the superior general of the time, had said, 'Now we can begin to give consideration to the needs expressed by some Sisters for a fuller community life, for experience of small groups and for a simpler lifestyle.'[1] In the summer of 1985, Sisters Veronica O'Brien, Mary De Largy and Deirdre McGlinchey had requested permission to live out the Mercy ideal in a small community with emphasis on more direct access to their apostolates. They requested the use of the upper floor of Ballysillan House (the ground floor of which was still being used by Mercy Primary School for music rooms and staffrooms) for an experimental period of two years. The specific reasons the Sisters gave for their request for this new style of community were: firstly, that it was a response to the spirit of the Second Vatican Council; secondly, that it would be a more realistic way of community living (which has always been an integral part of traditional religious life); thirdly, that it would put them more in touch with the local people and the parish; fourthly, that it would make them more accessible to people where they could offer Mercy hospitality if needed; fifthly, that it would be more convenient for their apostolates (in the primary and secondary schools); and sixthly, that it would provide better mutual support and shared prayer life.

The Sisters gave the new lifestyle a try, moving into Ballysillan House on 12 December 1985. However, after about a year and a half they decided to terminate the experiment (August 1986).[2] It had been a courageous venture. Whereas the small community had experienced many advantages in their new accommodation and lifestyle, they had also experienced disadvantages that could not have been foreseen, specifically in the matters of location and size of the community. The experiment had been valuable as a pilot scheme, throwing light on what needed to be taken into consideration by other Sisters planning to live in small communities away from the motherhouse. The move out into smaller communities was to gain momentum in the ensuing years.

Glenveagh Drive

Meanwhile, in the autumn of 1985, a new community house of the congregation was opened in the new parish of St Oliver Plunkett in west Belfast. The parish had been established to serve Lenadoon, a new, large Catholic housing estate that adjoined the older Hannahstown Parish. The parish priest, Reverend Francis McCorry (who had formerly been parish priest of St Agnes's Parish, Andersonstown, to which Fruithill Park Convent belonged) was anxious to have the Sisters living in the parish. They already ran the girls' school there (the primary schools on the Glen Road, Hannahstown, were now transferred to St Oliver Plunkett Parish). The parish at that time had about 8,000 people, with two middle-class estates and another with a largely working-class majority, many young married couples and a high percentage of unemployment. Besides the school there was a great need for Sisters to do visitation and other pastoral work. The Mercy Congregation acquired a plot of land beside the church, on Glenveagh Drive, to build a new convent and five Sisters (Sisters M. Colmcille Kennedy, M. Jarlath Mannion, M. Francis McCashin and M. Bernadette Sands, with Sister M. Alacoque McDonagh as local superior) were appointed to form a community there.

The new convent in Glenveagh Drive was ready by September 1985 and the following few months were spent in preparing it for occupation. On 22 December two Sisters moved in and on 26 December the first Mass was celebrated. The installation of the Blessed Sacrament was followed by a house blessing. In January the other members of the community took up residence.

The formal opening of the convent on 11 May 1986 was, as the parish bulletin reported, a 'red-letter day' in the history of St Oliver Plunkett Parish.

After the community moved out of Fruithill Park, that house was rented to student Sisters for a short time. When she was elected superior general of the Down and Connor Mercy Congregation in 1987, Sister M. Emilian Moloney decided to have the house refurbished for use as a generalate. It served this purpose until 1995.

In 1987, following the second general chapter of the Congregation of the Sisters of Mercy of Down and Connor, and a period of review of the apostolates and of other factors concerning the communities at this time (such as the extension of the Mater Hospital), some Sisters moved into new, smaller community groupings. These were in Ligoniel, Limestone Road and Ballysillan House, Belfast and in the Model Farm estate in Downpatrick.

Ligoniel

The Sisters of Mercy's association with Ligoniel, originally a linen-manufacturing village on the outskirts of north Belfast, now greatly expanded with housing estates, dates from 1989. In March of that year Sister Kathleen Savage, who had commenced community visitation in St Vincent de Paul Parish, Ligoniel, requested permission from the superior general to live in the parish as it would be more convenient for her apostolate. She had acquired a two-bedroom house at 153 Ligoniel Road from the Northern Ireland Housing Executive in recognition of the valuable social work she was doing in the district. As far as the congregation was concerned, Ligoniel was recognised as an area of high social disadvantage, with widespread unemployment and many young families in the new estates. In addition, Our Lady of Mercy Secondary School was nearby, on the outskirts of the parish, and many of its pupils came from St Vincent de Paul Primary School. It was seen as appropriate to develop the Mercy apostolate there and for a short time two Sisters worked in full-time ministry in the parish. Sister Mary De Largy, who was then teaching in Our Lady of Mercy Secondary School, joined Sister Kathleen in September 1989. Sister Margaret Campbell later replaced Sister Mary De Largy.

In order to enlarge the Ligoniel Mercy community the congregation considered for a time buying land in Ligoniel and building a larger house. However, the project proved to be economically unviable and they sought a larger house to rent instead. In August 1992 the Sisters acquired a three-bedroom house at 2 Lever Street.

Life in Ligoniel was not without its eventful moments. The district was one of the sectarian flashpoints in north Belfast, the residents of the estates being divided in their political allegiances. On the night of 27 September 1992, shortly after the Sisters had taken up residence in Lever Street, gunmen burst into the house and were confronted on the stairs by a terrified member of the community. It transpired that they had come in search of the former occupant. Fortunately they withdrew on realising their mistake. The Sisters suffered considerable shock but no one was injured.

Limestone Road

In September 1988, on the invitation of Father Peter Forde, administrator of Holy Family Parish, Newington, Belfast, Sisters Therese Larkin and Kathleen Savage undertook a ministry of pastoral care in his parish. These Sisters were, at the time, residing in St Paul's Convent, Crumlin Road, but they became increasingly aware, from their experience, of the need to reside in the Holy Family Parish itself. Their superiors agreed to their request to seek rented accommodation; 252 Limestone Road, a small terraced house near the parish church, fell vacant and was rented from Newington Housing Association. The Sisters took up residence there in May 1989. When Sister Kathleen moved to Ligoniel that year, Sister Therese was joined by Sister M. Carmel Laverty, who gave many years' valuable service to the Holy Family Parish.

The Sisters were made very welcome by the priests of the parish and the parishioners and were soon fully engaged in many and varied parish activities. These fell broadly into three kinds: work with the Society of St Vincent de Paul for the disadvantaged in the area; the instruction and care of families with children preparing for baptism, first communion and confirmation; running the Pastoral Centre for the provision of adult education in personal and spiritual development. In the early months of their presence in the parish, Sister Therese was also involved in bereavement counselling with Beginning Experience (a bereavement counselling service) but, as the pressure of other areas of ministry increased, she had to withdraw from this work.

By 1990 it was obvious that the Sisters would have to move out of St Paul's Convent on the Crumlin Road, so alternative accommodation had to be found. Much searching was done to find a suitable house, preferably in the Antrim Road area, which would satisfy the requirements of a small religious community. Early in the summer of 1990 a house was purchased, 2 the Glen, Limestone Road. This was a semi-detached, three-storey, commodious house with a large garden behind it, situated directly across the Limestone Road from Holy Family Parish Church and Presbytery. After some months of restoration the house was ready to be occupied and, on 6 December 1990, Sisters M. Aidan Mullarkey, M. Majella McAlinden,

M. Veronica O'Brien and M. Bernadette Park moved in. These Sisters were engaged in various apostolates.

A year later, when the adjoining house became available, it was purchased and refurbished. It was intended primarily as a formation house (from the autumn of 1984 there had been a formation house for the northern communities in Clogher, County Tyrone, but by 1990 this was no longer used and the Down and Connor postulants were going to Downpatrick Convent). In October 1991 the formation directress (Sister Grace Quinn), with four postulants, moved in there.

Ballysillan House

In view of the fact that the Sisters were moving out of St Paul's Convent, Crumlin Road and alternative accommodation was needed it was decided that Ballysillan House should be used once more as a community house. All through the summer of 1990 extensive renovations were carried out on the house and by December it was ready for occupation. A small community of three Sisters was appointed to live there (Sister Marie Duddy, Sister Frances Forde and Sister M. Gertrude Monaghan) and in December 1992, when St Paul's Convent closed, four other Sisters (Sisters Deirdre O'Leary, M. Ignatius McAvoy, Evelyn McDevitt and Annunciata Caffrey) came to join them. Sister M. Gertrude moved to another house at this time.

Meanwhile, the large stables and adjoining house that had originally served the main house were demolished and a new house was built on the site, 616 Crumlin Road, the new St Paul's Convent. Four Sisters took up residence there in the autumn of 1992 (Sisters M. Emilian Moloney, M. Gabriel Deignan, M. Teresa O'Neill and Kathleen Savage).

Coolock

The Downpatrick Mercy community was also expanding its apostolate. On 2 January 1989 Sisters M. Louis Donaghy and Brigid Quinn, who had recently retired from principalship of primary schools in Belfast and Downpatrick, went to reside in a housing estate on the edge of the town of Downpatrick. They took tenancy of a housing-estate flat, 119 Flying Horse Road, in the Model Farm estate. The idea was to live among the people in the estate, the home of many families who had had to leave the ghetto areas of Belfast because of the Troubles. Unemployment was high and there were all the usual problems of a migrant population. A new parish had been established in the estate and the Sisters got involved in its activities, both liturgical and social. Their presence was warmly welcomed by both the priests and the people and the Sisters held 'open house' for all who wished to visit or call to discuss their needs. The flat was named Coolock in memory of an early Dublin residence of the foundress of the Sisters of Mercy, Catherine McAuley.

On 8 September 1990 Sister M. Angela Deignan was appointed to Coolock. On 12 December of that year the Sisters moved from the flat to a Housing Executive house in Tobarburr Park. They later acquired an adjoining flat for use for their apostolate.

Early in 1993, Sister M. Louis had to leave the Model Farm because of ill health and she was greatly missed. In June of the same year, Sister M. Angela became seriously ill and also had to leave. Two other Sisters, Sister M. Finbarr Moloney and Sister M. Colmcille Kennedy, came forward to offer their services and joined Sister Brigid in Coolock the following October. The Sisters continued their good work for as long as they were able but eventually, when Sister Brigid also became ill, the undertaking became too much for the two remaining Sisters. They had to withdraw from the estate, much to the regret of the clergy and residents. They had accomplished a good work of mercy during their time there and their presence would not easily be forgotten.

Evaluation

With the idea of small communities coming more to the fore in the course of the later 1980s, this important development had been the subject of a special congregation assembly day held on 16 September 1989. Many questions, ideals, aspirations and criteria surfaced on that occasion, which are interesting to revisit in the light of later actual experience. The communal discernment highlighted specific points:

> – Most Sisters accepted that small communities were now part of the new vision of religious life, that they have advantages for closer community living, proximity to work and smaller houses to take care of; that the future of religious life is in small communities.
> – The forming of small communities called for preparation for a different lifestyle. They need flexibility and should be founded on mutual trust; they need purpose.
> – Small communities are not for all and those who wish to remain in the older form of community should be allowed to do so; a small community does not necessarily offer only advantages: its success depends on how much each person is prepared to put into it.

Various issues entered into the question of the formation of small communities: criteria regarding situation; pastoral and other work undertaken; the appropriate lifestyle; financial considerations.[3] The final conclusions were that, above all, a small community needs to have a corporate mission and to share faith and vision, and that there was need for more congregational discernment on this. This was undertaken and it ended on a positive note: that small communities would improve the spiritual and personal growth of the Sisters and would help to build a sense of corporate mission. For this, the members would need to be carefully chosen and willing to make the community a success. They should be of mixed age groups as all ages have a place in such communities.

Such were the ideals but, in face of the demands of day-to-day practicalities, ideals often have to give way to the exigencies of reality. However, practical experience, even of a few years, enriched the substance of theoretical thinking. In the event it was found that living in small communities lent flexibility to community life and apostolate, but also required a process of adjustment from the 'Common Life' of a large traditional group to a situation that usually combined considerable individual autonomy with less privacy and the need for closer interpersonal cooperation. Usually Sisters went into the new situations with many expectations of what a 'genuine' religious community could or should be. Perhaps all expectations were not realistic. A happy medium would be achieved through a process of trial and error, evaluation and discernment and consequent readjustment of aims and goals, and would be an ongoing learning process. The structures of traditional religious life were no longer in place. The new lifestyle would be necessarily flexible and provisional, shaped by the individuals involved and the requirements of their apostolate. Consequently, the early 1990s saw considerable movement and change in the small communities, and the middle of that decade saw a further stage as some Sisters stepped out to live entirely on their own.

[1] Sister M. Genevieve Martin to Mercy Congregation (MCA, February 1983).
[2] 'Small group experiments', superior general's records, Down and Connor Mercy Archives (MCA, 1986).
[3] See details of these considerations in the documents of this congregation assembly (MCA, 1989).

27

END OF AN ERA

As has been recorded, the 1980s were years of rapid change. But the most dramatic and traumatic event for the Sisters of Mercy of Down and Connor in all their history was the closing of the convent, St Paul's, on the Crumlin Road in December 1992. Following many consultations with the Congregation of the Sisters of Mercy of Down and Connor over the previous years, and after the congregational assembly that had taken place in July, in August 1988 Sister M. Emilian Moloney, superior general, informed the bishop that the Sisters were prepared to consider offering the convent for sale to the Mater Hospital.

This momentous step was not lightly taken but, over the ten years of the process of discernment regarding the convent property in the light of the hospital's expansion, several indicators had emerged, pointing to what at first had seemed an unthinkable conclusion. Two main considerations came into play. The first was the urgent need to expand the hospital's facilities. This Sisters took this seriously. Much convent property had already been given for the new tower-block extension and the convent itself was requested for absorption into the hospital complex. The Sisters would at least be assured that their beloved motherhouse would be used for the continuation of the care of the sick, one of the works of mercy for which they had originally come to live in Belfast. From the small infirmary the Sisters had started in Bedeque House the Mater Infirmorum Hospital had expanded into a large institution giving care in a greatly varied and highly specialised way to the sick. To hold on to the convent building merely for sentimental and historical reasons would be unworthy. Since the vocation of the Mercy Institute was to serve the poor, the sick and the needy, they saw that this would be the decisive criterion in their discernment.

The second consideration was multi-faceted and affected the community more immediately. On the one hand was the fact that the population distribution in the area had changed radically over the years. Urban planning and development had caused the disappearance of the small working-class streets in the immediate vicinity of the convent – Fairview Street, Lonsdale Street, Twickenham Street, Bedeque Street and others – and in the Antrim Road and New Lodge areas, streets which had been the scene of regular visitation by the Sisters of Mercy right up until the late 1960s. A large percentage of the population had moved to new housing on the outskirts of the city. There was no longer the close contact between the Sisters and their neighbours that there had been for a century before.

Another factor was that, for the first phase of hospital expansion in the 1970s, the Convent Primary School had moved a mile and a half further up the Crumlin Road. There was now no direct connection between the school and the convent, as formerly, except for the fact that the Sisters teaching in the school lived in the convent and travelled from and to it each day. The secondary school was also at a distance from the convent – almost a mile further on. The girls' club had moved to Thorndale Avenue, off the Antrim Road. So the convent remained simply the home of the Sisters, most of whom left each day to travel to their various apostolates elsewhere.

As in the schools, fewer Sisters were engaged in the Mater Hospital at this time. There was still some close collaboration: between April 1990 and June 1991 the convent gave accommodation to student nurses and staff on call when the nurses' home was in the process of being refurbished as the hospital Psychiatric Unit. However, the connection between the hospital and the convent was becoming tenuous.

Added to this was the trend, not only in the Crumlin Road Mercy community but also throughout active apostolic religious life as a whole, for Sisters to move out of larger communities into smaller houses and community groupings, and already some Sisters were in the process of moving out of St Paul's Convent. Gradually the senior Sisters formed the largest group among the remaining residents and it became obvious that the convent was too large and too inconvenient for the comfortable accommodation of an elderly, and in some cases infirm, community.

Even taking into consideration the above factors, which emerged more explicitly through the 1980s, up to the middle of that decade more than 60 per cent of the community were against selling the convent to the hospital authorities – mainly because, at that juncture, the idea of leaving the convent was unthinkable. Gradually, however, as the building of the new hospital tower block progressed and the convent became more and more closed in by the surrounding buildings, the idea of remaining there became less and less feasible. Eventually, in 1989, after protracted discussions with the interested parties, the community decided to proceed with the sale of the convent. The matter moved ahead from there.

At a meeting of the community council in May 1990 a decision was firmly taken to phase out St Paul's Convent. The novices and postulants had already moved to Downpatrick Convent (on 1 January 1990), where they remained until October 1991. After that they went to the new novitiate house at the Glen, Limestone Road, Belfast. The first priority was to relocate the senior Sisters to the communities of Beechmount, St Columbanus's and Downpatrick.

Beechmount and St Columbanus's Homes

In anticipation of the closing of the convent on Crumlin Road, the members of the community were given a choice as to where they wanted to go. The older Sisters, for the most part, chose to go to the Beechmount and St Columbanus's communities.

In the latter years of the 1980s and the early 1990s, changes were taking place in these establishments too. Beechmount House had opened as Our Lady's Hospital in 1932 under the care of the Sisters of Mercy and a new, modern hospital was added in 1935 to accommodate 100 elderly patients, male and female. On 9 September 1976 the hospital was registered with the Eastern Health and Social Services Board as a residential home for aged, infirm and physically disabled persons; the maximum number of residents was 74. The day-to-day management of the home was the responsibility of the Sisters of Mercy. In the early 1990s Sister M. Emmanuel O'Rawe was matron, with Sister Veronica Loughran as staff nurse. Sisters M. Veronica Cawley and Margaret Mary Daly were supervisors of catering and Sister M. Bernadette Agnew was local superior of the community. Sister M. Emmanuel O'Rawe retired on 26 March 1995 after 33 years' service as matron. She died a short time afterwards, on 22 August 1995. The overall control of the home throughout was exercised by the Down and Connor Diocesan Management Committee.

The home was subject to inspectorial visits by the Social Services Department of the Eastern Health and Social Services Board and in the summer of 1989 it was inspected with a view to upgrading. The assessment was that an additional building, or a completely new building, was needed as soon as possible. In January 1990 the option to build a new home was taken. In the meantime funding was given for the temporary upgrade of the home.

Naturally this change of circumstances impinged upon the resident Mercy community. Their residence, the original Beechmount House, would be disconnected from the new nursing home, plans for which provided for a new site in the extensive grounds of Beechmount, completely separate from the existing buildings. Beechmount House and the original chapel were declared listed buildings in June 1987 by the Department of the Environment (Historic Monuments Branch). After the building of the new nursing home and convent they, along with the former hospital building, were purchased by the trustees of the Irish-speaking secondary school in west Belfast. Much of the land on either side of the long drive up to the house was bought from the diocesan trustees by the Down and Connor Housing Association for the building of houses.

It was clear that that the congregation would not be able to offer Sisters to administer the new home and the question of provision for the senior and invalid Sisters became urgent, especially with the imminent closing of St Paul's Convent. The best option seemed to be a new convent, which would be built and owned by the Sisters of Mercy, adjacent to the new nursing home, on land leased to the congregation until such time as the Sisters wished to withdraw from Beechmount. This was approved by the bishop and, after the necessary negotiations with the Diocesan Management Committee, plans for the new convent were drawn up. The new convent would be known as the Convent of Mercy, Beechmount and would open in 1997.

In 1991 some of the senior Sisters moved to Beechmount. Sisters Briege O'Callaghan and M. Alacoque McDonagh went to the nursing home where Sister M. Lucy Mullan was already a resident. Sister M. Lelia Martin and Sister M. Kevin Drain joined the community. Later (in August 1992) Sister M. Dolores Morton, congregational treasurer, moved her office to Beechmount and Sister M. Sarto McCrory went to assist in the nursing home and chapel. There were others who went to join the community at St Columbanus's Home, Helen's Bay. In 1989 plans were drawn up for a new large extension. This was completed and officially opened on 24 September 1991, with quite a notable ceremony. The bishop, Dr Patrick Walsh, celebrated Mass. Present were Monsignor Mulally, chairman of the St Columbanus's board of trustees, Patrick Kinder, manager, Sir Thomas Brown, former chairman and many other dignitaries. Also present were the nursing Sisters who had served in the home since its opening in 1959. After the Mass the new building was viewed and those present gathered in the foyer for the unveiling of a bronze plaque commemorating the event. The matron, Sister M. Benedict, thanked the diocesan representatives the members of the Eastern Health and Social Services Board for their unfailing help over the years. Afterwards the guests went to a large reception room, where a buffet lunch was served.[1]

The new wing added considerably to the accommodation and other facilities. At the same time the older buildings were refurbished and St Columbanus's became a registered nursing home under the Eastern Health and Social Services Board. Sister M. Benedict Monan was matron of St Columbanus's during these years.

In St Columbanus's the Sisters occupied the third floor of the 1959 three-storey extension to the original Craigdarragh House. In 1990 Sister M. Perpetua Murphy was local superior of the community, which at that time numbered five members. The others were Sister M. Benedict Monan, Sisters Elizabeth Gray and Rosemary McCloskey, who were engaged in the nursing home, and Sister M. Mercy Cummins, who cared for the beautiful little oratory (where Mass was celebrated each day) and took responsibility for the liturgy. In the summer and autumn of 1990 the community was augmented by the arrival of Sisters from Crumlin Road Convent: Sisters M. Vincent Donnelly, M. Brendan Blanche and M. Eugene Murphy.

In April 1992 Sisters M. Brendan Blanche and M. Mercy Cummins celebrated the diamond jubilee of their religious profession. The celebrant was Reverend Patrick McCafferty and he was assisted by Reverend Gerard McCloskey. Sister Ann McKeever sang, accompanied by Marian McPolin. A jubilee Mass was celebrated in the oratory of the home on 25 April, the feast of St Mark, and after the Mass a celebratory lunch was provided in a local restaurant. It was a most memorable event, especially for the jubilarians themselves, and an occasion for a great reunion of relatives and friends.

The senior Sisters resided in St Columbanus's between 1990 and 1996. There were bereavements for the community in the course of those years when Sister M. Vincent and Sister M. Brendan died. In 1994 the nursing home was handed over to lay administration. Sister M. Benedict, who had been the nursing home's administrator, did not enjoy her well-deserved retirement for long. She died on 29 March 1995. By this time the new convent in Beechmount was almost ready and when it opened Sisters M. Mercy, M. Eugene and Elizabeth moved to the community there. Sister M. Perpetua joined the Downpatrick community.

Thus ended another chapter in the story of the Down and Connor Mercy Congregation, 36 years of generous service to the elderly and infirm in the beautiful surroundings of Craigdarragh on Belfast Lough.

Mount St Patrick Convent, Downpatrick

The closure of St Paul's Convent and the formation of small communities also affected Mount St Patrick's Convent, Downpatrick, as some Sisters from Belfast joined the community there. Sister Elizabeth McKeown went to Downpatrick in 1990 as local superior and Sister M. Augustine O'Neill moved there on her retirement from St Malachy's College in the summer of 1991. She had served there, with great devotion, as matron for the priests and seminarians for many years, after her retirement from teaching in Down and Connor and with the Sisters of Mercy on the island of Guernsey.

In the early 1990s a proposal was put forward for the refurbishment of the convent chapel and the provision of better facilities for the elderly and infirm Sisters. These renovations were tastefully carried out. Comfortable seating was provided, along with a ramp leading from the chapel corridor to a new side door giving easy access for Sisters requiring wheelchairs and their care attendants. The Downpatrick community are noted for the care given to their elderly Sisters and for the warm welcome and generous hospitality given to all visitors.

The last days of St Paul's Convent

The second and final phase of preparation for departure from St Paul's Convent was to begin to dispose of its furnishings and other effects. On 21 June 1991 it was decided that the convent would no longer function as a full community from 7 July of that year and that those Sisters remaining would have withdrawn completely by September 1992. This became the signal to begin the sad and inevitable process of dismantling. Much of the furniture and other household items were required for the new communities being set up; the rest was disposed of in various ways – to auctions, to the needy and to individuals who had made requests. The library furniture was transferred to Ballysillan House, along with as many books as could be housed there. Rare-book dealers bought the surplus rare and older books. Valueless, out-of-date stock was not retained.

Disposing of the accumulated contents of the convent, the legacy of almost 150 years, was an arduous task, overseen with generosity and skill by Sister M. Gabriel Deignan, the last superior of the Crumlin Road community. Two special items are worthy of note. The convent bell, used for so many years to summon the community to prayers, meals and other exercises, found a new home in Nigeria. It was taken there by Father Paul Hardy, a Kiltegan missionary, for his new church, St Michael's, in Imirtingi Parish, Ologi, Bayelsa state. There it would summon a new community to prayer – and perhaps, in time, even another Mercy community. The large, life-size crucifix, so familiar in the convent chapel (St Anthony's) before its demolition and later at the shrine on the cloister, went to Downpatrick Convent. Later it was donated to the parish church in Downpatrick for the new transept, which was opened in 1993.

On 31 July 1991 the last Mass was celebrated in the convent chapel. From that date Our Lady's Oratory was used for Mass and prayers (until the end of October 1992). On 10 December 1992 Sister M. Emilian wrote to all the Sisters in the Down and Connor Congregation:

The negotiations regarding Crumlin Road Convent are finally drawing to a close. The Mater Hospital will take over the security and maintenance of the convent from 21 December 1992.

This is an historic but sad time for all of us – certainly a time for letting go and trusting in the Lord's plans for the future. It is also a time to thank God for the generations of Sisters who have served his people from this location and ask his blessing on the Sisters who will continue their services from other locations.

I wish to thank all the Sisters who have co-operated in the painful process of vacating the convent and wish them joy and happiness in their new homes.[2]

She added:

A special word of gratitude and appreciation is due to Sister M. Gabriel who has been at the 'cutting edge' this past few years and who has had a very onerous task in planning and organisation. It has been a difficult time and the amount of work done behind the scenes cannot be over-estimated. May the Lord reward her and be with all of us as we plan for the future.[3]

In her letter Sister M. Emilian paid tribute to the generations of Sisters who had lived in, and served from, St Paul's Convent – about 250 in all in the approximately 140 years of its existence. This recalls an event that had taken place two months previously, when one very important part of the convent heritage had to be dealt with: the little community cemetery in the convent garden. As a consequence of the sale of the convent it was necessary to transfer the remains of the Sisters buried in the cemetery to the community graveyard, Our Lady's Acre, Greencastle. The work of removal commenced on 5 October 1992 and was carried out with great sensitivity and respect by five gravediggers employed by Cahal McAteer. A ceremony of re-interment in a common grave in Our Lady's Acre was conducted by Reverend H. Rooney, P.P. of Greencastle, on Thursday, 15 October. A large number of the congregation attended. Two Sisters of the Good Shepherd, who had been buried in the convent cemetery, had been transferred to the cemetery of the Good Shepherd Sisters, Ormeau Road, Belfast, on Monday, 12 October.

On Thursday, 12 December, the anniversary of the founding of the Mercy Institute, at 6 p.m, the final Eucharist was celebrated to mark the formal closing of St Paul's Convent. Most of the Sisters of the Down and Connor Congregation attended. Bishop Walsh was the celebrant. Sister M. Emilian Moloney, superior general, addressed the congregation, giving an account of the foundation in Belfast from the arrival of the Sisters from Dublin in January 1854 up until the present day. She outlined what had been achieved in the intervening 137 years, the expansion within the diocese and also to foundations in England and Australia. She noted that, in keeping with the spirit of the recommendations of the Second Vatican Council for the renewal of religious life, and in response to the circumstances necessitating a move from St Paul's Convent on the Crumlin Road, the Down and Connor Mercy Congregation was now distributed over 12 smaller communities in the diocese, the largest being Mount St Patrick's Convent, Downpatrick, which would replace St Paul's as the main convent of the Down and Connor Sisters of Mercy.

And so arrived the end of a year that had seen the moving out of the remaining members of St Paul's community to their new homes. The closing of St Paul's was an occasion for sadness, no doubt, but also for joy as the Sisters looked to a new life in the future – new pastures, new apostolates, new communities. The past must be relinquished for openness to what the future may bring. Sisters M. Gabriel Deignan and M. Kieran Morrison were the last two Sisters to reside in St Paul's Convent. They undertook the unenviable task of disposing of all the remaining contents of the convent and closing the front door for the last time.

And so, the end of an era. The decades to come were to engage the Down and Connor Sisters of Mercy in wider dispersal and in a much larger Irish and international community.

Union of the Sisters of Mercy of Ireland and South Africa

A definitive step in the history of the Sisters of Mercy of Down and Connor, as an autonomous congregation, came with their decision to become integrated into the new all-Ireland Union of the Sisters of Mercy. The formation of the union was a momentous event for all the Mercy congregations in Ireland, introducing a totally new era for the Mercy way of life in the country. The story of the union's formation is a history in itself and will be recounted here only insofar as it directly affected the subject of this particular history.

When Mercy Ireland was instituted in 1985, one of the objectives was a still-closer bonding of all the Sisters of Mercy in the country (including their missionary regions). This progressed rapidly with regular meetings of the superiors for discussion on matters of common concern and discernment with regard to more cooperative action in the future. Other groups of Sisters around the country were meeting regularly on commissions for areas of common interest – for example, healthcare, justice and formation. The

CONGREGATIO
PRO INSTITUTIS VITAE CONSECRATAE
ET SOCIETATIBUS VITAE APOSTOLICAE

Prot. n. D 41-1/89

D E C R E E

The Sisters of Mercy of Down and Connor, Ireland, have accepted the common constitutions of the Sisters of Mercy of Ireland, already approved by this Congregation for Institutes of Consecrated Life and for Societies of Apostolic Life on December 12, 1985 (Prot. n. A 127-1/82), and have completed them by the addition of particular provisions in the form of a constitutional appendix.

This Congregation for Institutes of Consecrated Life and for Societies of Apostolic Life, by virtue of its authority to erect, guide and promote institutes of consecrated life, having carefully studied the completed text presented by the Sisters of Mercy of Down and Connor, acceding to the request of the Superior General and her Council, herewith approves the constitutional appendix, within the limits of canon law. The constitutions of the Sisters of Mercy of Ireland, together with this approved constitutional appendix, henceforth are the constitutions of the Sisters of Mercy of Down and Connor.

May the generous of these constitutions encourage all the Sisters to an ever deeper commitment to their consecrated life in the spirit of Mother Catherine McAuley and under the strong and tender protection of Our Lady of Mercy.

Given at Rome, March 18, 1989
Feast of St Joseph, Spouse of Our Lady

Document relating to new common Mercy constitutions

Mercy Ireland team maintained continuous communication with all the communities and working parties. Gradually, through these reflective processes, a conviction began to emerge that, in a country the size of Ireland, a more cohesive structure would be both possible and desirable.[4]

Already, in the course of 1985, the Down and Connor Mercy Congregation entered into participation with the other Mercy congregations in the country, in a process of discernment regarding the formation of a national union. In October 1987 Sister M. Emilian Moloney, superior general of the Down and Connor Congregation, informed the Sisters that the Mercy Ireland national assembly had met on 25 September and that the primary aim of Mercy Ireland now was to forward the movement for a national institute. In fact, a decision was to be made about this by 1989. This set things moving on a fast track. To facilitate the process of discernment, in October 1987 three options were formulated by the Mercy Ireland executive and put to all the Sisters for their consideration:

- To stay with the present structure – autonomous diocesan congregations with the Mercy Ireland team acting as a coordinating body.
- To form a canonical federation.
- To unite into one single congregation.

When a vote was taken 75 per cent of the Sisters favoured the third option. This pointed the way towards a referendum on the desirability of exploring a union model appropriate to Ireland and to the Sisters from various Irish convents overseas. The proposal for such a referendum got 90.7-percent support.

In December 1990, after this process of widespread discussion and discernment, a model and structure of the union were submitted to Rome. Permission to proceed was given. In the Down and Connor Congregation, on 20 May, an indicative vote was taken for union in Ireland. The result was 93 per cent in favour (67 in favour, four against and one abstention). A special chapter was held between Sunday, 30 June and Tuesday, 1 July. The result then was 91.4 per cent in favour of union.

The results of the voting from all the congregations in Ireland were submitted to the Mercy Ireland team by 15 September 1991. These indicated that the necessary majority (two-thirds) had been secured in all 26 congregations. This opened the way for the third and final stage, the independent vote of each Sister, stating her own intention regarding participation in a new Congregation of the Sisters of Mercy of Ireland. In January 1992 the results of the voting process, including a formal petition from each of the 26 Irish congregations to become part of the new institute, were forwarded to Rome. While awaiting approval, plans were made to hold the first congregational chapter in the summer of 1994.

Meanwhile, the Mercy Congregation in Johannesburg, South Africa, requested to join the new Mercy Ireland Union. Though founded from Ireland (from Strabane Convent in 1889), because of apartheid in South Africa they had been cut off from the Irish Mercy missions in other African countries. Their petition got a very favourable response from the Mercy congregations in Ireland and their inclusion in the new union was seen as a welcome enrichment. In addition to the South African group, approximately 400 other Sisters of Mercy who were missioned by the Irish congregations to other parts of the world – the USA, Canada, South America, Kenya, Zambia, Nigeria, Zimbabwe and England – would also join the new union. By the summer of 1994, when the inauguration of the Union eventually took place, the new congregation, now named the Union of the Sisters of Mercy of Ireland and South Africa, had become extensive, diverse and enriched by many cultures and charisms, as the founding event prominently displayed.

In the summer of 1992 the Mercy Ireland team handed over to a new transition coordinating committee, whose mandate was to prepare for the inauguration of the Union. As the date for the inauguration approached, each diocesan congregation was invited to hold a closing event to mark what could be called the bittersweet transition from an old and valued identity as an autonomous community to a new identity marked by membership of a wider congregation. It was an exercise in letting go, but a letting go in the faith and hope that the new would give birth to a more vital Mercy presence at home and abroad. The Down and Connor Mercy Congregation held its closing event on 21 May 1994.

The date set for the inauguration of the Union was Thursday, 14 July 1994. On that day over 2,600 Sisters of Mercy came together in the National Basketball Arena in Tallaght, Dublin, to form the Union of the Sisters of Mercy of Ireland and South Africa. The gathering represented the 2,615 Sisters in 26 autonomous Mercy congregations in Ireland and the Johannesburg Congregation in South Africa. These together formed a section of the approximately 16,000 Sisters of Mercy worldwide. They were joined by Sisters and lay associates from every place that had an Irish Mercy mission – Africa, Asia, Central and South America, Canada, the USA, the Pacific Islands – and by many friends and benefactors. Representatives of state and church also attended: the taoiseach, Albert Reynolds, the president of Ireland, Mary Robinson, Cardinal Cahal B. Daly and many other dignitaries, and clergy from many parishes and religious orders. In all it was a gathering of over 3,000 people.[5] The reading of the papal decree of union at the inaugural eucharistic celebration presided over by Cardinal Daly was the end of a long process and the beginning of a new life for the Mercy Institute in Ireland, South Africa and the mission territories.

The inauguration of the Union was followed by a general chapter of which the first task was to elect a central leadership team. The role of this team was (and is) to represent all the Sisters in the Union and to oversee the implementation of the directives of the general chapter – to set the vision and policies. Their term of office is six years. The Mercy communities and congregations in Ireland were divided into four provinces and, in the course of 1994 and early 1995, all the communities of the new northern province (to which diocese the Sisters in Down and Connor belonged) were preparing for their first provincial chapter, which was due to take place at Easter 1995. The northern province at this time numbered approximately 630 Sisters.[6] The provincial election chapter took place in Dromantine Conference Centre, Newry, at the end of April 1995, when over 80 representatives from the eight dioceses of the province met to elect their first provincial leadership team. The preparations for this first chapter were facilitated by the transition coordinating committee of the province, of which Sister M. Gabriel Deignan, Belfast, was a member. The result of the election was that Sister Agnes Hannon was chosen as provincial leader and Sister Paula Carron was chosen as deputy leader. Other members of the team were Sisters Maureen McGurran, Ann Brady and Gabrielle Stuart. Sister Agnes Hannon, of the diocese of Meath, worked in Zambia; Sister Paula Carron, of the diocese of Dromore, was a nurse and social worker; Sister Ann Brady, of the diocese of Meath, was a teacher and community worker; Sister Maureen McGurran, of the diocese of Clogher and formerly of Miami, Florida, was a teacher; and Sister Gabrielle Stuart was a lecturer and group facilitator. After the elections the chapter continued with the business of dealing with the wider issues of policy, statutes and administration, and as a province the Sisters recommitted themselves to the mission declaration subscribed to at the general chapter. These important steps were to point the direction for the province for the following six years.

The first practical act of the new union was to send a group of ten Sisters out to Rwanda, central Africa, which at the time was being torn apart by a devastating internecine war. They went to work with aid agencies already present there and they stayed as long as their help was needed.

Almost coinciding with the inauguration of the Mercy Ireland Union was the opening of the new Mercy International Centre in Baggot Street, Dublin. The idea had originated with the Mercy Association of Ireland in the 1970s and had long been in the minds of Mercy communities, especially those abroad who looked back to Ireland (and in particular to the foundation convent in Baggot Street, Dublin), to find something of the inspiration of their venerable foundress. The Baggot Street Convent, a house of the Dublin Mercy Congregation, in the garden of which is the tomb of the Venerable Catherine McAuley, Foundress, had long been a place of pilgrimage for the many Sisters who visited Ireland from abroad. After years of planning, the project of acquiring it as an international centre was put into effect through the skilful collaborative work of the various Mercy congregations in Ireland and worldwide. After major renovations to the property, the centre was formally opened on 23 July 1994.

The opening was attended by Sisters representing communities all over the world. Guests were the president of Ireland, Mary Robinson, and other civil and ecclesiastical dignitaries. A focal point was an elaborate ritual, performed in the newly landscaped garden of the convent, of the mingling of water from many sources in a single flowing channel, symbolising the coming together of Mercy communities from all corners of the earth. At five o'clock in the afternoon there was a special eucharistic celebration in St Andrew's Church, Westland Row, the church frequented by Catherine McAuley, her companions, and the children and residents of the House of Mercy in her time. The day ended with a banquet in the Belfield campus of University College Dublin. The whole event was an historic occasion: worldwide Mercy had come home to its birthplace, where all visitors could find a welcome and a 'comforting cup of tea'.[7]

The centre became a focus for Sisters of Mercy and their families, friends and associates from all parts of the world, as well as housing a heritage centre and the Mercy International Archives and providing a conference venue for many gatherings and events.

The inner journey: an overview

At the same time as the renewing of the structures of the congregation there was, for all the Sisters, renewal at a personal level. Spiritual and community life were still of primary importance, but now should be such as to maintain an attitude of openness to the modern world. The whole journey towards union had been backed by deep reflection on the Mercy charism and what it meant for the contemporary world both in developed countries and the countries still struggling to realise their full potential, in which many Sisters were playing vital roles. As can be seen from reflecting on the earlier chapters of this story, the Mercy mission had changed over the previous century and a half in tune with a changing society. The story of the Down and Connor

Sisters of Mercy was fairly typical of the Mercy communities in Ireland. While traditional corporate ministries were still being maintained, newer ministries were being embarked upon in response to the changing social circumstances and challenges of the time. In recent decades a major new dimension was being added – cooperation with the laity and the integration of lay associates into the Mercy apostolate. The Conference of Religious of Ireland, in their submission to the Synod on Consecrated Life in the early 1990s, called for 'a move towards a model of the Church where there is genuine partnership between religious, priests and laity'.[8]

This was not new in the Mercy way of life. Catherine McAuley, a lay woman, had started off with this very vision in mind. No doubt it had been modified – and obscured to some extent – by what were considered to be the accepted norms of consecrated religious life in the nineteenth and twentieth centuries.[9] Above all, the fullness of the original charism – dedication to the "service of the poor, the sick and the ignorant" – had survived and was being put into practice with renewed vigour in the very new social, religious and political circumstances of the late twentieth century, with hopes of even greater things to be achieved, with God's help, in the future.

[1]   Sister M. Mercy Cummins, pers. comm.
[2]   Sister M. Emilian to Down and Connor Mercy Congregation (MCA, 10 December 1992).
[3]   Ibid.
[4]   See M.R. Kelly, 'Mercy united', *Intercom* (Ireland) (July/August 1992).
[5]   A full account of the ceremony can be read in the congregation records, press releases and other documents to be found in the Mercy archives (MCA).
[6]   At the time of Mercy Ireland Union (July 1994) the northern province numbered 743 Sisters.
[7]   See video of the opening event (MCA, 1994).
[8]   Conference of the Religious of Ireland, 'On the 1994 synod, 1', *Religious Life Review* (January/February 1994).
[9]   See the various biographies of Catherine McAuley.

EPILOGUE

Why was a span of 140 years (1854–1994) chosen for this story?

St Paul's Convent of Mercy, Belfast, is no more. On the site of the convent there is now the impressive modern McAuley Building of the Mater Hospital, proudly bearing the name of the Mercy foundress, the Venerable Catherine McAuley. St Patrick's Convent of Mercy, Downpatrick, continues in existence as it has outlived the 'material' changes which called for the closure of St Paul's (see Chapter 27), that is, the need for hospital expansion and the demographic changes – shift of population – in the area which the community had served for almost a century and a half.

In addition, as has been recorded (Chapter 25), the restructuring is also due to fundamental changes in the concept of apostolic Religious Life in the latter half of the twentieth century and the closer ties formed with the sister Mercy communities in Ireland and worldwide.

Taking these historical elements into consideration, and the fact that the year 1994 is, as we have seen, the date of the Union of the Sisters of Mercy of Ireland and South Africa, this seemed an appropriate point at which to conclude the first phase of the history of the Sisters of Mercy of Down and Connor Diocese. The vision and allegiance is now international – surely appropriate in a world now become a 'global village'.

That being said, the Sisters of Mercy are still very much alive and active here. At present (2010) there are 42 Sisters distributed throughout 14 houses (including the Convent of Mercy, Downpatrick) in the diocese. Also, they still hold trusteeship of two successful schools – Mercy Primary School, Crumlin Road, and Our Lady of Mercy Girls' School, Bilston Road, both in north Belfast. Although the Sisters are no longer teaching in the schools, the principals and staffs of these schools are dedicated to preserving the Mercy ethos which, they believe, gives a firm foundation for the education of the pupils and their future lives.

I apologise if there are any mistakes in information recorded here. I have tried to be as accurate as possible and faithful to the records in our archives. For want of space, and in order to bring this story to a timely conclusion, much has had to be left for another day. I thank all who have encouraged and helped me in my research for, and writing of, this history, and simply for the moral support I received to keep faithful to a task of many years' duration.

APPENDICES

Appendix to Chapter 1

Decree of approval, *Decretum laudis,* for Catherine McAuley's congregation and for her two Mercy chapters, conveyed to Archbishop Murray by Cardinal Fransoni and signed by Reverend Angelo Mai, secretary of the Sacred Congregation of Propaganda Fide.[1]

Extract:

> Your Grace will of yourself understand, without my having to express it in words, how highly the Sacred Congregation and our Most Holy Lord approve the resolution taken by the very pious lady, Catherine McAuley, of establishing a society of ladies, called *of Mercy*, from the works in which it is to be dedicated. For I need not tell you how deserving of praise that society must be which directs all its efforts and aims to the special end of helping the poor and relieving the sick in every way, and of safeguarding, by the exercise of charity, women who find themselves in circumstances dangerous to virtue. I shall merely say that from an institute of this kind the greatest benefit will result both in civil society and to religion.[2]

[1] APF, SOCG, vol. cml, f. 190v.
[2] Bolster, *op. cit.*

Appendix 1 to Chapter 5
The Maguire Family

Mother M. Philomene Maguire (1827–88), foundress of the Convent of Mercy, Belfast, came from quite a remarkable family. She was the second eldest of four sisters who had entered the Convent of Mercy in Baggot Street shortly after the death of the foundress. They were the daughters of Richard Maguire, a wealthy grazier of Newgrange, County Meath, and his wife Margaret. The eldest was Elizabeth. She entered the Baggot Street community on 1 May 1843, received the religious habit and the name Sister M. Cecilia Xavier on 21 November 1844 and was professed on 26 November 1845. On 26 September 1848 she was elected mistress of novices and on 24 May 1855 superior of the community, which office she held for one term (until 1858). A year later, in 1859, she set sail to make a foundation in Geelong, Australia, where she died on 30 August 1879.

The third sister was Maria. She entered Baggot Street seven years after her two older sisters – that is, on 15 August 1850. It was there that she received the religious habit and the name Sister M. Bernard. While still a novice she was sent out with a small group of Sisters to found a Convent of Mercy in Loughrea, County Galway. She returned to Baggot Street and was sent out again to the foundation in Ballinasloe (a daughter house of Loughrea) in March 1853. There she made her profession on 3 October of that same year 'with special permission' (by an act of chapter, since she should normally have been professed in the motherhouse). Eight years later, in April 1861, she set out for her third foundation, to Longford, and was first superior there; she remained in that office for 12 years. After this she was assistant superior for a further four years. Her health broke down and she was hospitalised in Belgium, where she died on 30 October 1882.

The fourth and youngest sister was Henrietta, who was only six years of age when her two older sisters, Elizabeth and Annie, entered the convent. She joined them there 16 years later and received the religious name Sister M. Joseph Aloysius. She followed her sister Annie (Mother M. Philomene) to the Belfast foundation in May 1861 and was professed there in October of that year. Two of the Maguire sons became Jesuits.

In 1864 Sister M. Joseph Aloysius went on the foundation to Ashton-under-Lyne in Lancashire, England, and later to Bolton. She returned with the Bolton community to Ireland and made a foundation in Belturbet, County Cavan, in 1868. There she succeeded Mother M. Bernard Geraghty as superior (1869) and held the posts of matron, head nurse and superior in the County Home during the remaining days of her life. On the death of Mother M. Bernard, the foundress of the Belturbet community, Sister M. Joseph Aloysius, who was assistant superior, became acting superior for one year. It was during that time that she got in touch with her sister, Mother M. Philomene, who was then in Worcester, and informed her of the Ballyjamesduff situation. Mother M. Philomene very generously consented to reopen Ballyjamesduff convent and a few weeks later transferred, with her whole community, from Worcester to County Cavan, where she received a tumultuous welcome from the bishop and all the people of the town.

Appendix 2 to Chapter 5
Foundation in Ballyjamesduff

By 1871 the Ballyjamesduff community was quite large. Towards the end of May of that year Sister M. Philomene Graham made her profession in the parish church. She was the younger sister of Charlotte Graham (Sister M. Agnes), who had joined Mother M. Philomene Maguire for the mission to Worcester in 1862. This Charlotte Graham, born on 20 April 1839, was the daughter of Hugh Graham and Charlotte Selina Savage of Belfast. She was educated at the Convent of the Sacred Heart, Roehampton, England, and had decided to join the Mercy Congregation in order to serve the poor. She entered the convent in Baggot Street as a candidate for their English missions. It would appear that when Mother M. Philomene and her companions visited Baggot Street on their way to Worcester (via Liverpool) Charlotte, now Sister M. Agnes, joined them. She was to remain a faithful companion to Mother M. Philomene for the rest of her life.

The Sisters named as being part of the Ballyjamesduff community at this time, given in the list of those present at the dinner following the profession ceremony, were 'Rev. Mother, Mrs Maguire [Mother M. Philomene], Mother Assistant, Mrs Graham [Sister M. Agnes], sister of the Professed, Sr. M. Catherine McQuillan, Sr. M. Stanislaus Aldridge, Sr. M. Joseph Howard'.[1]

---

[1] *Anglo-Celt*, 27 May 1871. See also Leaden, *op. cit.*, p. 8.

Appendix to Chapter 10
Bibliography on education

Printed works

Atkinson, N., *Irish education: a history of educational institutions* (Dublin: Allan Figgis, 1969).

Coolahan, J., *Irish education: its history and structure* (Dublin: Institute of Public Administration, 1981).

Goldstrom, J.M., *The social content of education 1808–1870: a study of the working-class school reader in England and Ireland* (Shannon: Irish University Press, 1972).

Royal Commission of Inquiry, Primary Education, Ireland, *Report of the commissioners* (Dublin: HMSO, 1870–71).

Articles

Keenan, P., 'Female adult education', *Irish Quarterly Review*, no. 21 (1856).

Manuscript sources

Special reports of the Commissioners of National Schools (PRONI, Education section, 6/1/3/3, 1,840 *et seq.*).

Special reports of the Commissioners of National Education in Ireland on convent schools, H.C. 1864 (46), xlvi (PRONI).

Reports of the Commissions of National Education in Ireland: seventeenth report H.C. 1850, eighteenth report H.C. 1851 etc. (Queen's University, Belfast).

Appendix to Chapter 11
Horarium drawn up personally by Mother Catherine McAuley, 1840[1]

Daily distribution of time

5½	To rise
6	Assemble in Choir. Angelus. Small Hours. Meditation
7	Make up cells, etc.
7½	Mass
8¼	Breakfast
9	Lecture
9½	Prepare for school, Visitation of the sick, Instruction of Adults
10	These duties entered upon
11¾	Particular examen. Visit to Blessed Sacrament
12	Angelus, Acts of Faith, Hope and Charity and Litany of Jesus
4	Dinner
5	Vespers. Litany of the Blessed Virgin
5½	Lecture
6	Angelus, etc. Matins and Lauds. Litany for a happy death
6¾	Supper
7	Recreation
9	Examen. Litany of the Saints. Morning Meditation prepared
10	All to bed

Sisters engaged in Visitation of the Sick are exempt from any Choir duty from 10 till 4.

But all in Choir at Office and all attend Lectures. The Rosary is said by obligation, but no time is marked; it is often said going on Visitation.

---

[1] Archives, Convent of Mercy, Handsworth, Birmingham, England.

Appendix to Chapter 23
Mater Infirmorum Hospital bibliography

Printed sources

Fleetwood, J.F., *The history of medicine in Ireland* (2nd ed., Dublin: Skellig Press, 1983).

Mater Infirmorum Hospital publications (a collection following the occasion of the opening ceremony of the new hospital, 1900) (Belfast: Mater Infirmorum Hospital, 1900).

Mater Infirmorum Hospital, *Centenary year, 1883–1983* (Belfast: Mater Infirmorum Hospital, 1983).

Mater Matters (the newsletter of the Mater Infirmorum Hospital) (Eastern Health and Social Services Board).

Taylor, F. and M.M. Taylor, *Eastern hospitals and English nurses: a narrative of twelve months' experience in the hospitals of Koulali and Scutari* (London: Hurst and Blackett, 1857).

Manuscript sources

Mater Infirmorum Hospital, annual reports (MIHA, from 1883).

Mater Infirmorum Hospital, H.C. 1883 (29), xxix (Queen's University, Belfast).

Mater Infirmorum Hospital, prospectus (MIHA, 1893).

BIBLIOGRAPHY

See also appendix to Chapter 10 (bibliography on education) and appendix to Chapter 23 (Mater Infirmorum Hospital bibliography).

Printed sources

Allen, M.G., *The labourers' friends: Sisters of Mercy in Victoria and Tasmania* (Melbourne, Australia: Hargreen, 1989).

Bardon, J. and H.V. Bell, *Belfast: an illustrated history* (Belfast: Blackstaff Press, 1982).

Barton, B., *The Blitz: Belfast in the war years* (Belfast: Blackstaff Press, 1989).

Beckett, J.C. and R.E. Glasscock (eds), *Belfast: the origin and growth of an industrial city* (London: BBC, 1967).

Beckett, J.C. *et al.* (eds), *Belfast: the making of a city, 1800–1914* (Belfast: Appletree Press, 1983).

Bernard of Clairvaux, St, *Life of Malachy* (London: Society for Promoting Christian Knowledge, 1920).

Bolster, A., *The correspondence of Catherine McAuley, 1827–1841* (Cork: Congregation of the Sisters of Mercy, dioceses of Cork and Ross, 1989).

Bolster, A., *Positio: documentary study for the canonisation process of the servant of God, Catherine McAuley, 1778–1841* (Rome, 1985).

Bolster, E., *The Sisters of Mercy in the Crimean War* (Cork: Mercier Press, 1964).

Boyd, A., *Holy war in Belfast* (Belfast: Pretani Press, 1987).

Brett, C.E.B. and M. O'Connell, *Buildings of County Antrim* (Belfast: Ulster Architectural Heritage Society and Ulster Historical Foundation, 1996).

Burke-Savage, R., *Catherine McAuley: the first Sister of Mercy* (Dublin: Gill and Sons, 1949).

Carroll, M.A., *Life of Catherine McAuley, foundress and first superior of the Institute of Religious Sisters of Mercy* (New York: D. & J. Sadlier, 1871).

Clear, C., *Nuns in nineteenth-century Ireland* (Dublin: Gill and Macmillan, 1987).

Collins, P., *The making of Irish linen: historic photographs of an Ulster industry* (Belfast: Friar's Bush Press, 1994).

Crowe, M.C., *The Sisters of Mercy, Kilmore, Ireland, 1868–1994* (Kilmore: Congregation of the Sisters of Mercy, diocese of Kilmore, 1994).

Dallat, C., *Caring by design: the archaeological heritage of the health and social services in Northern Ireland* (Belfast: Department of Health and Social Services, 1985).

Fleetwood, J.F., *The history of medicine in Ireland* (2nd ed., Dublin: Skellig Press, 1983).

Gately, M.J., *The Sisters of Mercy: historical sketches, 1831–1931* (New York, Macmillan, 1931).

Harkness, D. and M. O'Dowd (eds), *The town in Ireland* (Belfast: Appletree Press, 1981).

Heatley, F., *The story of St Patrick's, Belfast, 1815–1977* (Belfast: Diocese of Down and Connor, 1977).

Holmes, J. and D. Urquhart (eds), *Coming into the light: the work, politics and religion of women in Ulster, 1840–1940* (Belfast: Institute of Irish Studies, Queen's University, 1994).

Inglis, T., *Moral monopoly: the Catholic Church in modern Irish society* (Dublin: Gill and Macmillan, 1987).

Jordan, A., *Who cared? Charity in Victorian and Edwardian Belfast* (Belfast: Institute of Irish Studies, Queen's University, 1993).

Larkins, M.F., *A Mercy way of life: Colac 1888–1988* (Colac, Australia: Colac Herald Press, 1988).

Larmour, P., *Belfast: an illustrated architectural guide* (Belfast: Frair's Bush Press, 1987).

Llewellan, J., *A guide to Cushendall* (privately published, 1996).

Luddy, M. and C. Murphy (eds), *Women surviving: studies in Irish women's history in the 19th and 20th centuries* (Dublin: Poolbeg Press, 1989).

Macaulay, A., *Patrick Dorrian, bishop of Down and Connor 1865–85* (Dublin: Academic Press, 1987).

Magee, J., *St Patrick's Church, Downpatrick, 1872–1993: a souvenir of the dedication of the extension and new shrine of St Patrick, 23 May 1993* (Downpatrick: St Patrick's Church, 1993).

McAuley, C., *Familiar instructions of Rev. Mother McAuley: foundress of the Institute of the Religious Sisters of Mercy, Dublin, Ireland* (St Louis, USA: Carreras, 1888).

McNeill, M., *The life and times of Mary Ann McCracken, 1770–1866: a Belfast panorama* (Belfast: Blackstaff Press, 1988).

Montalembert, C.F., Comte de, *The monks of the west, from St Benedict to St Bernard* (Edinburgh and London: Blackwood, 1860).

Neuman, I. (ed.), *Letters of Catherine McAuley* (Baltimore, USA: Helicon, 1969).

O'Byrne, C., *As I roved out: a book of the north* (Belfast: Blackstaff Press, 1982).

O'Hanlon, W.M., *Walks among the poor in Belfast, and suggestions for their improvement* (Wakefield: S.R. Publishers, 1971).

O'Laverty, J., *An historical account of the diocese of Down and Connor, ancient and modern*, (5 vols, Dublin: Duffy, 1878–95 and Belfast: P. Quinn and Co., 1945).

Quill, M. (ed.), *The end of an era, 1872–1990: St Ann's College, Warrnambool* (Warrnambool, Australia: St Ann's College, 1990).

Reeves, W., *Ecclesiastical antiquities of Down, Connor and Dromore* (vol. i, Dublin: Hodges and Smith, 1847).

Royal Commission of Inquiry, Primary Education, Ireland, *Report of the commissioners* (Dublin: HMSO, 1870–71).

Rogers, P., *St Peter's Pro-Cathedral, Belfast, 1866–1966* (Belfast: Howard Publications, 1967).

Society of Saint Vincent de Paul, *150th anniversary pamphlet* (Belfast, 1983).

Society of Saint Vincent de Paul, *Centenary volume* (Belfast, 1951).

Sunday Times Insight Team, *Ulster* (London: Penguin Books, 1972).

Articles

Armstrong, D.L., 'Social and economic conditions in the Belfast linen industry, 1850–1900', *Irish Historical Studies*, vol. vii (1951).

Cohen, M., 'Paternalism and poverty: contradictions in the schooling of working-class children in Tullylish, County Down, 1825–1914', *History of Education: Journal of the History of Education Society*, vol. xxi, no. 3 (September 1992).

Kelly, M.R., 'Mercy united', *Intercom* (Ireland) (July/August 1992).

Leaden, A.H., 'The Sisters of Mercy in Kilmore (1868–1968)', *Breifne: Journal of Cumann Seanchais Bhréifne*, vol. iii (1969).

McClelland, M. 'The first Hull Mercy nuns: a nineteenth-century case study', *Recusant History*, vol. xxii, no. 2 (1994).

McEwen, A., 'Half-timing in Belfast', *Northern Teacher*, vol. xiv, no. 1 (autumn 1983).

Usherwood, S. '"No-popery" under Queen Victoria', *History Today*, vol. xxii, no. 4 (April 1973).

Manuscript sources

For details of further manuscript sources see endnotes to chapters.

O'Connell, M., 'Convents in the north of Ireland from mid-nineteenth century to mid-twentieth century' (MA dissertation, Queen's University Belfast, 1992).

'Some notes on the Hamills of Trench House' (Belfast: Resources Centre, St Joseph's College of Education, 1978).

Sisters of Mercy sources

Printed sources

O'Hanlon, J. (ed.) *St Comgall's Primary School centenary, 1890–1990* (1990).

Sisters of Mercy, *Centenary souvenir commemorating Downpatrick Convent of Our Lady of Mercy Primary School 1876* (Downpatrick: Sisters of Mercy, 1976).

Sisters of Mercy, *Guide for the religious called the Sisters of Mercy* (Dublin: Browne and Nolan, 1888).

Sisters of Mercy, *Leaves from the annals of the Sisters of Mercy* (New York: Catholic Publication Society, 1881).

Sisters of Mercy, *Our Lady of Mercy, Belfast: silver jubilee, 1960–1985* (Belfast: Our Lady of Mercy Secondary Intermediate School, 1985).

Sisters of Mercy, *St Mary's High School, Downpatrick: commemorative booklet* (Downpatrick: St Mary's High School, 1993).

Sisters of Mercy, *Star of the Sea Girls' Primary: centenary magazine* (Belfast: Star of the Sea Girls' Primary School, 1989).

Sisters of Mercy, *Supplementary manual to The Sisters of Mercy: historical sketches, 1831–1931* (New York: Macmillan, 1931).

Sisters of Mercy, *The rule and constitutions of the religious called Sisters of Mercy* (Dublin: Browne and Nolan, 1866 (repr. 1926)).

Articles

Cummins, M.M., 'The coming of the Sisters of Mercy to Belfast', *St Malachy's Convent Primary School Centenary Brochure, 1878–1978* (Belfast: St Malachy's Convent Primary School, 1978).

Philbin, W., 'Foreword', Sisters of Mercy, *Centenary souvenir commemorating Downpatrick Convent of Our Lady of Mercy Primary School 1876* (Downpatrick: Sisters of Mercy, 1976).

Manuscript sources

Sisters of Mercy, 'Convent of Our Lady of Mercy, St Paul's, Belfast: centenary souvenir, 1854–1954' (MCA).

Sisters of Mercy, 'Directory of foundations, 1863–1913' (MIA).

Sisters of Mercy, 'St Patrick's Convent of Mercy, Downpatrick: acts of chapter' (MCA).

Sisters of Mercy, 'St Patrick's Convent of Mercy, Downpatrick: annals' (MCA).

Sisters of Mercy, 'St Patrick's Convent of Mercy, Downpatrick: archives' (MCA).

Sisters of Mercy, 'St Paul's Convent of Mercy, Belfast: acts of chapter, 1854–1911, 1923–1994' (MCA).

Sisters of Mercy, 'St Paul's Convent of Mercy, Belfast: annals' (MCA).

Sisters of Mercy, 'St Paul's Convent of Mercy, Belfast: archives' (MCA).

INDEX